JSA/JASA 30 Years Anniversary Book

BAYON BOOK

JSA/JASA's 30 Years Challenge to the Mystery and Hope

Supervisor: NAKAGAWA Takeshi
Edited by Japanese Government Team for Safeguarding Angkor

カンボジア アンコール遺跡救済 日本政府チーム協力30周年記念誌

バイヨン

謎と希望への
JSA / JASA 30年の挑戦

November 2024

中央公論美術出版

Editorial Supervisor:
NAKAGAWA Takeshi ／中川 武

Editorial Board:
KOIWA Masaki, ISHIZUKA Mitsumasa, NARUI Itaru ／小岩 正樹, 石塚 充雅, 成井 至

Translation from Japanese into English, English ro Japanese (order of appearance):
Robert McCARTHY, NARUI Itaru, MIZOGUCHI Akinori, IWASAKI Yoshinori, FUKUDA Mitsuharu,
OKOUCHI Hiroshi, MIZUNO Saya, TABATA Yukitsugu, UCHIDA Etsuo, MATSUI Toshiya,
KAWASAKI Emi, KATAYAMA Yoko, IKEUCHI Takeshi, OISHI Takeshi, YAMADA Shunsuke,
AKAZAWA Yasushi, TOMODA Masahiko, SHIMODA Ichita, ISHIZUKA Mitsumasa, YANO Kenichiro,
SHIGEMATSU Yushi, SHIMODA Mariko ／
ロバート・マッカーシー, 成井 至, 溝口 明則, 岩崎 好則, 福田 光治, 大河内 博, 水野 さや,
田畑 幸嗣, 内田 悦生, 松井 敏也, 河崎 衣美, 片山 葉子, 池内 克史, 大石 岳史, 山田 俊亮,
赤澤 泰, 友田 正彦, 下田 一太, 石塚 充雅, 矢野 健一郎, 重松 優志, 下田 麻里子

Photographs & Drawings:
©Japan-APSARA Safeguarding Angkor

本書の出版計画にあたってはユネスコ文化遺産保存日本信託基金のご支援をいただいております。

This publication project is supported by the UNESCO/Japanese Funds-in-
Trust for the Preservation of the World Cultural Heritage.

JSA/JASA 30 Years Anniversary Book
BAYON BOOK
JSA/JASA's 30 Years Challenge to the Mystery and Hope

Supervisor : NAKAGAWA Takeshi
Edited by : Japanese Government Team for Safeguarding Angkor

©Japan-APSARA Safeguarding Angkor, November 2024

Book Binding Design design by OKAMOTO Yohei (okamoto design)

Published 2022 in Japan by Chuokoron Bijutsu Shuppan Co., Ltd.
ISBN978-4-8055-0991-3

Pl. I After Restoration of Northern Library, Bayon (Phase 1)

Pl. II After Restoration of Northern Library inside the Outermost Enclosure, Angkor Wat (Phase 2)

Pl. III After Restoration of N1, Prasat Suor Prat (Phase 2)

Pl. V Landscape Improvement of the East Outer Gallery, Bayon (Phase 4)

Pl. VI Archaeological Excavation Work, Bayon (Phase 4)

Pl. IV After Restoration of Southern Library, Bayon (Phase 3)

Pl. VII Landscape Improvement of Tower 55, Bayon (Phase 5)

Pl. VIII Landscape Improvement of Gallery 56, Bayon (Phase 5)

Pl. IX Landscape Improvement of Tower 69, Bayon (Phase 6)

Pl. X Stabilization Work of Central Tower before Dismantle, Bayon (Phase 6)

Pl. XI Face Towers of Bayon (Left: Deva Middle: Devata Right: Asura)

Pl. XII Face Towers of Tower 30 and Tower 31, Bayon

Pl. XIII Turtle Artifact Excavated from Southern Pond, Bayon (Phase 4)

Pl. XIV Looking Down View from the Central Tower, Bayon

Pl. XV Restoration Work of Southern Library, Bayon (Phase 3)

Pl. XVI Restoration Work (Phase 3)

カンボジア アンコール遺跡救済 日本政府チーム協力30周年記念誌
JSA/JASA 30 Years Anniversary Book

バイヨン
BAYON BOOK

謎と希望へのJSA/JASA30年の挑戦
JSA/JASA's 30 Years Challenge to the Mystery and Hope

本刊行物は，JSPS 科研費 JP24HP5158 の助成を受けたものです。
This publication was supported by JSPS KAKENHI Grant Number JP24HP5158.

巻頭寄稿

Foreward & Contribution

H.E. PHOEURNG Sackona *16*

UENO Atsushi *17*

Mr. Lazare ELOUNDOU ASSOMO *18*

Foreword for JSA/JASA's 30 Years Projects of Conservation & Restoration in Bayon

The Paris Peace Agreement was signed in 1991, and the following year the Angkor was registered as a UNESCO World Heritage Site. Up to the present, many of countries including Japan have been carrying the restoration and conservation projects at the site of monuments in Cambodia, and each restoration team has achieved certain results today. The Japanese Government Team for Safeguarding Angkor, headed by Takeshi Nakagawa, was formed in 1994 and has been restoring the Bayon Temple, Prasat Suor Prat and North Library inside the outermost enclosure of Angkor Vat over the past 30 years. In 2006, JSA and APSARA National Authority organized teamed up and moved to joint operation named as JASA. In this context, in each restoration project, in order to understand the authenticity of Bayon and Angkor, and to seek a conservation and restoration policy based on this authenticity, experts in numerous fields, including not only architecture and archaeology but also geotechnics, art history, conservation science, and petrology, have been tackling the problem of restoration and conservation of the temples. This book, which summarizes the results of their work over the past 30 years, will be an important resource for the future of Bayon and Angkor. The project is currently in its 6th phase, and among them, the success of restoration project for stabilization of the Central Tower in the Bayon Temple can be regarded as one of the highlights in the history of the restoration of Angkor monuments.

The JSA/JASA's restoration projects conducted over the past 30 years have contributed to both Japan and Cambodia as international cooperation projects. In addition, we hope that future restoration projects will serve as a model case for restoration projects of cultural properties in the world and the projects will promote the development of young Cambodian experts lead in the next generation through the exchange the technique and knowledge.

H.E. PHOEURNG Sackona
Minister of Culture and Fine Arts of Cambodia
President of APSARA National Authority

Contribution from Ambassador UENO for the Foreword in JSA/JASA's 30 Year Memorial Publication

I would like to congratulate the JAPAN-APSARA Safeguarding Angkor (JSA/JASA) team on its 30th anniversary and its remarkable achievements. The publication of a compilation of its work provides an opportunity to reflect on the progress it has made and to think about the direction for the future.

Japan has been playing a leading role in the peace process in Cambodia since the late 1980s. Japan took the lead in safeguarding the Angkor monuments based on a belief that it would be an essential element in the reconstruction and unification of Cambodia. Working alongside other international partners, Japan committed itself to Angkor's restoration. We are proud of the important role that Japan has played in Cambodia's post-conflict reconstruction process, and we are also proud that Japan has contributed significantly to the safeguarding of Cambodia's cultural heritage, particularly the Angkor historical sites.

Over the past three decades, the historic site of Angkor, once threatened with destruction and abandonment, has become one of the world's most important cultural heritage sites and a leading tourist destination. As part of Japan's commitment to the restoration, the Government of Japan has contributed more than US$28.6 million through Japanese Funds-in-Trust (JFIT) to the JSA/JASA project and more than 1,500 Japanese experts were sent to work at the archeological sites. Today, the JSA/JASA project is one of the longest JFIT-funded heritage conservation projects in the world and has become a veritable model for international cooperation in heritage conservation. I would like to commend, and pay tribute to, everyone involved in this joint project. The great achievements of the past 30 years would not have been possible without their tireless efforts.

This restoration project also provides a valuable case study in terms of human resource development. The accumulated knowledge and experience must be shared internationally, and I believe that this publication will contribute significantly to such efforts. Japan remains committed to addressing the conservation and restoration challenges that still remain and will work closely with the Cambodian authorities and international partners.

UENO Atsushi
Ambassador Extraordinary and Plenipotentiary of Japan to the Kingdom of Cambodia

Foreword by the Director of the UNESCO World Heritage Centre, Mr. Lazare ELOUNDOU ASSOMO

For the past thirty years, the temple of Bayon has been the centrepiece of a conservation and restoration project born out of a long-standing partnership between UNESCO, the Royal Government of Cambodia, and the Government of Japan. The ambitious initiative was realised with the technical support of Waseda University, and in close collaboration with the APSARA National Authority.

The project "Safeguarding the Bayon Temple of Angkor Thom" was launched in 1994 within the framework of the Japanese Funds-in-Trust for UNESCO, in response to the global appeal to save Angkor, which was inscribed on the World Heritage List two years prior for its outstanding historical, artistic, and religious significance.

Following the success of the emblematic Nubia Campaign, the multilateral cooperation for Angkor was founded upon the principles of the 1972 World Heritage Convention which positions the stewardship of outstanding sites as humanity's shared responsibility.

For three decades, the Government of Japan has adhered to these global standards and provided considerable financial and technical support for the preservation of the archaeological complex of Bayon of Angkor Thom. To date, the donor has contributed over 29 million USD and engaged more than 1,500 Japanese experts. Continuous multilateral efforts have been carried out in order to meet the urgent conservation needs of this outstanding World Heritage property and face emerging challenges including climate change and overtourism.

For Cambodia, still reeling from years of civil conflict and political unrest, the great influx of international support for the preservation of Angkor constituted a major catalyst for peacebuilding. The project also served to inspire a sense of solidarity, pride and social cohesion, as it empowered the Cambodian people to actively engage in the management of their rich cultural heritage.

True to this spirit, Waseda University has been committed to creating a collaborative, multicultural environment that enhances the knowledge and skills of Cambodian experts in the preservation and valorisation of cultural heritage at large. This publication is the product of a constant dialogue and exchange of ideas which characterized this project.

The important milestone calls for a celebration of this long-established cooperation which placed the Bayon Temple at the forefront of international heritage conservation as well as archaeological and scientific research in Cambodia. At the same time it is also a moment to commit ourselves, once again, to the values of the UNESCO1972 Convention as we did some 30 years ago.

As the conclusion of the 2030 Agenda for Sustainable Development draws near, the world is casting an eye on the future. The General Assembly of the United Nations just adopted the "Pact for the Future", giving culture a historic recognition as a driver of sustainable development. It also underlined the importance of multilateral cooperation and intercultural understanding to achieving a just, inclusive vision of future.

The collective efforts towards the preservation, study, and sustainable development of World Heritage sites, as exemplified in this project, continues to increase its relevance.

Mr. Lazare ELOUNDOU ASSOMO
Director, UNESCO World Heritage Centre

Table of Contents

Foreward & Contribution *15*

CHAPTER 1   Conservation of Elusiveness in Bayon *25*
NAKAGAWA Takeshi

CHAPTER 2   Past Study about Angkor and Bayon *33*
edited by NAKAGAWA Takeshi

Chapter 3   JSA/JASA Research and Study of Bayon

3.1   Environment Conditions for the Wider Region of Angkor *49*
IWASAKI Yoshinori   FUKUDA Mitsuharu   OKOUCHI Hiroshi

3.2   Research on the Provincial Ancient Khmer Cities and Temples *56*
MIZOGUCHI Akinori   NARUI Itaru

3.3   Dimention Planning Method in Khmer Architecture and the Bayon *69*
MIZOGUCHI Akinori

3.4   Inventory Research of Bayon *80*
NISHIMOTO Shinichi

3.5   Face Towers and Gods in Bayon *85*
MIZUNO Saya

3.6   Archaeology of Bayon *93*
TABATA Yukitsugu

3.7   A Petrological Approach to the Angkor Monument, with a Focus on the Bayon *100*
UCHIDA Etsuo

3.8   Conservation Scientific Research in Bayon *111*
MATSUI Toshiya   KAWASAKI Emi

3.9   Microorganisms of the Angkor Monuments *118*
KATAYAMA Yoko   Gu Ji-Dong

3.10 3D Scanning of the Bayon *125*
OISHI Takeshi   IKEUCHI Katsushi

3.11 Structural Mechanic Research of Bayon *134*
YAMADA Shunsuke   HASHIMOTO Ryota   KOYAMA Satoshi

3.12 Geotechnical Engineering of Bayon *143*
IWASAKI Yoshinori   FUKUDA Mitsuharu   Robert McCarthy

3.13 Bayon Master Plan and JSA's Declaration of Challenge *154*
NAKAGAWA Takeshi

CHAPTER 4   JSA/JASA Restoration and Conservation Project

4.1   The Conservation and Restoration of the Prasat Suor Prat on Royal Palace, Angkor Thom ... *163*
AKAZAWA Yasushi

4.2 Northern Library of Bayon:
    Presenting a New Model for Restoration in Angkor 170
    TOMODA Masahiko

4.3 Northern Library Inside the Outermost Enclosure of Angkor Wat 177
    TSUCHIYA Takeshi

4.4 Restoration of the Southern Library of Bayon:
    Attempting Sustainable Heritage Conservation and New Insights from within the Platform 187
    SHIMODA Ichita

4.5 Landscape Improvement of the East Outer Gallery of Bayon 193
    ISHIZUKA Mitsumasa

CHAPTER 5 Human Resource Development and Collaborative Project

5.1 On-the-Job Training at Restoration Site and Cambodian Expert Development 203
    NAKAGAWA Takeshi   So Sokuntheary   Chhum Menghong

5.2 Bayon Great Buddha Project: Making Replica, Restoration, Reconstitution and
    Reinstallation of the Original Bayon Buddha Image 208
    YANO Kenichiro   NAKAGAWA Takeshi   SHIGEMATSU Yushi   ISHIZUKA Mitsumasa

5.3 Restoration Project of Naga Balustrade and Lion Statues at the Outer Gallery and
    the Eastern Causeway of Bayon in Cooperation with a Non-Governmental Organization ... 216
    SHIMODA Mariko

5.4 Children of Angkor and the Stone Carpenter Village 221
    NAKAGAWA Takeshi

CHAPTER 6 Restoration and Conservation Project of Bayon

6.1 Permanent Countermeasures for Foundation Structure of Central and Sub Towers 227
    IWASAKI Yoshinori   FUKUDA Mitsuharu   Robert McCarthy

6.2 Countermeasure for the Superstructure of the Central Tower, Bayon 236
    YAMADA Shunsuke

6.3 Restoration and Conservation Project of the Bas-reliefs of the Inner Gallery, Bayon 243
    MATSUI Toshiya   KAWASAKI Emi

6.4 Conservation of Landscape of Bayon 253
    NAKAGAWA Takeshi   ISHIZUKA Mitsumasa

CHAPTER 7 Could Bayon Become Hope or not, Instead of Conclusion 261
    NAKAGAWA Takeshi

Biography of Authors 270
Acknowledgements 281
Memorial Writing 283

目　　次

巻頭寄稿 15

第1章　バイヨン謎の保存 25
中川 武

第2章　アンコール・バイヨンに関する既往研究の地平 33
中川 武 編

第3章　JSA/JASA の調査研究
3.1　アンコール地域広域環境 49
岩崎 好規　福田 光治　大河内 博

3.2　アンコール遺跡広域大型寺院都市研究 56
溝口 明則　成井 至

3.3　クメール建築設計方法とバイヨン 69
溝口 明則

3.4　バイヨンのインベントリー 80
西本 真一

3.5　バイヨンの尊顔と神々 85
水野 さや

3.6　バイヨンの考古学 93
田畑 幸嗣

3.7　アンコール遺跡の岩石学とバイヨン 100
内田 悦生

3.8　バイヨンの保存科学 111
松井 敏也　河﨑 衣美

3.9　アンコール遺跡の微生物 118
片山 葉子　グ・ジドン

3.10　バイヨンの3Dスキャン 125
大石 岳史　池内 克史

3.11　バイヨンの建築構造学 134
山田 俊亮　橋本 涼太　小山 倫史

3.12　バイヨンの地盤工学 143
岩崎 好規　福田 光治　ロバート・マッカーシー

3.13　バイヨンマスタープラン・JSA の挑戦宣言 154
中川 武

第4章　JSA/JASA の保存修復事業
4.1　アンコール・トム王宮前広場プラサート・スープラの保存修復 163
赤澤 泰

4.2 バイヨン北経蔵
──アンコールにおける新たな修復モデルの提示 170
友田 正彦

4.3 アンコール・ワット最外周壁内北経蔵 177
土屋 武

4.4 バイヨン南経蔵の修復工事
──持続的な遺産保護への試行と基壇内からの新知見 187
下田 一太

4.5 バイヨン外回廊東面景観整備 193
石塚 充雅

第5章　人材育成及び協力関連事業

5.1 保存修復現場での研修とカンボジア人専門家の育成 203
中川 武　ソ・ソクンテリー　チュン・メンホン

5.2 バイヨン本尊仏のレプリカ作製と修復による再安置プロジェクト 208
矢野 健一郎　中川 武　重松 優志　石塚 充雅

5.3 民間組織協力による，バイヨン東参道，外回廊ナーガ欄干
およびライオン彫像修復事業 216
下田 麻里子

5.4 アンコールの子供たちと石工村 221
中川 武

第6章　バイヨンの保存修復工事計画

6.1 中央塔群基礎地盤構造の恒久的安定化計画 227
岩崎 好規　福田 光治　ロバート・マッカーシー

6.2 バイヨン中央塔の上部構造の対策 236
山田 俊亮

6.3 バイヨン浅浮彫の保存修復計画 243
松井 敏也　河﨑 衣美

6.4 バイヨンの景観保存について 253
中川 武　石塚 充雅

第7章　バイヨンは希望となりえるか，結語に変えて 261
中川 武

執筆者略歴 270

謝辞 280

追悼 282

Abbreviations

Organization

ACO	Angkor Conservation Office
APSARA	Authority for the Protection and Management of Angkor and the Region of Siem Reap
ASI	Archaeological Survey of India
EFEO	École Français d'Extrême-Orient
GACP	German Apsara Conservation Project
ICOMOS	International Council on Monuments and Sites
JICE	Japan International Cooperation Center
JSA	Japanese Government Team for Safeguarding Angkor
JASA	Japan-APSARA Safegurding Angkor
JST	Japan Science and Technology Agency
UNESCO	United Nations Educational, Scientific and Cultural Organization

Others

ICC	International Coordinating Committee for the Safeguarding and Development of the Historic Site of Angkor

Ages of Reign

本書では，以下に示す王の治世期を基準とする。
In this book, we use the King's reigns as the below.

The Reign of Khmer Kings

Bavavarman I	バヴァヴァルマン I	598
Ishanavarman I	イーシャナヴァルマン I	616- 635
Jayavarman II	ジャヤヴァルマン II	802- 834
Yasovarman I	ヤショヴァルマン I	889- 910
Jayavarman IV	ジャヤヴァルマンIV	921- 941
Harchavarman II	ハルシャヴァルマン II	941- 944
Rajendravarman II	ラージェンドラヴァルマン II	944- 968
Jayavarman V	ジャヤヴァルマン V	968-1000
Suryavarman I	スールヤヴァルマン I	1002-1050
Udayadityavarman II	ウダヤディティヤヴァルマン II	1050-1066
Suryavarman II	スールヤヴァルマン II	1113-1150
Jayavarman VII	ジャヤヴァルマンVII	1181-1218

第 1 章　バイヨン謎の保存

Chapter 1 Conservation of Elusiveness in Bayon

中川　武
NAKAGAWA Takeshi

1. アンコール遺跡の正統と異端

バイヨンには謎が満ちている。この謎に近づくためには、アンコール遺跡全般をともかく見渡す必要があるだろう。12世紀後半から13世紀にかけて、現東南アジアのおよそ半分の版図を占めるに至ったアンコール帝国は、ヒンドゥー教、仏教寺院を都市、社会の中核施設として発展、拡大してきた。その歴史的プロセスは

①ラオス南部ワット・プー（8〜12世紀）に代表される「参道段台テラス縦深型寺院」は、聖山の麓から山の頂上もしくは中腹に向かって長い参道とテラスを重ね、聖山に降臨した異境からの神のための祠堂をつくる（奥宮）。農耕神の場合、季節の祭に合わせて里宮、田宮へと巡行する。カンボジア・タイ東北部国境ダンレック山脈上に造営されたプレア・ヴィヘア（9〜12世紀）の場合、アンコール地域上空が聖なる方向と見做されていた可能性がある。

②バコン（10世紀）やプノム・バケン（11世紀）のように、都市の中心を占める階段状の基壇の上に立つ高い塔状建物で、護国寺もしくは国家中央寺院として位置づけられることが多いピラミッド型寺院と呼ぶ。

③寺院を中心に広い敷地を確保し、その中に駅舎、施療院など広く民衆のための社会施設を包含する水平展開型祠堂で、中央・地方を問わず、クメール寺院、都市、社会施設の大部分はこれにあたる。バンテアイ・スレイ（10世紀）は中央と地方の中間にあり、この種の寺院都市の水平展開型寺院の典型である。

以上までの3つの祠堂の類型は、クメール建築史研究の先覚者千原大五郎の指摘であるが、バプーオン（12世紀）は以上の①、②、③の類型が、各々史的に融合されながら包含されて形成された。即ち、長い参道、テラスを連ね、ピラミッド型基壇上の高い中央祠堂と、周囲に広がる広い伽藍敷地を備えた総合性が特徴であり、このバプーオンをさらに拡大、発展させたものがアンコール・ワット（12世紀前半）である。まさにクメール建築史が到達した美と力の正統性の完成像である。

他方、バイヨン（12世紀後半〜13世紀初）は、円形の中央塔群、巨大な尊顔塔の群立、度重なる増改築と祀られる神々の複合と重層による立体曼荼羅状群造形の密集度の高い動的空間、そして神々と王と民衆が躍動する万華鏡ストーリーの回廊浅浮彫装飾等々、その形態、空間、

1. Orthodoxy and Heresy at Angkor

The Bayon is full of mysteries. To get closer to this mystery, it is necessary to see the Angkor Monuments in person. The Angkor Empire, which occupied about half of present-day Southeast Asia from the late 12th to the 13th century, developed and expanded with Hindu and Buddhist temples as the core of its cities and society. The historical process is as follows.

① The "vertically-oriented layout temple", represented by the Vat Phu in southern Laos (8th-12th century), consists of a long causeway and terrace from the foot of the sacred mountain to the top or middle of the mountain, where a shrine is built for a deity from another world who descended from the sacred mountain (Okumiya). In the case of agricultural deities, the shrine is moved to the village shrine (Satomiya) and the rice field shrine (Tamiya) according to seasonal festivals. In the case of the Preah Vihear (9th-12th century) built on the Dangrek Mountains on the Cambodian-Thai northeastern border, it is possible that the sky above the Angkor area was regarded as the sacred direction.

② The Bakong (10th century) and Phnom Bakheng (11th century) are high tower-like buildings standing on a stepped platform occupying the center of the city, and are called pyramid type temple, which are often positioned as temples of protection or central temples of the state.

③ The majority of Khmer temples, cities, and social facilities, both central and local, are the type of "Vertically-Oriented on the Plains" that is belongs to the type of horizontally developed shrine that has a large site centering on a temple and includes social facilities for the people at large, such as a station, hospital, and so on. The Banteay Srei (10th century), located between the central and provincial areas, is a typical example of this type in a temple city.

The three types of shrine buildings mentioned above were pointed out by Chihara Daigoro, a pioneer in the study of Khmer architectural history, and Baphuon (12th century) was formed by historically integrating types ①, ②, and ③ above. The Baphuon (12th century) is characterized by its comprehensive nature, with a long series of causeway and terraces, a high central tower shrine on a pyramid platform, and a spacious surrounding temple compound. The Angkor Wat (early 12 century) is considered as expansion and development of this characteristic. It is a perfect example of the orthodoxy of beauty and power that the history of Khmer

佇まいともそれまでのクメール建築のどこにも無いものであって，アンコール・ワットまでのプロセスが正統とすればまさに異端としか呼びようのないもののように思われる。

　正統への道は，どんなに遥かなものであっても一つ一つ積み重ねていけばやがて到達可能なものであろう。それに対して異端は，地道な努力だけでは及ばない。どこか不思議な謎や天才的な飛躍が隠されているようにも思われる。様々な興趣を誘うバイヨンではある。ジャヤヴァルマンⅦ（1181〜1218）という存在感の強い尊像が彼の拠点のいくつかによって発見されていることもあり，アンコール史上でも建寺王として最もよく知られ，親しまれている王への注目も大である。現にアンコール・トムの中心に鎮座し続けてきたのであり，クメールの伝統の中で生まれたことは間違いない。その上で，クメールのみならず世界の建築史上において稀有で，圧倒的な建築がどのようにして誕生することになったのか。それはクメール帝国にとってどのような意味を持ったのか。そして，現在，バイヨンの価値を明らかにし，それを保存しようとすることが，クメール，ひいては世界の文化史上どのような意義があると考えられるのか。この巨大な謎に一歩でも近づきたいと願うのである。

2. バイヨン，尊顔塔の謎

　バイヨンの中央塔四方位にはかつて巨大な尊顔が刻まれていた。東面の尊顔頭部を装飾したと想定される冠の一部がかろうじて残っているものの，積み石のかなりの部分は崩落している。現状では，塔状祠堂は52塔がほぼ健在であり，173面の尊顔が残存している。これらから，かつての中央塔の尊顔像を想像すると，その偉容はいかばかりであったかと胸躍り，また，消滅したことに残念な気持ちにもなる。ともあれ，この尊顔は当初，全部で180面あるいは181面計画説が有力であるが，外回廊四錐の広い出入口ホール上部にも尊顔があったとする研究者もいて，数自体が定まっていない。なぜこのような多くの，巨大な尊顔が必要だったのか。そもそもこの尊顔は何で，どうして彫刻のような，建築のような異観を現出させなければならなかったのか。その意味は何であったのか。バイヨン尊顔塔からは無数のインパクトの強い謎が浮上してくる。

　これらの顔面は何か，について既に仏陀の理想を実現するためにこの世に現れた100の観音菩薩説，ヒンドゥー教シヴァ神説，デーヴァ・ラージャ（神王）説などが唱えられてきた。私たち，日本国政府アンコール遺

architecture has reached.

On the other hand, the Bayon (late 12th-early 13th century) has a highly dynamic space with a group of circular central towers, a cluster of face towers, a complex of three-dimensional mandala group formations with repeated additions and renovations, and a kaleidoscopic story of gods, kings, and people in motion, as well as the bas-relief in the gallery. This expansive complex and appearance are unique compared with other Khmer architecture. If the process leading up to Angkor Wat is considered orthodox, it would seem to be nothing short of heresy.

The road to orthodoxy, no matter how far it may be, is one that can be reached eventually if one builds it up one by one. Heresy, on the other hand, cannot be attained only by steady efforts. There seems to be necessary of some mystery or leap of genius hidden in the heresy. The Bayon invites a variety of fascinations. The image of most well-known and familiar king of Angkor, Jayavarman VII (reigned 1181-1218), has been discovered at several of his strongholds, and noted as a king who encouraged architecture in Khmer history. In fact, he has continued to sit at the center of Angkor Thom, and there is no doubt that he was born in the Khmer tradition. On this background, how did such a rare and overwhelming structure come into being, not only in Khmer architecture, but in the history of world architecture? What meaning did it have for the Khmer Empire? And what significance does it have in the cultural history of the Khmer Empire, and indeed of the world, to reveal the value of the Bayon and to try to preserve it today? It is my hope that we will be able to approach this enormous mystery with a step closer to unlocking the mystery.

2. The Mystery of the Face Towers in Bayon

The four sides of the Central Tower of the Bayon were once carved with gigantic faces. Although a part of the crown, which is assumed to have decorated the head of the precious face on the east face, barely remains, a significant portion of the piled stones have collapsed. At present, 52 towers are almost intact, and 173 faces remain. When I imagine the original Central Tower, I am excited to see how magnificent it must have looked in the past, and I also regret that it was injuried. There is the strong theory that the faces were carved as 180 or 181 faces. Some researchers advocate that there were faces above the wide entrance hall of the Outer Gallery, and the number of faces itself has not been identified. Why were such a large number of huge faces necessary? What were these faces, and why did they have to appear sculptural or architectural in appearance? What was its meaning? The face towers of Bayon suggest a myriad of high-impact mysteries.

For the mysteries of face towers, the 100 Bodhisattvas of Avalokitesvara appeared in the world for realizing the Buddhism ideal, the Shiva of Hinduism, and the Deva Raja

跡救済チーム（JSA）は，汎用性の高い調査データの収集を第一義と考えていたので，現存する全尊顔を大型カメラで正面から撮影し，美術史，建築史合同調査記録を作成した。その結果，遠くからは，シヴァの第三眼や観音の化仏のように見えなくもなかった。尊格を表現する額飾りのディテールをはじめとして，顔面の各要素や輪郭，冠帯，頸飾りなどの装身具等の美術史的分析，そして3Dスキャン測量による比較分析等の総合考察を重ねた。これらの尊顔塔は，学術書にも四面塔と書かれているが，三面や二面しか刻まれていない塔もある。全体に共通しているのは，戦士が常用する葉冠を装着していることである。このためこれらの尊顔塔には四方位を護持する戦う神々が彫られていると考えて間違いないであろう。そして，これらの神々に3つの傾向があることが，美術史研究により判ってきた。㈠目が細く吊り上がり気味で，頬の線がほっそりしている顔貌のデヴァター（女神）像，㈡ドングリ眼で，顎が張った憤怒形相のアスラ（阿修羅）像，㈢両者の中間的印象の穏やかなデーヴァ（男性神）像である。尊顔に3つの類型があることは確からしく思われるが，3つの疑問がある。バイヨン時代になって，門衛神がドラヴァルターから左右にアスラとデーヴァ像を据え，一歩引いた両側にデヴァター像を配する形式が生まれた。これは建物の出入口ホールにも，ほぼ例外なく使用されている。前面を戦う強い神であるアスラとデーヴァ像で護り，出入口開口部の左右の対の位置に女神のデヴァター像というのはそれなりの筋が通っているように考えられる。しかし，四方位を護持するために3つの戦う神というのは，どのような理屈によるのだろうか。二方向はどうしても同じものを配置せざるをえないが，その根拠となる理由が今のところ見いだせないのである。尊顔塔が四面塔と呼ばれるのは四方位神の考え方からであろうが，とすれば余計，3類型の護持神で四方位を，と何故考えたのかという謎が浮かぶのである。他の2つの疑問もこの四方位神の謎と関係がある。四方に神を配置するのは，四方八方，全世界を強い神が睨み，安寧を願うということであって，寺院の中央と四錐に方位神を置くというのが，少なくとも大乗仏教の考え方であろう。バイヨンでは，四方，八方どころか，ありとあらゆる場所に方位神が置かれ，方位神自体が混沌とした世界を醸成しているかのような気配がある。また，尊顔像はほぼ3類型に分類されるが，中には，目の形や頬から頸への線が左右で異なっていたり，頸帯飾りという顔貌の表情には関係のない装飾が左右で異なっていたりする。大型の石彫は，左右2人の彫師で分担し，最後に親方が調整するのが通常で，バイヨンの尊顔は，左右で異なる表情を意図的に演出したとも考えら

(God King) have already been proposed as theories. We, the Japanese Government Team for Safeguarding Angkor (JSA), considered the collection of versatile survey data to be our first priority, so we photographed all the existing faces from the front with a large camera and made a joint survey record of art history and architectural history. As a result, from a distance, it may seem like Shiva's third eye or an incarnation of Avalokitesvara on the face. We examined with the comprehensive consideration the art historical analysis of details and 3D scan surveying the forehead ornament expressing the dignity, the elements and contour of the faces, crown band, neck ornament and others elements. Although these face towers are mainly described as four-faced in academic books, there are also face towers with only three or two faces inscribed on them. What they all have in common is that they wear the leaf crown that warriors usually wear. Therefore, it must be assumed that these towers are carvings of fighting deities protecting the four directions. Art historical research has revealed three tendencies among these deities. (1) Devata (goddess) statues with narrow, slender eyes and slender cheek lines, (2) Asura statues with berserk expression, acorn-shaped eyes and jowls, and (3) Deva (god) statues that has impression between the two. Although it seems certain that there are three types of faces, there are three questions. In the Bayon period, a new style emerged in which the gateway deities were placed on either side of the Dravarta, with Asura and Deva on the left and right, and Devatas on both sides, one step away from the Dravarta. This is used almost without exception in the entrance halls of buildings. It seems reasonable to have the front of the building protected by statues of Asura and Deva, the strong gods of war, and the goddess Devata in a pair of positions on either side of the doorway opening. However, what is the logic behind having three fighting deities to protect the four directions? The two directions are inevitably by the same god, but I have not been able to find a reason for this at this point. The reason why the face towers are carved four faces may be due to the idea of a four-directional deity, which raises the mystery of why the three types of guardian deities were thought to have four directions. The other two questions are also related to the mystery of the four directions deities. The placement of a deity in the four directions means that a strong deity would gaze in all directions and over the entire world to pray for peace and tranquility, and the placement of a deity of the four directions in the center of the temple and in the four corners is at least a Mahayana Buddhist concept. In Bayon, the deity of direction is placed in all directions, not only in the four directions and eight directions, but in every possible place, giving the impression that the deity of direction itself is fostering a chaotic world. In addition, the statues of the deity's face almost can be classified into three types, but some of them have different eye shapes and lines from the cheeks to the neck, or have different ornaments on the neck band,

れる，というのが美術史専門家の意見であった。多様な顔貌を表出するためには3類型の原則が必要で，その原則を少し変更することで，位置や大きさや光と影を時々刻々と変化させ，多様な神々の像をさらに増幅させようとしたのだろうか。とすれば，それは何のために。依然として謎が残るのである。

3. クメール世界のパノラマ的パンテオンの謎

バイヨンの本尊は，ムチリンダ竜王に護持された仏陀座像で，総高4.7m，12世紀後半から13世紀後半頃のクメール彫刻屈指の偉容と深い精神性を湛えたまま，バイヨン中央塔直下竪坑内に投下されていたものを1930年代に，EFEO（フランス極東学院）により発掘されたものである。出土時は大きく7つに分断されていたが，その後修理され，アンコール・トム王宮前広場近くのプレアヴィヘア・プランピー・ロヴェンで住民に護持されてきた。この本尊仏のレプリカ作製復原研究を通して，バイヨン建立の背景の一部が究明される可能性がある。

バイヨン建立のプロセスは未だ不分明である。ジャヤヴァルマンⅦ（1181～1218頃）が，その治世初期に建立したとしても当初から大乗仏教の寺院であったか不明の点がある。というのは，中央塔群の基壇基礎の北東下部にヒンドゥー教シヴァ神信仰の礼拝祭儀にかかわるソーマ・スートラの痕跡が確認された考古学調査がある。一方で，中央上段テラス上の西副祠堂の下部壁体に，移築の可能性もあるが，美術史的編年から見て12世紀後半頃の仏像彫刻の断片が残ること，また十字回廊隅塔のペディメントに残る古式のアプサラ像などから，当初期から仏教色を備えた寺院であった可能性は否定し切れない，と美術史学から指摘されている。いずれにしろ現状伽藍の宗教モチーフの配置とバイヨン全体の増改築による変容過程のすり合わせが必要となるが，以下に主な論点を整理する。

バイヨン中央祠堂に本尊として安置されていたと考えられる仏陀座像と，これまでのJSA美術史班の調査により，中央塔礼拝主軸空間には，王と王家の仏陀信仰，中央塔を囲繞する8基の副塔には，菩薩像，クメールの主な地方神，アンコール朝の祖王が祀られていることが明らかにされている。そして，内回廊浅浮彫装飾については，正面東側が主に王の業績に関する伝説，北側がシヴァ神，西側がヴィシュヌ神，南側についてはバイヨンの宗旨が変更になったため，仏教関連の主題からシヴァとヴィシュヌ関連のモチーフに変えて彫刻された，あるいはあらかじめ刻まれていた仏教モチーフを削除して，

which is not related to the facial expression, between the left and right sides. Art historians have suggested that the faces of Bayon towers were usually carved by 2 sculptors positioned on each left and right side, and then the chief sculptor adjusted the balance. Historians mentioned the possibility that the sculptor intentionally produced different facial expressions on the left and right sides. The principle of the three types is necessary to represent a variety of facial expressions, and by slightly modifying the principle, was the artist trying to further amplify the diverse images of the gods by making the position, size, and light and shadow change from time to time? If so, to what end? It remains a mystery.

3. Mystery of the Panoramic Pantheon of the Khmer World

The main image of the Bayon is a seated Buddha protected by the Dragon King Mucalinda, 4.7m high, one of the most magnificent and deeply spiritual Khmer sculptures from the late 12th to the late 13th century, which was excavated by EFEO in the 1930s after being buried in the looted shaft directly below the Central Tower of Bayon. When it was excavated, it was broken into seven large and several smaller pieces, but it was repaired and has been preserved by the local people at the Preah Vihear Pram Pi Lveng near the Royal Palace in Angkor Thom. There is the possibility to clarify some of the background of the construction of Bayon through research on the restoration of the replica of the Great Buddha image.

The process of Bayon construction is still unclear. Even if Jayavarman VII (1181-1218) built the temple in the early period of his reign, it is uncertain whether it was a Mahayana Buddhist or multi-religion temple from the beginning. There is an archaeological survey that revealed traces of a soma-sutra, which is related to the worship rituals of Hindu Shiva, on the lower northeastern part of the base of the Central Tower. On the other hand, art historians have pointed out that although there is a possibility of repurpose, it is undeniable that the temple was a Buddhist temple from its early period. This is substantiated by the fact that there are fragments of Buddhist sculptures from the late 12th century on the lower wall of the western sub-tower on the 3rd terrace, and an ancient Apsara image on the pediment of the cruciform gallery. In any case, it is necessary to reconcile the arrangement of religious motifs in the current temple with the transformation process of the Bayon as a whole through additions and renovations. The issue for consideration is the enshrinement of the seated Great Buddha image as the principal image in the Central Tower of Bayon. The research conducted by the JSA Art History Group so far have revealed that the Central Tower worship axis space is dedicated to the king and the royal family's belief in Buddha, and the eight sub-towers surrounding the

その上に新しく浮彫をし直した，すなわち南側だけ他より若干深く掘られているとする調査もある。回廊は連続的な礼拝空間であり，そこに王家の信仰，仏教，シヴァ教，ヴィシュヌ教，地方の精霊や祖霊，さらに特定の宗教を超越した守護神としてのデヴァター，アスラ，デーヴァの三神など，およそ当時のクメール世界において考えられる限りの神々を呼び寄せ，立体的かつパノラマ的に連続させて展開していることに，バイヨンの特徴がある。中央塔第3テラス上主軸の南側に，ジャヤヴァルマンⅦの父君の菩提を弔うプレア・カーン（1191年）の本尊観世音菩薩立像と，同じく北側に母堂をなぞらえた般若波羅密多菩薩立像の各々を小堂に祀り，仏陀を主尊とし，観音と般若波羅密多を脇侍とするバイヨン三尊形式をつくり，十字型内回廊の四方と四錐に各々を配置し，計8基，そしてこれを，バイヨンを中心にアンコール地域にプレア・カーンと母の菩提寺タ・プローム（1186年）へと拡げ，さらに東北タイのピマイをはじめとした領国に拡大させたようである。特にスールヤヴァルマンⅡの時代の征服地はその後再び仏教色の強い国に戻ったために，ジャヤヴァルマンⅦは施療院の薬師如来を先頭に仏教的福祉政策を強めたことが窺われる。

バイヨン外回廊には，チャンパとの戦争や王を描くだけでなく，民衆の生活が積極的かつ生きいきと描かれているのが特徴だと思われる。当時の世界観において，民衆とはいえ，王権や宗教から独立していたとは考えられない。帝国の護国寺院のハイライトともなる場面に民衆の姿がパンテオンの一部として出現すること自体が，支配と被支配を超えた，伝統的神と新しい神の争いを超えた，水と森のゆらめきを超えた，その中からしか生まれ出ようがないが，そこから超え出ることによって，新しい王と民衆が新しい仏陀とヒンドゥーの神と新しい伝統の神々が，すなわちクメール世界が新しい次元に躍り出たことを示しているのかもしれない。それがクメール帝国，ジャヤヴァルマンⅦ，そしてバイヨンの創成によって成就したのかもしれない。

4. バイヨン中央塔建築構造の謎は
誰が命じたものなのか

バイヨンの数々の謎は，突出した帝国を征覇するに至った不世出の王，ジャヤヴァルマンⅦの，精神と肉体の息詰まるような葛藤の劇から生み出されたとするのが，三島由紀夫『癩王のテラス』のシナリオであった。バイヨンを眼にした者は，三島でなくとも，その謎に挑戦したくなるであろうことは容易に肯ける。しかしバイヨ

Central Tower are dedicated to bodhisattvas, major Khmer local deities, and the founder king of the Angkor Dynasty. In addition, other decorative reliefs mainly depict legends of the king's achievements on east side, Shiva on south side, and depicts Vishnu on west side Inner Gallery. On the south side, art historian pointed out the possibility that it was carved with motifs related to Shiva and Vishnu instead of Buddhist themes due iconoclasm of Bayon. Some studies suggest that the motifs were removed and new relief was carved on top of them, so that., only the south side was carved slightly deeper than the others. The gallery is a continuous space for worship, and it is a three-dimensional, panoramic, and continuous development that invokes all possible deities in the Khmer world at the time, including the royal religion, Buddhism, Shiva, Vishnu, local and ancestral spirits. The three guardian deities Devata, Asura, and Deva transcend any particular religion and are one of the defining characteristics of Bayon. On the south side of the main axis on the third terrace of the Central Tower, a standing image of Bodhisattva Avalokiteshvara, the principal deity of Preah Khan (1191), which is dedicated to the repose of the soul of King Jayavarman VII's father, and a standing image of Bodhisattva Prajnaparamita, who was modeled after Ta Prohm on the north side, are enshrined in a small hall, forming the Bayon triad with the Buddha as the main deity and Avalokiteshvara and Prajnaparamita as supporting deities. These deities were arranged for a total of 8 on the four sides and four corners of the cruciform gallery. It has been extended to the temples of Preah Khan and his mother's family temple of Ta Prohm (1186) in the Angkor area, centering on the Bayon, and then projecting to Phimai and other territories in northeastern Thailand. In particular, since the conquered areas during the reign of Suryavarman II were later reintroduced to the country with a strong Buddhist practices, Jayavarman VII strengthened his Buddhist welfare policy that was led by the Bhaisajyaguru in the hospitals and chapels built along the Royal Roads.

The Bayon Outer Gallery seems to be characterized not only by its depiction of the war with Champa, but also by its positive and vivid portrayal of the daily lives of the people. In the worldview of the time, the people could not be considered independent of royal power or religion. The very fact that the figure of the people appears as part of the pantheon in a scene that is also the highlight of the imperial temple of protection can only emerge from within. Beyond the conflict between the ruler and the ruled, the traditional and new gods, the shimmering waters and forests, but by transcending from there, the new king and the people a new Buddha, a new Hindu god, and new gods of tradition, may indicate the Khmer world had leaped into a new temporal dimension. This may have been fulfilled by the Khmer Empire, Jayavarman VII, and the creation of the Bayon.

ンには精神のドラマだけでなく，建築構造というリアル
な物質の謎もあることも見逃すべきではない。わけても，
中央塔および中央塔群の謎は巨大な難問である。難問で
はあるが，これまでEFEOをはじめ，この巨大な謎に魅
せられた世界中の専門家による解決への挑戦が続けられ
てきた。しかし，バイヨンの謎といえば大部分が尊顔
塔であり，神々の変更や重層振りであり，浅浮彫であり，
その複雑な歴史や，異形な形や空間ではあっても，それ
らの物質的な成り立ちとその謎について，正面から挑ん
だ専門家はあまりいなかった。高塔を持つ，ピラミッド
型寺院の基壇基礎の中央坑を発掘し，その構造，つまり
支持壁があるか，あるいは無しで表面を一層か二層の砂
岩とラテライトで覆った砂質地盤の版築土層の直接基礎
のどちらかであることを明らかにしている。何のために，
何か埋蔵宝物の有りや無しやの関心が強かったのはやむ
を得ないとして，その地盤基礎の構造とそれに連動した
上部構造について，かつてはあまり関心が払われなかっ
たようだ。

　バイヨン中央塔は高さが27mあり，それが高さ15m
の厚い版築土層のみで，つまり直接基礎で支持されてい
る。現代建築でいえば，約10階建の鉄筋コンクリート
造のビルが地下杭などの安定した支持壁無しで，砂上の
楼閣のように建っているようなものだといえよう。カン
ボジアでは地震が無いとはいえ，高塔の荷重そのもので
地盤が沈下しないのか。それに擦り合わせの空目地で積
まれた石壁の目地がズレれば，それから半年は雨季でス
コールのある土地柄である。基壇版築土層内に雨水が浸
透していくということは当然想定されたはずである。に
もかかわらず，このような構造を採用し，改善しようと
しなかったのは何故か。バイヨン中央塔は，ともかく倒
壊することもなく，約800年間その偉容を保ち続けたの
である。ここにこそ謎と驚きがある。JSA/JASAの，地
盤地質と建築構造を中心とした専門家たちは，この大き
な謎があったが故に，連携して取り組み，物理と建築構
法の仕組みを解明していった過程が明らかにされるであ
ろう。

　クメールの祖先たちがインドからの刺激を受け，気候
風土に合うようにクメール建築を工夫し，それらの体験
が伝統となり，価値観となり，思想となっていく様相は，
クメールの伝統だけのものではなく，およそ文明の伝播
について広く視ることができる。そこに特別のものはな
いように思われるのに，いざ修復の段になって初めて問
題が露出してきたのである。

　バイヨン中央塔の竪坑は1930年代に発掘された。そ
の埋め戻し土の強度はほぼ0で，周辺の版築土層の強度
とのあまりの極端な差は，地下水脈の季節変動と近年の

4. Who Ordered the Mystery of the Bayon Central Tower Architectural Structure?

The scenario of Yukio Mishima's "The Terrace of the Leper King" was that the many mysteries of the Bayon were created from the drama of the struggle between the mind and body of Jayavarman VII, an unprecedented king who conquered a prominent empire. It is easy to agree that anyone who has seen Bayon would want to challenge this mystery, even if they are not Mishima. However, we should not overlook the fact that the Bayon has not only a spiritual drama but also a real material mystery in the form of its architectural structure. In particular, the mystery of the Central Tower and its group of towers is a huge conundrum. Despite the difficulty, experts from all over the world, including EFEO, have been trying to solve this mystery. However, many of researchers the elucidate the Bayon's mysteries of not material origins of the tower and its mysteries, but the tower, the changes and layering of the gods, the reliefs, complex history, and atypical shapes. The excavation of base foundation of the high-towered central shrine, revealed that it is constructed by one or two layers of sandstone and laterite covering the surface, with a support wall or not. It seems there was a strong interest in the existence or not of some buried treasure, not much attention was once paid to the structure of the foundation and the superstructure.

The Central Tower of the Bayon is 27 meters high and was supported only by a thick layer of compacted soil 15 meters high, in other words, on a direct foundation. In modern architecture, it would be like a 10-story reinforced concrete building standing like a tower on the sand without any stable support walls such as foundation pile. Even though there are no earthquakes in Cambodia, does the load of the tall tower itself not cause the ground settlement? If the joints of the stone walls, which were piled up with the friction joints, were to shift, it is easy to imagine rainwater infiltrating into the soil foundation during periods of rain. Nevertheless, why did they adopt this kind of structure and not try to improve it? The Central Tower of the Bayon did not collapse, and it continued to maintain its grandeur for about 800 years. Herein lies the mystery and wonder, and it is precisely because of this great mystery that JSA/JASA specialists in geology and building construction and geotechnology worked in tandem to unravel the physics and the mechanics of the building's construction.

We can see not only Khmer tradition but also wider context of the spread of civilization in the process that Khmer ancestors created their original convention, experiences, and values while received inspiration from India. Although there seems to be nothing special about the Central Tower of Bayon, it was not until the restoration work that the problem was exposed.

地球環境の変動による長時間降雨の頻発が，乾けば深部まで浸透しないですぐに強度を復元していた土層が，雨水によって極端に弱体化する砂質であることが判明した故に，将来の惨禍を招かないか危惧されるに至ったのである。バイヨン中央塔において，基壇基礎の問題が浮上する以前から，アンコールの修復においては，基壇基礎の内部構造として，鉄筋コンクリートの床板と壁体，そして排水管の導入などにより版築土層とは無関係な構造になってしまっていた。しかし，クメール建築が版築土層を選び続けたのは，水と地質という彼等にとっての環境の土台に，柔軟に寄り添い，その声を聞きながら生きてきたことの証しが，版築土層の構造に象徴されているようにも思われる。私の考えでは，クメールの版築土層こそ，彼等にとっての環境理念であって，それを維持することが環境調和思想であるように思われる。それがバイヨンにおいて最大の危機を迎えている。私たちの近代化生活がこの危機の源であるといっても過言ではない。クメールの人々が版築土層に込めた意義を継承し，保存すべきであろう。それが文化遺産のオーセンティシティの意味である。

The shaft of the Central Tower of the Bayon was excavated in the 1930s. The strength of the backfilled soil was almost zero, and the difference between the strength of the backfill soil and that of the surrounding plate clay layer is a potential for a catastrophic collapse in the future. Before Central Tower of Bayon, in the restoration of Angkor Monuments, the corrective action to theproblem of the base foundation had been made with reinforced concrete floor panels and walls, and drainage pipes, which had nothing to do with the compacted soil foundation. However, the fact that the Khmer architects continued to choose the compacted soil foundation is symbolized by the structure of the foundation proves that they understood the environmental properties of water and geological elements especially soil. In my opinion, the Khmer's built-up soil layer was their environmental philosophy, and maintaining this philosophy was their idea of environmental harmony. Nowadays the harmony of the Bayon is facing its biggest crisis. It is no exaggeration to say that our modern life is the source of this crisis. The significance that the Khmer people have attached to the soil foundation should be respected and preserved. This is the pronciple of authenticity of cultural heritage.

第 2 章　アンコール・バイヨンに関する既往研究の地平

Chapter 2 Past Study about Angkor and Bayon

中川　武 編
edited by NAKAGAWA Takeshi

1. はじめに

アンコール遺跡については，周知のようにEFEO（フランス極東学院）の先学達による1世紀以上にわたる調査，研究，修復事業がある。アンコール遺跡をめぐる旅人は何人も彼等の足跡をたどることなしにそれに近づくことはできない。また，各々の専門に応じて既往研究を批判的に継承するのが基本であるが，近年，バイヨンに関する研究が集中している感がある。勿論，H. パルマンティエの研究をはじめ，それを引き継いだ感がある。J. デュマルセの広範な研究，そして基本的にJ. デュマルセが建築遺構に即しているのに対し，碑文研究を基本として，歴史と宗教面から研究を深め，拡げてきたC. ジャックとの間の研究方法の違いが興味深い。本項においては各専門家の各々の関心に照らして，近年のものを中心としたバイヨン関連の主要な研究およびその問題点・課題について概報していただいたので各々掲載する。

2. バイヨンの増改築過程

**概要：J. デュマルセ，H. パルマンティエ
およびC. ジャック説の整理**

バイヨンの建造過程についてはJ. デュマルセの報告書によって既往研究が包括的に吟味され，通説として受け入れられるに至ったが，バイヨンが4期にわたって造られたと見るその骨子は，H. パルマンティエによって築かれた。J. デュマルセは基本的にH. パルマンティエの説を受け入れており，当初は十字形であった回廊の四隅に増築がなされてバイヨンの平面が矩形に変更され，またA～Pの16棟の祠堂が設けられたという見方は継承されている。一方，C. ジャックによるならば，16棟の祠堂の建設は第1期にまで遡るものとされるが，この差異は改めて検討を要する。C. ジャックも指摘しているように，16棟の祠堂が内回廊あるいは外回廊と，どのように接続しているかの建築学的・考古学的考察が再び重要となろう。JSAによる調査では，C. ジャックの説を支持するような調査結果はこれまで何一つとして得られなかったと言ってよい。ただC. ジャックの論の中で注目されるのは，中心塔には仏陀の像が置かれていたはずであるが，しかしその両側に位置する部屋10，11の戸口にはそれぞれヴィシュヌ神の妻ダラーニと，シヴァ神の妻，パールヴァーティの名が刻まれているので，中心塔には仏陀に代わり，ハリハラ神の像が置かれ

1. Introduction

As is well known, there has been a history of over a century of investigation, research, and restoration work in the Angkor Archaeological Park by the pioneering scholars of EFEO. Travelers to Angkor cannot approach the sites without retracing their footsteps. While it is fundamental to critically inherit previous studies according to each specialist's field, I feel that in recent years there has been a growing interest in research on the Bayon. Of course, those studies have been preceded by the work of H. Parmentier and others. In the various studies, extensive research by J. Dumarçay and the difference in research methods between J. Dumarçay, who primarily focuses on architectural aspect, and C. Jacques, who has deepened and expanded research from the perspectives of history and religion, based on epigraphy, are especially interesting. In this section, summaries of the major studies related to the Bayon, mainly in recent years, as well as their issues and challenges are provided in light of the interests of each specialist.

2. Reconstruction Process of Bayon

**Summary: Organization of the Theories
by J. Dumarcay, H. Parmentier, and C. Jacques**

The construction process of Bayon has been comprehensively examined in previous studies by J. Dumarcay and his study has been accepted as a prevailing theory. However, the framework that Bayon was built in four phases was already established by H. Parmentier. J. Dumarcay basically accepts Parmentier's theory, which suggests that extensions were made at the corners of the initially cruciform gallery, and changing the plan of Bayon from a cross to a rectangle, then 16 chapels (A to P) were added. On the other hand, according to C. Jacques, the construction of the 16 chapels dates back to the first phase, but this difference needs to be reconsidered. As pointed out by C. Jacques, the architectural and archaeological considerations of how the 16 chapels are connected to the inner or Outer Galleries will be important once again. According to the investigations by JSA, it can be said that no investigation results supporting the theory of C. Jacques have been obtained. On the other hand, what is noteworthy in C. Jacques' theory is that the Central Tower should have had an image of Buddha, but since the names of Dharani, wife of Vishnu, and Parvati, wife of Shiva, are inscribed on the doorways of chambers 10 and 11, located on either side of the Central Tower, it is assumed that an image of Harihara was placed in the Central Tower instead of Buddha. This point should be discussed further in the future. In addition, although the theory proposed by H. Parmentier and J. Dumarçay was

たと推定されると述べている点で，この指摘については今後さらに検討をおこなうべきであろう．H. パルマンティエ－J. デュマルセによる説は基本的に正しいことがJSAによって確認されたものの，細かい点においては追加・訂正すべき箇所が見つかった．特に最上基壇上に立つ塔群などに関しては新たな発見もなされ，これらはバイヨン・インヴェントリーとして詳細に記されることが期待される．　　　　　　　　　　　（西本 真一）

3．ジャヤヴァルマンⅦの外征と内政

概要：ジャヤヴァルマンⅦの登位，外征，内政

1177年にチャンパ（ジャヤインドラヴァルマンⅣ）の水軍がメコン川からトンレサップ湖に侵入．ヤショダラプラを占領し，トリブヴァーナディティヤヴァルマンが殺される．未だ登位していないジャヤヴァルマンⅦは，その後4年をかけてチャンパ軍を追い払い，1181年に至って登位する．その後，現バッタンバン州の南「マルヤン」で起こった反乱を平定し，1190年に再び侵入したチャンパ（ジャヤインドラヴァルマンⅣ）軍を破り，1203年から1220年にかけてはチャンパを併合する．並行してヴィエンチャンまでを支配し，チャオプラヤ川流域では，離反しつつあったラヴォ帝国（碑文では1167年にダルマーショカと名乗る王が統治）を呑み込んで，マレー半島北部とシー・サッチャナラーイまで版図を広げてハリプンチャイ帝国と対峙した．ジャヤヴァルマンⅦは1218年没．マハーパラマサウガタ（偉大で最高の仏教徒）の諡号を受けた．

　ジャヤヴァルマンⅦは1190年にチャンパ軍を追走し，その後，短期間（1203〜1220）だが併合する．チャオプラヤ川流域のドヴァラヴァティ国家群は，スールヤヴァルマンⅡの時期にハリプンジャヤ（「ランプンにまで達したよう」G. セデス）まで，いったん平定した地域．内政については，仏教（密教）立国を目指したこと，アンコール・トムの整備とタ・プロム以下，多くの仏教寺院を造営したこと，ダンレック山脈を越えた北方では街道の整備と駅舎（灯火の家）および施療院の造営が注目されてきたが，このこと以外に積極的な議論はみあたらない．ただ，仏教徒であった理由については，ダラニーンドラヴァルマンⅡに由来するか，あるいは母であるチューダーマニの影響（とくに密教．C. ジャック）などが指摘されてきた．

既往研究の意義と問題点・課題

既往研究は，限定された碑文の解読研究と

confirmed to be fundamentally correct by the surveys of JSA, some detail points were found that should be added or corrected. In particular, new discoveries were made regarding the towers standing on the uppermost terrace, and these are expected to be detailed in the Bayon Inventory.

(Shinichi Nishimoto)

3. The foreign campaigns and domestic policies of Jayavarman VII

Summary: Ascension, foreign campaigns, and domestic policies of Jayavarman VII

In 1177, the naval forces of Champa (under Jaya Indravarman IV) invaded from the Mekong River to Tonle Sap Lake. They occupied Yasodharapura and killed Tribhuvanadityavarman. Jayavarman VII, who had not yet ascended the throne, spent the next four years driving out the Champa army and finally ascended to the throne in 1181. He then quelled a rebellion in Marjan, south of present-day Battambang province, and defeated the invading Champa army (under Jaya Indravarman IV) again in 1190, before annexing Champa from 1203 to 1220. Concurrently, he extended his rule to Vientiane and absorbed the rebellious Lavo Kingdom (ruled by a king who adopted the name Dharanindravarman in 1167 according to inscriptions) in the Chao Phraya River basin, and extended his territory to the northern Malay Peninsula and Si Satchanalai, then faced the Haripunchai Kingdom. Jayavarman VII died in 1218. He received the posthumous title of Mahaparamasaugata (Great and Supreme Buddhist).

In 1190, Jayavarman VII pursued the Champa army, eventually annexing them briefly from 1203 to 1220. The Dvaravati states in the Chao Phraya River basin were temporarily pacified up to Haripunjaya ("as far as Lampang"; G. Cœdès) during the reign of Suryavarman II. Regarding domestic policies, Jayavarman VII aimed for a Buddhist (Esoteric Buddhism) state, arranged Angkor Thom, and constructed many Buddhist temples including Ta Prohm. In the northern regions beyond the Dângrêk Mountains, his efforts in road construction, rest houses (houses of lights), and hospitals have been noted, but there is little other active discussion. However, it has been pointed out that the reason why he was a Buddhist may have originated from Dharanindravarman II or from the influence of his mother, Tudamani (especially Esoteric Buddhism; C. Jacques).

Significance and Issues/Challenges in Previous Studies

Previous studies have been conducted by comparing the decipherment of limited inscriptions with limited Chinese literature. Due to the limited nature of the sources, there are limitations in interpreting details, but efforts have been made to construct an overall picture as much as possible. The issues regarding foreign campaigns are relatively well understood

中国文献とを突き合わせて研究されてきた。史料が限定されているため細部の解釈に限界があるが，可能な限り全体像を構築しようとしてきている。外征に関する問題は，チャンパとの抗争と併合の経緯は比較的よく理解できているが，北方の平定については，各地の碑文やジャヤヴァルマンⅦの瞑想像の分布などから，その支配の範囲が想定されているものの，平定の経緯や時期についてははっきりした史料がなく詳細がわかっていない。

　仏教立国という王国の大きな方向転換の理由は，従来の研究史ではジャヤヴァルマンⅦ個人の私的な問題として捉えられてきたようで，積極的に言及されていない。しかしこの転換は国家観や王権の統治の正当性が巨大な変容を起こしたことを意味する。クメールのヒンドゥー教立国の思想は，チャンパとも共有していたシヴァ派を前提とした神王思想に由来する。国家を代表する寺院には「王名＋イシュヴァラ」の名を冠するリンガを安置した。この種のシヴァ神による神王思想は，現時点ではチャンパが最も古く，インドよりも早い時期に成立したと考えられている。インドネシアも同様の神王思想を持っており，ジャヤヴァルマンⅡの国家統一と立国にとっても重要な存在であった。キングメーカーであるバラモン「ディヴァーカラ」に始まる新王統以後，ヴィシュヌ神が前面に現れるようにみえることやスールヤヴァルマンⅡの個人的な？信仰が仏教の様相を垣間みせていること，そしてジャヤヴァルマンⅦの両親，ダラニーンドラヴァルマンⅡが大乗仏教徒であり（G. セデス），チューダーマニが密教の信奉者であったこと（C. ジャック）は，もっと注目されるべきである。つまりこの時期，公的には王権の精神的支柱をヴィシュヌ神やシヴァ神に依存しつつも，私的な信仰としては仏教が王家に浸透し，国家と王権を守護する旧来の宗教と個人の救済を目的とする新宗教とが併存する状況であったらしい。

　ジャヤヴァルマンⅦの外征は，スールヤヴァルマンⅡが支配し，彼の死後（1150年）内政の不安定な時期にクメールの支配から離れていったと考えられるドヴァラバティの各国家を再び支配すること，つまりスールヤヴァルマンⅡ時版図の再獲得をめざしたものだが，結果的にその目標よりもやや広い地域を獲得した，と考えてよいと思われる。このとき，ドヴァラヴァティの宗教である仏教と王権の宗教との融合は，シヴァ派の神王思想やヴィシュヌ神の権威が通用せず，従来の王権の正当性の主張が困難な状況にあったことから選択の余地のない政策として求められたと考えられる。この状況を契機として，スールヤヴァルマンⅡの頃から垣間見える仏教化の気配が一挙に前面に現れた可能性が高い。

　ジャヤヴァルマンⅦの政策は，ダンレック山脈の北側

in terms of the conflicts and annexations with Champa. However, regarding the pacification in the north, while the extent of his control is inferred from various inscriptions and the distribution of the Meditation Statue of Jayavarman VII, the details of the pacification process and timing are unclear due to the lack of definitive sources.

The significant shift in the kingdom towards becoming a Buddhist state has traditionally been understood as a personal issue of Jayavarman VII and has not been actively discussed. However, this transformation signifies a huge change in the national view and the legitimacy of kingship. The Khmer ideology of a Hindu state was based on the concept of divine kingship shared with Champa, which worshiped Shiva. In the temples representing the state, the lingas bearing the name of "King's name + Ishvara" was enshrined. As far as is known at the moment, this kind of divine kingship ideology based on Shiva is considered to have originated earliest in Champa, even earlier than in India. Indonesia also had a similar divine kingship ideology, which was significant for Jayavarman II's unification and state formation. Under the situation, it should be noted that after the new royal lineage began with the Brahmin "Divakara" as the kingmaker, the god Vishnu seems to have come to the forefront, the personal(?) faith of Suryavarman II shows glimpses of Buddhism, and among the parents of Jayavarman VII, Daranindravarman II was a Mahayana Buddhist (G. Coedès), and Chudamani was a follower of Tantric Buddhism (C. Jacques). In other words, during this period, while publicly depending on Vishnu and Shiva as the spiritual pillars of kingship, Buddhism permeated the royal family as a private belief, coexisting with the traditional religion that protected the state and kingship and the new religion aimed at individual salvation.

Jayavarman VII's foreign campaigns aimed to reassert control over the various Dvaravati states that had drifted away from Khmer control during the unstable period of internal affairs after the death of Suryavarman II (1150). It can be considered that he achieved a slightly wider area than his original goal. At this time, the fusion of the Dvaravati religion, Buddhism, with the royal religion was seen as an unavoidable policy, as the authority of the Shiva-based divine kingship and Vishnu's authority did not apply, making it difficult to assert the legitimacy of kingship. This situation may have prompted a sudden emergence of Buddhist tendencies that had been glimpsed since the period of Suryavarman II.

Jayavarman VII's policies aimed to win over the hearts of Buddhists by establishing rest houses and hospitals along roadsides on the north area of the Dangrek Mountains, while repeatedly constructing large Buddhist temples centered around Angkor to convert the Hindu Khmer population to Buddhism on the south area of the Dangrek Mountains. Looking at the simultaneous construction projects in various regions, the conversion of the expanded Khmer kingdom into a Buddhist state was likely a pressing issue for Jayavarman

では主に街道沿いに駅舎と施療院を各地に設けることで仏教徒たちの民心を掌握し，ダンレックの南側ではアンコールを中心に大規模仏教寺院の造営を繰り返し，ヒンドゥー教のクメール民衆を仏教化しようとするものであった。これら各地で同時に進められた造営事業をみると，ジャヤヴァルマンⅦにとって拡大したクメール帝国の仏教立国化は切実な問題であったように思われる。ところが従来の研究史は，ジャヤヴァルマンⅦの仏教立国の意図を，私的な信仰の問題かその延長として扱ってきたようにみえる。しかし，王権の正当性がどのような宗教的論理によって担保されたのか，なぜ宗教政策が転換されたのか，など，王権と宗教の問題は巨大なテーマであり，内政，統治の方策の問題としてもっと注目し，研究されなければならない。 　　　　　　　　　　（溝口 明則）

4. J. Clark編『Bayon: New Perspectives』

　近年のバイヨン関連の研究成果を取りまとめられた論稿集が『Bayon: New Perspectives』である。以下が主要論稿に関する概要および見解である。

⑴ Ang Choulean "In the Beginning was Bayon"

概要　Ang Chouleanが同書においてクメール創世神話を考察することにより，クメールの人々が自然と超自然との交信を通じて，彼等の魂を紡いできたプロセスを鮮やかに示している。バイヨンは，クメール・アンコールの歴史そのもののようにも，そこからできるかぎり超出したようにも考えられることの理想の一端を教えていただいたように思う。 　　　　　　　　（中川　武）

⑵ O. Cunin "The Bayon: an archaeological and architectural study"

概要　本書は1990年代以降のバイヨンの復原研究および遺構造営史の研究を取りまとめると共に，J. コンマイユによってバイヨン各所において集積された石材の探査作業，ジャヤヴァルマンⅦ統治期に建設された地方拠点遺構であるバンテアイ・チュマールとの比較考察から，バイヨンの上部構造をはじめとした全容の復原考察を行っており，20世紀までのバイヨン復原研究に新たな展開を加えている。また，石組みの連続性・考古学的な痕跡といった遺構の実地調査，カンボジアータイにおける周辺時代の遺構調査と比較分析，P. ステルンによって1965年に発表されたバイヨン様式史に関する研究，アンコール地域でJSA内田教授によって実施された帯磁率測定結果に基づき，寺院の建造順序に関する

VII. However, the question of the relationship between kingship and religion, such as what religious logic ensured the legitimacy of kingship and why religious policy was shifted, is a huge topic, therefore this topic must be given more attention and study as a matter of internal politics and governance measures. 　　　　　　　　(Akinori Mizoguchi)

4. "Bayon: New Perspectives", edited by J. Clark

A collection of reports summarizing recent research on the Bayon has been compiled in "Bayon: New Perspectives." The following is an overview and analysis of the main reports.

⑴ Ang Choulean "In the Beginning was Bayon"

Summary　In this report, Prof. Ang Choulean vividly illustrates, through his examination of the Khmer creation myth, the process by which the Khmer people have woven their souls through communication with nature and the supernatural. The Bayon seems to have taught us an ideal aspect, as if it were a part of the history of Khmer Angkor itself or had transcended it as much as possible.

　　　　　　　　　(Takeshi Nakagawa)

⑵ O. Cunin "The Bayon: an archaeological and architectural study"

Summary　In this report, with the compilation of the research since the 1990s on the restoration image of Bayon and the history of its construction, and by an exploration of stones arranged by J. Commaille at various locations in and around Bayon and a comparative study with the Banteay Chhumar, a regional base temple constructed during Jayavarman VII's reign. He examined the restoration image and construction process of the entire Bayon, including its superstructure, and added a new vision to the studies on the restoration image of Bayon temples up to the 20th century. Based on the results of the field survey of the remains, including the continuity of masonry and archaeological traces, survey and comparative analysis of the remains on the surrounding periods in Cambodia and Thailand, study on the history of the Bayon style published by P. Stern in 1965, and the magnetic susceptibility measurements conducted by Prof. Uchida of JSA in the Angkor area, this study provided a diagram of the order of construction of Bayon and their relative relationships with the surrounding monuments. In particular, while following and partially recognizing the chronological process of expansion and renovation of the Bayon previously proposed by J. Dumarçay, C. Jaques and others, he added new insights to the construction range and sequence division.

Expected Future Results　The author utilizes recent petrological research results, such as magnetization measurements of stone materials, as

ダイアグラムおよび周辺遺構との相対的な建造順序関係が示される。特にJ. デュマルセ，C. ジャック等によるバイヨンの増改築編年に準拠し，その一部を再確認しながらも，建設範囲や順序区分に新たな知見を加えている。

今後期待される成果　著者は石材の帯磁率測定という近年行われた岩石学の調査結果を活用し，遺構の造営時期の相違を類推する手がかりとしているが，クメール遺構は転用材が用いられることが多々あるため，表面的な数値の判断のみで築造の前後関係を類推することは困難であることに留意したい。また，本書ではEFEOによって発掘された本尊仏が後から運び込まれたものではなく，建造初期から安置されていたものだと想定するが，JSA/JASAによって発見された中央塔内室床面下部のソーマスートラの痕跡から，計画初期段階でバイヨンが仏教寺院として建造されたかどうかは議論を要する。バイヨンはアンコール・トム都城中央に立地しているという性質上，その計画に関する解明はクメール史における大きな課題の一つである。今後本研究によって示された編年考察を基に，さらなる基礎的調査による検証が期待される。

（成井　至）

⑶ C. Jacques "The historical development of Khmer culture from the death of Suryavarman II to the 16th century"

概要　クメール碑文研究の第一人者であるC. ジャックによる本論考は，ジャヤヴァルマンⅦをめぐる既存の憶測や架空のイメージに対して，碑文を見直すことで精査したものであり，未発表の仮説も含む意欲作である。同王の全貌に迫るためには，少なくともスールヤヴァルマンⅡの死まで遡る必要があり，さらに，その治世以降も続いた建設工事や宗教的反動，そして16世紀末に至るアンコールの都市の変遷を長い時間軸で捉えた内容となっている。現代のクメール研究者の間に広く浸透するジャヤヴァルマンⅦへの安定した評価は，歴史学者G. セデスによって形成されたものである。チャム軍を破り，首都を奪還した「救世主」として「最高王」の位に就いたことや，ジャヤヴァルマンⅧによる徹底的な破壊行為が，ジャヤヴァルマンⅦの伝説や誇張を生み出す要因となった。しかし一般の書物に記される同王の生活や思想は裏付けのない推論を多く含むものであり，注意が要される。

本論考は，上記の問題提起に続いて，その出自から，アンコール陥落前のジャヤヴァルマンⅦ，同王によるヤショダラプラのチャンパからの「解放」，治世の初期，晩年，14世紀までのアンコール略史，幾つかの寺院に関する覚書とバイヨン，そしてバイヨンにおける「ク

clues to infer differences in the construction periods of the remains. However, considering that Khmer remains often use reused materials, it is noted that inferring the chronological relationship of construction based solely on superficial numerical judgments can be difficult. Additionally, the report assumes that the main Buddha excavated by EFEO was not later brought in but was enshrined from the initial construction. Whether the Bayon was built as a Buddhist temple in the early stages is debatable based on the traces of the somasutra found under the floor of the main room of Central Tower discovered by JSA/JASA. Due to its location in the central part of the Angkor Thom, the clarification of its plan is one of the big important challenges in Khmer history. Based on the chronological analysis presented in this study, further verification through additional foundational research is expected.

(Itaru Narui)

⑶ C. Jacques "The historical development of Khmer culture from the death of Suryavarman II to the 16th century"

Summary　This ambitious report by C. Jacques, a leading scholar in Khmer epigraphy, scrutinized existing speculations and fictional images regarding Jayavarman VII through the reexaminations of inscriptions, including unpublished hypotheses. In order to get a full picture of the king, it is necessary to go back at least to the death of Suryavarman II, and the report also takes a long-time frame to capture the construction work and religious reaction that continued after his reign, and the evolution of the city of Angkor until the end of the 16th century. The stable evaluation of Jayavarman VII, widely accepted among contemporary Khmer researchers, was formed by historian G. Cédès. His ascension to the title of "Supreme King" as the "savior" who defeated the Cham army and recaptured the capital, as well as the thorough destruction of the city by Jayavarman VIII, contributed to the legend and exaggeration of Jayavarman VII. However, it is important to note that the king's life and thought as described in popular writings contain a great deal of unsupported inferences. Following the above question, this report mentioned Jayavarman VII before the fall of Angkor, his "liberation" of Yashodharapura from Champa, the early years and later years of his reign, a brief history of Angkor up to the 14th century, notes on several temples and the Bayon, and then conclude by touching on the issue of "kuti" in the Bayon.

Significance and issues of the research　The significance of this study lies in the fact that it clearly shows that behind the very limited information obtained from the inscriptions that have been deciphered until the present day, there remain a vast number of unresolved issues. On the other hand, we reaffirmed the issue of how to relate the fragmented and biased research results of each field and construct history.

ティ」の問題に触れ，締め括られる。

研究の意義と課題　　本研究の意義は，現代まで解読されてきた碑文資料から得られる非常に限られた情報の背後に膨大な未解明の問題が残されていることを端的に示している点にある。他方，互いに断片的で，偏りのある各分野の研究成果をどのように関連づけ，歴史を組み立てるか，という課題を改めて確認することになる。

　スールヤヴァルマンⅡと「アンコール・ワット様式」，ジャヤヴァルマンⅦと「バイヨン様式」といった，広く普及している大掴みの様式史的な歴史解釈は，特定の人物に強い光を当てながら，一方で，その他大勢の歴史を大きな影で覆い隠してしまう。すでにJ．ボワスリエは「アンコール・ワット様式」について同様の指摘をしており，C．ジャックもまた「バイヨン様式」に関して，その下限を14世紀，さらに16世紀まで拡大した。しかしバイヨンをはじめとして，これらの寺院群の建造過程に関するC．ジャックの提案は，H．パルマンティエやP．ステルン，O．クニンの緻密な観察結果と相違することは留意される。同様に，バプーオンやアンコール・ワット，プレア・ピトゥ等に見られる「空中参道」について，C．ジャックは，これをインドラヴァルマンⅡが着手し，ジャヤヴァルマンⅧの時代にも続いた改造であった，と述べる。しかし，この見解もまた，これらの建造に使われた石材の帯磁率を網羅的に計測し，分析を行った内田悦生の研究結果と相違しており，検証の必要がある。ジャヤヴァルマンⅦの出生地を「マヒダラプラ」でなく，「ジャヤディティヤプラ」とし，これをコンポンスヴァイのプレア・カーンに比定する見解も独自のものである。ジャックはその理由として，この都市名がジャヤヴァルマンⅦの碑文に「見当たらないこと」を挙げ，これが新たな都市の建設ではなく，既存の都市を継承した根拠であるとする。実際古代クメールの巨大な石造構造物が，長い時間をかけて増改築を繰り返した結果であることは否めず，上記と併せて，さらに詳しく調査すべき課題である。

　年代に関しては，碑文が示す年代と建造物の年代とが，単純な関係ではない。C．ジャックはこの点について，碑文が与える日付とは，「寺院において神々に命が吹き込まれたときのもので，この時点では寺院の基部だけが完成し，塔はまだ建てられていなかったことを意味する」と述べている。しかし松浦史明の研究では，クメールの碑文に記される年代には，およそ3つのパターンがあると述べられ，さらに詳しく調査すべきである。以上の他にも，クメールにおける土着の信仰と外来のヒンドゥー教，仏教，さらに仏教の中でも大乗仏教，密教，

Widespread stylistic historical interpretations, such as Suryavarman II and the "Angkor Wat style" or Jayavarman VII and the "Bayon style," shine a strong light on specific figures, while it overshadows the history of many others. J. Boisselier had already made a similar point regarding "Angkor Wat style," and C. Jacques has also extended the upper limit of the "Bayon style" to the 14th and then to 16th centuries. However, it should be noted that C. Jacques' proposal regarding the construction process of these temple complexes, including the Bayon, differed from the detailed observation results of H. Parmentier, P. Stern, and O. Cunin. Similarly, regarding the "aerial approach" seen at the temples such as Baphuon, Angkor Wat, Preah Pitu, C. Jacques mentioned that these were modifications initiated by Indravarman II and continued during the reign of Jayavarman VIII. However, this opinion also differs from the research results of E. Uchida, who comprehensively measured and analyzed the magnetic susceptibility of the stones used in these constructions, so it needs to be verified. The view that Jayavarman VII's birthplace is "Jayadityapura" instead of "Mahidharapura" and that this is identified as Preah Khan of Kompong Svay is also a unique opinion. C. Jacques points out that the name of the city is "not found" in the inscription of Jayavarman VII as the reason for this, and that this is the basis for inheriting an existing city rather than building a new one. In fact, it cannot be denied that the huge stone structures of ancient Khmer were the result of repeated additions and renovations over a long period of time, and in conjunction with the above, this is an issue that should be investigated in more detail.

As for the age, there is no simple relationship between the age indicated by the inscription and the age of the structure. C.Jacques states in this regard that the date given by the inscription is "when the gods were brought to life in the temple, meaning that at this point only the base of the temple was complete and the tower had not yet been built". However, research by F. Matsuura states that there are approximately three patterns in the dates recorded in Khmer inscriptions, which should be investigated in more detail. In addition to the above, the complex relationship between the indigenous beliefs in Khmer and the introduction of foreign Hinduism, Buddhism, and even within Buddhism, each sect such as Mahayana Buddhism, Esoteric Buddhism, and Theravada Buddhism and the construction and remodeling of temples is still not fully understood, therefore it still continues to be one of the important issues in Khmer studies.　　(Katsura Sato)

⑷ **P. Sharrock "The Mystery of the Face Towers"**

Summary and Opinion　　As pointed out in this report, conventional studies of the deity's face have sometimes failed to fully reconcile conceptual and doctrinal understandings with understanding of the face in terms of its figurative characteristics. For example, even though it does not match the representation of Avalokitesvara

上座部仏教といった各宗派の伝来と，寺院の建立や改造が複雑に絡まり合う様相は，いまだ十分に解明されておらず，なおもクメール研究の重要な課題の一つであり続けている。 （佐藤　桂）

⑷ P. Sharrock "The mystery of the face towers"

概要および見解　　本論における指摘のように従来の尊顔研究は，概念上・教義上の理解と造形的特徴による理解との照合が十分になされないことがあった。バイヨン期の観音の表現と一致しないにも関わらず，その時期のローケシュヴァラ信仰を背景に，観音の尊顔と見なすなどである。尊顔の造形的特徴に重きを置いた上で，関連する彫刻作品を広く射程に収めて検討する姿勢は，JSA美術史班が重視してきたものである。ただし氏は，JSA美術史班の「デヴァター，デーヴァ，アスラを象徴する尊顔」という見解に対し，尊顔の「均質性」が否定できない（区分を識別できない）ことを問題視する。しかし実際には，一定の均質性を保ちながらも尊顔には造形的差異が存在する。顔貌は，鑑者がその人の印象を左右させる要素が集約されたところであるからこそ，そこに表れる微細な差さえ軽視できない。こうした観点によるならば，やはり，尊顔の顔立は3種に区分される。

本論において氏は，ヴァジュラサットヴァ（金剛薩埵）の尊顔との見解を示す。後のイスラーム王朝の勃興に先立つ12世紀末頃から既に，インドからネパールさらに東南アジア方面へ，仏教（大乗，特に後期密教）の積極的展開が始まっていたことを背景とする。こうした後期密教の積極的展開が，ジャヤヴァルマンⅦ後期のアンコール朝におけるヘーヴァジュラ（喜金剛）信仰を隆盛させたと理解する。青銅製のヘーヴァジュラ，ヴァジュラサットヴァ，ヴァジュラダーラ（持金剛）の造立例や諸尊を表す法具が確認されており，密教系諸尊に対する儀礼の存在は確かであろう。ヴァジュラサットヴァとヴァジュラダーラは本来的には別個の尊格であるが，氏が紹介するピマイ出土の碑文（K.1158）において「最高の仏陀」（金剛界五仏を統合した第六仏）が「ヴァジュラサットヴァ」と称されているように，混同される場合もあった。後期密教的宇宙観における究極存在であるヴァジュラサットヴァの尊顔を表すことでその宇宙における最高位の様相をバイヨンに付帯させ，王の行う国の儀礼に直結する重要性を氏は見出している。また，造形的根拠としては，開眼する（ここに氏もジャヤヴァルマンⅦによる国の精神的防衛の概念が働いていると指摘する）四面四臂ヴァジュラサットヴァの存在を挙げる。

なお，朴亨國は，尊顔を塔堂に表す着想源の一つとし

in the Bayon period, it is regarded as the face of Avalokitesvara in the context of the Lokeśvara beliefs of that period. The approach of emphasizing the figurative characteristics of the deity's face and considering a wide range of related sculptures has been a focus of the JSA Art History team. On the other hand, in response to the JSA Art History team's view that the deity's faces symbolize devatas, devas, and asuras, he takes issue with the undeniable "homogeneity" of the deity's faces (the inability to identify the divisions). In reality, however, there are formative differences among the deity's faces while maintaining a certain degree of homogeneity. Because the facial features are the concentration of factors that influence the impression a person makes, even minute differences that appear in the face cannot be disregarded. From this viewpoint, we think there are three types of facial features of the deity's faces.

In this report, he presented his view that the deity's faces are the faces of Vajrasattva. This theory is based on the fact that Buddhism (Mahayana, especially late esoteric Buddhism) had already begun to actively develop from India to Nepal and Southeast Asia around the end of the 12th century, prior to the rise of the later Islamic dynasties. This active development of late esoteric Buddhism is understood to have led to the flourishing of the Hevajra faith in the Angkor dynasty during the late Jayavarman VII period. Examples of the construction of bronze Hevajra, Vajrasattva, and Vajradhara, as well as ritual implements representing the various deities, have been confirmed, and the existence of rituals for esoteric deities is certain. Although Vajrasattva and Vajradhara are essentially two different dignities, they were sometimes confused with each other, as in the inscription (K.1158) excavated in Phimai, which he introduced, where the "Supreme Buddha" (the sixth Buddha who united the five Buddhas of the Vajrayana world) is called "Vajrasattva". He found that by representing the face of Vajrasattva, the ultimate being in the late esoteric cosmology, Bayon is attached with the aspect of the highest position in the universe, and its importance is directly connected to the state rituals performed by the king. As figurative evidence, he pointed to the existence of the four-faced, four-armed Vajrasattva, which opens the eyes (here, he also pointed out, the concept of spiritual defense of the nation by King Jayavarman VII is at work).

Park Hyounggook had indicated the possibility of a vajra bell with a deity faces on the handle part as one of the sources of inspiration for representing the deity faces on the chamber tower (JSA, 2005 report). Although such a vajra bell has not yet been discovered in Cambodia (there are usual vajra bells), there are Indonesian vajra bells with the deity faces dating back to the 12th century. With this in mind, it may not be necessary to wait for the reception of late esoteric Buddhism from northern India via Nepal. According to Park, if the Bayon and its deity faces are compared to the vajra bell, a body of the bell, as the place where the truth (principle) is propagated to the cosmos,

て，鬼目に尊顔を有する金剛鈴の可能性を示した[1]。このような金剛鈴は，カンボジアにおいて今のところ未発見であるが（通形の金剛鈴はある），12世紀に遡るインドネシアの尊顔付き金剛鈴は存在しており，これを念頭に置くならば，必ずしも，北インドからネパール経由での後期密教の受容を待つ必要もないかもしれない。朴によれば，バイヨンとその尊顔を金剛鈴に置き換えてみると，鈴身は真理（法）を広める場所として人間世界における神仏を安置する堂塔に相当し，鈷は光明・放光として天空に通じるところであり堂塔頂部の蓮華と満瓶に相当する。鬼目が中心となる把部は，その中に納める舎利（聖・法）を近親・守護する部分であり，鬼目の菩薩面は近親を，忿怒面は守護の役割を有する。バイヨンの尊顔が守護神の葉飾付の冠帯を着していることから，守護における無畏と攻撃とも相通じる役割を兼ねた，デヴァター，デーヴァ，アスラと認識することも可能であろう。

(水野 さや)

⑸ V. Roveda "Relifs of the Bayon"

概要および見解　JSA美術史班の調査・研究活動が終了した2004年の時点において，外回廊浅浮彫に関する具体的かつ総括的な調査に及ぶことができていないため，ここでの言及が限定的になることをあらかじめ断っておきたい。

　本論考は，バイヨンの浅浮彫表現の特徴を確認した上で，先行研究における指摘の誤認などにも修正を加え，浅浮彫の各場面の情景が丁寧に記述されている。まず外回廊については，王・王国の歴史的内容によって構成されており，王の年代記を成立させるものとあらためて指摘する。また内回廊については，従来の研究における指摘事項（外・内の回廊浅浮彫は回廊建設直後に施されたものの，王の死によって中断を余儀なくされ，内回廊は13世紀後半，ジャヤヴァルマンⅧ時代という見解）に対し，氏は様式的観点から，ジャヤヴァルマンⅧの時代の彫刻と見なす根拠はなく，内回廊の一部の浅浮彫はジャヤヴァルマンⅦ期に行われ，他はその後の追刻であるが，この時期を16世紀と想定する。そしてこのことが，バイヨン内における浅浮彫モティーフの不連続性，内容や様式の不統一を引き起こしていると判断する。

　美術史班は既刊の報告書において，内回廊浅浮彫の不連続性，内容や様式の不統一については，当時の人々にとっての「合理的関連」に基づくものであったと推察し，必ずしも横つながりの大画面構図として展開することを基本としていない可能性を示してきた。なぜなら，バイヨンの彫刻作業は，一部の追刻・改変を除けば，様式的・技法的な観点において，20～30年間程の比較的短

is equivalent to the chamber tower where gods and Buddha are enshrined in human world, and the prong is as the point to shed the light connecting to the sky, and it is equivalent to a lotus flower in a treasure vase seen at the top of the tower chamber. The holding portion mainly consisting of handle part is place where Buddha's bone (sacred, principle) is held, which means protecting and relative, bodhisatvva face on the grip means close relative, and indignant face has obviously character of protection. Since the deity face of Bayon wears the crown band with leaf decoration for guardian, it can be recognized as a devata, deva, or asura, which can also play the role of both fearlessness and aggression in protection.

(Saya Mizuno)

⑸ V. Roveda "Reliefs of the Bayon"

Summary and opinion　It should be noted that, as of 2004, when the research and study activities of JSA Art History team were completed, it had not been possible to undertake a specific and comprehensive study of the Outer Gallery reliefs, so the scope of reference here is limited.

This report confirms the characteristics of Bayon's reliefs, corrects some misconceptions pointed out in previous studies, and carefully describes the scenes in each relief. Firstly, the Outer Gallery is composed of the historical content of the king and kingdom, and it is pointed out once again that it establishes the chronicle of the king. As for the Inner Gallery, in contrast to the previous research (the Outer and Inner Gallery reliefs were made immediately after the construction of the gallery, but were interrupted by the death of the king, and the relief of the Inner Gallery was made in the late 13th century, during the reign of Jayavarman VIII), he considers from a stylistic point of view, there is no basis for considering the carvings to be from the era of Jayavarman VIII, and some of the reliefs in the Inner Gallery were done during the Jayavarman VII era, while others were added later. He assumes this period to be the 16th century. Then he judges to be the reason for the discontinuity of the relief motifs in the Bayon, and the inconsistency in content and style.

In previous reports, JSA Art History team had suggested that the discontinuity and inconsistency in content and style of the Inner Gallery reliefs were based on 'rational association' for the people of the time, and not necessarily based on the development of a large horizontal composition. This is because, with the exception of a few reproductions and alterations, Bayon's sculptural work, in terms of style and technique, appears to have been basically carried out over a relatively short period of about 20 to 30 years. The content and layout of the Inner and Outer Gallery reliefs also show a relationship in some places. Similarly, it has been noted in previous reports that the Inner Gallery reliefs correspond to the religious segregation of the shrines on the upper terrace. In this report, he also refers to this, but adds the following further

期間に基本的には作業されたと見られるからである。また，内・外の回廊浅浮彫の内容と配置に関係性を見出せる箇所もあるからである。また同様に，内回廊の浅浮彫がテラス上祠堂の宗教的棲み分けに呼応していることについても，既刊報告書において述べた通りである。本論では氏もこのことに言及しているが，さらに次の点を補足しておく。

内回廊東面は王の治世と業績，北面はシヴァ神，西面はヴィシュヌ神，南面はシヴァ系の内容が色濃いが，必ずしも統一が図られておらず，テラス上祠堂の棲み分けに基本的に準じているものの徹底されてはいない。また，浅浮彫表現において，プレ・アンコール期以来の伝統的な表現を用いるところもあれば，バイヨン期において新たに取られた表現も混在している。そのため，同じ神話題材を用いながらも，当時のジャヤヴァルマンⅦおよびその周辺の政治的・宗教的配慮のもと，その一面的な意味に留まらない，重層的理解も可能であろう。

（水野 さや）

⑹ T. S. Maxwell "Religion at the time of Jayavarman VII"

概要　　ジャヤヴァルマンⅦの寺院における宗教的慣習について，主要な世界宗教ではなくクメール文化の文脈の中で理解し，碑文，建築の配置計画，社会人類学的研究などから研究を進めることを目的としている。

その上でまとめとして，初期の時代には，多くの神々がインド名とクメール名の両方で崇拝され，その神聖さはクメール語の称号で示されていた。いくつかのインド名は実際にはオリジナルのクメール名の翻訳であり，必ずしもインドの宗教的概念や神々を反映したものではなかった，としている。

またカンボジアでは，導入された神々と土着の神々が統合され，クメール語の称号体系の中で文脈化され，分類された。これにより，カンボジア社会の構造を反映し，機能的な関連性を得ることができた。これらの神々のために寺院が造営され，寺院に祀られた神々や女神は，カンボジアの文化的アイデンティティの枠組みの中で，個人が地上生活と死後の世界を結びつけることを可能にする精神的階層を提供した，としている。

（早稲田大学小岩研究室アンコールゼミ）

5. M. Hendrickson, M. Stark, D. Evans 編『THE ANGKORIAN WORLD』

概要　　本項は，書籍『THE ANGKORIAN WORLD』

points.

The eastern side of the Inner Gallery is devoted to the king's reign and achievements, the northern side is devoted to Shiva, the western side is devoted to Vishnu and the southern side is heavily devoted to Shiva. Although this is basically the same as the division of residences in the shrines on the upper terrace, they are not fully unified. In addition, some of the reliefs use traditional expressions that have been used since the Pre-Angkor period, while others were newly adopted during the Bayon period. Therefore, although the same mythological subject matter is used, it is possible to understand it in a multilayered manner and not just in one aspect, in accordance with the political and religious considerations of Jayavarman VII and his surroundings at the time.　　(Saya Mizuno)

⑹ T. S. Maxwell "Religion at the time of Jayavarman VII"

Summary　　The aim is to understand the religious practices in the temples of Jayavarman VII in the context of Khmer culture rather than the major world religions, and to study them from inscriptions, architectural layout plans and social anthropological research.

As summary, he mentioned many deities were worshiped in the early period under both Indian and Khmer names, and their sacredness was indicated by Khmer titles. He states that some Indian names were actually translations of the original Khmer names and did not necessarily reflect Indian religious concepts or deities.

He also mentioned that in Cambodia, introduced and indigenous deities were also integrated, contextualized and categorized within the Khmer title system. This enabled them to reflect the structure of Cambodian society and gain functional relevance. Then he remarked temples were built for these deities, and the gods and goddesses worshiped in the temples provided a spiritual hierarchy that enabled individuals to connect their earthly lives with the afterlife within the framework of Cambodian cultural identity.

(Angkor Seminar, Koiwa Laboratory, Waseda University)

5. "THE ANGKORIAN WORLD", edited by M. Hendrickson, M. Stark and D. Evans

Summary　　This section is a chapter-by-chapter extract and summary of architectural-historical references related to Bayon in the book "THE ANGKORIAN WORLD".

Chapter 9: Angkor and the Mekong River: Settlement, Resources, Mobility, and Power

For each region of the Mekong River Basin, the local climate and culture are analyzed with a focus on ecological and historical features. Among them, the Khmer presence in the central forested areas of the lower Mekong River

において，バイヨンに関連した建築史的な言及があるものを章ごとに抽出し，まとめたものである。

第9章　アンコールとメコン川居住，資源，移動，権力

メコン川流域の地域ごとに，その土地の風土や文化を生態学的・歴史的特徴に焦点を当てて分析している。中でもメコン川下流域の中央部の森林地帯にはクメール人が存在し，碑文による記録や建築物の形態から，プレ・アンコールの王朝と繋がりを持っていたことが窺える。これらはアンコール王朝の時代にも引き継がれ，バイヨンの小祠堂にシアンブプラやナーガスターナプラなどメコン川地域の神々が祀られている点，ジャヤヴァルマンⅦによって12世紀末に建てられた病院祠堂のうち3つがメコン地域に存在する点などから，メコン川の地域の支配を非常に重要視していたと考えられる。

第10章　アンコール世界における都市主義の軌跡

クメールの都市を研究するための考古学的手法の変遷を論じ，2000年にわたるその発展に関する現在の知識を評価している。その中で，アンコール・トムについて，J. ゴシエ（2004）及びP. ウィートリー（1983）の論考を用い，インド文献「Sastra」などに則ったアンコール・トムは理想化された都市計画の様を体現するものであり，さらにバイヨンは都市空間を明確に区切り，囲いの中心に存在することから，本質的に寺院都市であると述べている。

第20章　石切り場から寺院へ：アンコール世界の石材調達，物質性，精神性

さまざまな時代のクメール建築から彫刻における石材の使用と加工について，その変遷を考察している。12世紀初頭，スヴァイ・ダムナック地域で産出する斑点のある砂岩の亜石種が脚光を浴び，ジャヤヴァルマンⅦ治世下の作品において象徴的な存在となった。この石は，ジャヤヴァルマンⅦの瞑想姿や仏像，バイヨンのナーガ像などのバイヨン様式の彫刻に多用された。しかしタ・プロームやプレア・カーンの石材にはこの砂岩が見られず，ジャヤヴァルマンⅦの治世初期にはこの石がアンコールの地にはなく，ジャヤヴァルマンⅦがコンポンスヴァイのプレア・カーンなどの建設プロジェクトの過程で，ようやくこの石材を発見した可能性を示唆している。

第24章　栄光の肉体　アンコールの彫像

アンコール時代の彫像の宗教的，政治的，文化的，技術的な文脈を評価し，神性の体現とアンコール時代の碑

basin and their inscriptional records and architectural forms suggest that they had links with the Pre-Angkor dynasty. These relationships were carried over into the Angkor dynasty, and the facts that the small shrine at Bayon deities from the Mekong River region, such as Siambupura and Nagasthanapura, and that three of the hospital shrines built by Jayavarman VII at the end of the 12th century are in the Mekong region, suggest that they placed great importance on controlling the Mekong River region.

Chapter 10: Trajectories of Urbanism in the Angkorian World

The progress of archaeological methods for studying Khmer cities is discussed and current knowledge regarding their development over 2000 years is assessed.

Authors mentioned by citing the reports of J. Gaucher (2004) and P. Wheatley (1983), Angkor Thom embodies an idealized urban plan based on ancient principles such as the Indian literature "Sastra" and remarked that from the reason that Bayon remains the focus of an extended enclosure which neatly delimits and defines the true urban space, Angkor Thom is essentially a temple-city.

Chapter 20: From Quarries to Temples: Stone Procurement, Materiality, and Spirituality in the Angkorian World

The authors examined the changes in the use and processing of stone in Khmer architecture and sculpture in various periods. In the early 12th century, a speckled sandstone subspecies from the Svay Damnak region was in the spotlight and became iconic in the works of Jayavarman VII. This stone was frequently used in Bayon style carvings such as the meditation statue of Jayavarman VII, Buddha statues, and the Naga statues of Bayon. However, this kind of sandstone is not found in the stones of Ta Prohm or Preah Khan. Therefore, it suggests possibility that this kind of stone was not found in Angkor in the early period of Jayavarman VII's reign, and Jayavarman VII may have finally discovered this kind of stone during construction projects such as Preah Khan in Kampong Svay.

Chapter 24: Bodies of Glory: The Statuary of Angkor

The religious, political, cultural and technological aspects of Angkorian statues are assessed, focusing on the embodiment of divinity and the concept of the "Bodies of glory" based on Angkorian inscriptions. The Bayon and Preah Khan inscriptions are examples of local deities being placed in the sub-shrine of the capital's central temple and fostering mutual allegiance. And as examples of archaism and iconoclasm, which deliberately reproduces sculptures in the style of older periods, the example of iconoclasm, the destruction of Buddhist reliefs carved during the reign of Jayavarman VII, and the second stage of vandalism, perhaps by reworking the first iconoclasm in order to re-establish Buddhist primacy, are

文に基づく「栄光の体」の概念に焦点を当てる。その中で首都の中央寺院の副祠堂に地域の神々が置かれ，相互に忠誠心を育んだ事例がバイヨンやプレア・カーンの碑文である。また意図的に古い時代の様式を模した彫刻を再現するアルケイズム，イコノクラスムの例として，ジャヤヴァルマンⅦの治世に彫られた仏教の浅浮彫を破壊するイコノクラスム，おそらく仏教の優位性を再確立するために，最初のイコノクラスムを再加工することによって，破壊行為の第2段階が示されている。

（早稲田大学小岩研究室アンコールゼミ）

6. Khmer Archaeology Lidar Consortium によるアンコール遺跡群の調査

概要 シドニー大学とフランス極東学院，カンボジア政府文化芸術省が中心となった7か国，8組織の国際的な研究チームよりなるKhmer Archaeology LiDAR Consortiumは，2012年にアンコール遺跡群，コー・ケー遺跡群，クーレン山の一部，合計370㎢のエリアにおいて航空レーザー測量（LiDAR）を実施した。2015年には，フランス極東学院とカンボジア政府が連携し，古代クメール帝国の地方都市を中心とする合計1910㎢の考古学的サイトで測量が追加された。

これらの地形情報を利用して各組織の研究者が各種の分析を進め，多くの研究成果が報告されるに至っている（https://angkorlidar.org/）。主要な研究は，精緻な地形図を用いて，寺院，水路，貯水池，土手，道，水田痕地といった遺構や土地改変の痕跡を検出したものである。遺構の広域分布や配置関係を明らかにすることができることから，都市スケールの遺構の認識や水利構造，交通インフラといった大規模で複雑な構造を把握することに長けている。また，面的な遺構の分布が把握されていることによって，発掘調査地点の選定や，点的な調査結果の解釈を格段に高めることに寄与している。

研究の意義と今後の課題 航空測量調査に基づく研究によって，遺跡群として認識されている各地の古代都市の様相が明らかにされつつある。精緻な地形図は，都市構造の解明，土地利用状況の復元，生活実態の解明に対する分析や，各都市が形成されてから，維持，改変，衰退，放棄の過程を解明する手掛かりを提供するものであった。こうした観点からの考察によって，権力の集約化と分散化，支配者層と被支配者層，最盛期と形成－展開期，といった社会の諸側面を既往の史料研究とは別の角度から立体的に検証することができるようになった。

shown. (Angkor Seminar, Koiwa Laboratory, Waseda University)

6. Survey of Angkor Archaeological Sites using LiDAR Technology by the Khmer Archaeology LiDAR Consortium

Abstract The Khmer Archaeology LiDAR Consortium, consisting of an international research team from 7 countries and 8 organizations led by the University of Sydney, EFEO, and the Cambodian Ministry of Culture and Fine Arts, conducted airborne LiDAR surveys over an area of 370 km^2, covering the Angkor Archaeological Park, Koh Ker site, and part of Kulen Mountain in 2012. In 2015, the collaboration between EFEO and the Cambodian government expanded the survey to cover a total of 1,910 km^2, including major regional archaeological sites.

The LiDAR data has been utilized by researchers from various organizations to conduct various analyses, leading to numerous research findings reported on the website https://angkorlidar.org/. The main focus of the research has been the detection of structures and traces of past human activities, such as temples, waterways, reservoirs, embankments, roads, and agricultural fields, through the use of detailed topographic maps. This ability to reveal the wide distribution and spatial relationships of structures allows for a better understanding of large-scale urban structures, water management systems, and transportation infrastructures. Additionally, the knowledge of the spatial distribution of structures has greatly contributed to the selection of excavation sites and the interpretation of point-based survey results.

The Significance and Future Challenges of the Research

Research based on airborne LiDAR surveys is gradually revealing the aspects of ancient cities recognized as archaeological sites. The detailed topographic maps provide valuable insights into the analysis of urban structures, land use patterns, and the living conditions of the inhabitants. As a result, historical reinterpretations can be made from different perspectives, such as the centralization and decentralization of power, the relationship between rulers and the ruled, the peak period and the developmental period of the society, rather than focusing solely on the traditional historiography of ancient and medieval Angkor.

Another crucial outcome is the significant expansion of the spatial recognition of archaeological sites. It became evident that artificial elements constituting the peripheries of major temple structures extend over a much broader area, leading to the reconstruction of a continuous urban landscape that encompasses both cities and rural areas of ancient and medieval periods.

Since different organizations are currently working on research projects for each of the targeted archaeological

また，遺跡群として認識される空間領域が格段に拡張されたことも重要な成果であった。主要な寺院遺構の分布のはるか広域にも都市周辺部を構成する人為的な要素が展開していることが明らかになり，都市と農村とが緩やかに連続した古代・中世の都市景観が復元された。

航空レーザー測量の対象となった各都市遺跡の研究は，それぞれに異なる組織が取り組んでいるのが現状であることから，今後は各組織が情報共有を図り，各都市遺跡の比較や相互分析を通じた総合的な考察が期待される。これによって，古代クメールの各都市の特質や都市築造の時代的展開，中央国家と地方との関係や交易実態を明らかにしていくことが可能になろう。　　　　（下田一太）

sites, future collaboration and information sharing among these organizations are expected to facilitate comprehensive investigations through comparative and mutual analyses. This will shed light on the unique characteristics of each ancient Khmer city, the temporal development of urban construction, and the relationship between central and regional powers, as well as trade practices.　　　　　　　　　(Ichita Shimoda)

References
1) JASA, Annual Technical Report on the Survey of Angkor Monument 2005-2006, September 2006, Angkor Project Office

第 3 章　JSA/JASA の調査研究

Chapter 3 JSA/JASA Research and Study of Bayon

3.1 アンコール地域広域環境
Environment Conditions for the Wider Region of Angkor

岩崎 好規 　　福田 光治 　　大河内 博
IWASAKI Yoshinori　FUKUDA Mitsuharu　OKOUCHI Hiroshi

1. アンコール地域の気象

東南アジアに位置するカンボジアは，熱帯性モンスーン気候帯にある。夏季は西風が卓越し，東西に並ぶエヴェレスト山脈によって整流化され，インド洋からの暑い蒸発水を運んでいくが次第に冷たくなるにつれて，雨を放出することになる。冬には中国東北部からの高気圧が優勢となり，カンボジアにおいては，東北風によって乾冷気がもたらされる。

Fig. 3.1.1に温度，湿度の月別変化，および雨量の月別変化（1980〜2004年の平均）を示した。雨量は雨季の初めから次第に増大していく傾向にある。

乾季の11月から2月までの気候は快適である。東北風が弱まる3〜4月ころには，最高気温は35℃から40℃にもなって草木も枯れるくらいになる。

Fig. 3.1.2に，1979年から2021年までの年間総降雨量の変化を示した。年間降雨量の平均値は1,380mm程度で，ほぼ1,200〜1,500mmという範囲で変動している。

1. Weather Climate in Angkor

Cambodia located in Southeastern Asia is situated in a tropical monsoon climate zone. West wind prevails in summer, being influenced by the Everest Mountain range in west to east direction which brings hot evaporated water from the Indian Ocean but discharges it as rainwater through the cooling process. In winter, high pressure prevails in the north and eastern regions in China and the northeast wind brings dry and cool air to Cambodia.

Fig. 3.1.1 shows monthly changes of temperature, humidity, and rainfall in Siem Reap. Rainfall shows a gradual increase from the beginning of the rainy season. Fig. 3.1.2 shows changes of annual rainfall in Siem Reap. It is a pleasant season from November to February. However, it becomes very hot in March to April when the north-east wind becomes weakened. Fig. 3.1.2 shows the change of the annual rainfall from 1979 to 2021. The average rainfall is 1380mm/year and fluctuates in a range of around 1,200 to 1,500 mm/year.

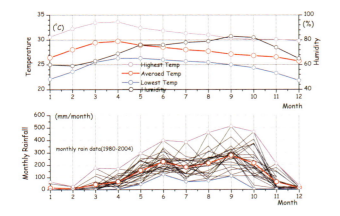

Fig. 3.1.1 Monthly change of temperature, humidity, and rainfall

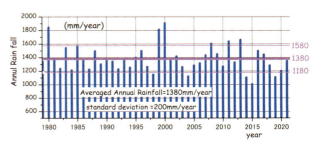

Fig. 3.1.2 Change of annual rainfall in Siem Reap

Fig. 3.1.3 Boring points in Angkor plain

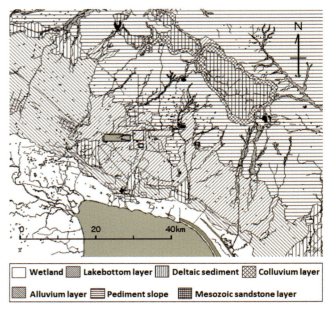

Fig. 3.1.4 Geotechnical N-S section in Angkor

2．アンコールの地形・表層地質

Fig. 3.1.3にアンコール等高線地形図[1]を示した。アンコール平野南北約50km，比高60mで，ほぼ1/1000という緩傾斜を有する。

クーレン山を源流とするシェムレアップ川は，同山の南西部から平野に入り，本来は西南方向に流下し，西バライの西北端部に流れていた。

現在のシェムレアップ川はクーレン山麓から西南に流れたのち，プム・クラート（Phum Khlat）分流堰地点で，人工河川によって南下して東バライの北側を西に流れ，同バライの北西部からアンコール・トムの東側を南下し，シェムレアップ市街の中を通ってトンレサップ湖に流下する。

トンレサップ湖は長さ150km幅30kmの瓢箪型で，乾季にはこの広大な水域がわずか2〜4mという浅い水深となる。

Fig. 3.1.4にJICAによる地表地形地質図[2]を示した。トンレサップ湖周辺には，雨季には水没する湿地帯がひろがり，アンコール平野が隆起する以前の水位が高かったころの湖底層や沖積扇状面が緩やかな平野を形成している。

3．ボーリング調査によるアンコール地下地質構造

アンコール地域における地質調査として100m級のボーリングをJSAが1994年に実施した[3]。その後，

2. Topology and Surface Geology in Angkor

Fig. 3.1.3 shows a topographical map with contour line in Angkor[1]. The Angkor plain expands from the northern lake shore of the Tonle Sap Lake to Phnom Kulen with a distance of about 50km with a gentle slope inclination of 1/1000.

The ancient Siem Reap River flowed out at the south of Phnom Kulen and flowed in the south-west direction to the north-western side of the West Baray.

The present Siem Reap River flows towards the west-south direction from the Phnom Kulen and changes to the south at the separating weir of Phum Khlat along the manmade river to the north side of the East Baray. The river flows westwards along the northside of the Baray to the north-west corner, turns to the south to continue along the east of Angkor Thom and flows through the city center of Siem Reap to the north of the Tonle Sap Lake.

The Tonle Sap Lake is gourd shaped and about 150km in west-east direction with about 30km in north-south direction. The lake shrinks in winter and the water depth becomes very shallow at about two to four meters in depth.

Fig. 3.1.4 shows the surface geology of the Angor area produced by JICA[2]. The surface ground near the lake is a wetland which consists of the lake bottom as well as alluvium deposits of the lake which was formed under the water before Angkor plain was lifted up.

3. Underground structures of Angkor by boring study

JSA performed the first deep boring of about 100m in

50　第3章　JSA/JASAの調査研究

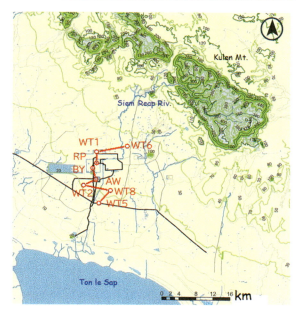

Fig. 3.1.5 Boring points in Angkor plain

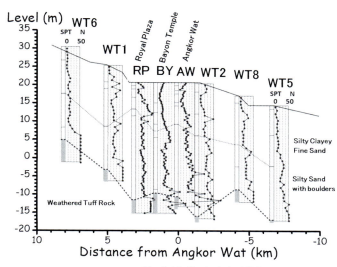

Fig. 3.1.6 Geotechnical N-S section in Angkor

JICAにおいても地質ボーリングが行われた[1]。これらの地点は，Fig 3.1.5に示したが，地表付近のN値の深度分布を南北断面としてFig. 3.1.6に示した[3]。

地表から40m程度までの深度は第四紀の地層で，N値50以下の細粒分を含む細砂層が分布している。この表層地層は，さらに二層に分けられ，上層は沖積層相当のシルト粘土質細砂でN値＜20以下であるが，下層は洪積層に相当する巨礫を含むシルト質細砂を主とするもので，N値は20〜50である。

第四紀層の下位には，N値＞50の第三紀と思われる風化凝灰岩が約GL-80mまで続き，さらに第三紀中世代を中心とする基盤岩が存在する。

4. アンコール地域の地下水位問題と遺跡への影響

JICAは，アンコール平野の地下水位流動を把握するために，井戸の地下水位の年間変化の計測を実施した[3]。

これらの計測地点の分布をFig. 3.1.7に示したが，そのうち，クーレン山からトンレサップ湖にかけての南北線を選んで，これらの地点の標高と地下水位変化をFig. 3.1.8〜9に示した[4]。

Fig. 3.1.7に各観測井戸における最高，最低水位を示した。どの観測井戸においても4月から5月が最低水位，11月から12月が最高水位となっている。

アンコール平野の地表面はほぼ水平で，水平流はわずかで，殆ど流れていない。降雨により地下水位が上昇し，蒸発により水位面が下降しているのである。

バイヨンで実施した地下水位と気象観測位置をFig.

Angkor in 1994[3]. JICA also performed the boring study for water resources[1]. Fig. 3.1.5 shows these boring points with SPT-N-values for the surface zone in Fig. 3.1.6 in NS section of Angkor.

The top surface of 40m in depth consists of Quaternary deposits of sand layers with fine soils which shows SPT, N-values less than 50. This top surface is divided into two layers. The upper layer is Holocene deposits of silty sand with SPT, N-values less than 20. The lower layer is Pleistocene deposit of silty sand with gravel and shows SPT, N-values of from 20 to 50.

Beneath the Quaternary deposit, weathered tuff layer of tertiary deposit continued down to about 80m where the base stone of Neogene Period is found.

4. Problem of Underground Water in Angkor related with Heritage

JICA proceeded to monitor annual changes of the water levels in many wells in Angkor[3] to study characteristics of underground water flow. Fig. 3.1.7 shows the positions of these wells.

Annual change of water levels at these wells along the line in north-south direction are shown in Fig. 3.1.8 and Fig. 3.1.9[4]. At every well, the minimum level is found from April to May, the maximum from November to December. Since the ground surface of the Angkor plain is almost flat, which results in little flow, the mechanism of rise and fall is infiltration of rain water in the rainy season and evaporation in the dry season.

Fig. 3.1.10 shows the monitoring position and Fig. 3.1.11 shows monitored weather and underground water levels in the

3.1.10に，ボーリングの地下水位の1997年度の観測結果をFig. 3.1.11に示した[5]。雨季における場合，2つの観測深度でそれぞれ地下水挙動は異なっている。降雨があれば，浅い観測深度ではただちに水位上昇が見られ，深い深度においては，その応答はやや鈍いが，降雨に応じて上昇していることが見える。すなわち，水位上昇は降雨時に発生し，鉛直流動と考えられる。

シェムレアップ周辺においては，GL-30m程度の深さで，地下水の揚水が行われており，Fig. 3.1.11の深層水位が低いのはこの影響である。

JICAはシェムレアップ周辺での井戸の水位観測を1998年に実施したが，Fig. 3.1.12に井戸の分布図を各井戸の年間水位変動幅別に示し，Fig. 3.1.13に井戸水位の年間最高位深さ，Fig. 3.1.14に年間最低位深さをシェムレアップ市のほぼ中心からの距離との関係で示した。年間変動は，乾季の終わりに最低水位で，雨季の終わりに最高水位を示し，多くはFig. 3.1.11に示したように，地表面レベルであるのに，Fig. 3.1.13にみられるように，市内中心から約5kmの範囲で雨季の終わりの地下水位が地表面よりGL-0.5〜-3m低い状態となっていることが分かる。このように，シェムレアップ市域を中心として井戸揚水の対象となっている深層地下水位が低下していることが判明している。

地下水変動による地盤変位の影響は，JICA[5]においても観測を行い検討しているが，プラサート・スープラで実施したJSAの結果[4]によれば，地下水位の低下により地下深度の水圧減少による圧縮と，地表面付近の地盤が乾燥し，サクションによる沈下が発生し，水位の上昇により隆起している。ほぼ2.5mの水位変動により5mm程度の変位が観測されている。

著者は，シェムレアップ地域の水源は井戸からの揚水ではなく，トンレサップ湖からの取水を推奨していた[4]が，JICAは検討の上，2006年に日本国からの無償資金協力で西バライの南側国道6号線沿いに揚水井戸群を設置し，日量8,000㎥の地下水を水源とする施設を完成させた。

JICAによる2011年の準備調査の報告[6]によれば，今後の水源は，アンコール平野の揚水ではなく，トンレサップ湖からの取水事業を推進していく方向に結論づけられており，地下水位低下によるアンコール遺跡への影響は回避される見込みである。

5. アンコール地域の大気汚染状況

東南アジア諸国連合（ASEAN）地域では，肺がんが

bore hole at the north of the Outer Gallery of Bayon in 1997. Water levels in Fig. 3.1.11 show different behavior for upper and lower levels during the rainy season. The shallow-water level responds to increase from rainfall without any delay. The deep-water level also responds to rainfall but with much delayed time. In the dry season water levels decrease due to evaporation and pumping of the underground water.

In the Siem Reap area, underground water has been pumped up from around a depth of 30 m to the surface. The effects of this pumping is shown as the lower water depth of the deeper sand layer as shown in Fig. 3.1.11.

JICA performed the monitoring of water levels of wells in and around Siem Reap city as shown in Fig. 3.1.12 for the distribution of wells; in Fig. 3.1.13 for the distribution of the annual highest level and in Fig. 3.1.14 for the distribution of the annual lowest level. Annual change of the underground water generally shows the highest at the end of the rainy season and the lowest at the end of the dry season.

The most wells show the highest water level at the ground surface as is shown in Fig. 3.1.13, the central area with the radius of less than 5km from the center shows the highest level of the water is 0.5 to 3m lower than the ground surface.

The effects of the change of water level on the settlement of the ground surface was one of the important subjects for JICA. Based upon the monitoring results at Prasat Suor Prat by JSA, the lowering of the underground pressure will cause shrinkage of the surface ground due to the decrease of the pore water pressure as well as the settlements by the increase of the suction in the drying surface. About 5mm of the displacement was observed for the change of the water level.

The water from Tonle Sap Lake for the Siem Reap area was recommended by the authors[4]. JICA had decided to use the underground water in Siem Reap after some discussions and completed the pump-up wells along the Route No.6 south of the West Baray of 8,000m[3]/day with distribution facility.

However, it was concluded to promote the water not from the water under Ankor plain but from Tonle Sap Lake in the future. It is expected to be able to avoid any adverse effects from underground water fluctuations upon the heritage structures in Angkor.

5. Air Pollution in the Angkor Region

In the Association of Southeast Asian Nations (ASEAN) region, lung cancer is the second leading cause of cancer-related deaths among men and women, with CO_2 and PM2.5 among air pollutants estimated to be the main causes. Lung cancer deaths are high in Indonesia, Thailand, Vietnam, and the Philippines, and low in Cambodia. However, there are few reports on air pollution in Cambodia, especially limited reports on air quality around the Angkor Monuments. According to Furuuchi et al. (2007), SPM concentrations are higher in urban

Fig. 3.1.7 Boring points

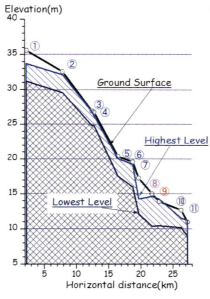

Fig. 3.1.8 NS-Section of boring sites

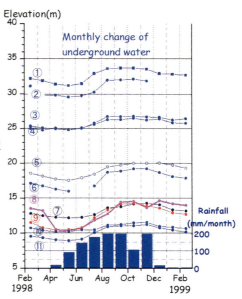

Fig. 3.1.9 Annual Change of Water Level

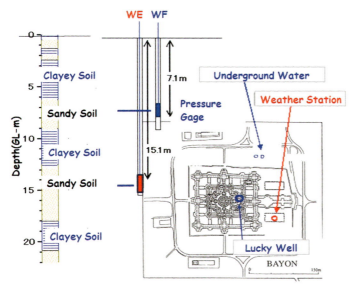

Fig. 3.1.10 Observation well

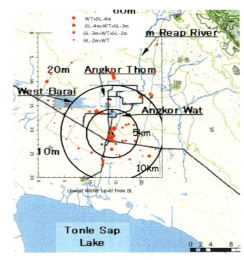

Fig. 3.1.12 Monitored well by JICA

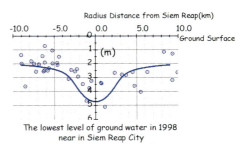

Fig. 3.1.13 Distribution of the highest level of water

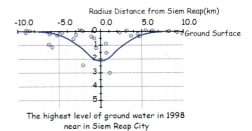

Fig. 3.1.14 Distribution of the lowest level of water

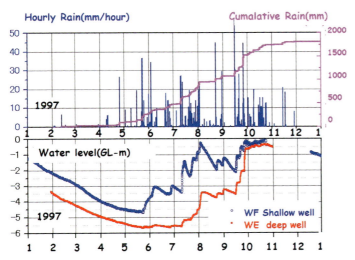

Fig. 3.1.11 Shallow and deep aquifer system in Angkor

3.1 アンコール地域広域環境

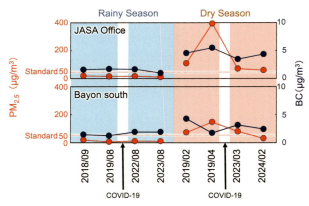

Fig. 3.1.14 Mass concentration of PM2.5 and black carbon (BC) in JASA office and Bayon south

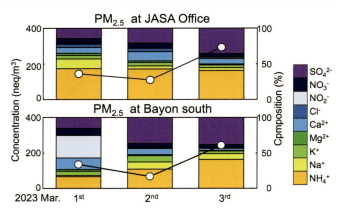

Fig. 3.1.15 Chemical composition of PM2.5 and black carbon (BC) in JASA office and Bayon south in dry season

男女におけるがん関連死の第2位の原因であり，大気汚染物質のうちCO_2と PM2.5 が主要因と推定されている．インドネシア，タイ，ベトナム，フィリピンでは肺がん死亡者が多く，カンボジアでの肺がん死亡者数は少ない．しかし，カンボジアでは大気汚染に関する報告はほとんどない状況であり，特にアンコール遺跡周辺の大気環境に関する報告は限られている．

Furuuchi et al.（2007）によると，SPM 濃度は遺跡周辺（20～110 μg/㎥）に比べて市街地（400 μg/㎥以上）と国道6号沿い（200 μg/㎥以上）で高いことが報告されている[7]．しかし，NO_2，SO_2，O_3などの典型ガス状大気汚染物質，PM2.5 質量濃度や化学成分濃度の報告はない．

著者は JASA オフィスを拠点にしてガス，粒子，雨水の総合的な大気汚染観測を行いつつ，バイヨン周辺でバッテリー駆動計測装置（PM2.5，BC，TVOC，O_3，CO_2）やパッシブサンプラー（SO_2，HNO_3，HCl，NH_3，O_3）を使用して2018年から大気汚染観測を行っている．Fig. 3.1.14 には，雨季と乾季における JASA オフィス，バイヨン南部における PM2.5 およびブラックカーボン（BC）の質量濃度の比較を示す．JASA オフィス，バイヨン南部ともに PM2.5 質量濃度は雨季に環境基準より低いが，乾季には環境基準を大幅に超過している．BC質量濃度も PM2.5 と同様の傾向にあった．乾季における PM2.5 質量濃度の上昇は野焼き（バイオマスバーニング）の影響が要因として考えられる．

Fig. 3.1.15 には，2023年3月に JASA オフィス，バイヨン南部で PM2.5 の水溶性化学成分の同時観測を行った結果を示す．両地点ともに PM2.5 水溶性化学成分濃度の変動は類似しており，JASA オフィスのほうがバイヨン南部よりも高い．3月2，3日とも両地点で化学成分組成は類似しており，硫酸アンモニウムが主成分であった．このことから，バイヨン南部の PM2.5 は近隣道路を走行している自動車やトゥクトゥクの排外ガスが直接

areas (>400 μg/m³) than around the monuments (20~110 μg/m³) (20~110 μg/m³) and along National Road No. 6 (200 μg/m³ or higher) compared to those around archaeological sites (20~110 μg/m³)[7]. However, there are no reports on typical gaseous air pollutants such as NO_2, SO_2, and O_3, mass concentrations, and concentrations of chemical components of PM2.5.

We have been conducting comprehensive air pollution observations of gases, particles, and rainwater based at the JASA office, while using battery-powered instruments (PM2.5, BC, TVOC, O_3, CO_2) and passive samplers (SO_2, HNO_3, HCl, NH_3, O_3) around Bayon since 2018 observations. Fig. 3.1.14 shows a comparison of PM2.5 and black carbon (BC) mass concentrations in the JASA office and southern Bayon during the wet and dry seasons. concentrations also showed a similar trend to that of PM2.5. The increase in PM2.5 mass concentration during the dry season may be due to the effect of open burning (biomass burning).

Fig. 3.1.15 shows the results of simultaneous observations of water-soluble chemical components of PM2.5 at the JASA office and southern Bayon in March 2023. The concentrations of water-soluble chemical components of PM2.5 at both sites were similar, with higher concentrations at the JASA office than at the southern Bayon; on March 2 and 3, the chemical composition was similar at both sites, with ammonium sulfate as the main component. This suggests that the PM2.5 in southern Bayon is not directly influenced by the exhaust gases from cars and tuk-tuks traveling on nearby roads, but rather air pollutants emitted in Siem Reap city are likely being transported to the area. However, as shown in Fig. 3.1.14, both PM2.5 and BC in the southern part of Bayon tend to be similar to or higher than those in the JASA office in March 2023, which is the dry season, and thus may be directly affected by automobile emissions. In order to reduce the impact of air pollutants on the Angkor Monuments in the future, air pollution control measures in Siem Reap city as well as local emissions are considered important.

的に影響しているのではなく，シェムレアップ市内で排出された大気汚染物質が輸送されている可能性が高い。ただし，Fig. 3.1.14に示すように，乾季にあたる2023年3月にはバイヨン南部でPM2.5，BCともにJASAオフィスと同程度か高い傾向にあることから，直截な自動車排ガスの影響を受けている可能性もある。今後，アンコール遺跡群に対する大気汚染物質の影響を低減するには，局地排出とともにシェムレアップ市内の大気汚染対策も重要と考えられる。

References
1) JICA Report. Nippon Koei Co., Ltd. and Nihon Suido Consultants Co., Ltd., "The Study on Water Supply System for Siem Reap Region in Cambodia," JICA Report to Min. of Industry, Mines, and Energy, The Royal Government of Cambodia, June 2000
2) JICA Report. 国際建設技術協会，国際航業㈱，"The Topographic Mapping of the Angkor, Archaeological Area in the Siem Reap Region of the Kingdom of Cambodia"，May 1998，社調1 JR 98-087
3) 日本国政府アンコール遺跡救済チーム（編），1995～2001，アンコール遺跡調査報告書，日本国政府アンコール遺跡救済チーム
4) 岩崎好規，「カンボジア王国アンコールにおける地下水揚水問題」，サイバー大学紀要第1号，サイバー大学，（2009），pp. 129-148
5) 岩崎好規，アンコール地域の地下水問題，サイバー大学紀要第2号，サイバー大学，（2010），pp. 63-81
6) JICA Report カンボジア国シェムリアップ上水道拡張整備事業準備調査最終報告書2 2011，JR11-139
7) M. Furuuchi, T. Murase, S. Tsukawaki, P. Hang, S. Sieng, M. Hata: Characteristics of Ambient, Particle-bound Poly-cyclic Aromatic Hydrocarbons in the Angkor Monument Area of Cambodia, Aerosol and Air Quality Research 7, 2, pp. 221-238, 2007.

3.2 アンコール遺跡広域大型寺院都市研究
Research on the Provincial Ancient Khmer Cities and Temples

溝口 明則　　　成井　至
MIZOGUCHI Akinori　　NARUI Itaru

1. はじめに

東南アジア内陸部に大帝国を築いたクメール帝国は，12世紀後半から13世紀にかけて最盛期を誇り最大の版図を築いた。バイヨンを国家鎮護寺院として中央に据えた首都アンコール・トム都城は，一辺約3kmの方形矩形平面であり，周囲を城壁と環濠によって囲まれる。13世紀末に中国元朝の使節に同行した周達観が記す『真臘風土記』は，往時の賑わいや都城内に建設された寺院施設の様子を伝えている。

都城の構成は，王宮へ向かう勝利の門を除き，四方中央に開かれた城門がバイヨンへ繋がる。バイヨンはジャヤヴァルマンVII（1181～1218）により12世紀末に建造された。同時代には首都機能の充実化や多数の寺院が造営され，アンコールを中心に王国各地に延びる「王道」の再整備や「王道」を介した地方拠点の寺院遺構も造営された。特にアンコール・トムにおけるバイヨンは象徴性が高いが，各寺院と都市の構造は未だ謎が多い。

なお，本節で取り上げる各寺院遺構は，主に早稲田大学と名城大学の合同チームが調査を行ったもので，JSA/JASAが一部調査協力を行った。これら地方重要遺構との比較を通じて，バイヨンにおける都市と建築の特徴に関して検討したい[1]。

2. サンボー・プレイ・クック遺跡群

(1) 遺跡群概要

アンコールから約140km南西のコンポン・トム州に位置するサンボー・プレイ・クック遺跡群は，中国史書に，プレ・アンコール期に栄えた真臘国の首都として記録された「伊奢那城」あるいは「伊賞那補羅國」に比定され

1. Introduction

The Khmer Empire, which established a large empire in the interior of Southeast Asia, reached its peak from the late 12th to the 13th century. Angkor Thom as the capital city, with Bayon at its center as the national guardian temple, has a square plan with a perimeter of about 3 km, surrounded by walls and a moat encircling the city. "Zhēnlà Fēngtǔ Jì" authored by Zhou Daguan accompanied with envoys of Yuan Dynasty in end of 13th century, told of the prosperity and state of cities at that time.

The central gates as the component of the city in 4 directions, except for the Victory Gate leading to the royal palace, lead to the Bayon. The Bayon was built by Jayavarman VII (1181-1218) at the end of the 12th century. During the same period, Jayavarman VII expanded the function of the capital city and built many temples. In addition, he redeveloped the "royal road" extending from Angkor to other parts of the kingdom and built or expanded the temples in regional centers located on or near the "royal road". The Bayon at Angkor Thom is highly symbolic, but the structure of each temple and the city remains mysteriou.

The temple complexes written in this chapter, were mainly surveyed by a joint team of Waseda University and Meijo University, with research assistance from JSA/JASA. By comparing the Bayon with these locally important structures, we would like to discuss the characteristics of the city and architecture of the Bayon era temples[1].

2. Sambor Prei Kuk Monuments

(1) Outline of Sambor Prei Kuk Monuments

Located in Kompong Thom Province, about 140 km southwest of Angkor, the Sambor Prei Kuk Monuments (a World Heritage site) is an ancient city complex that is compared

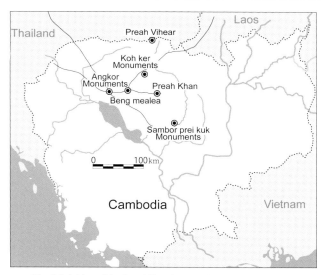

Fig. 3.2.1 Map of the Local Temples and Ancient Road in Cambodia

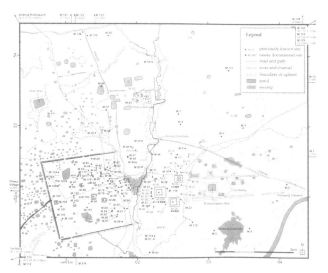

Fig. 3.2.2 Map of Samor Prei Kuk Monuments

る古代複合都市遺跡である。当該遺跡群は，中央を流れるオー・クル・ケー河に対し，3つの主要伽藍と周辺遺構によって構成される東側を「寺院区」，2km三方の環濠と東側の河川によって囲繞された多数の遺構や都市機能の痕跡が立地する西側を「都市区」あるいは「都城区」と称して構成される。碑文研究によって，当該遺跡群がバヴァヴァルマン（598頃）の治世期まで遡り，ラージェンドラヴァルマンⅡ（944～968）によって主尊の改変が行われた可能性などが判明しており[2]，少なくとも6世紀末には一定の統治領域を有し，802年以後，統一国家となってロリュオスに首都機能が移転した後も，一地方拠点として機能し続けていた。

(2) 周辺自然地形

遺跡群はメコン川の支流であるセン川の下流域に位置しており，南側の氾濫源に対して数m高くなった台地上の土地に計画されている。西側の「都市区」は，オー・クル・ケー河を東辺として三方を土塁と狭い環濠で囲むが，その内外に多数の小区画水田や溜池がみられる。漢籍史料から，表現に誇張があったとしても都城内外に居住する人口が大規模であったことが推定される[3]。当該遺跡群はセン川を取水源とした広範囲にわたる農耕水や生活用水の確保，また寺院造営などに係る資材や物資の運搬として有用であったことが指摘される[4]。

(3) 都市形成と寺院伽藍の原型

「寺院区」は，北寺院群（プラサート・サンボー），南寺院群（プラサート・イエイ・ポアン），中央寺院群（プラサート・タオ），および周辺の小遺構で構成される。大半の煉瓦造祠堂遺跡が単独で建ち，北寺院群および南寺院群が先んじて造営され，その後中央寺院群が建設

"Isanapura" or "Isanapura Country", which was recorded in Chinese historical books as the capital of the Chenla that flourished in the Pre-Angkor period. This site is mainly composed of a "Temple Area" located on the east side of the site has 3 main groups and other shrines. The "City Area" located on the west side has many traces of a city and shrines surrounded by a 2 km moat without an east side, and with "O Kru Ker River" flowed in the center of the site. Inscriptional research has revealed the possibility that the sites in question date back to the reign of Bhavavarman (598), and that the main deities were altered by Rajendravarman II (944-968)[2]. The city had a certain area of governance at least by the end of the 6th century, and after 802, it became a unified state and the capital functions were transferred to Roluos. Even after the transfer of the capital function to Roluos, it continued to function as a regional center.

(2) **Surrounding Topography**

The site is located in the lower reaches of the Sen River, a tributary of the Mekong River, and is planned on a plateau elevated several meters above the flood plain to the south. The western "City Area" is surrounded on three sides by earthen mounds and a narrow moat encircling the O Kru Ker River on the east side, with numerous small rice paddies and reservoirs inside and outside the area. From Chinese historical documents, it can be inferred that the population living inside and outside the city was large, even if there are some exaggerations in the expressions used[3]. The water management facilities were useful for securing water for agriculture and daily life over a wide area using the Sen River as a source of intake, as well as for transporting materials and goods related to temple construction[4].

(3) **Models of City Planning and Temple Complex**

The "Temple Area" consists of the North Group (Prasat Sambor), the South Group (Prasat Yeai Poeun), the Central

されたと考えられるが，祠堂の建築形式には多様なバリエーションがみられる。北寺院群から出土した神像の様式，碑文研究からもアンコール期に首都が移転されて以降，少なくとも10世紀頃までは衛星都市の一つとして機能していたことがわかる。

北寺院群中央の主祠堂は，煉瓦造祠堂のなかで唯一四方に開口を有し，主祠堂が建つテラス上および内周壁内には等方位に祠堂が配置される。城壁に設置された門や参道遺構等の構成要素，伽藍の配置計画は，後年のアンコール時代におけるピラミッド型寺院の原型ともみられる一方，南寺院群および中央寺院群は東西の軸性が意識された配置計画をとる[5]。また，北寺院群の遺構軸は正方位である一方で，南寺院群は約4.3°，中央寺院群は約2.9°北に偏向する。

プレ・アンコール期に発展した都市遺構は，多数確認されるが，都市区を囲む矩形平面の環濠，水利をはじめとしたインフラ施設，主要河川との位置関係，複合寺院伽藍の建立，聖山としてのリンガパルヴァタとの配置関係などを鑑みると，サンボー・プレイ・クック遺跡群をプレ・アンコール期における一つの都市構成としての到達点として見ることができる。

3. プレア・ヴィヘア

(1) 寺院概要

プレア・ヴィヘアはタイとの国境をまたぐダンレック山脈上に建設された，縦深型寺院である。建築史，美術史および碑文研究から，ヤショヴァルマンⅠ（889〜910）からスールヤヴァルマンⅡ（1113〜1150）の治世期にかけて度重なる増改築が施されたと考えられているが，未だ詳細な建造編年は解明されていない。

寺院は標高約600mの崖上に位置しており，全長約850m，高低差100mを超えて南端の疑似ゴープラを含む6つのゴープラを結ぶ，精確な南北線を軸として展開

Group (Prasat Tao), and other surrounding structures. Most of the brick shrines stand alone, and it is thought that the North and South Groups were built first, followed by the Central Group, but there are many variations in the architectural styles of the shrines. The style of the statues of deities excavated from the North Temple Group and the study of inscriptions indicate that the city functioned as one of the satellite cities at least until the 10th century, after the capital was moved to the Angkor area.

The main shrine in the center of the North Group is the only brick shrine with openings on all four directions, and the other shrines are located in equal directions on the terrace where the main shrine stands and within the inner walls. The layout of the temple complex and its components of the gates and approach structures on the walls, can be seen as a prototype for the pyramid-type temples of the Angkor period. On the other hand, the South and Central Groups are arranged based on an east-west axis[5]. While the axis of the North Group is square, the South and Central temples are deflected to the north by approximately 4.3 and 2.9 degrees, respectively.

The ancient cities developed during the Pre-Angkor period. Through these ancient cities, Sambor Prei Kuk Monuments can be regarded as one of achievement for city development. The complex consists of a rectanglar enclosure with moat, infrastructure facilities including water supply, located on rivers, with temple complexes, and relationship with Lingaparvata

3. Preah Vihear

(1) Outline of the Temple

Preah Vihear is a deep vertical temple built on the Dangrek Mountains straddling the Thailand border. According to architectural, art historical, and inscriptional studies, the temple is thought to have been repeatedly enlarged and remodeled between the reigns of Yasovarman I (889-910) and Suryavarman II (1113-1150), but the detailed sequence of the construction process has not yet been clarified.

The temple is located on a cliff about 600m above sea level,

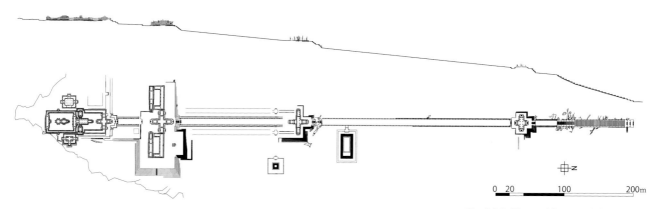

Fig. 3.2.3 Plan and Section of Preah Vihear

する。多くのクメール寺院が東西軸に合わせて構成されるのに対し，地形から南北を軸として造営された。山頂手前の第2ゴープラを超えると回廊が配され，最奥の中央祠堂を囲む第1回廊が崖上に建っており，中央祠堂に至るまで，縦深性および聖性が高まる特徴的な構成となっている。

(2) 周辺自然地形と伽藍構成

プレア・ヴィヘアはダンレック山脈上に建造されており，南側（カンボジア側）は比高500mに達する急崖をなす一方，北側（タイ）側は緩い勾配がコーラート平原に続いている。周辺は砂岩の露岩地が拡がり，整形した岩盤上に直接構造物が建設されるものもある。当該寺院の南西麓にヤショータターカ，南東麓にスールヤタターカとよばれるバライが確認される。ヤショータターカから3km西方には遺物散布地があり，スールヤタターカの南東約3.5kmには異なるバライや，土地神「ネアックターの森」が位置する[6]。

プレア・ヴィヘアは，多数の段台テラスとゴープラが南北一直線の参道を介して連続する縦深型寺院であり，平地に展開し東西を主軸とする多くのアンコール遺跡と異なる。また，伽藍中心線に対して口の字型および田の字型平面の「宮殿」とよばれる施設が東西に対に，連続で配される点[7]，第1ゴープラ前の対の経蔵が互いに向き合い，この配置に合わせて翼廊・周壁が調節された点，山頂伽藍が南北に二分されたような形式をとり，第1伽藍のゴープラが中央祠堂へ延びる部位のないT字型平面である点など[8]，伽藍構成および各建物の形状や配置に特異性がみられる。このような伽藍構成は，クメールの基層文化である山岳への崇拝とともに，狭小な尾根と山頂に造営されたことに起因する。一方，精緻な実測調査に基づいた伽藍計画分析を踏まえると（詳細は3.3），各建物は一貫した計画に基づいて配置されており，幅のある造営年代は，一貫した初期計画に基づく遺構の造営ばかりでなく，建て替えの過程などを示す可能性が考えられる。

4. コー・ケー遺跡群

(1) 遺跡群概要

コー・ケー遺跡群はアンコールから北東約80kmに位置する。ジャヤヴァルマンIIがアンコール王朝を統一して以降，ロリュオスやアンコールに築かれた王都から，ジャヤヴァルマンIV（928〜941）が遷都を試みた王都「チョック・ガルギャー」に比定されている。遺跡群

and is 850m long with a height difference of more than 100m. It was developed along a precise north-south axis connecting 6 gopuras, including a pseudo-gopura at the southern end. While most Khmer temples are constructed along an east-west axis, this temple was constructed along a north-south axis due to its topography. The first gallery surrounding the central shrine at the innermost part of the temple is built on the cliff, and it is a characteristic structure that increases the vertical depth and sanctity of the temple all the way to the central shrine.

(2) Surrounding Topography and Temple Structure

Preah Vihear was built on the Dangrek Mountains, with steep cliffs reaching 500 m in height on the south side (Cambodian side) and a gentle slope on the north side (Thailand side) leading to the Khorat Plain. The surrounding area is covered with exposed sandstone, and some structures have been built directly on shaped bedrock. The baray called Yasotataka is located at the southwest foot of the temple, and a baray called Suryatatharka at the southeast foot. A relic dispersal site is located 3km west of Yasotataka, and a different baray and "Forest of Neak Ta" are located about 3.5 km southeast of Suryatataka[6].

Preah Vihear is a deep vertical temple with many terraces and gopuras connected by a straight north-south approach, which differs from most Angkorian monuments that are located on flat land and have their main axis in the east-west direction. It differs from most Angkor Monuments, which are flat and have an east-west axis. The "palaces" are arranged in pairs, east-west, in succession, in relation to the center line of the temple complex[7], the pairs of sutra repositories in front of the first gopura face each other, and the gallery and walls were adjusted according to this arrangement. The first temple has a T-shaped plan with no part extending to the central shrine[8]. The configuration of the temple and the shape and layout of each building are peculiar. Such a configuration is attributed to the fact that the buildings were constructed on narrow ridges and mountain tops, typical of Khmer worship of mountains, which was the underlying culture of the Khmer people. On the other hand, based on the analysis of the temple planning based on a detailed survey (detail in 3. 3), each building is arranged according to a consistent plan, and the wide range of construction dates may indicate not only the construction of the remains based on a consistent initial plan, but also the process of rebuilding.

4. Koh Ker Monuments

(1) Outline of the Koh Ker Monuments

Koh Ker Mouments is located approximately 80km northeast of Angkor. It is assumed to be the royal capital "Chok Gargyar," which Jayavarman IV (928-941) attempted to relocate from the royal capital built at Roluos and Angkor

は，南南東から北北西に延びる谷の中に造営された人工池「ラハール」を中心として数十の寺院が周囲に配置され，「ラハール」北西に位置する五層の段状基壇を持つ寺院「プラン」を擁するプラサート・トムが，国家寺院としてその中核を担っている。

(2) 周辺地形と配置計画にみる都市性

コー・ケー遺跡群は標高70〜90m付近の南から北へと緩やかに傾斜する丘陵地に位置し，北流するセン川支流の最上流部に位置する。尾根の稜線や付近の水流沿いに砂岩の露岩地がみられ，遺跡群の南方10kmの分水界に位置するスラヤン村周辺では透水性の低いラテライトを産出する。そのため，遺跡群の主材料である砂岩やラテライトは豊富に入手することが可能であった。一方，丘陵地である遺跡群周辺では水田耕作可能な平坦地がなく，人工的に水田地域を造成した可能性もあるが，この谷のなかだけで首都を維持する生産力を確保することは困難であったと予想される[9]。

遺跡が分布する一帯では境界標石や溜池，採石場を含め計127サイトが記録され，一見して不規則に点在しているように観察されるが，各遺構の方位性および配置は，ラハールを中心とした地形の特徴に基づいて軸線上に選地されたことが指摘されている。また，遺跡群の中心寺院であるプラサート・トムにおけるピラミッド遺構「プラン」には，9×9ハスタの高さに現在は失われているリンガが据えられていた，と碑文に記録されているほか，周辺遺構においても多数のヨニ座が報告されており，H.パルマンティエは都市全体が一つの大きなシヴァ寺院を表象していると述べる[10]。遺跡群のうち，ラハールの東西に配置された遺構は，ラハールの南南東–北北西の中軸線に直交する軸線を形成し，距離をとりつつも相互に向き合う。一般的に東を正面とすることが多いクメール寺院とは異なり，ラハールの方角を正面とし，ヨニ座

after Jayavarman II unified the Angkor Dynasty. The ruins consist of dozens of temples around "Rahal," an artificial pond built in a valley stretching from south-southeast to north-northwest. Prasat Thom, with its five-story stepped platform temple "Prang" located northwest of "Rahal," is the core of this national temple complex.

(2) Surrounding Topography and Arrangement Planning

Koh Ker Mouments is located on a hillside that slopes gently from south to north at an elevation of 70-90 m above sea level, at the uppermost reaches of a tributary of the north-flowing Sen River. Sandstone outcrops are found along the ridge and nearby water streams, and laterite deposits with low permeability are situated around Surayan Village which is located 10 km south of the site group at the watershed boundary. Therefore, sandstone and laterite, the main materials of the archaeological sites, were available in abundance. On the other hand, there is no flat land around the site group, which is hilly terrain, where paddy fields could be cultivated. Although it is possible that paddy field areas were artificially created, it is expected that it would have been difficult to secure a productive capacity to maintain a capital city within this valley alone[9].

A total of 127 sites, including boundary marker stones, reservoirs, and quarries, were recorded in the area where the ruins are distributed. Although they appear to be scattered irregularly at first glance, the orientation and arrangement of each site points to the fact that the sites were selected along an axis based on topographical features centering on Rahal. In addition, a pyramid "Prang" at Prasat Thom, the central temple of the complex, has a 9×9 hasta high linga, which is now lost, as recorded in an inscription, and numerous seated yoni are reported in the surrounding structures. H. Parmantier states that the entire city represents one large Shiva temple [10]. Among the sites, the remains located to the east and west of Rahal form an axis orthogonal to the south-southeast-north-northwest midline of Rahal, facing each other despite the distance between them. Unlike other Khmer temples, which generally face east, there are examples where the front of the temple faces the direction of Rahal and the "beak" of the Yoni faces the direction of Rahal. Therefore, it can be interpreted that the entire site complex was planned around Rahal, with the concept that holy water would flow into Rahal from each site, pass in front of the central temple, Prasat Thom, and flow toward the north[11].

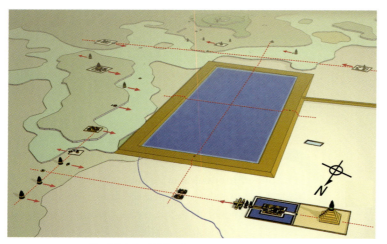

Fig. 3.2.4 Aerial View Image of Central Area of Koh Ker Monuments

の「嘴」をラハールの方角へ向ける例もある。したがって遺跡群全体の配置はラハールを中心に計画され，各遺構から聖水がラハールに流れ込み，中心寺院プラサート・トムの前面を通過して北方へと流れる，という構想が読み取れる[11]。

5. コンポンスヴァイのプレア・カーン寺院

(1) 寺院概要

コンポンスヴァイのプレア・カーン寺院（以下，大プレア・カーン）はアンコールの東方約95kmに位置し，アンコールから東に延びる王道沿いに立地する衛星寺院を含めた複合寺院である。中心寺院は東を正面として約27.4°北側に偏向しており，三重の周壁に囲まれ，その外側を4.8km四方の土塁が囲む。そして北東側の中央に2.8×0.6kmのバライを配している。建築学，美術史学の見地から，第1周壁内は11世紀頃の造営が想定されており，その後段階的に増築され，周辺の宿駅寺院を含めバイヨン期に至るまで建設が行われたと考えられている[12]。大プレア・カーンはジャヤヴァルマンⅦの生誕の地，あるいはアンコールに移る前の拠点として機能していたという指摘もあり，後述するバイヨンにみられる尊顔を付した小型寺院プラサート・プレア・ストゥンが

5. Preah Khan of Kompong Svay

(1) Outline of the Temple

The Preah Khan of Kompong Svay (hereinafter called Great Preah Khan) is a complex of temples, including satellite temples, located about 95km east of Angkor, along the royal road extending east from Angkor. The central temple is located at a deflection of about 27.4° to the north, with its front facing east, and is surrounded by a triple perimeter wall and a 4.8km square earthen mound on the outside. 2.8 × 0.6km baray is located in the center of the northeast side. From the viewpoints of architecture and art history, it is assumed that the first wall was built around the 11th century, and that it was enlarged in stages and built up to the Bayon period, including the surrounding station temples[12]. It has been suggested that the Great Preah Khan served as the birthplace of Jayavarman VII or as a base of operations before he moved to Angkor, and this influence can be seen in the fact that Prasat Preah Stoeng, a small temple with a deity face, is located on the west side of baray.

(2) Surrounding Topography and Features of the City

The temple is surrounded by small hills from northwest to east and slightly higher to southeast and southwest, except in the south. Phnom Dek, located about 35km southwest

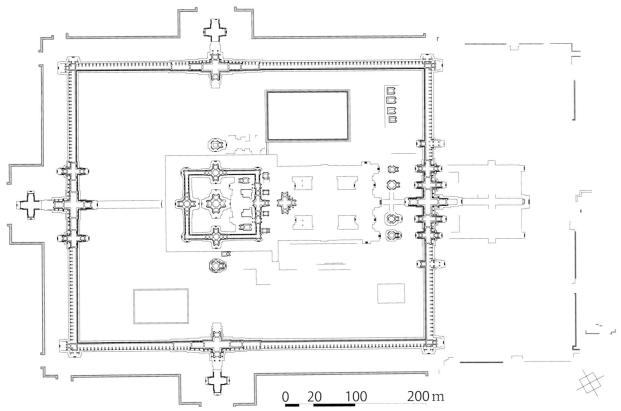

Fig. 3.2.5 Plan of Preah Khan in Kompong Svay

バライの西側に位置していることからもその影響を窺い知れる。

⑵ 周辺自然地形と都市としての特徴

寺院は北西から東へ，また南東，南西がやや高くなっており，南方を除いて小高い地形に囲まれている。寺院の南西約35kmに位置するプノム・デックは鉄の主要産地であることが知られており，少数民族であるクイ族が製鉄を主な生業としていたことが報告されている。寺院北東側にはストゥン川が流れており，主要な鉄生産の基盤として，また寺院内およびクイ族集落の生活用水として活用されていたと考えられる。大プレア・カーンの第3回廊北西側に位置する宿駅寺院ベン・スレ付近の溜池からは多数の鉄生産に伴う廃棄物が確認されており，補助的な鉱床として機能していたと考えられる[13]。一方，コー・ケー遺跡群周辺地形と同様に，水田稲作を行う適地はほぼなく，大規模な都市人口を維持することは困難であったとされる。

大プレア・カーンは崩壊が激しく，その全貌が明らかになっていないが，第3周壁以内に宿駅寺院や施療院が多数造営されているほか，第2回廊以内には，約220×170mの敷地内に多数の付属建物が点在していることが確認されている。付属建物群は寺院軸に対して対称に計画されているものが多いが，第1回廊南側に隣接する小建物や，第2回廊内北西に配置された四基のラテライト造の塔など独自に配されたものもある。また，第1回廊内では五連の仏陀座像が施されたリンテルが確認されており，密教の影響が指摘される[14]。

周辺ではスラグ痕跡や鉄器が出土し，また王道と主要河川の近傍に寺院が建設されていることなどから，この地はアンコール期だけでなく，長期に渡って鉄鋼産業の重要拠点として機能していたと推測される。上記のような産業遺構としての性格が，他遺構と比較しても広大な敷地を有し，付属建物を含む特異な伽藍が形成された要因である可能性が高い。

6. アンコール・ワット

⑴ 寺院概要

アンコール・ワットはスールヤヴァルマンII（1113～1150頃）が建造したヴィシュヌ神を信奉する寺院である。東西約1.5km，南北1.3km，幅200mの環濠に囲繞された寺院は，西辺中央に架かる長大な参道によって寺院内と接続する。寺院の北西1,300mほどには10世紀初頭に建立されたと想定されるプノム・バケンが位置し，ア

of the temple, is known to be a major iron producing area, and the Kuy ethnic minority is reported to have made iron manufacturing their main occupation. The Staung River flows on the northeast side of the temple and is thought to have been used as the main base for iron production and as water for daily life in the temple and in the Kuy community. A large amount of iron production waste has been found in a reservoir near Beng Sre, located on the northwest side of the Third Gallery of Great Preah Khan, and it is thought to have functioned as a supplemental deposit[13]. On the other hand, as with the topography of the area surrounding the Koh Ker Monuments, there was almost no suitable land for cultivation, and it would have been difficult to sustain a large urban population.

Although the entire image of the Great Preah Khan has not been revealed due to its severe collapse, it has been confirmed that a number of lodging temples and treatment centers were constructed within the Third Enclosure, and a number of attached buildings are scattered within the second corridor, which measures approximately 220×170m. The attached buildings are symmetrical to the axis of the temple. Most of the attached buildings are symmetrical to the axis of the temple, but some are uniquely arranged, such as a small building adjacent to the south side of the First Gallery and four laterite towers located in the northwest of the Second Gallery. In the First Gallery, a lintel with five rows of seated Buddha images has been found, indicating the influence of esoteric Buddhism[14].

The excavation of slag traces and iron tools in the vicinity of Great Preah Khan and the construction of temples near the royal road and major rivers suggest the site functioned as an important center of the iron and steel industry not only during the Angkor period but for a long period of time. It is highly possible that the above-mentioned characteristics of the site as an industrial site were the reason for the formation of a unique temple complex with a large site and attached buildings in comparison with other sites.

6. Angkor Wat

⑴ Outline of the Temple

Angkor Wat is a temple built by Suryavarman II (1113-1150), who worshipped Lord Vishnu. The temple is surrounded by a moat 1.5 km east to west, 1.3 km north to south, and 200m wide, and is connected to the interior of the temple by a long approach road causeway situated at the center of the western Outer Gallery. About 1,300m northwest of the temple is Phnom Bakheng, which is thought to have been built in the early 10th century. The main road running north-south on the west side outside of the confines of Angkor Wat leads straight to Bayon via the Southern Gate of Angkor Thom City. Furthermore, the distance from the South Gate of Angkor

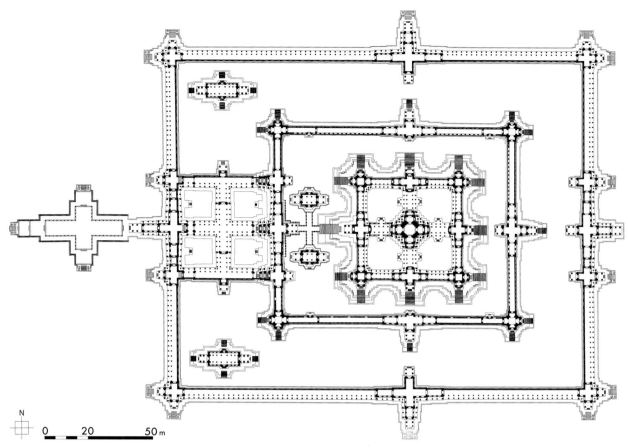

Fig. 3.2.6 Plan of Central complex of Angkor Wat

ンコール・ワット西辺に接する南北を走る幹線道路は，アンコール・トム都城の南大門を経て一直線にバイヨンへ至る。さらにアンコール・トム南大門から城壁南東隅までの距離とその位置はアンコール・ワット東西辺に近似し，一連の計画性の中で建設された可能性が示されている[15]。第3回廊の壁面にはラーマーヤナなどのヒンドゥー神話や軍隊の行進などをモチーフにした浅浮彫が施されており，クメール美術を代表する成果のひとつとされる。

(2) 周辺地形と伽藍構成

寺院は低平な扇状地に展開して大規模な環濠によって囲まれている。環濠の北東角には現在のシェムレアップ川から流入する水路があり，内部を通過して環濠の南東角から流出している。寺院内部の基礎地盤は掘り込みによってもたらされた土砂による盛土で嵩上げされて構築されている。

この寺院は広大な敷地に環濠を設け，長大な参道を介して寺院内部と接続する。内部は東西332 m，南北257 m，高さ1.8 mの大テラスの上に三層の段台ピラミッド形式の回廊で構成され，十字型回廊や経蔵を配置して中央第3層には四塔の副塔（隅建物）が取り囲む，高い求

Thom to the southeast corner of the city wall and its location are similar to the east and west sides of Angkor Wat, indicating the possibility that it was constructed in a series of planned activities[15]. The walls of the Third Gallery are decorated with shallow reliefs with motifs of Hindu mythology such as the Ramayana and military processions, and are considered to be one of the representative achievements of Khmer art.

(2) **Surrounding Topography and Temple Structure**

The temple developed on a low-lying fan-shaped site and is surrounded by a large moat. At the northeast corner, there is a water channel flowing in from the present-day Siem Reap River, which passes through the interior of the temple and flows out from the southeast corner of the moat. The foundation of the temple was raised by compacted soil brought by the digging.

The interior consists of a three-story stepped pyramid-shaped gallery on a large terrace measuring 332 m east to west, 257 m north to south, and 1.8 m high, with a cruciform gallery and sutra repository, and a high centripetal main tower surrounded by four sub-towers (corner buildings) on the central third level. Angkor Wat is a complex of the temple style of the hall-and-mountain type built in the Angkor area in the 9-10th century and the vertical-deep temple style that developed later on a flat surface. Angkor Wat is not only an artistically

心性のある主塔が聳える。9〜10世紀頃のアンコール地域に造営されたピラミッド型寺院とその後，平面に展開した縦深型の寺院形式とが複合した姿である。アンコール・ワットは，精緻な浅浮彫といった美術史的側面のみならず，クメール寺院建築の集大成ともいうべき遺構のひとつといえる。

7．ベン・メアレア

(1) 寺院概要

ベン・メアレアはアンコールから東方約40kmに位置する複合寺院と周囲に点在する小規模衛星寺院，およびバライや土手の痕跡などから構成される遺跡群であり，アンコール・ワット様式（12世紀前半）の建造であると見なされている。当該寺院はアンコールから東に延びる王道がコー・ケー遺跡群，ニャック・ブオスを経由してワット・プー寺院へと到達する北方と，前述の大プレア・カーンに到達する東方に分岐する地点に位置してお

historical monument with exquisite bas-reliefs, but also a culmination of Khmer temple architecture prior to the Bayon.

7. Beng Mealea

(1) Outline of the Temple

Beng Mealea is located about 40 km east of Angkor and consists of a complex of large and small temples, scattered in the surrounding area, and traces of a baray and causeways. The temple is located at the junction of the Royal Road running east from Angkor to Vat Phu via Koh Ker Monuments and Neak Buos, and to the east to the aforementioned Great Preah Khan, suggesting that it was a key site for local governance during the Angkor period.

(2) Surrounding Topography and Temple Structure

The temple consists of a three-layered cloister and a perimeter wall. The moat encircling the outer cloister is on three sides (east, west, and south), and the outer northern cloister is bounded by a river that leaves a sandstone quarry, O Thmor Dap, on the riverbed. The river flows between a

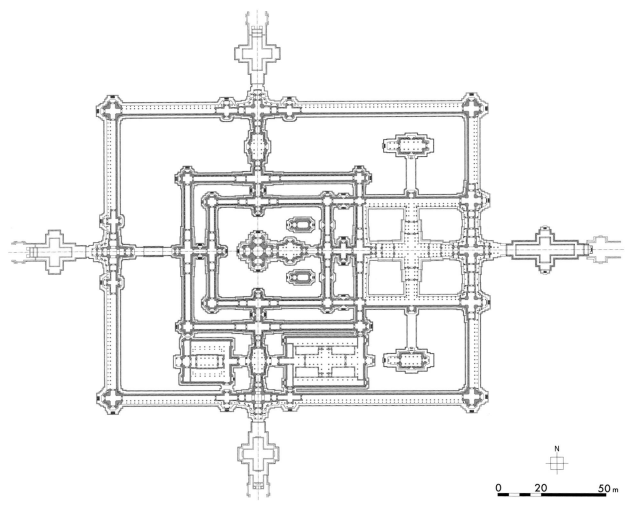

Fig. 3.2.7 Plan of Central complex of Beng Mealea

り，アンコール時代の地方統治の要所であったと推測される。

⑵ 周辺地形と伽藍構成

　当該寺院は三重の回廊と周壁を巡らす構成だが，外回廊を囲む環濠は東西南の三方で確認され，北側回廊外側は砂岩の採石場であるO Thmor Dapを河底に残す河川が区画しており，十字型ゴープラと疑似的な参道橋の間を流れている。寺院から東方約2kmには，Pr. Phtyと呼ばれる遺構を中央に配置した東西1.6km，南北0.9kmの土塁を巡らすバライがあり，ベン・メアレアの北側を流れる河川はこのバライに流入する。

　寺院周辺の住居跡は報告されていないが，寺院南西方向から南方へ延び，ほぼ90°の角度で西方へ伸びるL字型の土堤では，瓦片や土器を中心とした遺物が多数発見されており[17]，アンコールから延びる王道付近にかけて多様な施設が位置していたと思われる。

　ベン・メアレアを囲む環濠は，北側が河川によって縁取られたとみると，東西約1,020m，南辺の環濠外法から東西主軸までが約440mとなる。寺院内は三重の回廊によって囲まれ，第3回廊と第2回廊を接続する十字回廊や経蔵の配置形式等と，装飾と建築形式からアンコール・ワットが建立された直後，バイヨンが建設される前に建設されたとも考えられており，アンコール・ワットのようにピラミッド型の立面構成を取らない点で明確な相違がみられるほか，第3回廊内南側に配置された2つの「宮殿」など，構成施設や構法，装飾様式など様々な点で違いがみられる。王道の結節点として，周辺遺構を含めた当寺院は，大プレア・カーンやコー・ケー遺跡群へ至る交通・交易・軍事的な要所として機能していたと推察されるが，併存していた都市的機能を支える居住地等の痕跡は確認できていない。

8. バイヨン

⑴ 寺院概要

　バイヨンは，ジャヤヴァルマンⅦによって建設されたアンコール・トム都城の中心寺院である。当該時代より以前に築造された多くの遺構とは異なり，バイヨンの創成期はヒンドゥー教寺院として建造が始まり，途上で大乗仏教に宗旨が変更されたものと想定されており，1933年フランス極東学院により中央塔直下竪坑から4.7mの高さの座仏像が発見されている。後年にはヒンドゥー教寺院に改宗され，各所の仏陀の浅浮彫をシヴァリンガ像などに改変した。

cruciform gopura and a pseudo approach bridge. About 2 km east of the temple, there is a baray with a 1.6 km east-west and 0.9 km north-south earthen mound with the remains called Pr. Phty in the center. The river flows north of Beng Mealea flows into this baray.

Although no residential sites have been reported around the temple, many artifacts, mainly tile fragments and pottery, have been found in an L-shaped earthen embankment extending from the southwest of the temple to the south and west at an angle of almost 90°[17], suggesting that diverse facilities were located near the Royal Road extending from Angkor.

The moat of Beng Mealea, assuming that the northern side was fringed by a river, measures approximately 1,020 m from east to west, and approximately 440 m from the outer ring on the southern side to the main axis from east to west. The temple is surrounded by three Galleries, and the cruciform gallery connecting the Third and Second Galleries, the layout of the sutra repository, and the decoration and architectural style suggest that it was constructed immediately after Angkor Wat was built and before Bayon was constructed. The two palaces on the south side of the Third Gallery, for example, are different from each other in terms of their facilities, construction methods, and decorative styles. As a node of the Royal Road, the temple is located on the periphery of the presumed city. As a node on the Royal Road, the temple, including the surrounding structures, is thought to have served as a strategic point for transportation, trade, and military activities leading to Great Preah Khan and Koh Ker Monuments, but no traces of residences or other structures supporting the coexisting urban functions have been found.

8. Bayon

⑴ Outline of the Temple

Bayon is the central temple of Angkor Thom, built by Jayavarman VII. Unlike many other temples constructed before this period, it is assumed that the Bayon was built as a Hindu temple iinitially, and that the sect of Buddhism was changed to Mahayana Buddhism in the process of construction. Bayon is converted into a Hindu temple, and the reliefs of Buddha in various places were changed to Shivalinga statues in later period.

The temple consists of eight sub-temples supporting the Central Tower like buttresses. A group of worship halls are in front of the towers, a large terrace with Inner and Outer Galleries in the center, a north-south sutra repository in the Outer Galleries, a cistern and outer walls symmetrically arranged around the eastern approach. There is a 52 face towers, which are thought to have been decorated with asuras, devas, and devatas applied on all four sides, making them gods of the four directions[18]. The Buddhist temples built by Jayavarman VII include not only the temples at Angkor, such

Table 3.2.1 Comparison of Each City and Site

	Sambor Prei Kuk Monuments	Preah Vihear	Koh Ker Monuments
Location	Lower reaches of Seng River Floodplain Hinterland	Upper reaches of Seng River Hilly area of Dangrek Mountains	The uppermost tributaries of the Seng River It is located on gently sloping hills
City Outline	"City Area" 3 directions surrounded by the enclosure rotated counterclockwise	Clear outline of city area is not confirmed	Clear outline of city area is not confirmed
Trace and Feature of City	There are many traces of paddy field, baray, palace, and government facilities inside and outside of "City Area"	Scattered pottery and Chinese porcelains contain Ou Ang Krong	Scattered remains are constructed based on the relationship between landscape, Rahal, Prasat Thom central temple It is functioned as capital city in short period
Feature of Temple	North Group: Constructed based on cardinal directions Regarded as prototype of pyramid form South and Central Group: Constructed rotated counterclockwise Regarded as the prototype of vertical oriented layout temple	The temple unfolds north-south along the Dangrek Hill as vertical oriented layout temple. The long approach, continuous terraces, and pillared corridors make up the sanctity of the main shrine.	Pyramid form sacred mountain is constructed at the back of Prasat Thom formed vertical oriented on the plains. The vertical forms and arrangement of the temples enhance holiness.

寺院は中央にそびえる塔をバットレスのように支える八基の副塔とその前面の拝殿群，それらを載せる大規模なテラスを中央に内回廊，外回廊を巡らせ，外回廊内に南北経蔵を，東参道を中心に対称に配される貯水池や外周壁で構成される。四方に施されたアシュラ，デーヴァ，デヴァターを施して四方神としたとも考えられる52基の尊顔塔が林立する[18]。ジャヤヴァルマンⅦの造営による仏教寺院はタ・プローム，プレア・カーンなどアンコールの寺院のみならず，大プレア・カーン，バンテアイ・チュマールなど地方の遺構にも尊顔塔が設けられた。中央塔頂部は地上から約42mの高さとなるが，中央テラス以上は約31mとなり，寺院全高の3/4を占める大基壇となっている。

バイヨンの増改築に関する研究は1927年に発表されたH. パルマンティエ，P. ステルンらの論考に始まり，L. ドラポルト，H. デヴェリン，J. デュマルセらの復原研究を経て，各建物の痕跡をもとに補足を加えたO. クニンの四段階変遷説が通説となっている。O. クニンによれば①中央テラス，内回廊「十字型回廊」の建造，②内回廊「鉤型回廊」，③外回廊，内外回廊を結ぶ通廊ホールの建設と撤去，南北経蔵，外回廊東側の参道テラス，南北貯水池，④周壁の建造，外回廊壁入口の一部閉鎖，仏教関連の図像の改変が行われたとされ，①～③はジャヤヴァルマンⅦ，④はジャヤヴァルマンⅧの治世期に行われたと想定されている[19]。

⑵ バイヨンとアンコール・トム都城の関係性

バイヨンはアンコール・トム都城の中心に位置する。一帯はクーレン山沖積扇状地にあり，北東から南西に向

as Ta Prohm and Preah Khan, but also those in the provinces, such as Great Preah Khan and Banteay Chhmar. The top of the Central Tower is about 42 m high from the ground, but the base of the central terrace is about 31 m high, making it a large platform that occupies 3/4 of the total height of the temple.

The study of the extend and reconstruction of the Bayon began in 1927 with the work of H. Parmentier and P. Stern, followed by the reconstruction studies of L. Delaporte, H. Develin, and J. Dumarçay. Most recently O. Cunin proposed a four-stage transition theory, based on traces of each building and supplemented by other studies. According to O. Cunin, the construction was as follows: ① the construction of the central terrace and the Inner "Cruciform Gallery," ② the construction of the Inner "Hooked Gallery," ③ the construction and removal of the Outer Gallery and the passage hall connecting the Inner and Outer Galleries, ④ the construction of the perimeter wall, partial closing of the Outer Gallery wall entrance, and alterations to Buddhist-related iconography were carried out. It is assumed that ① to ③ were done during the reign of Jayavarman VII and ④ during the reign of Jayavarman VIII[19].

⑵ **Relation between Bayon and Angkor Thom**

As mentioned earlier, Bayon is located in the center of Angkor Thom. The area is located on the alluvial plain of Phnom Kulen, with a gentle slope of about 1/1000 from northeast to southwest. Water is taken into the inner moat at the northern end of the eastern side of the city, distributed to the city via waterways, collected at the Beng Thom basin in the southwestern corner, and discharged into the moat ring. Most of the waterways in the city run in a nearly four directions, but the one leading to Baphuon rotates clockwise,

Angkor Wat	Beng Mealea	Preah Khan of Kampong Svay	Bayon
Alluvial fan of Kulen Mountain	Segment point of Ancient Royal Road extended from Angkor to east	Located around the Staung River as major iron producing areas, mainly Phnom Dek	Functioned as guardian temple of the nation in center of Angkor Thom
Constructed based on city planning of Angkor	Remains of earthworks are found in some areas	4.8 km square earthen mound centered on the temple	Surrounded by inner and outer enclosure and city wall
It is located on grid plan of Angkor, and there is the possibility that the outline of Angkor Wat is composed based on South Gate and southeast corner of Angkor Thom.	Some pieces of roof tile and trace of earthenware are confirmed in southwest of temple. Some of remains estimated to construct in same period are located around the Ancient Royal Road and south of baray.	It is functioned as a key point for the steel industry by the trace of slag and waste around the temple.	It is constructed in long period and large-scale of city planning. The network of waterways is constructed for water distribution throughout the city.
Large-scale of enclosure and causeway connected with inside of temple, enhance the vertical spatially and huge terrace, 3 layer of pyramid, and central tower enhance the centripetal. The temple face to west and cardinal directions.	Almost cardinal directions temple is surrounded by natural lake and enclosure. It is mentioned the similarity with Angkor Wat, but elevation of central complex differs greatly and detail parts also differ.	Axis of temple deflects clockwise. Large-scale of temple unfolds on the plains. There are Dharmaçara along the Ancient Royal Road and Face Tower constructed in Bayon period around the temple.	The shape of city and temple are cardinal directions. Buddhism element is the feature as shown in huge terrace, many face towers, relief, sculpture and so on.

かう1/1000程度の緩やかな勾配を有する。都城内は直線状の水路網と多数の溜池が張り巡らされており，都城東辺北端にて内環濠へ取水され，水路を介して都城内に配水された後，南西隅のベントムへ集水，環濠へと排出される。都城内水路の多くはほぼ正方位に走るが，バプーオンに繋がる水路は時計回りに回転しており，アンコール・トム築造前の水路が組み込まれたと考えられる[20]。都市の建設はヤショヴァルマンⅠ（889～915）によるヤショダラプラ建造に始まり，10世紀半ばから11世紀半ばにかけて王宮周辺の多くの遺構が建設される。アンコール・トム外郭は9世紀から10世紀前半より計画が始まるが，都城内部の区画が環濠外部にも拡張されていることが明らかとなった[21]。各城門の建設はジャヤヴァルマンⅦの治世期ともされるが，城門を通る大通りの建造は不明であり，王宮前の象のテラスへと至る勝利の門を通じる大通りは王宮前広場の建設時には存在していた可能性が高い[22]。勝利の門と死者の門（東大門）の間が都城一辺の1/6となることからも，都市としての計画性を見て取れる。

（3）バイヨンの特異性

　個々にみてきた各地方都市遺構は，周辺地形の影響下にあり，また地域産業と密接に関連した特色などを備え，それぞれ，本来であれば東西に長い矩形の敷地を持つ寺院とともに構成されている。しかし，都市として明確な輪郭を持たないコー・ケー遺跡群やプレア・ヴィヘアなどの例もあり，そして必ずしも都市の中央に寺院を配置するとは限らず，バライとの位置関係も相対的なものであった。しかしバイヨンは，正方位への志向性が明確で

suggesting that the waterway was incorporated before the construction of Angkor Thom[20]. The construction of the city began with the building of Yashodharapura by Yashovarman I (889-915), and from the mid-10th to mid-11th century, many of the remains around the royal palace were constructed. The planning of Angkor Thom's outer wall began in the 9th to early 10th century, and it is now clear that the inner sections of the capital city were extended outside the moat encircling it[21]. The construction of each gate is said to have occurred during the reign of Jayavarman VII, but the construction of the main avenue passing through the gates is unknown, and it is highly likely that the main avenue leading to the Victory Gate to the front of the royal palace existed when the square flanked by the Elephant Terrace in front of the palace was built[22]. The fact that the distance between the Victory Gate and the Dead Gate is 1/6 of a side of the capital city also shows the planning of the city.

（3）**Uniqueness of Bayon**

Each of the individual city sites we have examined is under the influence of the surrounding topography and has features closely related to local industries, and each is composed of a temple with a rectangular site that would normally be long from east to west. However, there are also examples such as Koh Ker Monuments and Preah Vihear, which do not have a clear urban outline, and temples were not always located in the center of the city, and their location relative to the baray was also relative. Bayon, however, has a clear orientation toward the square, and Angkor Thom, a city with this temple correctly attached to the center, has an exceptionally square plan. This shows a clear plan to show a model of the city. However, Angkor Thom was built on a square plan, with the Bayon occupying the center of the city, which had already been

あり，この寺院を正しく中心に付置した都市であるアンコール・トムは，例外的に正方形平面を持っている。そこには都市の範型を示そうとする明確な計画性を窺うことができる。とはいえアンコール・トムは，すでに王宮を構えた都市として成立していた地域を，その図形的中心をバイヨンが占めるように後から正方形の平面にまとめ上げたものである。王宮を貫く東西軸とバイヨン前身建物の相対的な位置関係がこの二次的な都市計画の前提であった可能性が高い。そのような特質を含めて，アンコール・トムとバイヨンは，クメール帝国の都市・寺院遺構のなかでも極めて特異な存在である。この複雑な都市の履歴については，今後さらなる解明が待たれる。

established as a city with a royal palace. It is highly possible that the relative position of the east-west axis running through the royal palace and the bayon's predecessor buildings was the premise for this secondary urban planning. Including such qualities, Angkor Thom and Bayon are very unique among the city and temple remains of the Khmer Kingdom. The history of this complex city awaits further clarification.

References
1) JSA/JASAは，サンボー・プレイ・クック遺跡群では文化芸術省と早稲田大学の共同事業である「サンボー・プレイ・クック遺跡群保全事業」の修復事業および基礎調査に協力し，コー・ケー遺跡群とベン・メアレア寺院，プレア・ヴィヘア寺院と大プレア・カーンでは，それぞれ文部科学省科学研究費補助金・基盤研究(A)（海外）「クメール帝国地方拠点の都市遺跡と寺院遺構に関する研究」（2007-2011）および「クメール帝国の空間構造と地方拠点都市遺跡に関する研究」（2012-2016）（研究代表者：溝口明則）にて技術協力を行った。また，アンコール・ワット，バイヨンの修復事業はJSA/JASAの各年次報告書にて調査結果を詳述している。
2) Coedès, G.: Inscriptions du Cambodge, 5, PEFEO, Paris, 1953
3) 下田一太：クメール古代都市イーシャナプラの研究，早稲田大学学位論文，2010
4) 南雲直子：カンボジア中央部セン川下流域に立地するプレアンコール期王都と地形環境，東京大学学位論文．2011
5) Shimoda Ichita: Prasat Sambor as a Prototype of the Pyramidal State-Temple in Khmer Temple Construction, Archaeological Discovery, 2021.9
6) 久保純子，南雲直子：プレア・ヴィヘア寺院遺跡とその周辺における地理学的調査（2012-2015年），プレア・ヴィヘアーアンコール広域拠点遺跡群の建築学研究2 pp.41-52，中央公論美術出版，2018
7) 黒岩千尋，中川武，溝口明則：プレア・ヴィヘア寺院の「口の字」型・「田の字」型建築形式について，日本建築学会計画系論文集81巻719号，2016
8) 溝口明則：伽藍の計画法，プレア・ヴィヘアーアンコール広域拠点遺跡群の建築学研究2 pp.77-102，中央公論美術出版，2018
9) 久保純子：遺跡群周辺の地形と立地環境，コー・ケーとベン・メアレア ― アンコール広域拠点遺跡群の建築学研究 pp.32-38，中央公論美術出版，2014
10) Parmantier. H: L'art khmer classique. Monuments du quadrant Nord-Est, PEFEO 29 at 29 bis, EFEO, Paris, 1939
11) 下田一太，佐藤桂：古代クメール都市コー・ケー遺跡群の配置における宗教的コンセプト，コー・ケーとベン・メアレアーアンコール広域拠点遺跡群の建築学研究 pp.39-61，中央公論美術出版，2014
12) Bruguier. B, Juliette. L: Preah Khan, Koh Ker et Preah Vihear. Les provinces septentrionales, Guide archéologique du Cambodge, Tome V, Phnom Penh : Japan Printing House, 2013
13) Hendrickson. M, Bruguier. B: Reimagining the City of Fire and Iron, Journal of Field Archaeology, Vol. 40, No. 6 (December 2015), pp. 644-664, Published By: Taylor & Francis, Ltd.
14) Peter D. Sharrock: Garuda, Vajrapani and religious change in Jayavarman VII's Angkor, Journal of Southeast Asian Studies, 40 (1), pp111-151, The National University of Singapore, 2009
15) 斎藤直弥，江口千奈美，中川武：クメール都城の構成原理に関する研究（3）～アンコール・ワットとアンコール・トムを中心としたアンコール地域の地割り計画～，日本建築学会大会学術講演梗概集，2005
16) 下田一太，百瀬純哉，原智子，村岡知美，石塚充雅，島田麻里子，荒川千晶：ベン・メアレア遺跡群の建築的特徴，コー・ケーとベン・メアレアーアンコール広域拠点遺跡群の建築学研究 pp.150-163，中央公論美術出版，2014
17) Menghong. C: ベン・メアレア周辺の採集調査，ベン・メアレア遺跡群の建築的特徴，コー・ケーとベン・メアレアーアンコール広域拠点遺跡群の建築学研究 pp.188-197，中央公論美術出版，2014
18) H. Park, "Notes on the Character of the Chambers on the Terrace of Bayon temple And Pilgrimages Made To Them," ARJSA pp.107-150, 2001
19) O. Cunin and E. Uchida, "Contribution of the Magnetic Susceptibility of the Sandstones to the Analysis of Architectural History of Bayon Style Monuments," ARJSA, pp. 205-254, 2002
20) 下田一太，田畑幸嗣：密林に覆われたアンコール遺跡群の実像解明，3D考古学の再挑戦－遺跡・遺構の非破壊調査研究　2017年度総合研究機構研究成果報告会学術シンポジウム予稿集 pp.57-63, 2017
21) Damian H. Evans, Roland J. Fletcher, Christophe Pottier, Glenn Boornazian: Uncovering archaeological landscapes at Angkor using lidar, University of Central Florida, Orlando, Florida, and accepted by the Editorial Board June 13, 2013
22) 下田麻里子：アンコール・トム都市の編年研究にむけた予察的検討，東南アジア考古学39号 pp.67-82, 2019

3.3 クメール建築設計方法とバイヨン
Dimention Planning Method in Khmer Architecture and the Bayon

溝口 明則
MIZOGUCHI Akinori

1. はじめに

文化財建造物の修復とその基礎研究のあり方を考えるとき，修復の理念とその方針を支える"オーセンティシティ"については十分に考慮すべきであり，このことは十分な調査研究を実施すべきことを意味している。なかでも往時の設計者の意図や設計方法，設計過程などの解明は重要なテーマである。ところが世界的にみて，設計の方法や過程を復原的に捉えようとする努力はほとんど実施されたことがない。しかし，ときに未完成の部位を抱えるクメール建築にとって，計画上どのような姿が目指されたのかを理解することが，修復の基本方針を策定するために重要な指標となる場合が多い。このような視点から，私たちはクメール建築の造営時における設計の内容を，可能な限り復原することを目ざした。

そのためには，当時の造営尺の実長を特定することが必要だが，周知のように1000年前に隆盛したクメール文明は，膨大な寺院遺跡，巨大な土木工作の痕跡を残しながら当時のものさしを残していない。このため，20世紀の前半ではL. フィノ，G. セデス，後半ではE. モニカなどの研究者が，碑文の解読やアンコール・ワットの実測値などを手がかりに，当時の度制単位の実長を特定する作業に取り組んできた[1]。

それらの寸法単位は，碑文にヴィャマ（vyama）やハスタ（hasta，肘尺）と記されている。先行研究の成果はそれぞれハスタの長さを450mmあるいは436mmとし，ヴィャマをその4倍の長さと判断したが，先行研究の成果が示す寸法は10mmを超える相違を示している。またその研究内容は，碑文の解読や遺構の部分実測資料に基づいており，いずれの値も当時の造営尺度としてそのまま受け取ることは躊躇われる。造営尺度の実長を特定する研究は，あらためて遺構の実測調査と分析を行い，先

1. Introduction

When thinking about the restoration of cultural properties and basic research, we should give due consideration to the concept of restoration and the "authenticity" that underpins the policy, and conduct sufficient research on this matter. means that In particular, it is an important theme to elucidate the intentions, design methods, and design processes of the designers of the past. However, from a global perspective, almost no effort has been made to capture design methods and processes in a restorative manner. However, for Khmer architecture, which sometimes has unfinished parts, understanding what the plan was aimed for is often an important guideline for formulating a basic policy for restoration. From this point of view, we aimed to restore as much as possible the contents of the design at the time of construction of Khmer architecture.

In order to do so, it is first necessary to identify the actual length of the construction scale at that time. However, as is generally known, Khmer civilization flourished 1,000 years ago and left no measuring unit while leaving behind enormous ruins of temple, and traces of their huge engineering workoperations. Researchers, L. Fino and G. Cœdès in the first half ofthe 20th century, and E. Mannikka in the latter half, challenged theidentified true length of the unit of measurement with the decoding of the inscription and the dimensions of Angkor Wat[1].

Those dimension units have been written down in the inscription as vyama or hasta (cubit). The result of the previous studies was different for each, but wejudged the length of hasta as 450mm or 436mm, and judged thelength of vyama as four times of hasta. However, the results of thedimensions each of the previous studies show a difference of morethan 10mm. In addition, the study was based on the decoding ofthe inscription and partially from the data measuring the ruins.Therefore, we hesitate to consider them as the actual construction measures of that time. As for the study to identify

行研究の成果を検証しつつ新しい可能性を含めて検討する必要があった。

2. 分析の前提

伽藍規模で分析を行なう際の問題は，当時の規模計画を支えた寸法基準の位置である。回廊あるいは周壁の断面を想定した場合，寸法計画の基準は基壇外面，内面，周壁ないし回廊の壁面外面，内面，中心などさまざまな可能性が考えられる。1993年に行った東タイのクメール遺構（施療院付属寺院の伽藍19件，およびピマイ，パノム・ルン，ムアン・タム等の伽藍6件）の分析結果から，寸法計画の基準となった部位が基壇足下の部材（プリンスストーンに似た部材，「基座」と呼ぶこととする）の外面であった可能性がもっとも高いと判断された（Fig. 3.3.1）。「基座」の位置は，遺構が最大の値を取る位置である[2]。

分析の前提としたもうひとつの想定は，彼らが「完数制」を用いていたことである。この寸法計画技法は，日本の古代建築の技法の分析において考えられた概念だが，例えばエジプト古王国時代のピラミッドの寸法計画法にもみられる技法で，公定尺の単純な倍数を以て各部の長さを決定する技法である。

the true length of the construction measures, measuring surveys and the analysis of the ruins were newly conducted.

2. Analysis assumptions

The big issue in analyzing the size of the complex is where the measurement criteria should be assumed, which supported the planned size then. When we assume it to be the gallery or the cross section of the enclosure, the criteria of dimension planning has several possibilities including the outside or inside of the platform, enclosure, and the outside, inside or center of the gallery. The results of the study of the Khmer ruins in East Thailand, on 19 temples of medical charities, and six large complexes such as Phimai, Panom Rung and Muang Tam, conducted in 1993, made us determine that the parts of measurement criteria were more likely to be on the outside of the materials located under the platform, hereafter we call it the "base" meaning of the pedestal of the platform, which was similar in material as prince stone (Fig. 3.3.1). The position of the "base" is the position where the remains occupy the largest area[2].

Another premise of the analysis was that they used the "method using length multiples of the measurement unit (MMU)". This dimension planning technique is a concept conceived in the analysis of ancient Japanese architectural techniques, but it is also a technique that can be seen in

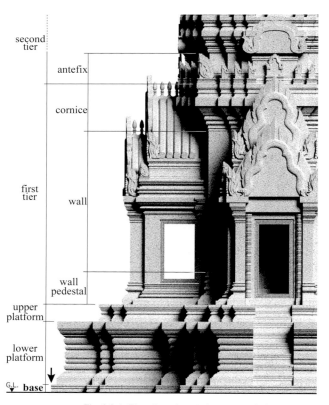

Fig. 3.3.1 Elevation of central sanctuary in Thommanon

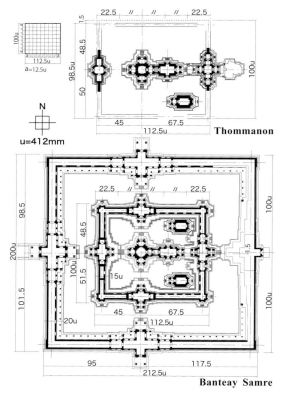

Fig. 3.3.2 Measiurement method forThommanon ans Banteay Samre

3. クメール遺構の分析

私たちは「基座」と「完数制」を手がかりに，クメール建築の寸法計画法を分析した。個々の建築の実測値は大きな寸法斑があるため，伽藍を対象として分析を試みた。そしてバンテアイ・サムレとトマノンの伽藍各部の実測値を比較することで，造営尺の実長を412±1mmと判断した（Fig. 3.3.2）。

⑴ トマノンとバンテアイ・サムレ

トマノンでは，南北を100ハスタ，東西をこの値に1/8（12.5ハスタ）を加えた112.5ハスタとする東西に長い矩形の輪郭に従って伽藍規模を決定している。バンテアイ・サムレはトマノンと同じ寸法を内回廊の輪郭にあて，その四周に50ハスタを加えて南北200ハスタ，東西212.5ハスタの外回廊の規模を決定していると考えられた。ただ，トマノンではこの矩形の輪郭の北辺から1.5ハスタを削減して東西を貫く中心線の位置が結果的に偏向を起こすようにしており，バンテアイ・サムレでは100ハスタ幅の輪郭の中心線の位置を，北に1.5ハスタずらすという操作が行われている[3]。この寸法計画技法は，完数制の扱い方からみて妥当性があると判断されたため，ここで獲得した造営尺である412±1mmを手がかりに，碑文が記す81ハスタの高さを持つ遺構，G.セデスによって比定されたプラン（the Prang）について実測を行い，碑文に記されたハスタと矛盾を起こさないかどうか確認を試みた。

プランはコー・ケー遺跡群のプラサート・トムの伽藍のうち後方半分を占める大きな敷地のなかに建っている。巨大な階段ピラミッド型の寺院遺構で921〜932年頃に造営されたと考えられている。Fig. 3.3.3に示すように，五層の基台上に下部基壇と上部基壇を重ね，その頂部に未完成の祠堂の壁体下部が残っている。

この遺跡に関わる記録と考えられた碑文は，G. セデスによって，リンガが81ハスタの高さに存在していたと解読された。また彼は，当時のハスタの実長が0.45m程であったとした。建築の具体的な大きさに言及した碑文は珍しく，当時の造営尺度の実長を考察する上で，見過ごすことのできない貴重な記録であるとともに，当該の遺構が現存している点は設計技術の分析研究にとって僥倖である。しかしこの対象は，研究史初期の碑文研究で一定の推定がなされたにもかかわらず，その後，十分に検討される機会がなかった。

---

the dimension planning method of the pyramids of the Old Kingdom of Egypt. It is a technique to determine the length of each part with a simple multiple of official scale unit.

3. Analysis of Khmer remains

We analyzed the dimension planning method of Khmer architecture with the clues of bace and "MMU" system. Since the measured values of individual buildings have unexpectedly large variations in size, we tried to analyze the size of the temple complex as targets, by comparing the measured values of each part of the temple complex of Banteay Samre and Thommanon, the actual length of the construction measuring scale was 412 ± 1 mm (Fig. 3.3.2).

⑴ **Thommanon and Banteay Samre**

In Thommanon, the scale of the temple is determined according to the outline of a long rectangle extending from east to west, with 100 hasta for north and south and 112.5 hastas for east and west, which is 1/8 of this value (12.5 hastas). And Banteay Samre assigned the same dimensions as Thommanon to the outline of the Inner Gallery, and added 50 hastas to the circumference to determine the scale of the Outer Gallery of 200 hastas from north to south and 212.5 hastas from east to west. However, in Thommanon, 1.5 hastas are reduced from the north side of the outline of this rectangle so that the position of the center line running through the east and west will change as a result. And in Banteay Samre, an operation is performed to shift the position of the center line of the 100 hasta wide contour to the north by 1.5 hastas[3]. This dimension planning technique was judged to be valid from the point of view of MMU system. And using the construction measuring scale of 412 ± 1 mm obtained here as a clue, I measured the plan (the Prang) identified by G. Cœdès and tried to confirm whether there is any contradiction with the hasta written in the inscription.

The Prang is built on a large site that occupies the rear half of the temple complex of Prasat Thom in Koh Ker Monuments. It is believed to have been built around 921 to 932 with the remains of a huge step pyramid-shaped temple. As shown in Fig. 3.3.3, the lower platform and the upper platform are superimposed on the five layers base, and the lower part of the wall of the unfinished temple hall remains at the top.

The inscriptions are regarded as a record about these ruins and was decoded by G. Cœdès, which reads the linga existed at the height of 81 hasta. He also noted that the true length of hasta was around 0.45 m at that time. The inscription referring the specific size of the construction was rare, therefore it was an important record on discussion the true length of the construction measures of those days. Moreover, the fortunate existence of such ruins is good for analysis of the design

3.3 クメール建築設計方法とバイヨン　71

Fig. 3.3.3 The Prang at Koh Ker Monuments

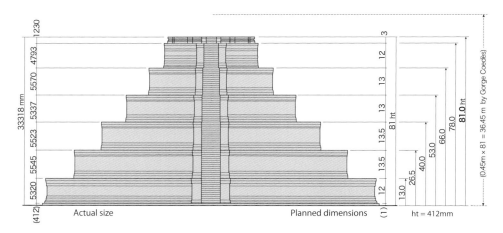

Fig. 3.3.4 Dimension analysis of the Prang

(2) プラン (the Prang)

プランの実測値を先のハスタで換算すると，その高さの計画はFig. 3.3.4のような結果となった。この結果は，ハスタを450mmとするG.セデスの提案では81ハスタの位置が中空に飛び出してしまうことに対し，基座から上部基壇の高さまでの合計が81ハスタになることが確かめられた。

碑文の内容は「81ハスタの高さにリンガを持ち上げた」とする。このため，81ハスタが上部基壇の上辺に合致することから，ハスタの実長を412±1mmとする判断には妥当性が認められる。この成果以後，私たちは想定された造営尺の実長の妥当性を確認するだけでなく，クメール遺構の伽藍計画法，寸法計画の技法を分析することに重点を移して行った[4]。

(3) コー・ケー遺跡群

私たちはコー・ケー遺跡群のなかで，まず，プラサート・プラムについて実測と分析を行った。この簡素な寺院は，東を正面とし，南北に長い基壇上に3基の塔状祠堂を一列に配置しており，前方に2つの経蔵を設けている。この遺構の伽藍の輪郭は南北101ハスタ，東西130

art. However, this subject did not have an opportunity to to be entirely discussed enough afterwards although a certain estimation was concluded from an early inscription study.

(2) the Prang

When the actual measured value of the plan was converted by hasta, the result of the plan for the height was as shown in Fig. 3.3.4. As a result, it was confirmed that the total height from the base to the upper platform is 81 hastas, whereas G. Cœdès' proposal of 450 mm hasta has the position of 81 hastas protruding in the air.

The inscription reads, "The linga was lifted to the height of 81 hasta". Therefore, since the 81 hastas matches the upper side of the upper platform, the judgment that the actual length of the hasta is 412±1mm is recognized as valid. After this result, we not only investigated the validity of the assumed actual length of the construction measuring scale, but also shifted our focus to analyzing the temple planning method and dimension planning technique of the Khmer remains[4].

(3) Koh Ker Monuments

Among the archaeological sites in Koh Ker Monuments, we first measured and analyzed Prasat Pram.This simple temple has three pagoda-like shrines arranged in a row on a platform

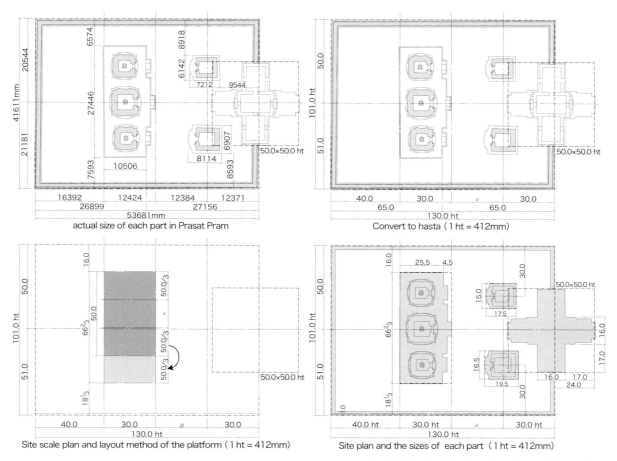

Fig. 3.3.5 Analysis for dimension planning in Prasat Pram

ハスタとするもので,南北の長さはいったん100ハスタとし,中心線をわずかに北に寄せるために,敷地の南辺を1ハスタ増加させている。トマノンが北辺を1.5ハスタ削除した技法と同じ技法だが,ここでは敷地を拡大することを選択している(Fig. 3.3.5)。

この遺構の計画法の分析結果を手がかりに,プラサート・トムの計画法について分析を試みた。プラサート・トムは,コー・ケー遺跡群を中心とした地域が首都となる以前からの古刹で,当初は小さな寺院であったと考えられる。その時代の敷地の輪郭は南北100ハスタ,東西120ハスタであったと推定した。

中央部は大基壇の上に小規模な9つの祠堂が施設されていた。そしてコー・ケー遺跡群を中心とした地域が首都となった時期(928～944年),国家を代表する寺院として拡張工事が行われた。このとき小寺院であったプラサート・トムを囲んで水濠が施設され,その外周を周壁で囲んだ大規模な寺院に変貌したが,中央部は前の時代の小規模な寺院であった頃の様相を残していた。

拡大されたプラサート・トムの敷地輪郭は,南北364ハスタ,東西396ハスタと判断されたが,これは南北360ハスタ,東西400ハスタとする基本計画から伽藍の

extending north and south, with the east facing the front, and two librarys in front.The outline of the temple of this remains is 101 hasta from north to south and 130 hasta from east to west.The north-south length is once set to 100 hastas, and the south side of the site is increased by 1 hasta in order to move the center line slightly to the north (Fig. 3.3.5).

Using the results of the analysis of the planning method of Prasat Pram as a clue, I tried to analyze the planning method of Prasat Thom. Prasat Thom was an ancient temple before Area centered on the Koh Ker Monuments became the capital, and it is thought that it was originally a small temple. The outline of the site at that time was estimated to be 100 hastas from north to south and 120 hastas from east to west.

In the central part, nine small shrines were built on a large platform. And when Area on the Koh Ker Monuments became the capital (A.D.928-944), expansion work was carried out as a temple representing the nation.At this time, a water moat was built around Prasat Thom, which was a small temple, and it was transformed into a large-scale temple with a surrounding wall around its perimeter, but the central part retained the appearance of a small-scale temple in the previous era.

The site outline of the expanded Prasat Thom was determined to be 364 hastas north to south and 396 hastas east to west. It was thought that the basic plan of 360 hastas from

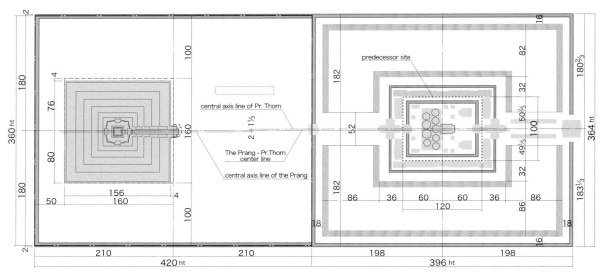

Fig. 3.3.6 Dimension planning in Prasat Thom and predecessor site

中軸線を変更させるために南端を4ハスタ拡張し，これに合わせて東西の長さから4ハスタを差し引いたものだと考えられた（Fig. 3.3.6）。これは調整を加える前の敷地面積を近似的に保存しつつ，敷地輪郭の完数制を保つ技法であったと考えられる[4]。この規模計画の技法は，私たちに当時の考え方を伝えるもので，設計技法を復原する立場にとって大きな手がかりである。

⑷ ベン・メアレア

アンコール・ワットとほぼ同時代に造営されたと考えられているベン・メアレアは大規模な寺院遺構である。三重に巡らす回廊と東に施設された十字回廊，南に配置された2つの付属建物（おそらくアシュラマ）は，この寺院が特別な地方拠点のひとつであったことを物語っている。Fig. 3.3.7は実測値から計画寸法を導いたもので，各部に完数計画を認めることができ，ハスタの実長は411mm程と算出された。

各部の実測値から推定される計画手順は思いのほか複雑なもので，おそらく当初は二重回廊の寺院として計画された。しかし工事が開始された後の早い時期に三重の回廊を巡らす計画に変更され，このことに合わせて敷地の拡大と各部の相対的な位置の微調整が行われた。相対的に狭い敷地に三重の回廊を設けたため，中回廊と外回廊のゴープラが一体となるなど，異例の構成をみることができる。

以上の現象を踏まえて計画過程を推定した結果，ベン・メアレアはFig. 3.3.8に示したような手順によって実現したと思われる。想定された基本となった敷地計画は，Fig. 3.3.8(i)に示したように，南北360ハスタ，東西440ハスタとするもので，中回廊の規模はそれぞれそ

north to south and 400 hasta from east to west was expanded by 4 hastas at the south end in order to change the central axis of the temple, and the 4 hasta were subtracted from the length from east to west (Fig. 3.3.6). This is thought to be a technique that maintains the MMU system of the site outline while approximately preserving the site area before making adjustments[4]. This scale planning technique tells us about the way of thinking at the time, and is a great clue for those who are in a position to restore the original dimennsion design techniques.

⑷ **Beng Mealea**

Beng Mealea, which is believed to have been built around the same time as Angkor Wat, is a large-scale temple remains. The triple gallery and cruciform garllary installed in the east, and the two ancillary buildings (probably āśrama) located in the south, indicate that this temple was one of the special local centers. Fig. 3.3.7 shows the planned dimensions derived from actual measurements, and the MMU system can be recognized for each part. The actual length of the hasta was calculated to be about 411mm.

The planning procedure estimated from the actual measurements of each part was unexpectedly complicated, and it was probably originally planned as a double garllary temple. However, the plan was probably changed early after construction began, with a triple gallary encircling the site, and the site was enlarged and the relative positions of each part were fine-tuned accordingly. Because three layers of Galleries were set up on a relatively narrow site, we can see an unusual composition, such as the Gopura of the Middle Gallary and the Outer Gallary are integrated. As a result of estimating the planning process based on the above phenomena, Ben Mealea seems to have been realized by the procedure shown in Fig. 3.3.8. The assumed basic site plan,

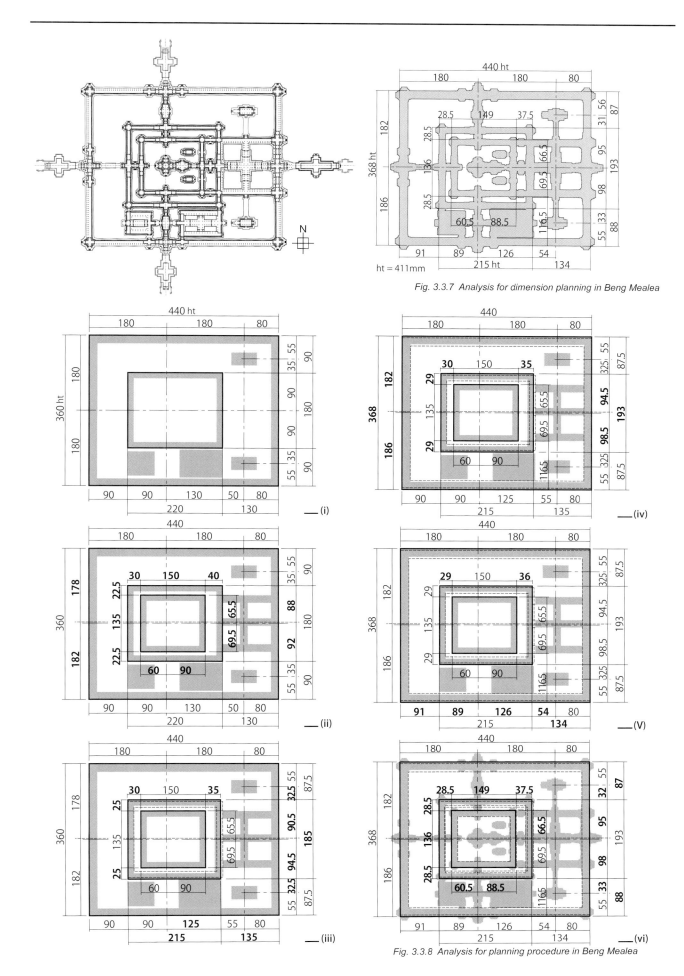

Fig. 3.3.7 Analysis for dimension planning in Beng Mealea

Fig. 3.3.8 Analysis for planning procedure in Beng Mealea

3.3 クメール建築設計方法とバイヨン　75

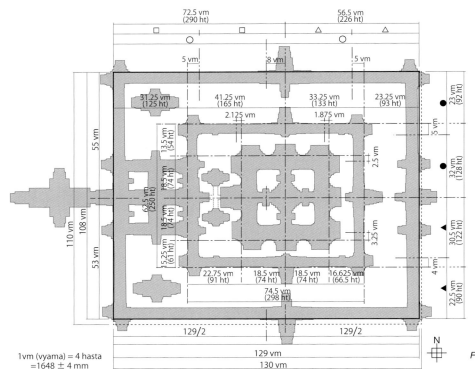

Fig. 3.3.9 Analysis for dimension planning in Angkor Wat

の半分の寸法，南北180ハスタと東西220ハスタとする計画であったと考えられた。この背後には，敷地面積を100ヴィヤマ（400ハスタ，1ヴィヤマ＝4ハスタ）四方とする最も基本となる規模計画が存在したと考えられる。

(5) アンコール・ワット

アンコール・ワットは例外的に西を正面とする寺院で，東向きの寺院を180°回転させたように中軸線も南に偏っている。その配置計画はFig. 3.3.9のように複雑な操作を加えているが，その基本となった敷地計画は南北110ヴィヤマ（440ハスタ），東西130ヴィヤマ（520ハスタ）とするもので，南端を2ヴィヤマ削減することで中心線の偏向を実現している。これはトマノンと同様の技法である。したがってアンコール・ワットの規模計画は，120ヴィヤマ（480ハスタ）四方とする敷地面積に由来すると考えられる。なお，ハスタの実長は412～411.5㎜程と算出される[5]。

(6) プレア・ヴィヘア

プレア・ヴィヘアは真南に向かって登る参道に合わせて5つの施設を配置した独特の寺院である。本章ではその配置計画に限定して紹介したい。直線上に並ぶ施設は，北から順にゴープラⅤ～Ⅰ，南端の山頂伽藍はゴープラⅡ（エンクロジャーⅡ）とゴープラⅠ（エンクロジャーⅠ）と呼ばれている。ゴープラⅤの基準の位置（東西に伸びる部位の北側の基座）から山頂伽藍の基本計画の南端ま

as shown in Fig. 3.3.8 (i), is 360 hastas from north to south and 440 hastas from east to west. And it was thought that the contours of the Middle Gallery was planned to be half that size, 180 hastas north to south and 220 hastas east to west. Behind this plan, it is thought that there was the most basic scale plan with a site area of 100 vyamas (400 hastas, 1vyama = 4 hasta) square.

(5) **Angkor Wat**

Angkor Wat is an exception to the west-facing temple, and the central axis line is tilted southward, as if the east-facing temple is rotated 180 degrees. The layout plan adds complicated operations as shown in Fig. 3.3.9, and the basic site plan was 110 viyamas (440 hastas) from north to south and 130 viyama (520 hastas) from east to west, which the change of the centerline was realized by reducing the south end by 2 viyamas. This is the technique similar to Thommanon. Therefore, the scale plan of Angkor Wat is considered to be derived from the site area of 120 vyamas (480 hastas) square. The actual length of the hasta is calculated to be about 412 - 411.5mm[5].

(6) **Preah Vihear**

Preah Vihear is a unique temple with five facilities aligned with the approach to the due south. In this chapter, I would like to introduce only the layout plan. The facilities lined up in a straight line are called Gopura V to I in order from the north, and the mountaintop temples at the southern end are called Gopura II (Enclosure II) and Gopura I (Enclosure I). There is a distance of 420 vyamas from the standard position of Gopura

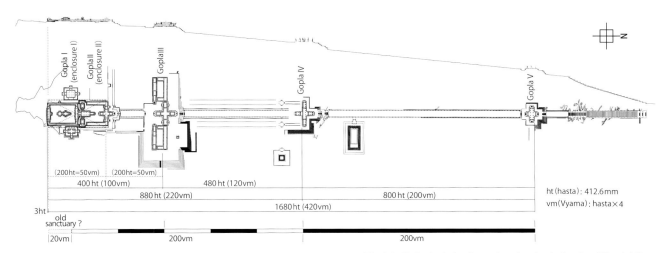

Fig. 3.3.10 Analysis for dimension planning in the site of Preah Vihear

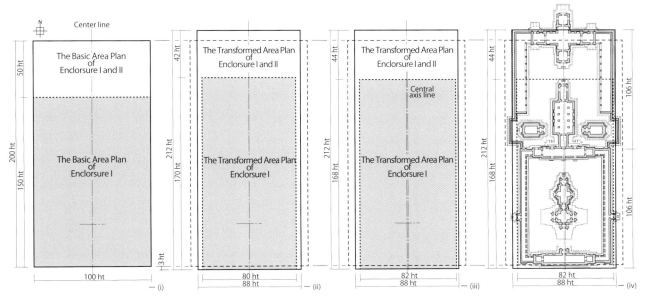

Fig. 3.3.11 Analysis for dimension planning in the munntentop temple of Preah Vihear

で420ヴィヤマの距離があり，ゴープラⅣは北端から200ヴィヤマに位置している。ゴープラⅣから南端まで220ヴィヤマのうち，ゴープラⅢはゴープラⅥから120ヴィヤマの位置に，そしてゴープラⅢから伽藍の南端まで100ヴィヤマとなる。完数制による寸法計画は非常に簡明な計画であったことがわかる (Fig. 3.3.10)。9世紀に遡る前身伽藍は，おそらく山頂伽藍の奥行きを20ハスタとし，そのアプローチを400ハスタとする計画であったと推定される。現在の山頂伽藍は奥行を200ハスタ，全幅を100ハスタとする基本計画から始まり，最終的に，南端が基本計画から3ハスタ伸びた構成を取ることになった[6] (Fig. 3.3.11)。

V (base on the north side of the part extending east and west) to the southern end of the basic plan of the mountaintop temple and Gopura IV is located 200 vyamas from the northern end. Of the 220 vyamas from Gopura IV to the southern end, Gopura III is located 120 vyamas from Gopura VI, and 100 vyamas from Gopura III to the southern end of the temple. It can be seen that the dimensional plan based on the MMU system was a very simple plan (Fig. 3.3.10). The predecessor temple dating back to the 9th century is presumed to have been planned to have a depth of 20 hastas at the summit temple and 400 hastas approach. The current mountaintop temple started from a basic plan with a depth of 200 hastas and a total width of 100 hastas[6] (Fig. 3.3.11).

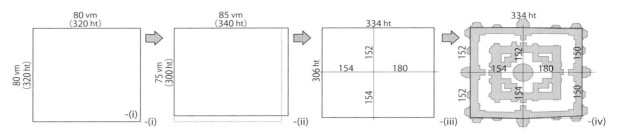

Fig. 3.3.12 Planning procedure of Bayon

4. Toward the analysis of Bayon

Bayon has many characteristics, but I would like to draw your attention to the fact that the Outer Gallery is slightly curved and does not form a straight line. This kind of feature can be seen as an error in construction, but the same is not seen in the Inner Gallery, and there is no other temple in the same period where the gallery does not form a straight line. In other words, we can only assume that the curving of the Outer Gallery was intentional. From the estimated actual measurements, the dimensions of each part of Bayon were analyzed as shown in Fig. 3.3.12. I would like to think about the planning procedure in which the outline of such a site appears. As mentioned earlier, Beng Mealea had a site area of 100 vyamas square, and Angkor Wat had a site area of 120 vyamas square, and it was thought that this was the starting point for planning. Bayon is thought to have started from 80 vyamas square in a similar way. The plan would be 75 vyamas from north to south and 85 vyamas from east to west, and 306 hastas from north to south (76.5 vyamas) to move the central axis to the north. After deducting the increase, the east-west area was set at 334 hastas (83.5 vyamas).

The problem is the adjustment from here, even though the distance between the Gopura and the Central Tower in the south center and north center is set to 152 hasts on the north side and 154 hastas on the south side, the distance from the north end to the West Gopura on the west side remains 152 hastas, The distance from the West Gopura to the south end is also 152 hastas, and on the east side, the distance from the north end to the East Gopura is 150 hastas, and the distance from the East Gopura to the south end is also 150 hastas (Fig. 3.3.12 (iv)). Despite the fact that the intention was to move the central axis to the north until the stage of setting up the Gopura on the four sides after the construction of the central part, it is thought that an attempt was made to eliminate the deflection of the central axis at the stage of constructing the Gallery. It is highly likely that this process was originally conceived as a temple for Siva, but the plan was changed to a Buddhist temple during construction. This is because in Buddhist temples, the principal image is placed on the center

以上は現段階の考察であり，今後，さらに調査と分析を進めるべき問題である。バイヨンは特別な寺院であり，この寺院を基点とするクメール帝国の歴史は，建築の歴史を超え，帝国そのものの変容を伝えていると思われる。

line of the temple site without avoiding the center like in Hindu temples[7].

The above are considerations at the present stage, and are issues that require further investigation and analysis in the future. The Bayon is a special temple, and the history of the Khmer Kingdom, which can be considered based on this temple, seems to convey the transformation of the kingdom itself beyond the history of architecture.

References

1) Finot L.,"Notes d'archéologie cambodgienne : I. Nouvelles inscriptions cambodgiennes, II. Deux bas-reliefs d'Angkor Wat", BCAI 1912

Coedès G., "Études cambodgiennes," BEFFEO 24 1924

Finot L., "Inscriptions D'Ankor," BEFFEO 25 1925

Coedès G., "Incriptions du Dambodge," vol.1, Hanoi. Paris, 1937

Mannikka E., "Angkor Wat Times, Spaces, and Kingship," University Hawaii Press 1996

2) Mizoguchi, A., Nakagawa, T., Narita, T., Isavorapant, C., "Study on Measurement Planning of Large Temple Complex, Khmer Architecture in Thailand : Study on Planning Method of Khmer Architecture I-2," Summ. Tech. Paper of Annual Meeting, AIJ, 1994, pp. 1195-1196

3) Mizoguchi, A., Nakagawa, T., Asano, T., Saito, N., "On the Dimensional Plan of the Complex in Thommanon and Banteay Samre: Study on the dimensional plan and the planning method of Kmer architecture No. 1," J. Archit. Plann., No. 612, AIJ, 2007, pp.131-138 (in Japanese).

4) Mizoguchi, A., Nakagawa, T.,etc "Koh Ker and Beng Mealea architectural study on the provincial sites of the Khmer Empire," Chuokoron Bijutsu Shuppan, 2014

厳密な面積ではなく外周寸法の合計を保つことを優先した技法である。このことで端数寸法が現れず，完数制が保たれる点にも注目したい。

This technique was designed to preserve the total dimensions of the perimeter rather than the exact area. It should also be noted that MMU system is preserved without the fractional dimensions.

5) Mizoguchi A., Nakagawa T., Shimoda I.,"The Ancient Khmer's Dimensional Planning at The Central Structures in Angkor Wat," Summ. Tech. Paper of Annual Meeting, AIJ, 2012, pp. 483-484

6) Mizoguchi, A., Nakagawa, T., etc "Preah Vihear architectural study on the provincial sites of the Khmer Empire 2," Chuokoron Bijutsu Shuppan, 2018

7) 『マヤ・マタ』などのインドの古文献では，ヒンドゥー教の神像は伽藍の中心を避けて安置させる。その萌芽は紀元前後に編纂された『マヌ法典』などにみられるが，一方その『マヌ法典』には大王の居所を世界の中心に置く記述がある。仏陀の前世が転輪聖王であったとする『ジャータカ』の記述にみられるように，王権と仏教は親和的であったため仏教寺院では尊像を中心に配置する。

As noted in ancient Indian literature such as the "Maya Mata", Hindu deity statues should be placed away from the center of the site. Its germination can be seen in the "The Law Code of Manu" compiled around AD, and in this "Law Code", the place of the great king was the center of the world. As the description of "Jataka" that the Buddha's previous life was Cakravartin -the greatest king- appears later, the kingship and Buddhism ware compatible, so in Buddhism, the statue was placed at the center of the temple site.

3.4 バイヨンのインベントリー
Inventory Research of Bayon

西本 真一
NISHIMOTO Shinichi

　バイヨンは壮大な複合体であり，中央へ行くに従って徐々に高くなる基壇の上に載った50ほどの塔や，あるいはパヴィリオンと呼ばれる矩形平面の建造物，またそれらを繋ぐ回廊などから構成されている。この寺院の研究調査や，修復に備えた破損箇所の記録作業に際しては，それぞれの部分をどのように呼称するかがJSAによるプロジェクトの開始当初から大きな懸案事項であった。

　EFEO（フランス極東学院）によるバイヨンの報告書では，現存する各建物に対し，当該寺院の中心から外側に向かって時計回りに順番に番号が与えられていた。寺院の正面，すなわち東側から若い番号が振られている点も特徴的である。また現在では存在しない構築物については数字ではなく，アルファベットが用いられ，区別がなされている。すでにこれらの略号が研究者の間で広く認知されているため，これを尊重すべきであるが，しかし細かな場所を指し示そうとする際，EFEOによる番号だけでは困難が伴う。破損箇所を逐一明記しようとする場合に，番号付けはさらに拡張されなければならない。少なくとも外回廊に立つ柱については，EFEOによって1本ずつ番付がなされたことが工事日誌からうかがい知ることができる。例えば1932年1月のG. トルーヴェによる報告では，東側回廊・北側外回廊について触れた日誌の中で「柱160, 160', 160", 161, 161', 161", 162', 163'番は立て直して土台を補修した」との記述が見られ，160番と161番の番付を有する柱に関してはそれぞれ3本がひとまとまりとして考えられているようであり，なおかつ番号に符号「'」や「"」を振ることによって3本の柱の識別をおこなっていたらしいことが推察される。これに基づいて該当箇所の平面図と照合するならば，外回廊の柱については時計回りに順次番号を付して，外側の柱列に関しては割り当てた数字に「'」，「"」の記号を振ったと考えることができそうである。

　しかしながらパヴィリオンの柱の番付については推定の手掛かりがないように思われ，また内回廊の柱に関

The Bayon is a magnificent complex consisting of about 50 towers on a gradually rising platform toward the center, rectangular flat structures called pavilions, and corridors connecting the towers. From the very beginning of the JSA project, the question of what to call the different parts of the temple was a major concern during the research and documentation of the damaged parts in preparation for the restoration.

According to the Bayon report by EFEO, the existing buildings were numbered in a clockwise order from the center of the temple outward. It is also characteristic that the numbering is given from the front of the temple, i.e., from the east side. In addition, the alphabet, rather than numbers, is used to distinguish structures that do not exist today. Since these abbreviations are already widely recognized among researchers, they should be respected. However, it is difficult to point out detailed locations using only EFEO numbers. The numbering system must be further extended when attempting to specify each and every damaged location. At least for the columns in the Outer Gallery, EFEO numbered the columns one by one, as can be seen from the construction diary. For example, in a report by G. Trouvé in January 1932, in a journal entry referring to the east and north exterior galleries, we find the following statement: "Columns 160, 160', 160", 161, 161', 161", 162', 163' were rebuilt and their foundations repaired," indicating that the columns with numbers 160 and 161 were numbered three each. It can be inferred that the three pillars numbered 160 and 161 were considered as a single unit, and that the three pillars were identified by a sign ' or " on the number. Based on this, if we check the plan of the corresponding area, we can conclude that the columns in the Outer Gallery were numbered clockwise, and that the numbers assigned to the outer column rows were assigned with the symbols ' and ".

However, there seems to be no clue for estimating the numbering of the columns in the pavilions, and no description is found for the columns in the Inner Gallery. For this reason, we have had to abandon our attempt to reconstruct EFEO column numbering. The use of the ' and " symbols

しては記述が見当たらない。このため，EFEOによる柱の番付を復原することは断念せざるを得なかった。「'」，「"」の記号の使用は柱の配列を理解する上で有利であり，また番号をいたずらに増加させないという長所がある。だが一方では誤記を招く恐れが指摘され，以上の諸点を勘案してバイヨンの建築インベントリーを進めるに当たっては，符号の付加による区別をやめ，柱には通し番号を振ることにした。

各建物を調査し，建築学的な特徴，特に注目すべき痕跡を発見することに努力が注がれたものの，H. パルマンティエの論考を基本として纏められたJ. デュマルセによる説，すなわちこの寺院が4回にわたる建造過程を有し，しかも各過程が完成を迎えないまま次の過程に着手されたとする見方を大きく変える発見はなされなかった。この点は，C. ジャックが近年，提唱したバイヨンの建造過程に関する新説を完全に否定する結果となっている。

付録で示されるように，この建築インベントリーと並行して崩落の危険度に関する調査もなされ，危険が高い場所については順次，JSAによって小規模な修復が進められた。また多量の崩落石材に関するデータベース化も着手され，尊顔塔の一部を構成していたと見られるいくつかの石材が発見された点は特に注目されるべきである。浅浮彫が施された外回廊の壁体から脱落した石材についても，今後の接合作業によって復原が期待される。東パヴィリオン中央の床面，最上基壇の塔17の西に近接した床面，同塔の北方の床面，また第2基壇上の北東内庭などでは，計画線と思われる刻線が残されており，実測がおこなわれたが，今後の分析によってバイヨンが建造された際に用いられた尺度が明らかとなる可能性が指摘される。

以上の建築インベントリー策定による成果を挙げるならば，

1，多数の堂宇と塔，回廊，及びそれらによって細分化された内庭などの各々の残存状況，及び崩落の危険度，また保存修復の難易度が明らかになったこと

2，他方でそれら相互の取り合いを調査した結果，全体としてどのような順番で建造がおこなわれたかが再度確認され，H. パルマンティエ－J. デュマルセによる説が支持されるとともに，C. ジャックによる新説が否定されたこと

3，顔面塔や外回廊の浅浮彫を復原する際に必要な石材が一定量，崩落石材から発見され，この調査結果と建築インベントリーの成果を合わせることにより，この寺院の復原に具体的な方策のひとつが

is advantageous for understanding the arrangement of the columns, and has the advantage of not unnecessarily increasing the numbering. However, it was also pointed out that the use of ' and " could lead to misdescriptions. Considering the above, it was decided that the Bayon's architectural inventory would not be distinguished by the addition of signs, but that the columns would be numbered consecutively.

Although efforts were made to examine each building and discover architectural features, particularly noteworthy traces, no discoveries were made that significantly changed J. Dumarçay's theory, which was based on H. Parmentier's, that the temple was constructed in four phases, each phase of which was not completed before the next phase was begun. No major findings have been made to change this view. This completely refutes the new theory of the building process of Bayon proposed by C. Jacques in recent years.

As indicated in the Appendix, a survey of collapse hazards was conducted in parallel with this architectural inventory, and minor remediation of high-risk areas was undertaken by JSA on a sequential basis. A database of the large number of collapsed stones was also compiled, and the discovery of several stones that may have been part of a face tower is particularly noteworthy. It is expected that the stones missing from the walls of the Outer Gallery, which were decorated with reliefs, will be restored through further work. In the central floor of the east pavilion, the floor adjacent to the west side of Tower 17 on the uppermost platform, the floor to the north of Tower 17, and the northeast courtyard on the second platform, there are engraved lines that appear to be plan lines, which were measured and may reveal the scale used in the construction of the Bayon through further analysis.

The results of the above architectural inventory include the following:

1, The inventory clarified the condition of the many halls, towers, corridors, and inner courtyards subdivided by these buildings, the degree of risk of collapse, and the degree of difficulty of conservation and restoration.

2, The interrelationships between the towers and galleries were studied, and the order in which they were constructed as a whole was confirmed again, supporting the theory of H. Parmentier - J. Dumarçay and rejecting the new theory of C. Jacques.

3, The discovery of a certain amount of stone from the fallen stones, which was necessary for the restoration of the reliefs on the façade tower and the Outer Gallery, together with the results of the architectural inventory, provided a tangible plan for the restoration of this temple.

4, The discovery of engraved lines that suggest the dimensions of the Bayon design, and the results of actual measurements of the space between columns in the pavilions and galleries, provide clues to estimating the scale of the temple at that time.

もたらされたこと

4, バイヨンの設計寸法を示唆する計画刻線が発見され，パヴィリオンや回廊などにおける柱間などの実測結果を勘案することにより，当時の尺度を推定する手がかりが得られたこと

などが列挙される。

この寺院の建造過程が改めて明確になった点は，今後の保存修復を遂行するに当たって大切な手がかりが得られたことを意味し，きわめて貴重である。

建造過程を明示するいくつかの重要な痕跡は後世にもそのまま伝えられるべきであり，特に最上基壇に立つ塔12～15に見られる一連の接続部，祠堂Aに残存する砂岩材による床，外回廊と祠堂Mが接していた痕跡，外回廊と祠堂Pとのつながりを示す部位などにおいて保存修復がおこなわれる場合には，細心の注意が必要とされよう。

C. ジャックの新説について補足をおこなうならば，H. ウッドワードはJacques and Freeman, Angkor: Cities and Templesに関するReview articleを挙げておかなければならない。この中でH. ウッドワードは次のように述べている。

(p. 250) *"At moments Jacques puts forward significant hypotheses that depend on archaeological data. The most consequential proposals are those that relate to the thirteenth century, and to the question of how long work continued at the Bayon. He believes that the inner quadrangular gallery at the Bayon, the one with the more-or-less Hindu reliefs, was constructed after 1243, in the time of Jayavarman VIII, to whose reign he assigns the anti-Buddhist movement responsible for the careful chiseling away of hundreds of Buddha images at Jayavarman VII's great temples, the Bayon included. A much-extended chronology has recently been given support by excavations below the foundation level of the northeastern "Library" at the Bayon, which resulted in the discovery of sherds of Chinese ceramics that are considered unlikely to predate the mid-thirteenth century (note 2)."*

このnote 2ではJSAの清水による論文が引用されており，C. ジャックの新たな仮説がJSAの発掘結果によって支持されているかのように受け取られる可能性があるため，バイヨンの建造過程に関するJSAの観点を明らかにしておく必要があろう。清水による論文は北経蔵の基礎の下でおこなわれた発掘報告であって，H. ウッドワードの認識のように，これを内回廊隅部の建立年代にまで拡げて解釈することはできないからである。

バイヨンの建造過程についてはJ. デュマルセの報告書によって既往研究が包括的に吟味され，通説として受

The following are just a few examples of the findings.

The clarification of the construction process of this temple is extremely valuable because it provides important clues for the future conservation and restoration of the temple.

Some important traces that clearly show the construction process should be handed down to future generations. In particular, a series of connections seen in Towers 12-15 on the uppermost platform, the sandstone floor remaining in Chapel A, traces of the contact between the Outer Gallery and Chapel M, and the connection between the Outer Gallery and Chapel P, all of which require careful attention if conservation and restoration is to be carried out.

In addition to C. Jacques' new theory, a Woodward review of an article by Jacques and Freeman, Angkor: Cities and Temples should be mentioned. In it, H. Woodward states.

(p. 250) *"At moments Jacques puts forward significant hypotheses that depend on archaeological data. The most consequential proposals are those that relate to the thirteenth century, and to the question of how long work continued at the Bayon. He believes that the inner quadrangular gallery at the Bayon, the one with the more-or-less Hindu reliefs, was constructed after 1243, in the time of Jayavarman VIII, to whose reign he assigns the anti-Buddhist movement responsible for the careful chiseling away of hundreds of Buddha images at Jayavarman VII's great temples, the Bayon included. A much-extended chronology has recently been given support by excavations below the foundation level of the northeastern "Library" at the Bayon, which resulted in the discovery of sherds of Chinese ceramics that are considered unlikely to predate the mid-thirteenth century (note 2)."*

Since this note 2 cites a paper by Shimizu of JSA, it is necessary to clarify JSA's perspective on the construction process of the Bayon, since Jacques' new hypothesis may be taken as supported by the results of JSA's excavation. This is because Shimizu's paper is an excavation report based on the foundation of the Northern Library and cannot be extended to the date of construction of the Inner Gallery corner, as H. Woodward seems to recognize.

J. Dumarçay's report comprehensively reviewed the previous studies on the construction process of the Bayon and came to be accepted as the prevailing theory, but the framework of the Bayon's four phases of construction was laid by H. Parmentier. J. Dumarçay basically accepts H. Parmentier's theory and continues to believe that the original cruciform gallery was extended at the four corners, the plane of the Bayon was changed to a rectangle, and sixteen Chapels (A-P) were built.

On the other hand, according to Jacques, the construction of the 16 chapels dates back to the first period. As C. Jacques points out, it is again important to consider the architectural and archaeological connection of the 16 chapels with the inner

け入れられるに至ったが，バイヨンが4期にわたって造られたと見るその骨子は，H. パルマンティエによって築かれた。J. デュマルセは基本的にH. パルマンティエの説を受け入れており，当初は十字形であった回廊の四隅に増築がなされてバイヨンの平面が矩形に変更され，またA〜Pの16棟の祠堂が設けられたという見方は継承されている。

　一方，C. ジャックによるならば，16棟の祠堂の建設は第1期にまで遡るものとされている。この点がH. パルマンティエ－J. デュマルセによる説との最も大きな差異であり，改めて検討がなされるべきところである。C. ジャックも指摘しているように，16棟の祠堂が内回廊あるいは外回廊と，どのように接続しているかの建築学的・考古学的考察が再び重要となろう。

　JSAによる調査ではしかし，C. ジャックの説を支持するような調査結果はこれまで何一つとして得られなかったと言ってよい。

　16の祠堂と外回廊との接続部分についてはH. パルマンティエ－J. デュマルセが明らかにしている通り，祠堂の壁が外回廊の壁にわずかに嵌め込まれているのであって，特に祠堂Mでは，外回廊の壁体下部に祠堂の壁が載っているさまを明瞭に観察することができる。

　JSAのおこなった大トレンチを開けての調査は，これに断面方向に関する貴重な情報を与えるという点で大きな意味を持ち，EFEOによるこれまでの考古学的な解釈，すなわち内回廊と外回廊が計画され，それらの間が土砂によって充填されたその上に祠堂が建立されたという順番を変えることには無理が生じる。

　加えてJSAによる岩石学的調査結果にあっても，祠堂Aと外回廊の砂岩の帯磁率は同じであり，C. ジャックが述べるように外回廊よりも祠堂の方が先に建設されたとみなすことは不可能である。C. ジャックは解体された通廊の石材を再利用して内回廊の隅部を作ったのであろうと推定しており，面白い考えではあるが，岩石学的観点からは否定される。

　ただC. ジャックの論の中で注目されるのは，中心塔には仏陀の像が置かれていたはずであるが，しかしその両側に位置する部屋10，11の戸口にはそれぞれヴィシュヌ神の妻ダラーニと，シヴァ神の妻，パールヴァーティの名が刻まれているので，中心塔には仏陀に代わり，ハリハラ神の像が置かれたと推定されると述べている点で，この指摘については今後さらに検討をおこなうべきであろう。

　H. パルマンティエ－J. デュマルセによる説は基本的に正しいことがJSAによって確認されたものの，細かい点においては追加・訂正すべき箇所がいくつか見つ

or Outer Gallery.

The JSA survey, however, has so far yielded no findings to support C. Jacques' theory.

As H. Parmentier - J. Dumarçay has shown for the connection between the 16 chapels and the Outer Gallery, the walls of the towers are slightly fitted into the walls of the Outer Gallery, and especially in Chapel M, it can be clearly observed that the wall of the tower rests on the lower part of the wall of the Outer Gallery.

The JSA's survey by opening a large trench is significant in that it provides valuable information on the direction of the cross section, and it would be unreasonable to change the order of archaeological interpretation by EFEO, namely that the Inner and Outer Galleries were planned, the space between them was filled with earth and sand, and the chapels were built on top of the newly created raised floor between two Galleries. It would be unreasonable to change the order in which the tower was built.

In addition, the results of the petrographic survey by JSA show that the magnetic susceptibility of the sandstones of Chapel A and the Outer Gallery are the same, making it impossible to assume that the tower was built before the Outer Gallery, as C. Jacques states. This is an interesting idea, but it is rejected from a petrographic point of view.

However, what is noteworthy in C. Jacques' argument is that the central tower would have housed an image of Buddha, but the names of Dharani, wife of Vishnu, and Parvati, wife of Shiva, are inscribed on the doorways of rooms 10 and 11 on either side of the central tower, respectively, suggesting that an image of Harihara was placed in place of Buddha in the Central Tower. This point should be further discussed in the future.

Although JSA has confirmed that H. Parmentier - J. Dumarçay's theory is basically correct, there are some minor points that need to be added or corrected. New discoveries have been made, especially with regard to the towers on the uppermost platform, and it is hoped that these will be documented in detail in a Bayon inventory.

かった。特に最上基壇上に立つ塔群などに関しては新た
な発見もなされているが，これらはバイヨン・インベン
トリーとして詳細に記されることが期待される。

3.5 バイヨンの尊顔と神々
Face Towers and Gods in Bayon

水野 さや
MIZUNO Saya

1. はじめに

美術史は，造形作品でたどる人間の歴史である。言葉では言い表すことができない人間の根本的な感覚を，選び抜かれた，計算された「形」と「色」を通して具現化された作品群から感じ取り，体系化していくものである。
——『東洋美術史』（武蔵野美術大学出版局，2016年）本書監修・執筆の朴亨國による「序文」より

だからこそ，美術史的調査研究が，寺院建築の修復に果たす役割がある。なぜなら，単に石材を積み上げ直すだけではなく，その寺院が建立され，利用された当時の背景をも復元的に考察することができてこそ，真の修復になると考えているからである。このような理念のもと，JSA美術史班は，バイヨンを特徴付けている彫刻的要素の一つである尊顔をはじめ，各祠堂のペディメント・リンテル・付柱・外壁の浅浮彫，内回廊浅浮彫についての調査を行った。また同時に，それに関する周辺調査も行ってきた。以下本項は，班長・朴亨國を中心としてまとめられた1997年から2004年までの美術史班の研究成果の一部をまとめて記するものである。詳細は各年次の報告書を参照されたい。

2. 複合寺院としてのバイヨンのあり方

バイヨンは，その初期の段階から，寺院としての性格も構造も変化していったと考えられている。まずはヒンドゥー寺院として建設が始まったが（第1次バイヨン），すぐさま仏教寺院として改築が行われ（第2次バイヨン），さらに，大規模な総合寺院へと増改築がなされた（第3次バイヨン）。この第3次バイヨンは，ヒンドゥーと仏教

1. Introduction

The history of art is the history of human beings through works of art. It is a way of perceiving and systematizing the fundamental senses of human beings, which cannot be expressed in words, through works of art that are embodied in selected and calculated "forms" and "colors".

-A History of Oriental Art (Musashino Art University Press, 2016). From the "Preface" by Hyounggook Park, who supervised and wrote the book.

Therefore, art historical research has a role to play in the restoration of temple architecture. This is because we believe that a true restoration is not merely a matter of reconstruct the stones, but also a restorative consideration of the background of construction and used at the time when the temple was built. Based on this philosophy, the JSA Art History Group conducted a survey of the sculptural elements that characterize the Bayon, such as the face towers, pediments, lintels, colonettes, and the bas-reliefs on the walls and Inner Gallery. At the same time, we have also conducted surveys of the surrounding areas. The following segment are partial report of the research conducted by the Art History Group led by the group leader PARK Hyounggook from 1997 to 2004, for details, please refer to each Annual Report.

2. The Bayon as a Temple Complex

The character and structure of the Bayon as a temple are considered to have changed from the early phases of its construction to what we see today. Construction began as a Hindu temple (the 1st phase of Bayon), but it was soon reconstituted as a Buddhism temple (the 2nd phase of Bayon), and then expanded and constructed into a large-scale general temple (the 3rd phase of Bayon). The 3rd phase of Bayon was

Fig. 3.5.1 Face Towers of Bayon (50E) Type 1   Fig. 3.5.2 Face Towers of Bayon (25W) Type 2   Fig. 3.5.3 Face Towers of Bayon (44S) Type 3

の双方に配慮した総合的な国家寺院としての拡大期である。尊顔は，この時期の主な増築部である堂塔の上，すなわち，中心塔の周囲と，内回廊と十字形回廊屈折部などの上に設けられた堂塔，そしてテラス上の堂塔に表されている（Fig. 3.5.1〜3）。一面の高さは約3mであり，現存するのは173面，当初は181面と推定されている。

宗教的複合のあり方は，テラス上の堂において，次のように成されている。東側は，本尊のムチリンダ龍王に護られた仏坐像を安置する中央祠堂を中央に，16堂の四臂観音立像，21堂の般若波羅密多立像と三尊形式をなす王家の信仰のエリアである。ジャヤヴァルマンⅦの治世において，このような銅造の三尊像が複数確認されており，プレア・カーンおよびタ・プロームの例からも，この三尊形式は，観音菩薩を父，般若波羅蜜多菩薩を母とし，ジャヤヴァルマンⅦ自身を仏坐像と見立てて構成した「王家の信仰のかたち」と理解されている。そして，北側の20堂にはシヴァ神，西側の19堂にはヴィシュヌ神，南側の18堂には仏陀をそれぞれ祀る。19堂の外壁上部に四臂ヴィシュヌ神，20堂の外壁上部にリシ（シヴァ派の修行者）が表されていることから，これらの各祠堂の性格，本尊像，信仰の対象が識別できる[1]〜[4]。

なお，18堂は仏像を祀る建物であったため，本来，その外壁上部には仏教尊像が表されていた。しかし，現状においては仏教モティーフの大半が破壊ないしリンガなどに改変されている。仏教モティーフの改変は，バイヨンのテラス下のペディメント，リンテル，付柱などに多数認められる。こうした破壊行為は，ジャヤヴァルマンⅦ後のシヴァ信者による破仏の動きによる。換言すれば，破壊された浅浮彫が認められるところは，本来は

a period of expansion as a comprehensive national temple that took into consideration both Hinduism and Buddhism. The face towers are represented on the main additions of this period, namely, on the around Central Tower, and towers on the Inner Gallery and the cruciform gallery corner, and on the towers on the terraces (Fig. 3.5.1-3). The height of each side is about 3 m. The present number of sides is 173, and the original number is estimated to be 181.

The religious complex in halls on the terrace is composed as follows. The east side is the area of the royal family's religious complex, which consists of the Central Tower with a seated Buddha statue protected by the Naga deity, Muchirinda, in the center, and the triad of statues, include a standing statue of the four-armed Avalokitesvara in Tower 16 and a standing statue of Prajnaparamita in Tower 21. During the reign of Jayavarman VII, some of bronze statues have been found, and from the examples of Preah Khan and Ta Prohm, this triad form is considered to be a "form of royal worship" in which Avalokitesvara is the father and Prajnaparamita is the mother and Jayavarman VII himself is considered the seated image of the Buddha. Tower 20 on the north side enshrines Shiva, Tower 19 on the west side enshrines Vishnu, and Tower 18 on the south side enshrines a statue of Buddha The four-armed Vishnu is represented on the upper part of the outer wall of Hall 19, and the Rishi statue (practitioner of the Shivaism) is represented on the upper part of the outer wall of Tower 20. This allows us to identify the character, principal image, and object of worship of each of these tower[1]〜[4].

Since Tower 18 was a building for enshrining Buddha images, the upper part of the outer wall originally had Buddhist images. However, most of the Buddhist images have been destroyed or altered into lingas or other non-Buddist forms. Many alterations of Buddhist motifs can be seen on the

仏教尊像（仏立像，仏坐像，四臂観音菩薩立像など）が表されていたことになる（Fig. 3.5.4）。

シヴァ派による仏教モティーフの破壊はバイヨンに留まらない。例えばバンテアイ・クデイのペディメントにおいては，上段の本来は仏坐像であったところは台座部分を残して削り落とされているが，中段・下段のデーヴァ形供養者とアスラ形供養者は破壊を被っていない。ここから，デーヴァとアスラは，仏陀とともに表されていたとしても，厳密な仏教モティーフと認識されていなかったことがわかる。

段階的に増改築が行われたバイヨンであるが，現存するバイヨンの諸彫刻は，一部の追刻・改変を除けば，比較的短期間に収まるものと考えている。従来言われているようなジャヤヴァルマンⅧによるバイヨンの完成は，美術史の立ち場からは認められない。彫刻は，建築の増築にあわせて漸次彫り加えられるものでも，建築ができた順序で完成するものでもない。建築作業が段階的に行われたとしても，そこに付随する浅浮彫は，建築作業が完了した時点で，一気に行われるからである。後述の15堂入口左右の王妃になぞらえたデヴァター像の表現，内回廊東正面の南壁における宮殿内の2人の王妃，内回廊西面南側におけるマルヤンの反乱（1182年頃）の鎮圧などの浅浮彫を考慮すれば，彫刻は，1190年代から1210年代の早い時期の20～30年間ほどで行われたと想定している。

なお，テラス上東側の15堂外壁入口左右に配される2軀のデヴァター像は，王宮のような建物の中に表され，周囲に供養者や従者などの附属モティーフを十分に伴っており，バイヨンにおける他のデヴァター像と比べ，特別であることは明白である。美術史班としては，ジャヤヴァルマンⅦの王妃になぞらえたものとの見解を提示している[1)2)]。ジャヤヴァルマンⅦには，まず，ジャヤラージャデーヴィーという王妃がいた。ところが，チャンパとの戦争中，彼女は没したようである。その後，彼女の姉（？）であるインドラデーヴィーが新たな妃として迎えられた。このデヴァター像（Fig. 3.5.5）の周囲に，「愛馬別離」や「剃髪」などの仏伝に依拠する場面（Fig. 3.5.6）が含まれている。数ある仏伝場面においても釈迦の出家を表す場面が選ばれていることから，仏教を信仰する家系のインドラデーヴィーとの婚姻に伴い，ジャヤヴァルマンⅦが仏教へ帰依したことを表すのではないかと推測する。

これに関連し，バンテアイ・チュマールにおけるジャヤヴァルマンの表現を確認しておきたい。バンテアイ・チュマール回廊浅浮彫におけるジャヤヴァルマンは，弓矢を執る姿で表されることから，アンコール・ワット第

Fig. 3.5.4 Re-carved Buddhist motif in pediment of Bayon 46E

pediments, lintels, and colonettes of the terraces of the Bayon. This iconoclasm was due to the movement to break the Buddhist religon by the followers of Shiva after Jayavarman VII died. In other words, the areas where the vandalized reliefs are found originally represented Buddhist images (standing Buddha, seated Buddha, standing four-armed Bodhisattva Avalokitesvara, etc.) (Fig. 3.5.4).

The destruction of Buddhist motifs by the followers of Shiva was not limited to Bayon. For example, in the Banteay Kdei, the upper pediment, which was originally a seated Buddha, had been chipped away, leaving the pedestal element, but the Deva and Asura offerings in the middle and lower pediments have not suffered destruction. This indicates that devas and asuras were not recognized as strictly Buddhist motifs, even though they were represented with seated images of the Buddha.

Although the Bayon was enlarged and constructed in stages, the existing sculptures in the Bayon were completed in a relatively short period of time without some of the additions and alterations. From the viewpoint of art history, the Bayon was not completed by Jayavarman VIII as has been conventionally believed. Sculptures were not gradually added to the building as it was enlarged. Even if the building work was done in stages, the reliefs accompanying the building work were done once the building work was completed. Considering the reliefs such as the Devata statues on the left and right sides of the entrance of Tower 15, the two queens in the palace on the south wall of the east front of the Inner Gallery, and the bas-relief of the suppression of Malyan's rebellion (c. 1182) on the south of the west side of the Inner

Fig. 3.5.5 Devata Image placed right side of east outer wall of T15

Fig. 3.5.6 Buddhist biography Image "Shaving the hair" (Upper Part) "Separation of beloved horse" (Middle Part)

Gallery, the sculpture was done between the 1190s and the 1210s, which is about 20 to 30 years.

The two statues of Devatas on the east side of the terrace on the left and right of the entrance to the outer wall of Tower 15, which is located on the east side of the terrace, are represented in a building like a royal palace and are surrounded by a sufficient number of accompanying motifs such as offerings and attendants, which clearly make them special compared to the other Devatas in Bayon. The Art History Group, not shared by all historians, has proposed the opinion that it was modeled after the queen of Jayavarman VII[1)2)]. Jayavarman VII had a queen named Jayarajadevi. However, she seems to have died during the war with Champa. After that, her sister (?) Indradayavi became the new queen. This image of Devata (Fig. 3.5.5) is surrounded by scenes from the Buddhist tradition (Fig. 3.5.6), such as "Separation of beloved horse" and "Shaving the hair". Since the scenes representing the ordination of the Buddha were selected from among the many scenes in the Buddhist tradition, it is assumed that they represent Jayavarman VII's conversion to Buddhism following his marriage to Indradayavi, who belonged to a family that believed in Buddhism.

In connection with this, I would like to confirm the representation of Jayavarman VII at Banteay Chhmar. In the bas-relief of the gallery in Banteay Chhmar, Jayavarman VII is depicted as holding a bow and arrow,

Fig. 3.5.7 Bas-Relief of Gallery in Banteay Chhmar

Fig. 3.5.8 Bas-Relief of Outer Gallery in Bayon

一回廊西面北側のように，ラーマ（ヴィシュヌ神の化身）の姿になぞらえた表現であろう。この浅浮彫においては，頭頂に王冠を被る姿ではないため，即位前のジャヤヴァルマンであると理解できるが，浅浮彫の複数箇所において，後頭部に小さな丸い髷を結い，そこに四臂ヴィシュヌ神の小像がある[1)2)4)]（Fig. 3.5.7）。なお，バイヨン外回廊浅浮彫に表されるクメール戦士の中には，頭頂に仏立像とみられる尊像を戴く例がある（Fig. 3.5.8）。ここ

Rama (an incarnation of Vishnu), same as on the north side of the western face of the First Gallery in Angkor Wat. In this relief, Jayavarman VII is not wearing a crown, so it can be considered that he was Jayavarman before his accession to the throne, but there are small images of Lord Vishnu with a small round topknot on the back of his head and four arms in several places[1)2)4)] (Figure 3.5.7). Among the Khmer warriors depicted in the reliefs in the Outer Gallery of the Bayon, there is an example of a standing Buddha on the top of the head (Fig.

からも，ジャヤヴァルマンⅦの改宗と，アンコール奪還および即位に向けて得られた，仏教勢力の助力がうかがえる。

すなわち，ジャヤヴァルマンⅦの本来の信仰，ヴィシュヌ神への信仰と，仏教勢力に対する配慮，そのような国内の宗教的融和をはかろうとした王国の政策が，バイヨンの複合寺院としてのあり方に反映されているのである。そしてバイヨンの尊顔は，東側の王家の信仰のエリア，北側のシヴァ信仰のエリア，西側のヴィシュヌ信仰のエリア，南側の仏教信仰のエリアのいずれにも表されている。換言すれば，これらの尊顔は，仏教，ヒンドゥー教シヴァ派・ヴィシュヌ派のいずれにおいても受け入れられる対象であることが前提となる。

3. バイヨンの尊顔分析による尊名と目的

バイヨンの尊顔については，ブラフマー神，シヴァ神，観音菩薩，ジャヤヴァルマンⅦの尊顔との見解，さらに近年，ヴァジュラサットヴァ（金剛薩埵）であるとの見解も示されている。これまでの尊顔に対する主な見解に共通する問題は，現存総数173面の高さ3 mに及ぶ巨大な尊顔を「均一」に扱う意識であり，尊顔個々に看取される視覚的情報が軽視される点であろう。美術史班の尊顔に関する調査研究の姿勢は，何よりもこれらを，バイヨン期を代表する個々の彫刻作品として捉えることである。そしてその考察は，第一に，尊顔が表される箇所を確認する，第二に，尊顔を構成する造形的要素を観察しその特徴を明らかにする，第三に，その上でバイヨン期の作品との比較考察を通して，バイヨンの尊顔の尊名とその役割・性格を導き出すことを目指した。

まず，尊顔はバイヨンに限定されるものではない。ジャヤヴァルマンⅦがチャンパよりアンコールの地を奪還した後に築造された都城の五つの門にも認められる。門はいずれも同一構造を呈しており，中央に塔を設け，その四面に尊顔を表す。城門の他には，バンテアイ・クデイ，タ・プローム，タ・ソムなど，バイヨン期の寺院における塔門にも尊顔が表されている。その他，バイヨンのように堂塔に尊顔が配される寺院として，大プレア・カーンのプラサート・プレア・ストゥンとバンテアイ・チュマールがある。バンテアイ・チュマールでは，中央祠堂付近に位置する計六基の堂塔に，それぞれ四面の尊顔を表す。また，その外濠の東西南北に位置する附属寺院においても，現状はその南側の寺院において，祠堂の中央にそびえる塔の四面に，同形の尊顔が認められる。おそらく，この四方の寺院のいずれにも，あたかも

3.5.8). This also indicates the support of Buddhist forces in the conversion of Jayavarman VII, the recapture of Angkor, and his accession to the throne.

This is to say, Jayavarman VII's original faith, his faith of Vishnu, his consideration for the Buddhist powers, and the kingdom's policy to achieve religious harmony in the country are reflected in Bayon's form as a temple complex. The faces towers of the Bayon are represented in the area of royal worship in the east, the area of Shiva worship in the north, the area of Vishnu worship in the west, and the area of Buddhism worship in the south. In other words, these faces are supposed to be acceptable objects in both Buddhism and Hinduism, Shiva and Vishnu.

3. Venerable Names and Purposes through the Analysis of Face Towers of the Bayon

There are various views of the face towers of the Bayon, including those of Brahma, Shiva, Avalokitesvara, and Jayavarman VII, and more recently, Vajrasattva. The common problem to the major views on the face towers, is that they treat the 173 faces, which are as large as 3m in height, as "equally" and disregard the visual information that can be perceived in each individual face. The Art History Group's approach to the study of the faces was, above all, to consider them as individual sculptural works representative of the Bayon period. The first step of the study was to confirm the places of in the towers. The second is to observe the figurative elements that compose the faces and clarify their characteristics. The third is to derive the names, roles and characters of the faces of the Bayon through comparative study with the works of the Bayon period.

The faces are not found only in the Bayon. They are also found on the five gates of Angkor Thom built after Jayavarman VII retook the land of Angkor from Champa. The gates all have the same structure, with a tower in the center and faces on all four sides. In addition to the city gates, the faces are also found on the tower gates of Bayon-period temples such as Banteay Kdei, Ta Prohm, Ta Som. Another temple that has a face on its tower, like Bayon, is Prasat Preah Stoeng in Preah Khan of Kompong Svay and Banteay Chhmar. The temple has a total of six towers located near the central shrine, each of which has four faces. In the annex building located on the north, south, east, and west sides of the outer moat of Banteay Chhmar, the same faces can be seen on the four faces of the towers rising in the center of the shrine in the temple to the south. Probably, all of the temples in these four areas originally had the same faces, as if they were boundaries. The faces on the gate and tower of the temple show the same figurative elements as those of the faces at Bayon.

As described above, giant faces are usually found at the gates of castles and temples, and at the four corners of the

3.5　バイヨンの尊顔と神々　89

結界を設けるかの如く，本来は尊顔が表されていたであろう。なお，城門および寺院の塔門におけるいずれの尊顔も，バイヨンの尊顔と同じ造形的要素を見せる。

　以上のように，巨大な尊顔は，城門および寺院の塔門，大寺院の四隅の堂塔に表されることが基本であろう。また，このような尊顔の配置から，単に「四面である」，「四方を向いている」ということではなく，その巨大な尊顔の存在によって，さらに，見開かれた眼によって，寺院・都城の周囲に睨みを効かし，対峙するものを威嚇する効果が求められたものと考えられる。従来，尊顔を表す塔を「四面塔」と称すなど，バイヨンの尊顔を「四」という単位であることに重きを置き，尊顔解釈の根拠とされることがあった。例えば，四面ブラフマー，四面シヴァ，四面で表される金剛薩埵などである。しかし，アンコール朝の塔堂形式の建造物の多くが迫り出し工法で石材を積み上げて構築されていることを考慮すれば，方形平面である方が効率は良いであろう。すなわち，建築工法上の実利的側面が働いていたものと推測する。バイヨン中央塔の上部における尊顔が必ずしも「四」の単位で構成されていないこと，中央塔から東に展開する12堂が南北の二面であることなども考慮すべきである。

　次に，これら尊顔の造形的要素の分析である。一見すると同じようなバイヨンの尊顔であるが，個別の彫刻として眺めると，いくつかの造形上の差異に気付かされる。そこで，尊顔の構成要素を，①顔の輪郭，②冠帯，③額飾，④眼の形・見開き具合・瞳の有無，⑤眉，⑥鼻，⑦口，⑧口髭，⑨耳，⑩頸飾などの項目を設けて観察した。これらの調査項目からは，尊顔の性格・役割に関わる点（②），尊名に関わる点（①④⑤），制作に携わった工人・工房に関わる点（②③⑨⑩）などの情報を得ることができる。

　尊顔の性格・役割に関わる要素としては，②冠帯などがある。バイヨンに限らず，城門のいずれの尊顔も同じ冠帯を付ける。工人・工房により文様単位の大小などの違いがあり，また，尊顔には後頭部がないため，本来は頭部に巻き付けて背面で結び止めるはずの冠帯の端が，左右の耳輪の中に入り込むなど，曖昧な処理がなされている。しかし，基本的に同じ構成で，帯状部分とその上下の葉飾を含む装飾部分からなる。このような葉飾付の冠帯は，バイヨン内回廊・外回廊におけるクメールの戦士に見出すことができる。アンコール・ワット第一回廊南面「軍隊の行進」浅浮彫において，クメール軍の兵士達が付ける冠帯とも共通する。なお，この戦士の葉飾付の冠帯は，同時代の仏陀や観音菩薩などの仏教尊像，シヴァやヴィシュヌなどのヒンドゥー尊像においては見出せない。

towers of large temples. The arrangement of the giant face is not simply a matter of "four faces" or "facing the four directions," but the presence of the giant face, with its wide-open eyes, is thought to have been intended to make the temple or capital city stare at its surroundings and intimidate those who confronted it. Traditionally, the Bayon's face has been referred to as a "four-faced tower," and the four "units" of the Bayon's face have sometimes been used as the basis for interpreting the face. For example, the four-faced Brahma, the four-faced Shiva, and the four-faced Vajrasattva. However, considering that most Angkorian temple buildings were constructed by piling up stones using a corbel arch, it would be more efficient to use a square plan. In other words, it is assumed that the practical aspect of the construction method was at work. It is also important to consider that the face at the top of the Central Tower of the Bayon is not necessarily composed of "four" units, and that the Tower 12 to the east of the Central Tower have two faces, north and south.

Next, I will introduce the analyze of the figurative elements of these faces. At first glance, the faces of Bayon's sculptures look similar, but when we look at them as individual sculptures, we notice some differences in their forms. The following items were observed: ① facial outline, ② crown band, ③ forehead ornament, ④ shape and extent of eye opening and pupil, ⑤ eyebrows, ⑥ nose, ⑦ mouth, ⑧ moustache, ⑨ ears, and ⑩ neck ornament. From these survey items, we can obtain information on the character and role of the face in ②, the deity's name in ①, ④, and ⑤, and the craftsmen and workshops involved in its production in ②, ③, ⑨, and ⑩.

Elements related to the character and role of the noble face include ② the crown band. Not only in the Bayon, but all of the faces at the gates wear the same crown band. The size of the design varies depending on the craftsman and workshop, and because the head of the faces have no back part, the end of the crown band, which should be wrapped around the head and tied at the back, is ambiguously placed in the left and right ear rings. However, the basic composition is the same, consisting of a band and decorative parts including foliage above and below the band. Such a crowned band with foliage can be found on Khmer warriors in the Inner and Outer Galleries of the Bayon. It is also common with the crown bands worn by Khmer soldiers in the "March of the Armies" bas-relief on the south face of the First Gallery of Angkor Wat. This warrior's crown band with leaf decoration is not found in Buddhism images such as Buddha and Avalokitesvara, nor in Hindu images such as Shiva and Vishnu, which are from the same period.

The elements related to the honorifics include ① the outline of the face, ④ the shape and extent of the opening of the eyes and the presence or absence of pupils, and ⑤ the eyebrows. Of course, these factors may be influenced by the degree of completion of each face, differences in the

そして，尊名に関わる要素としては，①顔の輪郭，④眼の形・見開き具合・瞳の有無，⑤眉などが挙げられる。もちろんこれらは，各面の完成の度合い，工人および工房の技術の差，造形感の違いによって左右されるであろう。しかし，巨大な尊顔をテラス上で眺めてみたとき，こうした個体差を認めながらも，個々の尊顔が与える「印象」の差こそが気になる。こうした受け手が抱く「印象」の差は，人間の面部においては，特に顔の形（頬から顎にかけての輪郭や面長・面幅の比率），眼の形（見開きの強弱，眼球の突出具合，目尻の角度）によって引き起こされる。こうした観点から，尊顔全てに貫かれている顔立ちは，次の3種類に大別することができる。

第一に，比較的細面の輪郭で，目尻をやや吊り上げて表す顔立ちである（Fig. 3.5.1）。また，この顔立ちにおける眉は，優美な曲線を描いて上方に跳ね上がる細い眉であることが多く，口髭を表さない。第二が，それと対照的な，角張った力強い輪郭で，見開きが大きく，突出気味に眼を表す顔立ちである（Fig. 3.5.3）。口髭はあるものとないものがあり，形は統一されていない。なお，アンコール・トムの5つの城門において，それぞれ外側と左右の三面は，いずれもこの顔立ちに該当する。第三は，その中間的な穏やかな丸い輪郭で，眼の形・見開き具合も強すぎず，杏仁形の眼を持つ顔立ちである（Fig. 3.5.2）。なお，いずれの尊顔においても見開かれた眼は，同時代の仏陀，観音菩薩などの尊像が半眼ないし閉眼とし，思いにふける印象を与えることとは，大きくそれを異にする。

尊顔におけるこれら3種類のイメージソースが何にあるのか，何を想起させる顔立ちなのか。バイヨン期の彫刻作品と比較すると，第1類はデヴァターやアプサラスなど，女尊形の典型的な顔立ちである。第3類は，アスラの顔立ちに該当する。城門外側の「乳海攪拌」に依拠するデーヴァ像群とアスラ像群のうち，アスラの顔立ちが与える印象に共通する。対して，第2類はデーヴァの顔立ちである。すなわちバイヨンの尊顔は，デヴァター，デーヴァ，アスラという異なるカテゴリーに属する尊格を想起させる特徴を具えており，デヴァター，デーヴァ，アスラそれぞれを表し，かつ，その集合体とも言えよう。このように，特定の神や仏ではない，ヒンドゥー，仏教のいずれの側においても受容されうる普遍的な神々として表されていたからこそ，破壊されることがなかったのである。このことは，先に触れたデーヴァ形供養者像とアスラ形供養者像が破壊を免れたことと同様である。

バイヨンの祠堂外壁に目を向けると，入口左右にデーヴァ形守門神像，アスラ形守門神像が配置されており，その外側にはデヴァター像も表されている。このように，

skills of the craftsmen and workshops, and differences in the sense of modeling. However, when we look at the huge faces on the terrace, even while acknowledging these individual differences, we are concerned about the differences in the "impressions" given by the individual faces. These differences in the impression that the receiver has are caused by the shape of the human face, especially the shape of the face (the contour from the cheeks to the chin and the ratio of face length to face width) and the shape of the eyes (the strength of the opening, the degree of protrusion of the eyeballs, and the angle of the outer corner of the eyes). From this point of view, the facial features that pervade all of the faces can be broadly classified into the following three types.

The first is a face with a relatively slender outline and the outer corners of the eyes slightly lifted (Fig. 3.5.1). The eyebrows of this type of face are often thin, curving gracefully upward, and do not show a mustache. The second type of face contrasts with the first in that it has a strong, angular profile with a large, protruding eye (Fig. 3.5.3). Some have moustaches and some do not, and their shapes are not uniform. In the five gates of Angkor Thom, the three faces on the outer, left and right sides of each gate correspond to this type of face. The third face has a gentle, rounded outline, not too wide-opened and with apricot-shaped eyes (Fig. 3.5.2). The wide-opened eyes in all of the three faces are very different from those of Buddha, Avalokitesvara, and other bodhisattvas of the same period, which have half-open or closed eyes, giving the impression of being lost in thought.

What are the sources of these three types of images in the faces, and what do these faces evoke? Compared to the sculptural works of the Bayon period, the first type is the typical facial features of the female noble forms, such as devatas and apsaras. The third type corresponds to the facial features of the Asuras. The Devas and the Asuras, both of which rely on the "stirring of the milk sea" outside the gate, share the same impression given by the facial features of the Asuras. In contrast, the second type is the facial features of the devas. In other words, the Bayon's faces show features that remind us of three different categories of dignities: devata, deva, and asura, and can be said to represent devata, deva, and asura, respectively, as well as a collection of each. Thus, it was not destroyed because it was not a specific god or Buddha, but a universal deity that could be accepted by both Hinduism and Buddhism. This is similar to the case of the Deva and Asura mentioned above, which escaped destruction.

In the outer wall at Bayon, we can see that deva and asura statues are placed on the left and right sides of the entrance, with devata statues on the outside of them. Thus, it can be seen that the devata, deva, and asura in the Bayon period not only played the role of offerings to the deities or solemnizing the world of the deities, but also actively played the role of guardians.

As described above, the Bayon's face represents the

バイヨン期におけるデヴァター，デーヴァ，アスラは，神々を供養する，神々の世界を荘厳するという役割に留まらず，守護の役割を積極的に担っていた。

　以上のように，バイヨンの尊顔は，デヴァター，デーヴァ，アスラという異なるカテゴリーの神々，いわば国中のあらゆる神々の典型的な顔立ちの印象的な要素を抽出・集約したものであり，そのような尊顔によって，都城ヤショーダラプラの中心寺院であるバイヨンを，さらに都城を，そして王国全体を守護する役割を帯びていたと考えられる。そしてその背景には，チャンパの侵略により打撃を受けたアンコールを回復させたジャヤヴァルマンⅦによる，王国守護の思想があったことは間違いない。バイヨンは，チャンパによる侵略からアンコール（王都）を奪還したジャヤヴァルマンⅦにより，国中の宗教勢力に配慮し，国内のあらゆる神々の力を得ることを期待して建立された国家寺院，まさに王国の精神的支柱となる中心寺院であったと言えよう。

extraction and concentration of the striking elements of the typical faces of the different categories of gods, devata, deva, and asura, or in other words, of all the gods in the country, and it is the face of Bayon, the central temple of Yashodharapura, the capital city and the kingdom as a whole. This was no doubt Jayavarman VII restored Angkor after it had been damaged by Champa's invasion. Bayon was built by Jayavarman VII in consideration of the religious forces in the country and in the hope of gaining the power of all the gods in the country, and was the central temple that became the spiritual pillar of the kingdom.

References
1) 日本国政府アンコール遺跡救済チーム（編），1998，『アンコール遺跡調査報告書』日本国政府アンコール遺跡救済チーム
2) 日本国政府アンコール遺跡救済チーム（編），2001，『アンコール遺跡調査報告書』日本国政府アンコール遺跡救済チーム
3) 日本国政府アンコール遺跡救済チーム（編），2002，『アンコール遺跡調査報告書』日本国政府アンコール遺跡救済チーム
4) 日本国政府アンコール遺跡救済チーム（編），2003，『アンコール遺跡調査報告書』日本国政府アンコール遺跡救済チーム

3.6 バイヨンの考古学
Archaeology of Bayon

田畑 幸嗣

TABATA Yukitsugu

1. はじめに

　古代アンコール文明の研究は，フランス東洋学の最高峰であり，その開始から常に考古学と共にあった。仏領期から今にいたるまでアンコール研究をリードするEFEO（フランス極東学院）の設立は，そもそも考古学研究を目的としていたのであり，そこでは研究と修復，観光と植民地経営が一体となったフランス東洋学の典型がアンコール研究として実践されていた。なかでも，王都の中心にメール山（須弥山）の宇宙観を具現化し，古代クメール世界の中心軸であったバイヨンは，整備・修復とならんで調査研究が最も進んだ遺跡でありがら，今もなお最も謎の多い遺跡でもある。

　バイヨンのこれまでの研究については本書や既刊の報告書を参照されたいが，大筋において，内戦前の調査は1919年のH. マルシャルとJ. デュマルセを始めとする極東学院によるものが全てであり，内戦後はおもに日本国政府アンコール遺跡救済チーム（JSA/JASA）とアプサラ機構による調査が中心となっている。JSA/JASAによる考古学調査は1995年から今日まで継続的に調査が実施され（Fig. 3.6.1），その結果として同寺院が複雑な建築・増改築過程を経て現在の姿となった事が明らかになりつつある。本章では，内戦後のこれまでのバイヨンにおける考古学調査を概観しながら，その成果を紹介したい。

2. 北経蔵の発掘調査

　1995〜98年に北経蔵の修復に伴う発掘調査が実施されたが，ここでは，基礎部分の建造技術の解明と出土遺物による築造年代の確定が課題とされた。経蔵基壇に隣

1. Introduction

　The study of the ancient civilization of Angkor is the pinnacle of French oriental studies and has always been accompanied by archaeology. The École française d'Extrême-Orient (EFEO), the leader in Angkor studies from the French colonial period to the present, was founded for archaeological research, and the study of Angkor is typical of French oriental studies, which combines restoration, with research and tourism. The Bayon, symbolized the cosmology of Mount Sumer at the center of the capital, is one of the most advanced monuments in terms of maintenance, restoration, and research, but it remains one of the most mysterious site of the Angkor Monuments group.

　Although a small portion of the past research on Bayon can be refered in this book and other published reports, the pre-civil war research was conducted entirely by EFEO led by H. Marchal and J. Dumarçay in 1919, and the post-civil war research was conducted mainly by the Japanese Government Team for Safeguarding Angkor and the Apsara National Organization (JSA/JASA). Archaeological research by JSA/JASA has been ongoing since 1995 (Fig. 3.6.1). Research has revealed that the temple underwent a complex process of construction, renovation, and reconstruction to achieve its present form. In this chapter, we will present an overview of the archaeological research conducted at Bayon since 1995.

2. Excavation of the Northern Library of the Bayon

　Excavation surveys in Northern Library of Bayon were conducted from 1995 to 1998 in conjunction with the restoration, and the issues to be addressed were the clarification of the construction technique of the foundation and the determination of the construction period based on the excavated artifacts. The excavation area adjacent to

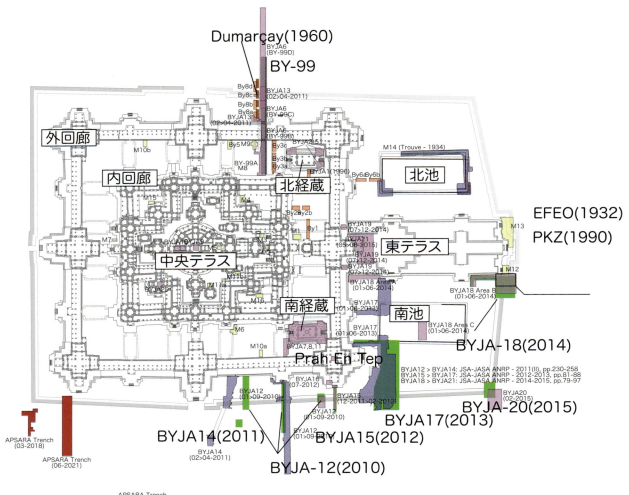

Fig. 3.6.1 Archaeological Survey in Bayon

接した発掘区の調査は北経蔵の部分解体と同時に行われた。これまでの定説では，バイヨンの建造過程は4期に分けられ，経蔵はその最終期に，内回廊と外回廊の間のテラス床面上に建てられたとされていた。

調査の結果，現存する北経蔵は内回廊と外回廊の間のテラス床面が敷設された後に建てられたものの，後に経蔵造営のために床面は取り除かれ，新たに基礎が構築されたと考えられるようになった。つまり，バイヨンを構成する様々な要素（祠堂，回廊，基壇その他）は，単純な時期区分では捉えきれず，それぞれの遺構ごとに複雑な構築過程を経ていることがこの調査で明らかになったのである。またこの発掘調査により，基壇は上段最上部から下段最下部まで58もの層で構成され，非常に入念に構築された事も判明した。

3．外回廊の発掘調査

1999年には，バイヨン北側の内回廊の基壇から外回

the foundation of the Northern Library was investigated at the same time as the partial dismantling of the structure. According to the conventional theory, the construction process of Bayon was divided into 4 phases, and the Northern Library was built in the final phase on the terrace floor between the Inner and Outer Galleries.

As a result of the research, it is thought that the Northern Library was built after the terrace floor between the Inner and Outer Galleries was laid, but the floor was later removed for the construction of the Northern Library, and a new foundation was built. In other words, this survey revealed that the various structures (shrine, gallery, platform, etc.) that make up the Bayon could not be captured by simple period divisions, and that each structure underwent a complex construction process. The excavation of the platform also revealed that it was constructed in as many as 58 compacted layers of sandy-silty soil with sandstone rubble inter-disbursed from the uppermost to the lowermost, and that it was very carefully constructed.

Fig. 3.6.3 Central Structure and Dismantling Process in South Pond

Fig. 3.6.2 Excavation Survey in 1999

廊を横断し，現在遺跡を周回する道路に至る発掘調査が行われた（Fig. 3.6.2）。この発掘の目的は，フランス人研究者によって提唱された建造過程説の再検証である。また，アンコールの寺院の多くは環濠をもつが，バイヨン周辺にはこれまで環濠が確認されておらず，その有無の確認も目的としていた。

調査の結果，建造過程と排水システムに新たな知見が得られた。まず，外回廊を南北に貫通する暗渠が2本検出された。そのうちのひとつは，すでにH．マルシャルの発掘によって報告されていたが，これらの暗渠は外回廊基壇側面に穿たれた穴と繋がっており，暗渠内は土砂で埋まっていた。これらはバイヨンの排水システムの一部と考えられる。

カンボジアを含むインドシナ半島の大部分は，年の半分は雨季であり，寺院は多量の雨水にさらされる事になるため，雨水の過剰な浸透による基壇の弱体化を防ぐ意味でも，このような排水システムが必要とされたのだろう。さらに，内回廊と外回廊の間の版築砂層を発掘した際には，内回廊の基壇を南北に貫通する横穴の存在が確認された。発見時，横穴の入口は砂岩ブロックによって塞がれていた。横穴は伽藍内の中心部から雨水を排出する排水溝であったと推測されるが，後内回廊と外回廊の間の床面が高められた際に塞がれたのだろう。

3. Excavation of the Outer Gallery

In 1999, excavation was conducted from the base of the Inner Gallery on the north side of the Bayon to the circle road across the Outer Gallery (Fig. 3.6.2). The purpose of this excavation was to reexamine the construction process theory proposed by French researchers. In addition, to confirm the presence or absence of moat encircling the Bayon area was also one of the purposes.

As a result of the excavation and subsequent analysis, new findings were obtained on the construction process and drainage system. At first, two culverts were found running north-south through the Outer Gallery. One of these culverts, which had already been reported by Marchal, was connected to an opening in the side of the Outer Gallery platform, and the inside of the culvert was filled with earth and sand. These culverts are considered as part of the drainage system of the Bayon.

Since most of the Southeast Asia which include Cambodia, has a rainy season half of the year and temples are exposed to a large amount of rainwater. A drainage system, like the one identified, was necessary to prevent the weakening of the base due to excessive rainwater infiltration. Furthermore, during the excavation of the sandy soil layer between the Inner and Outer Galleries, the existence of a horizontal hole penetrating the platform of the Inner Galleries from north to south was

Fig. 3.6.4 Excavated Turtle Statue made by Sandstone　　　Fig. 3.6.5 Excavated Rough Turtle Statue made by Sandstone

4．南池の調査

　寺院東参道の南側は平地となっているが，北側と対になる池が想定されているため，その確認調査を実施したところ，参道に対して南北に対称的な池配置を持つことが確認された。池の護岸は主としてラテライトで構築されており，池底部は現地表から約3.5 m〜4 m下で検出された。池底部は一面にラテライトを敷き詰めて水平面としている。池の護岸はラテライトを下から階段状に積み上げている。下部は10〜12段程で残存はよく，上部は後世に破壊されて残りは悪い。池の最下層を除く下層堆積土は自然埋没ではなく，人為的に埋められた可能性が高い。下層出土陶磁器からみて池は14世紀後半〜15世紀前半には機能を失いつつあったと考えられる。

　中央部池底は，さらに中央側にかけて低い段差（底面下段）をつくっている（Fig. 3.6.3）。底面下段では，砂岩を3段に積上げた東西2.8 m，南北3.3 mの石組みが検出されている。石組みの中央には小石室が設けられ，砂岩製の亀と鉛容器が置かれていた（Fig. 3.6.4）。亀の周囲と床面から金箔，水晶，貴石，銅板，鉄器片，土器片などが出土した。鉛容器は上下2枚の皿形を合わせていた。亀の甲羅上面には三角状の穴があけられており，畳み込んだ銅板が入れられていた。

　さらに，石組み最下段上面の東寄りに方形ピットの小穴が穿たれており，その中にも粗く成形された砂岩製の亀が埋納されていた。やはり上面に円形の穴があり，何らかの樹脂で密封していて，隙間を見ると貴石類が詰まっている（Fig. 3.6.5）。これらは池の祭祀に伴う鎮壇遺構と考えられ，今後，アンコールの建築にともなう鎮壇儀式の重要な基礎資料となろう。

confirmed. At the time of the discovery, the mouth of the pit was blocked by sandstone. It is assumed that the side hole was a drainage ditch that drained rainwater from the center of the temple, but it was probably blocked when the floor between the Inner and Outer Galleries was later raised.

4. Survey of the South Pond

The south side of the eastern causeway is level, but since a pond was assumed to be a counterpart to the north side, a confirmation survey was conducted. It was confirmed that the pond layout was symmetrical from north to south with respect to the causeway. The pond revetment was mainly constructed of laterite, and the pond base was detected approximately 3.5 m to 4 m below the surface of the site. The surface of the bottom was covered with laterite on one side to form a horizontal surface. The revetment of the pond was constructed with laterite piled up in a stair-like manner from the bottom, with the lower part having about 10 to 12 steps in a well preserved condition while the upper part was destroyed in later periods and what remains is in a poor state of preservation. The lower layers of sediments, except for the lowest layer of the pond, were not naturally buried, but were most likely filled in artificially. Based on the ceramics excavated from the lower level, the pond was probably losing its function by the late 14th to early 15th century.

The bottom of the central pond has a low step (lower level of the bottom) toward the center (Fig. 3.6.3). In the lower part of the bottom, a masonry structure of sandstone piled in three layers, measuring 2.8 m from east to west and 3.3 m from north to south, was found. In the center of the masonry was a small stone chamber with a sandstone turtle statue and lead container (Fig. 3.6.4). Gold leaf, rock crystal, precious stones, copper plates, iron shards, and earthenware shards were found around the turtle and on the pond pavement. The lead vessel had two upper and lower dish-shaped pieces together. A triangular hole was drilled in the upper surface of the turtle's

5. 出土遺物

アンコール遺跡から出土する遺物のなかで，今のところ年代（生産年代）が最もはっきりしているのは輸入された中国陶磁である。バイヨン出土中国陶磁の産地と年代の大枠は以下の通りとなる。生産年代が10世紀に遡るものは確認されていないが，これは寺院の建立年代を考えるとそれほど驚くべき事ではないだろう。

11世紀〜12世紀前半
　越州窯系青磁
11世紀後半〜12世紀末
　徳化窯系白磁，江西省（景徳鎮窯）系の青白磁，龍泉窯系・同安窯系青磁
12世紀中頃〜13世紀中頃
　同安窯・龍泉窯系青磁
13世紀初頭〜14世紀初頭
　龍泉窯系青磁
13世紀前半〜14世紀中頃
　龍泉窯系青磁，徳化窯系白磁（枢府系白磁）
15・16世紀
　青花磁器

出土した中国陶磁器は，バイヨン期以前から後アンコール時代にかけて，幅広い年代を持ち，バイヨン建立時にすでに伝世品となっていたと思われる古手の資料から，バイヨン廃絶までのものが含まれる。現状では，17世紀代以降の資料のまとまった出土がない事から，バイヨンは17世紀までに最終的に廃絶したのだろうと考えられる。

さらに，これらの年代的手がかりから，バイヨン出土の遺物群は，大きく，下層遺物群と上層遺物群に分類できる事がわかっており，これがバイヨンの利用年代を大きく反映していると考えられる。遺物群の特徴は次の通りとなる。

⑴下層遺物群

第12次調査で検出されている土壙と下層整地層出土遺物を基準資料とした遺物群である。上記の出土貿易陶磁器の年代から，11世紀後半〜13世紀中頃と考えられる。出土量は上層遺物群よりも貧弱であるが，ある程度の傾向は捉えられる。土器は特に資料数に欠け，クメール陶器は無釉・灰釉陶器の合子碗，脚台付碗，小型瓶，壺，丸瓦，平瓦，瓦，黒褐釉陶器の壺がある。総じて無

shell, and a folded copper plate was inserted.

In addition, a small square pit hole was drilled on the east side of the bottom surface, and a roughly shaped sandstone turtle statue was also buried in the pit hole. There is also a circular hole on the upper surface, also sealed with some kind of resin, and the gap shows that it is filled with precious stones (Fig. 3.6.5). It is considered to be the remains of a ritual altar for the pond ceremony, and will be important basic data to understand the ceremony and rituals associated with the dedication of structures in the Khmer Empire.

5. Excavated Artifacts

Among the artifacts excavated at Angkor Monuments, imported Chinese ceramics are the most clearly dated (production date) so far. The following is a general outline of the provenance and age of the Chinese ceramics excavated from Bayon. The production dates back to the 10th century have not been identified, but this is not so surprising considering the date of the temple's construction.

11th - early 12th century
　Yue type celadon
Late 11th - late 12th century
　White porcelain from the Dehua kiln series, blue and white porcelain from the Jiangxi (Jingdezhen) kiln series, and celadon from the Longquan and Tong'an kiln
Mid-12th - Mid-13th century
　Celadon of the Tong'an and Longquan kiln
Early 13th - early 14th century
　Longquan celadon
Early 13th - Mid-14th century
　Longquan celadon, Dehua white porcelain
15th and 16th century
　Blue-and-white porcelain

The Chinese ceramics excavated cover a wide range of ages from the pre-Bayon period to the post-Angkor period, and include old material that were probably already imported when the Bayon was built, as well as objects dating to the abandonment of the Bayon. The lack of excavated materials from the 17th century onward suggests that the Bayon was finally abandoned by the 17th century.

Furthermore, based on these chronological clues, it is known that the Bayon excavated artifacts can be roughly divided into two groups, the lower and upper layer artifact groups, which mainly reflect the age of the Bayon's use. The characteristics of the artifact groups are as follows.

⑴Lower layer artifact group

This artifact group is based on the excavated artifacts

釉・灰釉器種を中心とした一群であるといえる。

⑵上層遺物群

　第12次，第15次調査で検出されている上層整地を中心として出土した遺物を基準資料とする遺物群である。13世紀前半～14世紀中頃と考えられる。

　土器・陶器・輸入陶磁すべてにおいて資料数が豊富で，バイヨンでは最も明瞭な遺物群であるといえる。土器は壺，蓋，ストーブがあり，クメール陶器は無釉・灰釉陶器の碗，大型瓶，壺・甕類，丸瓦，平瓦，棟飾り，黒褐釉の壺，バラスター壺，有耳壺，底部穿孔壺，壺・甕類，有鈕蓋，動物形態器，丸瓦，平瓦などがみられる。総じて，無釉・黒褐釉陶器を中心とした遺物群と考えられる。また，上層遺物群では新たにベトナム産の鉄絵・白磁をみることができ，輸入陶磁の種類の幅も広がっている。

　これまでの研究では，バイヨンの建立と，第1～3期まで区分されている増改築過程は概ねバイヨン期（12世紀後半から13世紀前半）に行われ，第4期はそれ以降，おそらくはカンボジアが上座部仏教社会へと変容するなかで最終的な改築・改変がなされたと考えられてきた。第1～4期の実年代を細かく決定することは難しいが，遺物の出土量や種類の豊富さからみて，バイヨンがもっとも集中的に利用されたのは，13世紀前半～14世紀中頃，つまりバイヨン期後半から後バイヨン期なのは間違いないだろう。

　バイヨンの建立者であるジャヤヴァルマンⅦの在位は，1181～1218年頃と考えられている。残念ながら，王の死に関する情報は一切なく，その後継もどのように行われたのか，不明である。刻文にはその後の王として，インドラヴァルマンⅡ（1218～1243），ジャヤヴァルマンⅧ（1243～1295），シュリーンドラヴァルマン（1295～1307），シュリーンドラジャヤヴァルマン（1307～1327），ジャヤヴァルマパラメーシュヴァラ（1327～?）の王名が記されているが，これらはほぼ王名のみの記載でどのような王であったのか，何が起きたのかについての情報が無く，アンコール末期の実態解明を難しくしている。しかし少なくとも遺物の年代から判断すると，バイヨンが機能したのは，ジャヤヴァルマンⅦの在位中だけでなく，こうした，その後の実態がよくわからないアンコール末期の王達の治世下にかけての事だということになる。

6．おわりに

　バイヨンの考古学は，クメール建築の最終的な到達点である同寺院が最初から完成された形で建立されたので

from the earthen pit and lower level ground preparation layer detected in the 12th survey. Based on the age of the trade ceramics excavated above, it is considered to date from the latter half of the 11th century to the middle of the 13th century. The number of excavated artifacts is less than that of the upper layer artifact group, but some trends can be seen. Khmer ceramics include unglazed and ash-glazed bowls, bowls with footed bases, small bottles, jars, round tiles, flat tiles, roof tiles, and black-brown glazed pottery jars. In general, this is a group of mainly unglazed and ash-glazed pottery types.

⑵ Upper layer artifact group

This artifact group consists of artifacts excavated in the 12th and 15th investigations, mainly from the clearance of the upper layer, and is considered to date from the first half of the 13th century to the middle of the 14th century.

The number of artifacts is plentiful in all of the pottery, ceramics, and imported ceramics groupings, and it is the clearest artifact assemblage at Bayon. The Khmer ceramics include unglazed and grayware bowls, large jars, pots and jars, round and flat roof tiles, roof ornaments, black-brown glazed jars, baluster jars, ear jars, jars with perforated bottoms, knob lids, animal forms, and more. In general, the artifact group is considered to consist mainly of unglazed and black-brown glazed ceramics. In addition, iron painting and white porcelain from Vietnam was newly found in the upper layer, expanding the range of imported ceramics.

According to previous studies, the construction of Bayon and the process of expansion and remodeling, which are classified as the first through third periods, generally took place during the Bayon period (late 12th to early 13th centuries), and the fourth period was probably the final stage of reconstruction and remodeling, as Cambodia transformed into a Theravada Buddhist society. Although it is difficult to determine the actual dates of the first four phases in detail, the Bayon was most intensively used from the first half of the 13th century to the middle of the 14th century, or from the late Bayon period to the post-Bayon period, based on the amount and variety of artifacts excavated.

The reign of Jayavarman VII, the builder of the Bayon, is considered to be around 1181-1218. Unfortunately, there is no information on the king's death, and it is unclear how he was succeeded. The inscriptions list subsequent kings as Indravarman II (1218-1243), Jayavarman VIII (1243-1295), Shrindravarman (1295-1307), Shrindra Jayavarman (1307-1327), and Jayavarmaparameshvara (1327-?). However, these are almost exclusively king names, and there is no information on what kind of king he was or what happened to him, making it difficult to elucidate the actual situation at the end of the Angkor period. However, at least judging from the age of the artifacts, Bayon functioned as a religious center not only during the reign of Jayavarman VII, but also during the reigns

はなく，細かい増改築を繰り返していたことを明らかにしてくれたが，同時に出土した遺物の年代はこの寺院の歴史的解釈を一層困難にしている。

これまでの通説だと，ジャヤヴァルマンⅦでアンコール朝は最盛期をむかえ，その死後は「衰退」にむかい，やがて滅亡したとされる。彼の死後，大型のクメール寺院はもはや新たに築かれることはなく，サンスクリット刻文の数も激減する。そして14世紀にはクメール＝サンスクリット文化が途絶し，今のカンボジア社会へと直結する上座部仏教社会，いわゆる後アンコール時代へと社会は大きく変化したとされる。

しかし上述の通り，バイヨンが宗教的センターとして最も活発に機能したのは，アンコール朝の最盛期から，従来は衰退の時代とされてきた14世紀の中頃までであり，その後も少なくとも16世紀までは何らかの形で機能していたことが明らかになってきた。この事実は，従来の強大なジャヤヴァルマンⅦ以後のアンコール朝の国力低下やその後の衰退といった歴史観に，大きな変更を迫るものだろう。

そのような目でみると，バイヨンのすぐ周辺には，古手と考えられる上座部仏教寺院関連の遺構が多数配置されているし，ここ数年筆者らが実施している寺院周辺の地中レーダー調査では，後バイヨン期に構築されたと考えられている寺院外周壁に平行する，新たな遺構の存在が明らかになりつつある。バイヨンは，アンコール最盛期を代表する寺院というだけでなく，これまで不明であった，アンコール末期の宗教的・文化的・社会的な変容を明らかにする，最大の手がかりでもあるのである。

of the kings of the late Angkor period, whose subsequent status are not well known.

6. Conclusion

The archaeology of the Bayon has revealed that the temple, the final achievement of Khmer architecture, was not planned in the original form we see today, but rather underwent a series of additions and renovations. On the other hand, the excavated artifacts provide a more difficult historical interpretation of the temple.

According to the conventional theory, the Angkor dynasty reached its peak under Jayavarman VII, and after his death, the dynasty began to "decline" and eventually died out. After his death, new large Khmer temples were not built, and the number of Sanskrit inscriptions declined dramatically. In the 14th century, the Khmer-Sanskrit culture disappeared, and the society changed drastically to the Theravada Buddhist society, the so-called post-Angkor period, Theravada Buddhism is practiced in Cambodian society today.

However, as mentioned above, it has become clear that the Bayon functioned most actively as a religious center from the peak of the Angkor dynasty until the middle of the 14th century, which is conventionally regarded as a period of decline, and that it continued to function in some form thereafter at least until the 16th century. This fact would force a major change in the conventional historical view of the Angkor dynasty's decline in national power after the powerful Jayavarman VII and its subsequent decline.

From this point of view, there are a number of remains related to Theravada Buddhist temples in the immediate area around Bayon, and ground-penetrating radar surveys conducted by the authors in recent years have revealed the existence of new remains parallel to the temple perimeter wall, which is thought to have been constructed in the Later Bayon period. The Bayon is not only a representative temple of Angkor's glory period, but also the greatest clue to the religious, cultural, and social transformations of the late Angkor period.

References
1) 奥勇介，2017『アンコール後期における在地陶器の研究——バイヨン寺院出土遺物を中心にして——』，早稲田大学大学院文学研究科提出修士論文
2) 日本国政府アンコール遺跡救済チーム（編），1995～2009，2012～2021『アンコール遺跡調査報告書』日本国政府アンコール遺跡救済チーム
3) 山本信夫，2011『アンコール遺跡における出土貿易陶磁器の様相解明：平成19年度～平成22年度科学研究補助金（基盤研究(A)海外）研究成果報告書』

3.7 アンコール遺跡の岩石学とバイヨン
A Petrological Approach to the Angkor Monument, with a Focus on the Bayon

内田 悦生
UCHIDA Etsuo

1. はじめに

アンコール遺跡は，カンボジアのトンレサップ湖の北側一帯に分布する寺院群であり，9世紀から15世紀にかけてクメール人（カンボジア人）によって建造されたものである。この時期にクメール人によって建造された遺跡群は総称してクメール遺跡と呼ばれ，カンボジアのみならず，タイおよびラオスにかけて分布している。アンコール遺跡以外の代表的なクメール遺跡として，コー・ケー遺跡群，コンポンスヴァイのプレア・カーン，プレア・ヴィヘア，バンテアイ・チュマール，タイのピマイ，パノム・ルン，ラオスのワット・プーが知られている。ここでは，クメール遺跡の代表的な存在であるアンコール遺跡の建造に使用された石材に関して述べる。

アンコール遺跡は，多くの寺院から構成されており，Fig. 3.7.1はその分布を示している。代表的な寺院として，アンコール・ワット，バイヨン，タ・プローム，バンテアイ・クデイ，バンテアイ・スレイが挙げられる。

アンコール遺跡には主として砂岩とラテライトが使用されている（例えば，Uchida et al., 1998, 1999a, 1999b）。10世紀よりも古い遺跡では煉瓦も建築材として使用されている。ここでは，アンコール遺跡に使用されている砂岩に関して紹介する。

2. アンコール遺跡に使用されている砂岩

アンコール遺跡の建造には3種類の砂岩材が使用されている。すなわち，灰色〜黄褐色砂岩，赤色珪質砂岩，緑灰色硬砂岩の3種類である。岩石学的にはこれらの砂岩はそれぞれ長石質アレナイト，石英質アレナイト，長石質ワッケに分類される。このうち，最も重要なのは

1. Introduction

The Angkor Monument is a group of temples located north of Tonle Sap Lake in Cambodia, and was built between the 9th and 15th centuries by the Khmer people (Cambodian people). The temples built by the Khmer people during this period are collectively called Khmer Monuments and are distributed not only in Cambodia but also in Thailand and Laos. Representative Khmer Monuments other than the Angkor Monument include the Koh Ker Monuments, the Preah Khan of Kompong Svay, the Preah Vihear and the Banteay Chhmar in Cambodia, the Phimai and Phanom Rung in Thailand, and the Vat Phu in Laos. In this paper, the stones used to construct the Angkor Monument, which is representative of the Khmer Monuments, will be reviewed.

The Angkor Monument is composed of abundant temples. Fig. 3.7.1 shows their distribution. Representative temples include the Angkor Wat, the Bayon, the Ta Prohm, the Banteay Kdei, and the Banteay Srei.

The main construction materials used for the construction of the Angkor Monument are sandstone and laterite (e.g., Uchida et al., 1998, 1999a, 1999b) as well as compacted clayey-sandy soil as the foundation element. Bricks were also used in temples constructed in and before the 10th century. In this paper, the sandstones used in the Angkor Monument will be reviewed.

2. Sandstones used in the Angkor Monument

Three types of sandstones were used in the construction of the Angkor Monument: gray to yellowish-brown sandstone, red siliceous sandstone, and greenish graywacke. Petrologically, these sandstones are classified as feldspathic arenite, quartz arenite, and feldspathic wacke, respectively. Among these, the most important one is the gray to yellowish-brown sandstone, which was used in almost all the temples

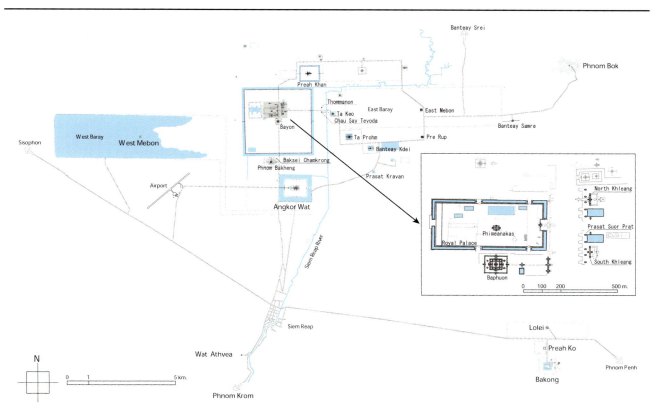

Fig. 3.7.1 Map of the Angkor Monument, showing the distribution of the representative temples (modified after Uchida et al., 2007).

灰色〜黄褐色砂岩であり，多かれ少なかれすべての寺院に使用されている（Fig. 3.7.2）。赤色珪質砂岩は唯一バンテアイ・スレイにおいて主要建築材として使用されている。緑灰色硬砂岩は，寺院としては，唯一タ・ケオの5つの祠堂に使用されている。しかしながら，緑灰色硬砂岩は，これ以外にも彫像やヒンドゥー教のシンボルであるリンガ・ヨーニに使用されており，そのような意味において重要な石材であるということができる。

これらの砂岩材はいずれも三畳紀から白亜紀のコラート層群から供給されたものである。コラート層群はタイでは9つの地層に分類されている[5]。これらの内，硬砂岩は，Huai Hin Lat層から，灰色〜黄褐色砂岩はPhu Kradung層から，そして，赤色珪質砂岩はSao Khua層から供給されたと推定されている。

3. 灰色〜黄褐色砂岩

Fig. 3.7.3上部は灰色〜黄褐色砂岩の偏光顕微鏡写真である。粒径は約0.2mm程度の細粒砂岩であり，主たる

Fig. 3.7.2 (a) The Angkor Wat temple built mainly of gray to yellowish-brown sandstone, (b) the Ta Kev Temple, where the sanctuaries are built of greenish graywacke, (c) the Banteay Srei Temple built mainly of red siliceous sandstone, and (d) a statue made of greenish graywacke.

(Fig. 3.7.2). Red siliceous sandstone is the main building material only in the Banteay Srei Temple. Greenish graywacke was used only in the five sanctuaries on the top of the Ta Kev. In addition, greenish graywacke is used for statues and Linga/Yoni, which is a Hindu symbol and is therefore important in that sense.

These sandstone materials were all supplied from the Khorat Group of the Triassic to the Cretaceous periods. In

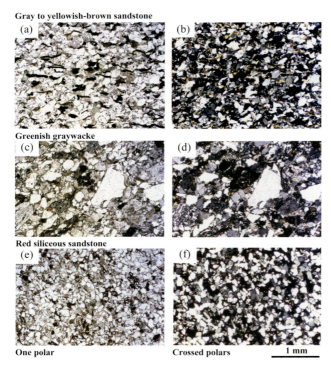

Fig. 3.7.3 Photomicrographs under a polarizing microscope of gray to yellowish-brown sandstone (upper), greenish graywacke (middle), and red siliceous sandstone (bottom) (Uchida et al., 1998)

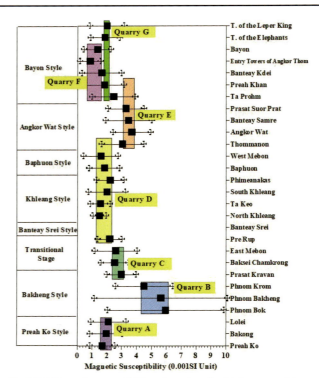

Fig. 3.7.4 Magnetic susceptibilities of gray to yellowish-brown sandstones used in the Angkor Monument (older to younger temples from bottom to top). The standard deviation (1σ) is also shown in the figure (modified after Uchida et al., 1998).

構成粒子は，石英，斜長石，カリ長石，岩石片，黒雲母および白雲母である．しかしながら，構成粒子には寺院による違いは見られない．

筆者らは代表的な寺院から採取した灰色〜黄褐色砂岩の化学組成の分析を行ってみた．しかしながら，微量元素を含めても化学組成に違いは認められなかった[11]．このことから，いままでアンコール遺跡の主要構成石材である砂岩材に対して多くの研究者が研究を行ってきたが，砂岩材に基づいて遺跡の建造に関する情報を得ることはできなかった[1)2)3)]．しかしながら，筆者らは，その帯磁率が建造時期によって異なることを見出した[8)11)]．帯磁率の違いは砂岩中に含まれる磁鉄鉱の量の違いによるものであると考えられる．

(1) 帯磁率

Fig. 3.7.4は，時代による灰色〜黄褐色砂岩の帯磁率の変化を示している[11)]．Fig. 3.7.4では下から上に向かって古い寺院から新しい寺院の順に並べられている．四角は平均帯磁率を示している．Uchida et al. (1998) は，時代とともに砂岩の帯磁率が異なることを見出した．この結果を解析することによりアンコール遺跡の灰色〜黄褐色砂岩は7つの地域から供給されたことが明らかになった[8)11)]．時期によっては複数の地域から石材が供給されたことを示している寺院も存在する．例えば，バイ

Thailand, the Khorat Group is classified into nine formations[5]. It is deduced that the greenish graywacke was supplied from the Huai Hin Lat Formation, the gray to yellowish-brown sandstone from the Phu Kradung Formation, and the reddish siliceous sandstone from the Sao Khua Formation.

3. Gray to yellowish-brown sandstone

Upper of Fig. 3.7.3 shows photomicrographs of gray to yellowish-brown sandstone under a polarizing microscope. It is a fine-grained sandstone with a particle size of around 0.2 mm. The main constituent materials are quartz, plagioclase, K-feldspar, rock fragments, biotite, and muscovite. There is no difference in the constituent materials between temples.

We determined the chemical composition of gray to yellowish-brown sandstones that are collected from representative temples. However, even including trace elements, no differences were found[11]. Many researchers have investigated the sandstones, which is the main building stones of the Angkor Monument, but could not obtain information on the construction of the Angkor Monument from the sandstone[1)2)3)]. However, Uchida et al. (1998, 2007) revealed that the magnetic susceptibility of the gray to yellowish-brown sandstone was different depending on the construction period. The difference in magnetic susceptibility is thought to be due to a difference in the amount of magnetite

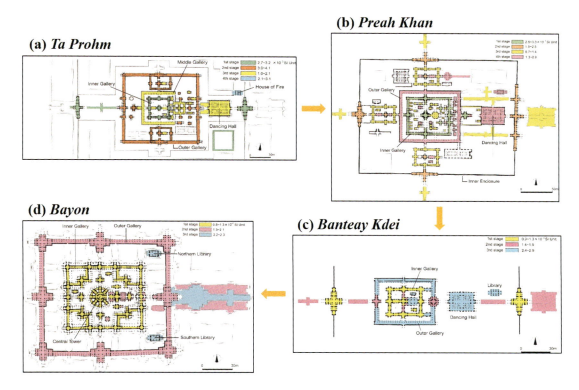

Fig. 3.7.5 The construction sequence of the (a) Ta Prohm, (b) Preah Khan, (c) Banteay Kdei, and (d) Bayon deduced from the magnetic susceptibility of the gray to yellowish-brown sandstones (Uchida et al., 2003).

ヨンでは2ヶ所の地域から砂岩材が供給されたことが判明した。

Fig. 3.7.5(d)は，バイヨンの平面図である[7]。基本的に，中央祠堂，内回廊，外回廊，東側テラスおよび経蔵から構成されている。この図では平均帯磁率によって色分けされている。一般的には寺院は中央から外側に向かって建造されたと推定される。中心部の中央祠堂と内回廊の砂岩材は1.0×10^{-3} SI単位程度の低い帯磁率を示しているが，外回廊とテラスの下側はおよそ1.7×10^{-3} SI単位の帯磁率を示している。約2.2×10^{-3} SI単位程度の最も高い帯磁率をテラスの上側と南北経蔵が示している。このことから黄色，赤色，青色に塗られた場所の順に建造されたことが推定される。

バイヨンは，アンコール・トム都城の中心に位置しており，全長12 kmの周壁によって囲まれている。この周壁には5つの砂岩造の門とその角には4つのチュルンと呼ばれる砂岩造の建物が存在している。それ以外はラテライトから建造されている。砂岩造の建物の平均帯磁率は約1×10^{-3} SI単位である。このことから周壁は，バイヨンの中心部が建造されていたときに建造されたことが明らかになった。

バイヨンが建造されたバイヨン期，すなわち，12世紀末から13世紀前半ではバイヨンをはじめとして，タ・プローム，プレア・カーンおよびバンテアイ・クデイの

contained in the sandstone.

(1) **Magnetic susceptibility**

Fig. 3.7.4 shows the change in magnetic susceptibility of gray to yellowish-brown sandstone by age[8]. The older to younger temples are arranged from bottom to top in Fig. 3.7.4. The square shows the average magnetic susceptibility. We found that the magnetic susceptibility of the sandstone is different depending on the construction period. By analyzing this result, it became clear that the gray to yellowish-brown sandstone of the Angkor Monument was supplied from seven quarrying areas[8)11)]. Some temples indicate that the sandstone was supplied from multiple quarrying areas depending on the period. In the case of the Bayon, it was found that the sandstone was supplied from two quarrying areas.

Fig. 3.7.5(d) is a plan of the Bayon[7]. Basically, it consists of a central sanctuary, Inner and Outer Galleries, east terrace, and libraries. The figure is color-coded by average magnetic susceptibility. Generally, temples are assumed to be constructed from the center outwards. The sandstone for the central sanctuary and Inner Gallery in the central part shows a low magnetic susceptibility of around 1.0×10^{-3} SI units, while the sandstone of the Outer Galleries and lower terrace show a magnetic susceptibility of around 1.7×10^{-3} SI units. The highest magnetic susceptibility of around 2.2×10^{-3} SI units is shown by the sandstone of the upper terrace and the northern and southern libraries. From this fact, it is deduced that the temple was built in the order of the location painted in yellow,

Table 3.7.1 Characteristics of the sandstone and laterite blocks used in the Angkor Monument (Uchida et al., 2005).

Style	Period	Monuments	Stage	Color of Sandstone	Lamina of sandstone	Pore size of laterite	Block size	Uniformity of block size	Stone masonry	Shape of block end	Orientation of the bedding plane	Sharpness of edge	Magnetic susceptibility of sandstone (×0.001SI unit)	Magnetic susceptibility of laterite (×0.001SI unit)
Preah Ko style	end of 9th c.	Preah Ko / Bakong / Lolei	I	Gray	Not remarkable	Small		Uniform	Range ashlar masonry	Rectangular	At random	Good	1.2-2.1	0.7-0.8
Bakheng style	end of 9th c. to early 10th c.	Phnom Bakheng / Phnom Krom / Phnom Bok	II			Large	Large						5.2-8.4	0.5-0.7
Transition style	early to middle 10th c.	Prasat Kravan / Baksei Chamkrong / East Mebon	III			Small				Square			2.5-3.6	0.7-1.4
Khleang & Baphuon style	late 10th c. to late 11th c.	Pre Rup / North Khleang / Ta Keo / Phimeanakas / South Khleang / Baphuon / West Mebon / Preah Palilay	IV a				Large						1.3-2.3	
Angkor Wat style	end of 11th c. to middle 12th c.	Preah Phitu / Thommanon / Boeng Mea Lea / Chau Say Teavoda / Wat Athvea	IV b				Extra large			Rectangular (W/H=1.33)			1.4-5.6	
		Banteay Samre / **Prasat Sour Prat** / Angkor Wat	V										2.9-4.4	
Bayon style	late 12th c. to early 13th c.	Ta Prohm / Preah Khan / Neak Pean	VI a-c		Intermediate			Medium	Intermediate	Almost natural bedding / Rectangular (W/H=1.67)	Intermediate		2.5-4.1	0.3-0.7
		Ta Nei / Baneay Prei / Banteay Thom	VI d	Gray to yellowish brown		Large	Large					Bad	1.5-2.5	
		Ta Som / Krol Ko / Prasat Prei / Prei Prasat / Banteay Kdei / Bayon	VII			Medium	Medium	Variable	Random range ashlar masonry				0.7-1.4	
		Terrace of Elephants / Srah Srang	VIII a		Remarkable		Small						1.3-2.1	0.6-0.7
		Terrace of Leper King / Ta Prohm Kel / Hospitals	VIII b			Small							1.7-3.1	

4つの大規模な寺院が建造されている。Fig. 3.7.5には，これらの寺院における砂岩材の帯磁率が色分けされている。同時期に建造された建物は同じ色で示されている。これらの建物は，碑文などから大まかにタ・プローム，プレア・カーン，バンテアイ・クデイ，バイヨンの順に建造されたことがわかっている。砂岩の帯磁率の測定結果から，例えば，タ・プロームの中心部が建造された時期には，バンテアイ・クデイおよびバイヨンはまだ着工されていなかったことがわかる。それに加え，バイヨンが着工されたときには，タ・プロームでは中回廊および

red, and blue in Fig. 3.7. 5(d).

The Bayon is located at the center of Angkor Thom and is surrounded by a 12 km long surrounding wall. The wall has five sandstone gates and four sandstone buildings called Churn at its corners. The rest of the surrounding wall is built from laterite. The average magnetic susceptibility of these sandstone buildings is around 1×10^{-3} SI units. This indicates that the surrounding wall was constructed when the central part of the Bayon was built.

During the Bayon period from the late 12th to the early 13th century, four large temples including the Bayon, Ta

Fig. 3.7.6 Summary of characteristics of the sandstone and laterite blocks used in the Angkor Monument.

ダンシングホールが建造されていたことがわかる。砂岩の帯磁率は，遺跡の建造順序あるいは建造時期を推定するのに役立つとともに，あとで述べるように石切り場の特定にも役立つ。このように帯磁率測定は，アンコール遺跡研究において大変重要な成果をもたらした。

(2) 灰色〜黄褐色砂岩材の特徴

Table 3.7.1 はラテライトも含めたアンコール遺跡における石材の特徴をまとめたものである。しかしながら，複雑であるため，特に重要な特徴をFig. 3.7.6 にまとめた。

石材の形：バプーオン期までの石材断面は正方形を呈している。しかしながら，アンコール・ワット期になると石材の断面の形は正方形の場合と長方形の場合とが存在する。バイヨン期以降は長方形を示している。

石材の大きさ：バイヨン期初期までは石材の大きさはほぼ統一されているが，バイヨン期主要期以降は不揃いになっている。

石材の層理面方向：バプーオン期までの石材の層理面方向はランダムであるが，アンコール・ワット期以降は基本的に水平になる。

石材の積み方：バイヨン期初期までは石材は同じ高さに積まれ，整層積みである。しかしながら，バイヨン期主要期以降になると乱積みとなる。

これらの石材の特徴から建造時期をある程度推定することができる。その典型例として，ラテライト造であるプラサート・スープラが挙げられる。プラサート・スープラは，アンコール・トム都城の王宮広場の東側に位置する12基の塔からなる。以前は，バイヨン期あるいはそれ以降の建造であると考えられていた。しかしな

Prohm, Preah Khan, and Banteay Kdei were constructed. Fig. 3.7.5 shows the magnetic susceptibility of the sandstone used in these temples, with different colors indicating the same period of construction. These buildings are considered to have been constructed in the order of Ta Prohm, Preah Khan, Banteay Kdei, and Bayon on the basis of inscriptions. From the measured magnetic susceptibility of the sandstone, we can infer that when the central part of Ta Prohm was built, Banteay Kdei and Bayon were not yet under construction. In addition, when the Bayon was under construction, the Middle Gallery and the dancing hall of the Ta Prohm had been constructed. Thus, the magnetic susceptibility of sandstone is useful for estimating the construction sequence and period of the temples and for identifying quarries. Thus, the magnetic susceptibility measurement brought significant results in the study of the Angkor Monument.

(2) Characteristics of the gray to yellowish-brown sandstone blocks

Table 3.7.1 shows the characteristics of the stones (sandstone and laterite) used for the construction of the Angkor Monument. However, since it is complex, the important features are summarized in Fig. 3.7.6.

Shape of stone blocks: Until the Baphuon period, the stone cross-section was square. In the Angkor Wat period, the stone cross-section is either square or rectangular. From the Bayon period onwards, the shape became rectangular.

Size of stone blocks: Until the early Bayon period, the size of the stone blocks is almost uniform, but became uneven after the main Bayon period.

Orientation of the bedding plane of stone blocks: Until the Baphuon period, the orientation of the bedding plane is random, but from the Angkor Wat period, it became mostly horizontal.

Stacking method of stone blocks: Until the early Bayon

ら，主要石材であるラテライトが正方形の断面を示すこと，層理面方向が水平であること，および，整層積みであることから，プラサート・スープラはアンコール・ワット期の建造であることが推測される。また，開口部や装飾に灰色〜黄褐色砂岩が使用されているが，その帯磁率が高く，アンコール・ワット期の砂岩の帯磁率と同じである。これらの事実はプラサート・スープラがアンコール・ワット期の建造であることを示している。さらに，プラサート・スープラの内壁にはスタッコが塗られており，その中には炭が混入していることがある。この炭に対する放射性炭素14年代測定結果は上述の結論を裏付けるものである[12]。

⑶ 供給源

アンコール遺跡の灰色〜黄褐色砂岩の供給源がアンコール遺跡の北東約35kmのところにあるクーレン山の南東山麓にあることが古くから知られていた[2)3)4)6)]。しかしながら，石切り場に関する詳細な情報はなかった。そこで筆者らはクーレン山の南東裾野において1ヶ月以上の時間をかけて調査を行った。その結果，145ヶ所において大小の石切り場の痕跡を発見した[13)14)]（Fig. 3.7.7）。Google Earthの画像において東西2km程度の長さの土手が見られたので，この土手が石材の運搬に関係したのではないかと考え，この土手を中心に調査を行った。Fig. 3.7.7は石切り場の場所を示した地形図である。砂岩の帯磁率と石材の大きさ，特に厚さから，以前に砂岩の帯磁率から推定された7地域（Area A〜Area G）の石切り場との関係を明らかにすることができた。その結果，時代とともに石切り場がこの土手を中心として反時計回りに移動していることが明らかになった。Fig. 3.7.8は，Fig. 3.7.7のno. 45に対応する一番大きな石切り場跡である。帯磁率が低く，ステップの高さが低いことからバイヨン期主要期の石切り場であることが推測された。

⑷ 運搬経路

灰色〜黄褐色砂岩の運搬経路に関しては，以前はクーレン山の南にある規模の大きな運河を利用して，クーレン山からトンレサップ湖経由で運搬されたと考えられていた。しかしながら，筆者らはGoogle Earthの画像を用いて，クーレン山とアンコール遺跡を結ぶ運河および河川を見つけ出した[13]（Fig. 3.7.9）。この経路は計35kmであり，以前に考えられていた経路と比べてかなり短くなっている。灰色〜黄褐色砂岩は船によりこれらの運河や川を利用してアンコール遺跡まで運ばれたと考えられる。

period, the stone blocks were stacked so that they were of uniform height and had a successive bed joint (coursed ashlar masonry), but from the main Bayon period, they show a non-successive bed joint (random range ashlar masonry).

The construction period can be estimated from these characteristics. The typical example is Prasat Suor Prat, which are mainly made of laterite. Prasat Suor Prat consists of 12 towers located on the east side of the Royal Palace square of Angkor Thom. It was previously thought to have been built during the Bayon period or later, but it was speculated to have been built during the Angkor Wat period because the main stone, laterite, shows a square cross-section, has a horizontal bedding plane, and has a successive bed joint. In addition, gray to yellowish-brown sandstone is used in the openings and decorations, and its magnetic susceptibility is high, the same as that of the sandstone from the Angkor Wat period. These facts revealed that the Prasat Suor Prat was built during the Angkor Wat period. In addition, the interior walls of the Prasat Suor Prat are coated with stucco containing charcoal fragments. Radiocarbon dating of the charcoal fragments supports this result[12].

⑶ Source of supply

It has long been known that the source of the gray to yellowish-brown sandstone used in the Angkor Monument is located about 35 km northeast of the Angkor Monument at the southeastern foothill of the Phnom Kulen[2)3)4)6)]. However, detailed information about quarries was not available. Therefore, we conducted a field investigation for over a month at the southeastern foothill of the Kulen Mountain. We found traces of quarries at 145 sites of various scale[13)14)]. We focused on a bank approximately 2 km long seen in Google Earth images, which we thought to have been related to the transportation of the stone blocks. Fig. 3.7.7 is a topographic map showing the location of sandstone quarries. We could identify the seven sandstone quarrying areas judging from the magnetic susceptibility and stone block size, particularly thickness. As a result, it was revealed that the quarrying sites moved counterclockwise around this bank with time. Figure 8 shows the largest quarry, No. 45, which is supposed to be a quarry from the main Bayon period because of its low magnetic susceptibility and low step height.

⑷ Transport route

Previously, it was thought that the gray to yellowish-brown sandstone was transported from the Phnom Kulen using a large-scale canal located south of the Phnom Kulen through the Tonle Sap Lake. However, we found canals and rivers connecting the Phnom Kulen and the Angkor Monument using Google Earth images[13] (Fig. 3.7.9). This route is 35 km long, shorter than the previously thought transport route. The sandstone was transported to the Angkor Monument using these canals and rivers by boat.

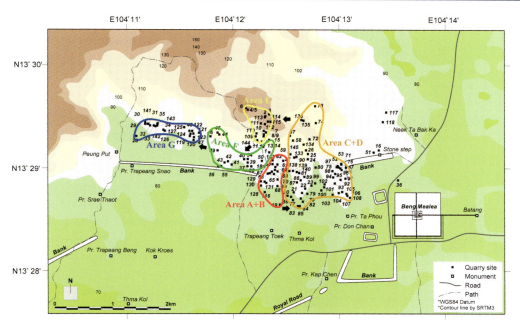

Fig. 3.7.7 Topographic map showing distribution of gray to yellowish-brown sandstone quarries during the Angkor period on the southeastern foothill of the Phnom Kulen (modified after Uchida et al., 2020).

Fig. 3.7.8 Photograph of the gray to yellowish-brown sandstone quarry, no.45, in Fig. 3.7.7

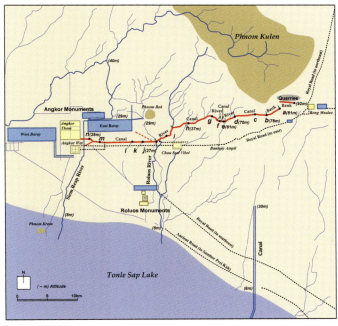

Fig. 3.7.9 Transport route of gray to yellowish-brown sandstone blocks, connecting the quarrying sites on the southeastern foothill of the Phnom Kulen to the Angkor Monument, shown with a red line (Uchida et al., 2013).

Fig. 3.7.10 Photographs of (a) greenish graywacke cut stones scattered in Sandan village, and (b) an unfinished pedestal made of greenish graywacke found in Trapeang Tuol Kruos village (Uchida et al., 2021).

3.7 アンコール遺跡の岩石学とバイヨン　　107

4. 緑灰色硬砂岩とその供給源および運搬経路

アンコール遺跡での緑灰色硬砂岩の使用量が少ないが、緑灰色硬砂岩はかなり遠い場所から運搬されてきたと考えられている。アンコール遺跡で使用されている緑灰色硬砂岩の先行研究はCaro and Douglas（2013）によって行われている[1]。緑灰色硬砂岩の切り石がKratie州のSandan村に点在しているとともにリンガ・ヨーニの台座が同じくKratie州のTrapeang Tuol Kruos村から見つかっている[15]（Fig. 3.7.10）。しかしながら、化学組成や帯磁率の測定は行われていない。そこで、筆者らは、これらの村において石材の分布を明らかにするための調査を行うとともに携帯型蛍光X線分析装置による化学組成分析および携帯型帯磁率計による帯磁率測定を行った。

Fig. 3.7.11は、緑灰色硬砂岩の帯磁率とRb含有量を示した図である[15]。これらの結果によるとアンコール遺跡のタ・ケオに使用されている緑灰色硬砂岩はSandan村の緑灰色硬砂岩材と大変良く似た帯磁率とRb含有量を示している。また、アンコール遺跡の彫像とリンガ・ヨーニに使用されている緑灰色硬砂岩の帯磁率およびRb含有量はTrapeang Tuol Kruos村の緑灰色硬砂岩と比較的よく似ている。それゆえ、これらの場所が、タ・ケオや彫像およびリンガ・ヨーニに使用されている緑灰色硬砂岩の供給地である可能性が考えられる。アンコール遺跡からこれらの地域までの直線距離は約220 kmである。また、両地域を結ぶ王道は存在しない。そこで石材の運搬ルートとしてメコン川の利用が考えられる[15]（Fig. 3.7.12）。これらの村はメコン川の近くに位置

4. Greenish graywacke, and its source of supply and transport route

In contrast, the use of greenish graywacke in the Angkor Monument is limited. It is believed that the greenish graywacke was transported from a considerably distant area. Research on the greenish graywacke used in the Angkor Monument was previously conducted by Carò and Douglas (2013)[1]. Cut stones of the greenish graywacke are scattered in Sandan village in Kratie Province, and also a pedestal of Linga/Yoni was found in Trapeang Tuol Kruos village in Kratie Province[15] (Fig. 3.7.10). However, no measurement of chemical composition and magnetic susceptibility was made. Therefore, we conducted the field investigation to clarify the distribution of greenish graywacke blocks in these villages and measurements of chemical composition using a portable X-ray fluorescence analyzer and magnetic susceptibility using a portable magnetic susceptibility meter.

Fig. 3.7.11 shows the magnetic susceptibility and Rb content of the greenish graywacke[15]. Based on these results, the greenish graywacke used for the construction of the sanctuaries on the top of the Ta Kev in the Angkor Monument shows a magnetic susceptibility and Rb content similar to those of the greenish graywacke blocks in Sandan village. In addition, the magnetic susceptibility and Rb content of the greenish graywacke used for the statues and Linga/Yoni in the Angkor Monument are similar to those of the greenish graywacke in Trapeang Tuol Kruos village. Therefore, these locations are considered to be the source of the greenish graywacke used for the Ta Keo and the statues and Linga/Yoni, respectively. The straight-line distance from these areas to the Angkor Monument is about 220 km. However, there is no Royal Road connecting these areas. Therefore, the use of

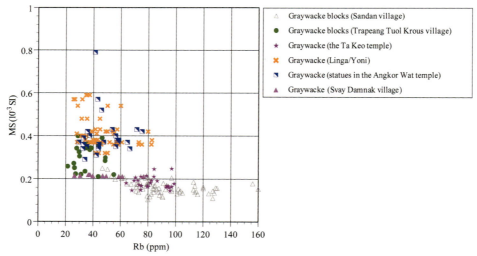

Fig. 3.7.11 Magnetic susceptibility vs. Rb content diagram for the greenish graywacke used in the Angkor Monument and also in Sandan, Trapeang Tuol Kruos, and Svay Damnak villages (Uchida et al., 2021).

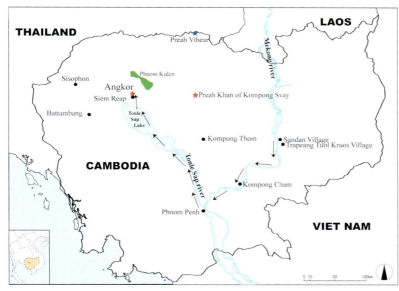

Fig. 3.7.12 Water transport route of greenish graywacke from Kratie Province to the Angkor Monument using the Mekong and Tonle Sap Lake (Uchida et al., 2021).

the Mekong River is considered as a possible transport route[15] (Fig. 3.7.12). These villages are located near the Mekong River. There is the Tonle Sap Lake to the south of the Angkor Monument, which is connected to the Mekong River via the Tonle Sap Lake. In the rainy season, the water level of the Mekong River rises, and water flows back into the Tonle Sap Lake. Therefore, it seems that stone blocks could be easily transported by water by going down the Mekong River and then by going up the Tonle Sap Lake in the rainy season. The total distance is 440 km. Therefore, it is thought that the amount of greenish graywacke used in the Angkor Monument was limited. It was used only for the sanctuaries of the Ta Kev and precious statues and Linga/Yoni.

5. Siliceous sandstone

In addition to the gray to yellowish-brown sandstone and greenish graywacke mentioned so far, red siliceous sandstone is used only in the construction of the Banteay Srei (Fig. 3.7.2 (c)). However, the quarry itself has not yet been found. The Banteay Srei is located near the Phnom Kulen. The red siliceous sandstone is located in the Sao Khua Formation outcrops on the Phnom Kulen (Fig. 3.7.13). Therefore, it is assumed that the red siliceous sandstone used in the Banteay Srei was supplied from the Phnom Kulen. In the Angkor Monument, the use of siliceous sandstone is limited. Although the color is different, siliceous sandstone is widely used in the Preah Vihear located in the northern part of Cambodia and other local temples around Battambang, Phnom Penh and Kampong Cham.

している。アンコール遺跡の南側にはトンレサップ湖が存在し，トンレサップ川によってメコン川と結ばれている。雨季にはメコン川の水位が上昇し，トンレサップ湖に向かって水が逆流する。それゆえ，雨季では，メコン川を下り，トンレサップ川を上ることにより水運によって容易に石材を運搬することができたと思われる。しかしながら，その全長は440kmであることから，アンコール遺跡において使用された緑灰色硬砂岩の量は限られたものとなっている。それゆえ，緑灰色硬砂岩は，タ・ケオの祠堂や貴重な彫像やリンガ・ヨーニにのみ使用されたと思われる。

5．珪質砂岩

上述した灰色〜黄褐色砂岩および緑灰色硬砂岩の外に，バンテアイ・スレイでは赤色珪質砂岩が用いられている（Fig. 3.7.2(c)）。しかしながら，その石切り場そのものはまだ見つかっていない。バンテアイ・スレイはクーレン山の近くに位置している。クーレン山にはSao Khua層の赤色珪質砂岩が分布していることから（Fig. 3.7.13），クーレン山からバンテアイ・スレイの赤色珪質砂岩が供給されたことが推測される。珪質砂岩はアンコール遺跡ではその使用が限られている。しかしながら，色は異なるが，カンボジアの北部に位置するプレア・ヴィヘアやバッタンバン，プノンペンおよびコンポンチャムの周辺に存在する寺院では珪質砂岩の使用が頻繁に認められる。

Fig. 3.7.13 Outcrop of red siliceous sandstone on the northwest foothill of the Phnom Kulen

References

1) Carò, F., Douglas, J.G. (2013) Nature and provenance of the sandstone used for Bayon style sculptures produced during the reign of Jayavarman VII. J. Archaeol. Sci. 40, 723–734.

2) Carò, F., Im, S. (2012) Khmer sandstone quarries of Kulen Mountain and Koh Ker: a petrographic and geochemical study. J. Archaeol. Sci. 39, 1455–1466.

3) Delvert, J. (1963) Recherches sur l'érosion des grès des monuments d'Angkor. In: Bulletin de l'École Française d'Extrême-Orient, vol. 51, pp. 453-534

4) Garnier, F. (1873) Voyage d'exploration en Indochine, effectué pendant les année 1866 et 1868, Paris

5) Meesook, A. (2011) 8. Cretaceous. Eds: Ridd, M.F., Barber, A.J., Crow, M.J. The Geology of Thailand, The Geological Society London, 169-184.

6) Saurin, E., 1954. Quelques remarques sur le grès d'Angkor. Bulletin de l'École Française d'Extrême-Orient, vol. 46, pp. 619-634.

7) Uchida, E., Cunin, O., Shimoda, I., Suda, C., Nakagawa, T. (2003) The construction process of the Angkor monuments elucidated by the magnetic susceptibility of sandstone. Archaeometry, 45, 221-232.

8) Uchida, E., Cunin, O., Suda, C., Ueno, A., Nakagawa, T. (2007) Consideration on the construction process and the sandstone quarries during Angkor period based on the magnetic susceptibility. J. Archaeol. Sci., 34, 924-935.

9) Uchida, E., Maeda, N., Nakagawa, T. (1999a) The laterites of the Angkor monuments, Cambodia. The grouping of the monuments on the basis of the laterites. Jour. Min. Pet. Econ. Geol., 94,162-175.

10) Uchida, E., Ogawa, Y., Maeda, N., Nakagawa, T. (1999b) Deterioration of stone materials in the Angkor monuments, Cambodia. Eng. Geology, 55,101-112.

11) Uchida, E., Ogawa, Y., Nakagawa, T. (1998) The stone materials of the Angkor monuments, Cambodia. The magnetic susceptibility and the orientation of the bedding plane of the sandstone. J. Min. Pet. Econ. Geol., 93,411-426.

12) Uchida, E., Suda, C., Ueno, A., Shimoda, I., Nakagawa, T. (2005) Estimation of the construction period of Prasat Suor Prat in the Angkor monuments, Cambodia, based on the characteristics of its stone materials and the radioactive carbon age of charcoal fragments. J. Archaeol. Sci., 32, 1339-1345.

13) Uchida, E., Shimoda, I. (2013) Quarries and transportation routes of Angkor monument sandstone blocks, Journal of Archaeological Science 40(2), 1158-1164

14) Uchida, E., Watanabe, R., Murasugi, M., Sakurai, Y., Shimoda, I. (2020) The Sandstone Quarries of the Angkor Monuments in the Southeastern Foothills of Kulen Mountain., Archaeological Discovery 8, 207-227

15) Uchida, E., Watanabe, R., Cheng, R., Nakamura, Y., Takeyama, T. (2021) Non-destructive in-situ classification of sandstones used in the Angkor monuments of Cambodia using a portable X-ray fluorescence analyzer and magnetic susceptibility meter, Journal of Archaeological Science: Reports, 39, 103137

3.8 バイヨンの保存科学
Conservation Scientific Research in Bayon

松井 敏也　　河﨑 衣美
MATSUI Toshiya　KAWASAKI Emi

1. はじめに

　バイヨンでは塔の尊顔や回廊の浅浮彫をはじめとして，砂岩石材に多様な彫刻が施されている。中でも回廊の浅浮彫は深刻な劣化現象が顕著に生じており，多角的な自然科学的アプローチによる劣化要因の解明とそれらからの保護，すでに劣化してしまった部分への保存修復方法の開発が求められている。

　文化財の保存修復では，常に必要最小限の修理にとどめるのが基本的な考え方である。他方，バイヨンの浅浮彫の場合には視覚的に違和感を感じさせるようなことがあってはならず，さらなる配慮が求められる。また，必要に応じて原状回復できる可逆性の保存材料を使用するのが原則である。こうした文化財修理の理念に沿ったバイヨン浅浮彫の保存修理の基本方針を以下のように設定した。

(a)浅浮彫の芸術性，崇高な宗教的美的価値を損なうことのない保存修理であること。
(b)浅浮彫を含む回廊全体の構築物について，構造上のゆるみや倒壊の防止策をはかり，また，構築物をなす岩石個々の劣化要因を解明し，その保存対策を検討する。具体的には，雨水の侵入防止，床面の排水機能の改善などをおこない，水による浅浮彫への危害を回避する措置を講ずる。
(c)浅浮彫の表面に付着する塩類等の析出物，着生した微生物類，コウモリの糞に起因した汚れなどの除去に際しては，浅浮彫の保存を第一義に考え，過度の除去処理はおこなわず，その優美さや質感を損なうことのない手法を検討する。
(d)バイヨンの浅浮彫修復に適合した保存修復技法を確立する。さらに，それらを他の遺跡修復に応用することを視野に入れた保存材料・施工技術の開発研究

1. Introduction

　The Bayon has a variety of sandstone reliefs, including faces decorating the towers and bas-reliefs spanning the Galleries. These Gallery bas-reliefs are clearly showing serious signs of deterioration. To identify the causes of the damage, protect the reliefs from deterioration factors, and develop conservation and restoration methods for the parts that have already been greatly damaged, a multifaceted, scientific approach is necessary. A central principal of cultural property conservation and restoration is limiting repairs to the minimum necessary. However, in the case of the Bayon bas-reliefs, further consideration is required in order to avoid visual inconsistencies. Another central principle is the notion that reversible preservation materials should be used when restoring objects to their original state. Below are basic policies for the conservation and restoration of the Bayon bas-reliefs, which have been established in line with these cultural property restoration central principles.

(a) The conservation and restoration of the bas-reliefs should be carried out in a way that does not affect the artistry of the bas-relief or its elevated religious aesthetic value.
(b) Measures should prevent the loosening and collapse of the Gallery structure, including the bas-reliefs. Measures should also help identify deterioration causes and support the conservation of individual stones that make up the structure. Specifically, measures should prevent rainwater from seeping in and improve the floor drainage to avoid water-related damage to the bas-reliefs.
(c) Preserving the bas-reliefs is the first priority to consider when removing surface adherents such as salt precipitates, epiphytic microorganisms, and dirt caused by bat droppings dust. Thus, methods should be considered that do not impair the beauty and elegance of the bas-reliefs through excessive removal processes.
(d) Conservation and restoration techniques suitable for the

をおこなう。

(e)これら一連の事業を通じて，カンボジアにおける保存修復に関する専門性のある人材育成をめざす。

2. 浅浮彫の劣化

(1) 石材の劣化現象とその要因

現在浅浮彫は，石材の劣化および地衣類やその他微生物の付着が著しく，その価値を失う危険性がある。Fig. 3.8.1では，隣り合う石材で同様の天女（アプサラ）をモチーフとした浅浮彫が施されているが，左側の浅浮彫は比較的形状が保たれているのに対し，右側の浅浮彫では石材が削れたように劣化していることが分かる。この他にも，このような劣化はなぜ，どのようにして起こるのかを解明することで，原因を取り除く，または和らげる対策につなげることができる。

劣化要因は，複合的で複雑だが，ひとつは塩類風化であり，アンコール遺跡全般に見られる現象である。すなわち，砂岩に侵入した雨水に岩石中のカルシウム分（Ca）やシリカ分（SiO_2）が水に溶け出し，その水が乾燥期に蒸発する際，岩石の表面に炭酸カルシウム（方解石；$CaCO_3$）や非晶質のシリカとなって析出し，岩石の表面組織を破壊する。実際，浅浮彫の各所で同じような現象が起こっている。もちろん，劣化要因は水の影響ばかりでなく，水が豊富に供給されるような環境のもとでは，微生物の着生も激しく，それが及ぼす浅浮彫への被害も甚大である。さらに，コウモリの糞に由来する塩類風化がある。特に屋根の内側部分，内壁の天井に近いところに白色の付着物が認められ，これらはコウモリの排泄物に由来するリン酸塩鉱物，および石膏（$CaSO_4 \cdot 2H_2O$）の析出が認められた[1]。

浅浮彫の劣化現象の根本要因のひとつは水にある。従来の理解では，回廊の屋根が遺存しているところでは雨漏りが大きな原因としてきた。漏水が壁面を伝って浅浮彫に及ぶというものである。他方，屋根が崩落しているところでは雨水が直に降り注ぎ，降雨時には大量の水が直接壁体に降りかかる。さらには回廊の床面に浸透した水が，回廊の壁体下部に浸入し，それが浅浮彫のある箇所にも及ぶ例があると考えてきた。最近，浅浮彫に最も大きな影響をもたらす水の供給源が新たに明確になってきた[2]。寺院の全体構造をみた場合，寺院の中央部に近いところの内回廊では，中央よりの壁体背後には塔のための高い基壇が密接している。回廊壁面の1.5m高さに相当する基壇が背後に造られている。それに比べて，回廊の四隅に配されるところでは背後の基壇の高さは内回

Bayon bas-reliefs should be established. Furthermore, research needs to be carried out on the development of conservation materials and construction techniques that can be applied for the restoration of other sites.

(e) Through this series of projects, Cambodian conservation and restoration professionals should be developed.

2. The Deterioration of the Bas-reliefs

(1) Stone Deterioration and its Causes

Currently, the bas-reliefs are at risk of losing their value due to the significant deterioration of the stone material and the adhesion of microorganisms such as lichens. Fig. 3.8.1 shows the photograph of adjacent stone bas-reliefs with the same motif of celestial maidens (apsaras). While the bas-relief on the left has maintained its shape, the bas-relief on the right is eroded. By understanding why and how this kind of deterioration occurs, measures can be taken to eliminate or alleviate the causes of such damage.

The causes of deterioration are complex and intertwined, but one important factor is salt weathering, a phenomenon that can be seen throughout the Angkor Monuments.

In short, when rainwater seeps into the sandstone, calcium (Ca) and silica (SiO_2) enter as solutes in the water, and when that water evaporates during the dry season, calcium carbonate (calcite; $CaCO_3$), amorphous silica, and other substance precipitates form on the stone surface, damaging its structure. In fact, a similar phenomenon occurs in various parts of the bas-reliefs. Of course, water itself is not the only factor in their deterioration. In an environment with an abundant supply of water, microbial organisms attach themselves and thrive, causing great damage to the bas-reliefs. Additionally, salt weathering also originates from bat droppings. White deposits were observed especially on the inside of the roof and on the inner walls near the ceiling, and they were determined to be phosphate mineral deposits derived from bat excrement and

Fig. 3.8.1 The deteriorated Bas-reliefs

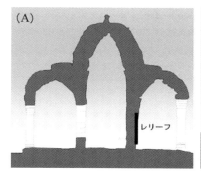 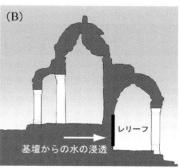

Fig. 3.8.2 Cross-sectional view of the Bayon Inner Gallery (Etsuo UCHIDA et al., 2011)
A : Low area on the platform at the four corners of the Inner Gallery
B : High area on the platform in the center of the Inner Gallery

廊の床面と同じ高さ，すなわち浅浮彫の壁面にとってはほぼ0mに位置する基壇なのである（Fig. 3.8.2）。従って，中央部に位置する内回廊の壁体の背後にある基壇内部の盛土には，降雨時には大量の水が含まれ，それが壁体背後から浅浮彫へ継続的に水が供給されるのである。結果，このような部分における壁体の中位の高さ付近の含水率は年間を通じて概して高い数値を示す傾向にある。他方，基壇の低い箇所では降雨時に直接浸入する雨水や床面に滞留した雨水の量は限られており，壁体の含水率は降雨時には高くなるが，乾燥期には含水率が低くなり，年間を通じた変動幅が大きくなる。背後に基壇を持つ回廊壁面の中位の高さの傍点では，壁面の含水率は雨季には1.7〜2.8％の変動幅を示す。また，乾季には1.4〜2.3％の変動を示し，年間を通じた変動幅は比較的小さい。

隣り合う石材で劣化の状況が異なるのは，石材の元々の性質の違い，水が到達する経路の違い，劣化因子の量的な差などが考えられる。この他にも日射等による温度変化に伴う膨張収縮や，応力集中などの構造的な問題も劣化の原因と考えられる。そして劣化の原因を抑え，すでに劣化してしまった部分へのダメージを最小限に食い止めるためには対策が必要である。

⑵ 観光の影響

カンボジアの外国人観光客数は10年前と比較して約3倍程度にもなり，遺跡への観光客の過度な集中（オーバーツーリズム）による遺跡への影響評価と対策が求められている。遺跡の整備は現場の劣化や損傷具合によって事業化への優先度が異なる。しかし整備後にその場所へ人が入ることは当然予測できることから，それによる影響を見越した保存整備でなくてはならない。今，目の前の現場の劣化のみに対応した保存整備では整備後の観光などによる活用に耐えることができないかもしれない。

遺跡では上記の観光客だけではなく，バスやバイクなどの交通機関や自然環境などからさまざまな振動が関わる。大規模遺跡では観光ルートが固定しがちであり，そ

gypsum (CaSO$_4$ 2H$_2$O) [1].

As a fundamental cause of the deterioration of the bas-reliefs has been determined to be water, the conventional understanding is that, if the roofs remain over the corridors, leaks must be the main cause of the damage, because they allow water to trickle down the wall, reaching the bas-reliefs. On the other hand, where the roofs have collapsed, rainwater falls directly onto the walls in large amounts. The water that permeates the Gallery floor is thought to originate from the lower part of the walls, even reaching areas where there are bas-reliefs. The water source with the greatest effect on the bas-reliefs has been identified recently [2]. Considering the overall structure of the temple, in the Inner Gallery near the center, there is a high tower platform, which is located behind the central wall. Behind it is a platform at a height of 1.5m of the gallery walls. Comparing them, in the four corners of the Gallery, the back pedestal is at the same height as the Inner Gallery floor. Thus, the pedestal is located at almost 0 m from the bas-relief wall surface (Fig. 3.8.2). Therefore, when it rains, a large amount of water is supplied continuously from behind the wall, as the embankment inside the foundation behind the wall of the central Inner Gallery holds a large amount of water during rainfall. As a result, high moisture content is found near the middle height of the wall in these areas throughout the year. On the other hand, in areas where the foundations are low, the amount of rainwater that enters and accumulates on the floor is limited, so the moisture content of the wall increases during rainy periods, but decreases during the dry periods, with large fluctuations throughout the year. At mid-height points on the gallery wall with the platform behind, the moisture content of the wall fluctuates between 1.7% and 2.8% during the rainy season. During the dry season, the fluctuations range between 1.4 and 2.3%, the fluctuation range throughout the year is relatively small.

The differing deterioration conditions between adjacent stones is thought to be due to differences in the original stone properties, in the routes that the water can take, and quantitative differences in the deterioration factors. In addition to this, deterioration is also thought to be caused by structural issues such as expansion and contraction due to temperature changes caused by solar radiation, and concentrated stress. Measures must be taken to suppress the causes of deterioration and to minimize damage to the already significantly damaged parts.

⑵ **The Impact of Tourism**

Tourists in Cambodia have tripled over the past ten years, and an impact assessment and countermeasures are needed to prevent against the excessive concentration of tourists at certain sites (overtourism). Maintenance is prioritized for

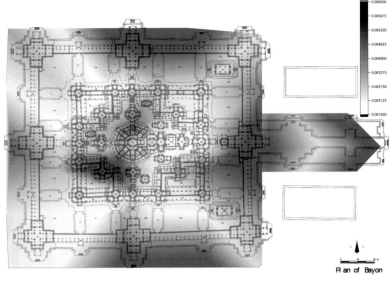

Fig. 3.8.3 Environmental vibration mapping at Bayon

commercially used sites, responding to their deterioration status and sustained damage. However, since people will likely enter these sites after they undergo maintenance, their impact must be considered when carrying out conservation maintenance. Currently, as conservation maintenance only deals with the immediately visible damage to a site, such sites might not withstand the impact of post-maintenance tourism.

At visited sites, vibrations are caused not only by the above-mentioned tourists, but also by transportation vehicles such as buses and motorcycles, and by the natural environment. Tourist routes tend to be fixed for large-scale ruins, which can place an excessive burden on the sites. The Bayon is no exception, as it receives a large number of visitors throughout the year, especially during the morning hours. The general route for visitors is entering from the east side, viewing the bas-reliefs on the south side of the Outer Gallery, and then exiting through the upper floors to the north side. We conducted a survey of the vibrations generated by the surrounding environment at 50 locations within the Bayon. The obtained results are shown in Fig. 3.8.3 in the form of an environmental map. Results indicated that tourists who entered through the east gate followed the route south, then passed through the upper Gallery to the top terrace, subsequently gathering on the west side of the terrace.

As a sanctuary is built on the east side, visitors use the west portion as a view point and a place for group photos. Results showed that people grouped subsequently near the Outer Gallery on the north side. The difference in vibration intensity at the Bayon was approximately 10 times greater. The effect of these measurements on the site remains unknown, but in the long term one could assume that, as vibrations propagate to certain areas of the site at certain times throughout the year, preventive countermeasures are necessary. In the future, it will be necessary to continue monitoring and studying the effects of the vibrations on the bas-reliefs. By measuring vibrations, excessive force concentrations in the site can be detected, which can influence site management plans. This experience shows that conservation should not only be considered for sites under the assumption that there are tourists. A conservation and maintenance plan that is closely linked to tourism plans and management plans is necessary. This requires a system that can respond flexibly to unexpected changes at the site.

れに伴う遺跡への過度の負担が想定される。バイヨンにおいても年間を通してしかも日中の午前中を中心にして訪問者が最も多くなっている。訪問者らは東側から入り，外回廊南側浅浮彫を見学後，上層階を経て北側に出るルートが一般的である。バイヨン内の50ヶ所で遺跡を取り巻く環境から発生する振動の調査を行った。得られた結果を振動マッピングとしてFig. 3.8.3に示す。その結果，東側ゲートから入った観光客はルートどおりに南に回り，その後上層回廊を経て最上段のテラスに至り，さらにテラスでは西側に集まることがわかった。これは東側に祠堂が建б，View pointおよびGroup photo場所として西側が選ばれていることを示す。その後北側の外回廊付近でも集積が見られた。バイヨンにおける振動の強度差はおよそ10倍であった。この数値が遺跡に与える影響は未知であるが，年間を通してある特定の時間帯に遺跡の一部に振動が伝播していることは長期的に考えた場合，対策を施したほうが良いであろう。振動を計測することで遺跡への過度の力の集中を検知でき，遺跡マネージメント計画に反映させることが可能となる。以上のことは，観光客がいない状況の遺跡の保存だけを考えていてはいけないということを示している。観光計画，管理計画と密接に連携した保存整備計画の必要性を示している。またこれは遺跡の変化に合わせていつでも臨機応変に対応する体制が求められる。

3. 浅浮彫の保存に向けて

劣化要因である水の遮断，その他劣化要因の除去（日射等），構造的課題の解決が理想的で根本的な浅浮彫の

Fig. 3.8.4 Samples in exposure testing

3. Towards the Preservation of the Bas-reliefs

The ideal and fundamental countermeasures against bas-relief damage would be to eliminate deterioration factors such as water and sunlight while solving structural issues. However, the Bayon has a complex structure with many already deteriorated elements so such complete countermeasures cannot be realistically implemented, and conservation needs to be applied to carefully selected areas. Specifically, deterioration causes need to be addressed through stone material consolidation and the adjustment of the water flow (moisture permeability regulator). The condition of the stones used in large-scale sites varies depending on their use and location, so it is necessary to select and adapt to the treatments according to their conservation status, rather than selecting the most suitable ones for treatment. In addition, in order to apply a conservation treatment, it is necessary to check whether it can be weather resistant and durable in the unique environment of Cambodia and its sites, and whether the conservation treatment will have any undesired other effects (e.g. investigate whether certain microorganisms are growing). Therefore, we first evaluated the performance and environmental compatibility of the conservation treatment by conducting an exposure test (Fig. 3.8.4) in the local environment using new sandstone samples. The consolidating conservation treatments are based on ethyl silicate, and we created variations of different monomer and polymer blending ratios. We created Bayon S, which has a composition similar to the reinforcement materials generally used worldwide, Bayon M, which contains a higher proportion of monomers, and Bayon P, which contains a higher proportion of polymer components. The ratio of monomer and polymer components affects the rate of crystallization and the size of the crystals after curing, and is also affected by the environmental conditions during processing. The higher the monomer content, the better the permeability into the stone, and the smaller the crystal size after hardening, which is effective if the stone is in a relatively good condition. Conversely, as the proportion of polymers increases, the crystal size increases, making it effective for treating stones with severely deteriorated surfaces. As the Bayon is in a location with a subtropical climate, heavy rains fall during a specific season. In order to restore the original water permeability, lost due to deterioration, and the moisture permeability of the stones, we prepared a moisture permeability regulator in addition to the consolidant. Silane monomers, oligomers, emulsions, etc. were used as moisture permeability regulators. When selecting these agents, consideration was given to workability in hot and humid conditions, ease of handling, and safety. Conservation treatments may be applied as either individual consolidants or moisture permeability regulators, or they may be combined.

劣化対策となるのだが，複雑な構造を持つバイヨンでは完全な対策は不可能と言ってよく，石材そのものへの保存処置が必要となる。具体的には，石材を強化し，劣化の原因である水の移動を調整する（透湿調整）処置をすることである。大規模な遺跡に使われる石材はその用途や部位によって劣化状況は様々であり，最適なものを一つ選択するのではなく，劣化状況に合わせて選択したものを適応する必要がある。加えて保存材料を使用するためには，それらがカンボジアの環境で耐候性，耐久性を持ち得るか，保存材料を使用したことで良い効果以外の影響を及ぼさないか（例えば特殊な微生物が繁茂しないかなど），を調査する必要がある。そこでまずは新しい砂岩で作ったテストピースを使って現地の環境における曝露試験（Fig. 3.8.4）を行うことにより保存材料の性能と環境への適合性を評価した。保存材料にはエチルシリケートを基本とし，そのモノマーとポリマーの配合比を個別に調整した強化剤を作製した。エチルシリケート強化剤は世界的に用いられる組成に似たものを Bayon S とし，それよりもモノマーの配合が多い強化剤 Bayon M と逆にポリマー成分を多く含むもの（Bayon P）を作製した。モノマーとポリマーの混合比は処理時の環境条件により結晶化の速度や硬化後の結晶の大きさなどに影響を及ぼす。モノマーが多いほど，石材への浸透性がよく硬化後の結晶の大きさは小さく，保存状態の比較的良好なものに効果がある。逆にポリマーが多くなると結晶の大きさも大きくなり，表面の劣化が激しい石への処理に効果的である。バイヨンは亜熱帯気候に属し，雨季には非常に多くの雨が降る。劣化により透水性能が失われた石材に本来の透水，透湿性能を回復させるため，強化剤とは別に透湿調整剤を用意した。透湿調整剤はシラン系モノマー，オリゴマー，エマルジョンなどを用いた。これらの薬剤を選択する際，高温および湿気条件での作業性，取り扱いやすさ，および安全性を考慮した。保存処理剤は強化剤，透湿調整剤それぞれ単独で用いられる

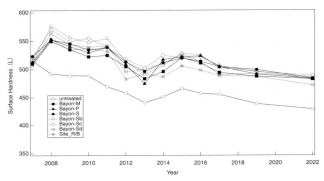

Fig. 3.8.5 Yearly variation of the surface hardness of exposed samples

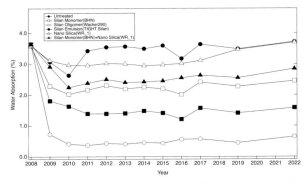

Fig. 3.8.6 Yearly variation of the water absorption of exposed samples

場合もあるが，併用して使うこともある．Fig. 3.8.5は，新鮮な砂岩を強化剤で処理されたテストピースの表面硬度（L値）の変化を示している．強化後は10％程度硬化しており，その後およそ10年で処理前の硬さまで低下した．表面硬度は処理の有無に関わらず毎年一定（約6L／year）の低下が確認されている．強化剤と透湿調整剤を併用したテストピースについても同様な結果となった．透湿調整剤を処理した砂岩テストピースの吸水率の経年変化をFig. 3.8.6に示す．薬剤の種類によってさまざまな透水率を砂岩に付与できることを示し，15年経過しほぼ一定の状態で推移している．

　このような曝露試験は，欠失部分を補うための補修材についても実施しており，仕上がりの質感や成形性，経年による表面硬度変化や防汚効果等の性能を評価している．以上のテストピースを用いた試験の結果を受けて保存材料を選定し，実際にバイヨンの壁面石材でのテストを行なった．強度が低かった部分が強化され，石材中の強度のばらつきがなくなりある程度均質化させる効果を確認しており，このことは，局所的な劣化の集中を防ぐことにつながるものである．またこの試験では，処置後に微生物がどう再付着するかの過程も捉えることができた．壁面後背に基壇のある十字回廊での壁面への施工試験において，クリーニングを行なった後，強化剤および透湿調整剤を塗布した．処置前から処置完了後2年4ヶ月までのバクテリアおよび真菌の変化を遺伝子解析により評価した．このうち微生物や蘚苔類の繁茂の著しい石材の例を示す．微生物や蘚苔類は石材の劣化（土壌化）を促進させる劣化因子である．強化および透湿調整処置を施した試験区において処置後は肉眼で微生物の繁茂は確認できなかったが，クリーニングのみの試験区では処置後8ヶ月の時点で微生物の繁茂が確認された．次世代シークエンサーによる遺伝子解析からは，クリーニングのみ行った試験区では処置前に優勢だったシアノバクテリアの仲間など，バクテリアの生物叢が処置後2年程度で処置前の状態に戻ったことが確認できた．真菌では

Fig. 3.8.5 shows the change in surface hardness (L value) of the fresh sandstone samples treated with consolidants. After the consolidation treatment was applied in 2007, the samples hardened by about 10%, but about 10 years, their hardness returned to pre-treatment values. The surface hardness was found to decrease at a constant yearly rate (approximately 6 L/year), regardless of whether or not a treatment was applied. Similar results were obtained for test pieces using a consolidant and moisture permeability regulator combination. Fig. 3.8.6 shows the change over time in the water absorption rate of sandstone samples treated with moisture permeability regulators. Results indicate that depending on the type of material applied, the sandstone water permeability varies, remaining almost constant for 15 years.

　We also conducted exposure tests for repair materials used to replace missing components, evaluating properties such as performance, finished texture, moldability, changes in surface hardness over time, and antifouling effects. Based on the sample results, we selected a conservation treatment and tested it on Bayon's actual wall stones. We confirmed that the weaker areas were strengthened and that the variations in strength were homogenized to some extent, which helps prevent concentrated, localized deterioration. This test also allowed us to understand how microorganisms reattach after treatment. As part of the test, we cleaned and applied a reinforcing agent and a moisture permeability regulator to a wall in a cross gallery with a platform behind another wall. Two years and 4 months after the treatment, a genetic analysis was conducted to evaluate the bacterial and fungal changes. An example of a stone that is heavily overgrown with microorganisms and bryophytes is shown below. Microorganisms and bryophytes accelerate the deterioration of stone (conversion to soil). There was no visual confirmation of pre-treatment microbial growth in the test area where a consolidant and a moisture permeability regulator were applied. However, in the test area where only cleaning was performed, microbial growth was observed 8 months after the treatment. Genetic analysis using a next-generation sequencer confirmed that in the test area that was only cleaned, the bacterial flora, including cyanobacteria, which were predominant before the treatment,

Fig. 3.8.7 Changes over time in the test areas treated with cleaning only and a consolidant and moisture permeability regulator combination (left: before treatment, middle: 3 months after cleaning, right: 8 months after cleaning).

時期や処置に関わらず優勢種が存在していたが，強化および透湿調整処置試験区では1年8ヶ月後から優勢種の割合が減少し，多様性が増していった。このことは，クリーニングだけでは処置前と同様の状況に戻ってしまうが，強化や透湿調整処置を行うことでクリーニングの効果を持続させ，石材を劣化しにくい状況に保つことができることを示している。

このほか，石材のクリーニング，浅浮彫補修材の調整，目地埋め材の調整と施工などの保存作業において，現地の技術専門家との交流を図り，ワークショップや意見交換を行ってきた。遺跡の保存にとって，遺跡を取り巻く状況の変化を捉え継続的に遺跡への影響を評価し対応し続けること，すなわち「遺跡に寄り添うこと」が重要なことである。実際に修復に携わり，寄り添い続ける現地の技術専門家との連携は不可欠であり，保存科学的視点を共有し，発展させていきたい。

returned to their pre-treatment state approximately two years later. As for fungi, dominant species propagated, regardless of the time of the year or the treatment. However, in the test areas treated with a consolidant and a moisture permeability regulator, the proportion of dominant species decreased while species diversity increased after 1 year and 8 months. These results indicate that cleaning alone will have the stone return to the pre-treatment conditions, but consolidant and moisture permeability regulator treatments can maintain the effects of cleaning and keep the stone in a condition that prevents deterioration.

In addition, we have held workshops and exchanged opinions with local technical experts regarding conservation work, including the cleaning of the stone material, adjusting the bas-relief restoration materials, and adjusting and constructing joint filling materials. For the conservation of sites like these, it is important to keep track of the changes in the circumstances that surround them, continually assessing and responding to the impacts on the site. In other words, it is important to "stay close to the site." Collaboration with local technical experts who are actually involved in the restoration and who continue to work closely with us is essential, and we would like to share and develop our conservation sciences perspective.

References
1) 内田悦生：バイヨン内回廊の保存修復対策に関する研究，Annual Technical report on the Survey of Angkor monument, 2005-2006, Safeguarding of Bayon temple of Angkor Thom, JASA: Japan + APSARA Authority, 2006
2) 内田悦生ほか：石材劣化機構の研究——バイヨン内回廊における含水率測定および表面吸水量測定——，アンコール遺跡・バイヨン寺院浮き彫りの保存方法の研究，平成19～22年度科学研究費補助金（基盤研究(A)）研究成果報告書，平成22年3月，研究代表者・沢田正昭

3.9 アンコール遺跡の微生物
Microorganisms of the Angkor Monuments

片山 葉子
KATAYAMA Yoko

顧　繼東
Gu Ji-Dong

はじめに

　微生物はあらゆる環境から見つかり，その中の細菌は地球上に最初に現れた生き物でもある。微生物はわずかな栄養と水分があれば，たとえ石の表面であっても増殖を始め，肉眼では見えないほど小さな個体は，やがて目に見えるコロニーを形成するまでになる。アンコール遺跡の主要な石材である砂岩は表面に微細な凹凸が多く，保水性に優れるため微生物の格好の生息場所となり，その表面には様々なバイオフィルムが形成される（Fig. 3.9.1）。バイオフィルムの色調はそれぞれの微生物が作る色素の違いに由来し，緑色植物と同じ光合成を行う細菌のシアノバクテリアは青緑色，カロチノイド色素を含む細菌は淡紅色から赤橙色，メラニンを含む真菌は黒色などを呈する。微生物には，太陽光線を利用して光合成生物として生きてゆくものもあれば，無機化合物や有機

Introduction

Microorganisms are ubiquitous in the environment, and bacteria among them were the first life form on the Earth showing great adaptation to different environments. Even on stone surfaces, microorganisms begin to multiply when a small amount of nutrients and moisture is available, and the cells, too small to be seen by the naked eye, eventually increase to form colonies or biofilms that are large enough to be visible, such as the various colors. Sandstone, the main building material for Angkor Monuments, provides a physical environmental conditions for microorganisms because it is rich in microscopic irregular pores which have excellent water retention properties, resulting in the formation of biofilms of various colors on its surface over time (Fig. 3.9.1). Cyanobacteria, a group of bacteria that performs photosynthesis similar to that of green plants, are showing almost dark green, while other bacteria containing carotenoid pigments are in light red or red-orange, and fungi containing melanin are in black. Some of them use solar irradiation to grow as phototrophs while others use either inorganic or organic compounds as a source of energy and electron to grow. Because of this, the metabolical versatility of microbial life style is extremely high.

When stone gallery walls are covered with biofilm, it is not only compromised the visual landscape of viewing, but also cause serious problems by the metabolites from the physiological and biochemical activities of

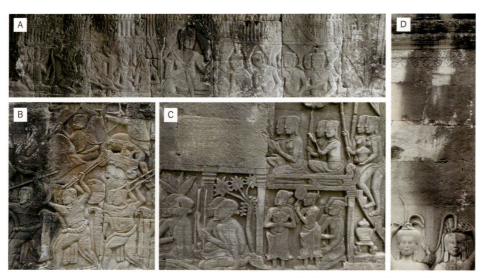

Fig. 3.9.1 Bas-relief of Angkor Monuments.
A, B, C, Inner Gallery, Bayon. Angkor Thom; D, terrace of the second floor, Angkor Wat

化合物をエネルギー源として増殖するものもあり，その代謝の多様性は極めて高い。

遺跡の回廊壁面にバイオフィルムが発生すると，景観を損うだけでなく，微生物の代謝に伴い細胞外へ排出される代謝産物が，深刻な問題を引き起こす場合がある。特に，硝酸や硫酸などの無機酸，クエン酸などの有機酸といった酸性化合物は，岩石の成分を溶出させると共に，それらが塩となって析出する事でさらに劣化を促進させる可能性がある[9]。そのため，バイオフィルムにどのような性質の微生物が生息しているかを知ると共に，それらが砂岩に与える影響を予測することは，アンコール遺跡を微生物による劣化から守る上で重要な情報となる。そこで，まずどのような微生物がいるのかに注目し細菌叢の解析を行った。また，代謝に関連して，細菌，アーキア，真菌が代謝の過程で生成する酸性の窒素化合物や硫黄化合物について調べた。これらの代謝反応に注目した理由は，遺跡には今も多くのコウモリが生息し，その排泄物に含まれるアンモニアや硫黄化合物を微生物が利用し，その結果作り出される酸性の化合物による石材への影響が予想されたからである。

1．バイオフィルムの微生物

バイオフィルムの細菌叢を調べるには，新材に比べて脆くなっている遺跡の砂岩に影響を与えることなく，安全にバイオフィルムを採取することが必要である。そこで，スペースシャトル内部の環境モニタリングに使用された粘着性シートを用いる事にした。予め滅菌された粘着性シートでバイオフィルムを慎重に移し取り，そこから抽出したDNAから細菌とアーキアの特定遺伝子の領域をPCR法で増幅した。その塩基配列を既存のデーターベースと比較し，系統分類学のデーターベースを

these microorganisms. In particular, acidic compounds such as inorganic acids of nitrate and sulfate as well as organic acids are produced to dissolve and leach out selective mineral components from the rock and contribute to degradation through solubilization, precipitation or crystallization of their salts to minerals upon drying[9]. Therefore, the critical information is to understand the capabilities of the microorganisms that inhibit in the biofilm and the damage they may cause to the underlying sandstone for protecting the Angkor Monument against deterioration caused by microscopic organisms. We started with an examination of the bacterial flora focusing on the different kinds of microorganisms occurring at different sites. Then, we focused on the metabolism of selective microorganisms, namely bacteria, archaea and fungi, for transformation of nitrogen and sulfur compounds, especially the acidic ones. The reason for analyzing these compounds is that many bats still live at these sites and it is known that their excrement containing ammonia and sulfur compounds would promote microbial growth and development. As a result, stone monuments can be attacked by the colonized microbes under the changing environmental conditions.

1. Microorganisms of biofilm

In order to examine the microflora of the biofilm, it is necessary to collect the biofilm samples without damaging the stone, which is much more fragile than the fresh material. Therefore, adhesive sampling sheets, used for monitoring inside surfaces of the space station, have been used to collect the biofilms. The collected samples of biofilms on sterile adhesive sheets can be extracted for genomic DNA, and then the specific gene region of the DNA of bacteria and archaea can be amplified by polymerase chain reaction (PCR) method, and the obtained nucleotide sequences of the microbial population in biofilm samples can then be compared with available database to estimate the phylogenies and their

Fig. 3.9.2 Visible pigmented biofilms covering the sandstone wall of the Inner Gallery of Bayon. Salmon pink, black-gray and signal violet in the upper row indicate the color tones of the biofilm identified based on the standard color chart. The names of the prevailing bacteria, estimated from sequence comparisons of the 16S rRNA gene, are shown in a box below the specific color accordingly.

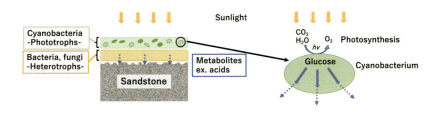

Fig. 3.9.3 A schematic illustration of deterioration processes of sandstone by the layered biofilms of phototrophic cyanobacteria and heterotrophic bacteria and fungi formed on the surfaces of stone

もとに菌叢を推定した[6]。バイヨンの内回廊の壁面には，異なる色のバイオフィルムがまだら状に現れている場所がある。その菌叢を調べた処，淡紅色のバイオフィルムには高濃度の塩や紫外線に耐性を持つルブロバクター属の細菌が優占し，淡紫色のバイオフィルムではノストック属のシアノバクテリアとクロロフレクサス門の細菌が優占していた（Fig. 3.9.2）。

粘着性シートを新しいものに交換しながら，同じ場所から移し取る事を繰り返すと，バイオフィルムの表面から内部に向かって菌叢を立体的に再構築できる。例えば，表層部分にはシアノバクテリアが優占し，その内側の層ではシアノバクテリアの比率は低下し，代わりにルブロバクター属やその他の従属栄養性の細菌の優占が確認された（Fig. 3.9.3）[6]。バイオフィルムは細菌の他にもアーキア，真菌類，微細藻類など数多くの微生物の生息場所となっており，複雑な微生物生態系を作り上げている。バイヨンの内回廊には暗緑色のバイオフィルムに覆われた壁面があり，高濃度の硝酸塩の蓄積も確認されている。このようなバイオフィルムを形成する微生物を理解することは，砂岩の劣化に対する微生物の寄与とそのはたらきを評価する上での重要な第一歩である。

2. 硝酸塩の蓄積と浅浮彫の劣化

生物による石材の劣化には多様な微生物が関わり，それぞれの微生物の特性によって劣化の様相も異なる。バイヨンの劣化した砂岩表面のバイオフィルムには，上述の様に硝酸塩の蓄積している場所があり，特に塔近くの，屋根がまだ残っている回廊の壁面に多い。その起源は，現在でも塔内部に棲むコウモリの排泄物由来と考えられるが，なぜ高濃度の硝酸塩が蓄積するのか，その詳しいメカニズムは我々が調査を開始するまで全く不明であった[3]。哺乳類であるコウモリの排泄物には高濃度のアンモニアが含まれるため，その巣の周辺はアンモニアによる汚染が発生しやすい。アンモニアを酸化することでエ

relationships in the population[6]. In doing so, the community compisition information of the biofilm samples can be obtained. Some sections in the Inner Gallery of Bayon show biofilm with various colors appearing in patches on the wall surfaces. The results of analysis showed that the pale red biofilms were dominated by bacteria of the genus *Rubrobacter*, which are known to be resistant to high salt concentrations and intense Ultra-Violet (UV) light. The light purple biofilms are dominated by cyanobacteria such as *Nostoc* and bacteria of the phylum Chloroflexi group (Fig. 3.9.2).

By repetitive sampling from the same location for more than 40 times and then analysis of the microbial community based on DNA, a three-dimensional (spatial) structure of the biofilm can be reconstructed using the multiple sampling approach and analysis. In the Inner Gallery at Bayon, a major and clear shift in the bacterial species from the top biofilm surface layer to the deep layers. Cyanobacteria are mainly in the top biofilm surface layer and low diversity is observed. When moving down to the deep biofilm layers, Rubrobacter and other heterotrophic bacteria sensitive to oxygen become dominated instead (Fig. 3.9.3)[6]. In addition to bacteria, actual biofilms are inhabited by a variety and mixture of microorganisms, including archaea, fungi, and microalgae, forming a complex microbial ecosystem. There is also a wall covered with a dark green biofilm which shows a significant accumulation of nitrate at high concentration. An understanding of the physiologically active microorganisms colonizing in these biofilms is an important and the first step before assessing their contribution to the deterioration of the sandstone and also mechanisms involved.

2. Deterioration of bas-relief with accumulation of nitrate

Different physiological groups of microorganisms have their own way to cause deterioration of stone. Biofilms formed on the surfaces of deteriorated sandstone of Bayon have been found to be associated with accumulation of extremely high concentration of nitrate, in particular, in areas where the roof of the Gallery is still intact and also on the walls around the temple towers specifically. Although the origin of nitrate-nitrogen has been predicted to be the excrement of bats, which are still widely found in towers, the details of the mechanism leading to the accumulation of high concentration of nitrate remained unknown mostly and further investigation are required to delineate the fundamentals[3]. As mammals, bats' excrement contains high concentration of ammonia, which means that the areas with bat roosting are commonly contaminated with high concentration of ammonia.

ネルギーを得る微生物にはアンモニア酸化細菌（AOB）とアンモニア酸化アーキア（AOA）が知られており，近年さらにコマモクス菌と呼ばれる細菌も発見されている。このようにアンモニアを除去する微生物は土壌をはじめ様々な環境に生息しており，亜硝酸を経由してアンモニアを硝酸に変換する，硝化と呼ばれるプロセスで重要なはたらきをしている[3]。亜硝酸・硝酸はさらに別の細菌によって亜酸化窒素（一酸化二窒素，化学式はN_2O）や窒素ガスなどの気体に変換される脱窒と呼ばれる反応があるため，バイヨンで見られる硝酸塩の深刻な蓄積は，通常は見ることは少ない。また，硝酸の生成は酸性化にもつながり方解石などを溶かす事から，石材の劣化をもたらす[12]。

では，なぜバイヨンで硝酸塩が蓄積してしまうのだろうか？　そこでまず，AOA，AOBのどちらがアンモニアの酸化に直接寄与する微生物なのかを調べた。手法は上で述べた方法と基本的に同じだが，アンモニアから亜硝酸へ酸化する時にはたらくアンモニアモノオキシゲナーゼという酵素の遺伝子を解析のターゲットとすることで，硝化の反応に直接関わる微生物を追う事ができるようにした。その結果，この反応を主に担っているのはAOBではなくAOAであることが明らかとなった[10][11]。石の劣化の話題から少し外れるが，二酸化炭素の273倍の温室効果を有し，しかもオゾン層破壊物質でもある亜酸化窒素が，窒素循環の過程で微生物によって亜硝酸から生成されることが明らかとなり，亜酸化窒素生成に関わる研究が盛んに行われるようになった。その結果，AOAよりもAOBの寄与の大きいことが，土壌を中心とする研究によって明らかとなって来た［例，Hink et al., 2017］。一方，土壌とは異なり，遺跡環境ではAOBよりもAOAが優占することを，我々の調査はいち早く示した。周辺の寺院も調査対象に加え，合計34の試料について同様にAOAとAOBの存在を調べた結果，30の試料でAOAが優勢であり，しかもPCR増幅によってAOBの存在が確認されたのはこの内10試料のみであった[11]。この様にアンコール遺跡はその多くの場所において通常の土壌とは異なり，AOAの優占する環境であることが初めて示された。

微生物叢においてAOAが優勢であることは示されたが，実際にAOAがアンコール遺跡でアンモニア酸化を担っているのかどうかは不明である。そこで，DNAからRNAに読み取られる遺伝情報をベースとすることで，アンモニアモノオキシゲナーゼの定量化を行うと共に，安定同位体である^{15}Nの取り込み試験を行った。その結果，アンモニアの亜硝酸／硝酸への酸化は，やはりAOAが重要な役割を果たしている事が再確認された。

Microorganisms that utilize ammonia including bacteria can obtain energy by oxidizing ammonia (ammonia-oxidizing bacteria, AOB; ammonia-oxidizing archaea, AOA; and complete ammonia-oxidizing bacteria, comammox bacteria), which are widely detected in soil and various other environments. All of them oxidize ammonia into nitrite/nitrate ions as a metabolite plus acidity by the normally known nitrification reaction[3]. Furthermore, another biochemical route by bacteria converts inorganic nitrogen into gases such as dinitrogen monoxide (N_2O) and nitrogen gas, which does not lead to the accumulation of severely high concentrations of nitrate as found in the Bayon. This reaction, which produces nitrate, also increases acidity and dissolves minerals from the stone, e.g., calcite into solution to cause material loss and a porosity increases[12].

The question, then, is why does nitrate accumulation occur in Bayon? To answer this question scientifically, we first investigated which microorganisms contribute directly to nitrification, AOA or AOB. The method for this part is basically very similar to those described above using genomic DNA and RNA, but the target gene is more specific, ammonia monooxygenase, an enzyme responsible for the oxidation reaction of ammonia to nitrite, which allows us to evaluate which of the two microorganisms involved more in the reaction. The results revealed for the first time that AOA play a much greater role than AOB in this reaction[10][11]. While we are off the topic of stone deterioration, it was discovered that N_2O, a greenhouse gas which is 273 times more potent than carbon dioxide and an ozone depleting substance, is produced from nitrite through the biochemical reaction of various microorganisms, and research on the microorganisms involved in N_2O production began in the 2010s. It was reported that AOB mainly contributes to N_2O formation in the soil environments ［ex. Hink et al., 2017］. In contrast, our research was the first to show that AOA dominates than AOB in the unique environment of archaeological sites, which is different from soil. In addition to Bayon, a total of 34 samples in the surrounding region were examined for the presence of AOA and AOB. For the results, AOA found were predominant in 30 of them while only 10 samples were confirmed to show the presence of AOB by PCR amplification[11], confirming that many of the Angkor Monuments are AOA-dominated in the microbial community responsible for nitrification reaction.

Although AOA was found to be predominant at the Angkor site, in order to confirm that AOA is actually performing ammonia oxidation, we quantified the amount of enzyme activity by targeting RNA and also tested the incorporation of the stable isotope ^{15}N. It was confirmed again that AOA are an important contributor in the oxidation of ammonia to nitrite/nitrate. Nitrification have been thought to be carried out by two separate bacteria in sequence of the reaction, ammonia oxidation to nitrite first by ammonia oxidizing bacteria and then nitrite oxidation to nitrate by nitrite oxidizing bacteria

3.9　アンコール遺跡の微生物　　121

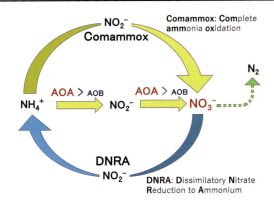

Fig. 3.9.4 A proposed internal nitrogen cycling reactions carried out by AOB, AOA, comammox bacteria and DNRA bacteria found on Angkor Monuments

従来，硝化反応はアンモニア酸化とそれに引き続く亜硝酸酸化の2つの反応を別の細菌がそれぞれ担うとされていたが，2015年にこの2つの反応を単独で進める細菌が見つかりコマモクス菌と名付けられた。2つの反応を同一の細菌がまとめて進めるため，より高い効率で硝酸を生成することが出来るが，アンコール遺跡でもこのコマモクス菌の生息が確認され，硝酸の蓄積に寄与していることが明らかとなった[1]。また，このように生成された硝酸を大気へ戻す脱窒活性は低く，硝酸を効果的に消費できるほどではないことが示された[1,3]。さらにその上，アンモニアへの異化的硝酸還元（DNRA）と呼ばれる，硝酸をアンモニアへ還元させる微生物もいることがわかり，DNRAによって硝酸は消費されるが，同時にアンモニアを再生させることになり，結果としてアンモニアの酸化反応に必要な基質を新たに供給していることが示された（Fig. 3.9.4）[2,3]。これらの結果は，AOA，AOB，そしてコマモクス細菌によるアンモニアの酸化と，DNRAによるアンモニアの再生からなる，窒素循環のループが存在していることを示す。一連のこれらの重要な発見によって，バイヨンでおきている硝酸塩蓄積のメカニズムを初めて説明できるようになった。

5. 細菌と真菌の硫黄酸化

元素循環のひとつである硫黄循環は，酸化反応の最終生成物である硫酸が酸性であるため，石材に損傷を与える可能性がある。上述の硝酸塩の蓄積と同様に，硫酸塩の蓄積の場合もコウモリの排泄物に由来すると予想される硫黄化合物を用いて，様々な微生物によって行われている。硫酸による劣化のメカニズムを理解するには，硫酸生成に関わる微生物の情報が必要であり，この調査で硫酸を生成する微生物と石材の劣化との関係を見るため

(NOB), but in 2015, a single bacterium was found to complete these two reactions by itself, and was named comammox bacteria. Since the reaction can be carried out by a single bacterium, nitrate can be produced with higher efficiency. The presence of comammox bacteria was also confirmed at the Angkor Monuments[1], clearly contributing to the efficient production and then accumulation of nitrate. Furthermore, removal of nitrate by denitrification and anammox reactions, in which the produced nitrate is returned to the atmosphere as N_2, was relatively low and cannot consume the nitrate produced effectively[1,3]. In addition, dissimilatory nitrate reduction to ammonium (DNRA) bacterium is also detected in the microbial community, which allow a decrease of the accumulated nitrate and then at the same time to provide new substrate for ammonia oxidation reaction to continue cyclically (Fig. 3.9.4)[2,3]. These results collectively show a nitrogen recycling reaction loop is formed internally, involving ammonia oxidation by AOA, AOB and comammox bacteria, and a regeneration of the necessary substrate, ammonia, by DNRA. This important finding explains the accumulation of nitrate detected on Bayon monuments more comprehensively.

5. Oxidation of sulfur by fungi and bacteria

Sulfur cycle is an important part of the natural element cycle, characterized by the sulfate as the end product of the oxidation reaction, which is acidic and thus induces damage to the stone material. Similar to the nitrate accumulation described above, sulfate accumulation is also carried out by a variety of microorganisms using sulfur compounds, which are expected to be derived from bat excreta. Understanding the mechanism of deterioration of bas-reliefs by sulfate needs to identify the microorganisms producing sulfate. To demonstrate the relationship between sulfate-producing microorganisms and the deterioration of the stone, sandstone pillars of Angkor Wat were chosen as the site for a survey of microorganisms. Many of the stone supporting columns at Angkor Wat have deteriorated the most at or near the floor level, and some columns have become thinner as a result of the exfoliation. Such exfoliation as a mechanism is caused by an increase of the internal pressure due to salt accumulation and crystallization inside the stone below the surface, which is induced by rainwater intrusion and the crystallization of soluble salts into minerals[3]. Biofilm formation has not been to the level to be visually visible, it was confirmed that bacteria closely related to the genera *Truepera* and *Rubrobacter*, known with salt and UV tolerance, are present in the deteriorated section of columns of the Angkor Wat gallery section. Since the supply of organic matter from photosynthesis performed by cyanobacteria was also expected to be low, the density of bacteria was examined here using the culture-dependent method, assuming the presence of autotrophic sulfur-oxidizing

に選んだのが，回廊にある砂岩の柱である。アンコール・ワットの回廊には，砂岩の柱が床面に接する部分で著しく細くなっている場所があり，砂岩のこのような剥離は，浸入した雨水の蒸発や，石材中の塩分が析出し内圧が上昇することで進行すると考えられている[3]。見た目ではこのような場所にバイオフィルムは確認できず，菌叢解析では高濃度塩類やUVに耐性のあるトルエペラ属やルブロバクター属の細菌の優占が確認され，シアノバクテリアによる光合成からの有機物の供給は少ないことが予想された。そのため，独立栄養性の硫黄酸化細菌が生息することを想定して，培養法による菌密度の調査を行なった。劣化した石材表面の微生物について，有機物を含まない無機的な培養条件のもとで，硫黄から硫酸を生成する独立栄養性の微生物をMPN法と呼ばれる培養法によって，1998年から2007年までの10年間にわたり計数した。例えばバイヨンでは1gの試料に換算して$10^1〜10^5$ MPNの微生物が計測された[7]。この方法は培養を行うため，目的の性質の微生物を分離することも可能であり，佐賀大学のグループがコウモリのグアノから分離した株も含め，20株を超す硫酸生成菌が分離された。これらの菌株の内5株はマイコリシバクテリウム属の細菌であり，残りの菌株はペニシリウム属などの子嚢菌に属する真菌であった（Fig. 3.9.5）[5)8)13)]。

マイコリシバクテリウム属の細菌も子嚢菌に属する真菌も，いずれもこれまで有機物質を必須とする従属栄養性の微生物と考えられてきた。しかしながら，今回見つかったマイコリシバクテリウムや子嚢菌のいくつかの分類群の真菌は，有機物質を含まない培養条件で，硫黄をエネルギー源として生育する能力も備わっていることが我々の研究で初めて確認された。今回の調査により，これまで従属栄養性と考えられてきた細菌や真菌にも，有機物の存在しない条件下で硫黄の酸化と増殖の見られることが初めて明らかになり，長く信じられてきたこれらの微生物に対するイメージを大きく変える重要な発見であると共に，今後の硫酸塩蓄積のメカニズムを理解する上でも考慮すべき事柄であると云える。

6. 結論と展望

カンボジアのアンコール遺跡で確認された窒素と硫黄の循環に関わる微生物は，その酸化反応によって生成した代謝産物が周囲の酸性化を引き起こし，更には高濃度の硝酸塩や硫酸塩の蓄積をもたらす。その原因となっているコウモリ定住の問題が解決すれば，硝酸塩や硫酸塩はいずれも水溶性のため，水による洗浄は有効な方法と

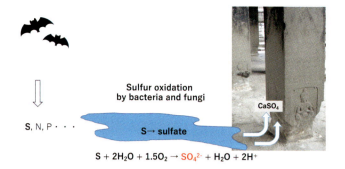

Fig. 3.9.5 Deterioration of the supporting stone pillar of Angkor Wat, and the bacterial and fungal sulfur oxidation reactions producing acidity

bacteria. The population of microorganisms that produce sulfate from sulfur can be enumerated from the deteriorated stone surfaces samples over a 10-year period from 1998 to 2007 using a culture-dependent method called the MPN method, which, for example, yielded 10^1-10^5 MPN in 1 g of sample at Bayon[7]. Because this method is a culturing-dependent method, it is possible to isolate microorganisms of interest into pure culture, and more than 20 strains of sulfate-producing microorganisms using sulfur as an energy source have been obtained, including isolates from bat guano by a research group from Saga University. Five of these strains were bacteria of the genus *Mycobacterium*, and the rest were fungi of the genus *Penicillium* or other groups of Ascomycota (Fig. 3.9.5) [5)8)13)].

Both the bacteria of the genus *Mycobacterium* and the fungi belonging to the phylum Ascomycota revealed in this study are heterotrophic microorganisms that utilize organic matter for growth. However, our study is the first to demonstrate that bacteria in the genus *Mycobacterium* and some fungal strains which belong to some taxonomic groups of the phylum Ascomycota can grow using sulfur as an energy source under culture condition that does not contain organic matter. *Mycobacterium* and fungi that are thought to grow heterotrophically using organic matter, have the metabolic capacity to oxidize elemental sulfur to obtain energy without the presence of organic substance, a discovery that has changed the commonly held view of the bacteria and fungi for many years.

6. Conclusions and perspectives

The microbiome of the Angkor Monuments in Cambodia contains biochemically functional microorganisms, and the metabolites produced in nitrogen and sulfur metabolisms by these microorganisms cause acidification and then the accumulation of high concentrations of nitrate and sulfate in these cultural heritage sites. Since both of these metabolites are water soluble, washing with water would be an effective

云える。ゲノミクスへの新たなアプローチに加え，安定同位体を用いたトレーサー研究やより詳細な化学分析の導入は，微生物による石材劣化をより詳細に解明することになり，鉱物学や水の特性に加えて，劣化に関わる微生物群やそれらが行う生化学反応の情報を加味することで，石材劣化をより深く理解することが可能となる。また，このような情報は文化遺産や歴史的建造物の保存においても有効なものとなるであろう。

method if the problem of bat, assuming to be the cause of their generation, could be solved. In addition to new approaches to genomics, the introduction of tracer technique using stable isotopes and more detailed chemical and mineralogical analyses is expected to further elucidate an in-depth understanding of the mechanisms of stone degradation by different microorganisms and the biochemical reactions involved. In addition to mineralogy and water properties, information on the microorganisms involved in deterioration, as well as the biochemical reactions they undergo, can provide a more in-depth understanding of stone degradation. Such information can be used to effectively protect cultural heritage and historic buildings.

References

1) Ding X, W Lan, Y Li, A Yan, Y Katayama, K Koba, A Makabe, K Fukushima, M Yano, Y Onishi, Q Ge, J-D Gu (2021) An internal recycling mechanism between ammonia/ammonium and nitrate driven by ammonia-oxidizing archaea and bacteria (AOA, AOB, and Comammox) and DNRA on Angkor sandstone monuments. Int. Biodeter. Biodeg. 165, 105328.

2) Ding X, W Lan, Y Li, A Yan, Y Katayama, J-D Gu (2022) Microbiome characteristics and the key biochemical pathways identified from world stone cultural heritage under different climate conditions. J. Environ. Manag. 302 (Part A), 114041.

3) Gu, J-D, Y Katayama (2021) Microbiota and biochemical processes involved in biodeterioration of cultural heritage and protection. 37-58. *In* E. Joseph (ed.), Microorganisms in Biodeterioration and Preservation of Cultural Heritage, Springer Verlag GmbH, Heidelberg, Germany.

4) Hink I, GW Nicol, JI Prosser (2017) Archaea produce lower yields of N_2O than bacteria during aerobic ammonia oxidation in soil. Environ. Microbiol., 19, 4829-4837.

5) Kusumi A, XS Li, Y Katayama (2011) Mycobacteria isolated from Angkor monument sandstones grow chemolithoautotrophically by oxidizing elemental sulfur. Front. Microbiol. 2, 104.

6) Kusumi A, XS Li, Y Osuga, A Kawashima, J-D Gu, M Nasu, Y Katayama (2013) Bacterial communities in pigmented biofilms formed on the sandstone bas-relief walls of the Bayon temple, Angkor Thom, Cambodia. Microbes Environ. 28, 422-431.

7) Li XS, H Arai, I Shimoda, H Kuraishi, Y Katayama (2008) Enumeration of sulfur-oxidizing microorganisms on deteriorating stone of the Angkor monuments, Cambodia. Microbes Environ. 23, 293-298

8) Li XS, T Sato, Y Ooiwa, A Kusumi, J-D Gu, Y Katayama (2010) Oxidation of elemental sulfur by *Fusarium solani* strain THIF01 harboring endobacterium *Bradyrhizobium* sp. Microbial Ecol. 60, 96-104.

9) Liu X, R Koestler, T Warscheid, Y Katayama, J-D Gu (2020) Microbial deterioration and sustainable conservation of monuments and buildings. Nature Sustain. 3, 991-1004.

10) Meng H, L Luo, HW Chan, Y Katayama, J-D Gu (2016) Higher diversity and abundance of ammonia-oxidizing archaea than bacteria detected at the Bayon temple of Angkor Thom in Cambodia. Inter. Biodeter. Biodeg. 115, 234-243.

11) Meng H, Y Katayama, J-D Gu (2017) More wide occurrence and dominance of ammonia-oxidizing archaea than bacteria at three Angkor sandstone temples of Bayon, Phnom Krom and Wat Athvea in Cambodia. Inter. Biodeter. Biodeg. 117, 78-88.

12) Qian, Y, T Gan, S Zada, Y Katayama, J-D Gu (2022) De-calcification as an important mechanism in (bio)deterioration of sandstone of Angkor monuments in Cambodia. Inter. Biodeter. Biodeg. 174, 105470.

13) Xu H-B, M Tsukuda, Y Takahara, T Sato, J-D Gu, Y Katayama (2018) Lithoautotrophical oxidation of elemental sulfur by fungi including *Fusarium solani* isolated from sandstone Angkor temples. Inter. Biodeter. Biodeg. 126, 95-102.

3.10 バイヨンの3Dスキャン
3D Scanning of the Bayon

大石 岳史　　池内 克史
OISHI Takeshi　　IKEUCHI Katsushi

1. はじめに

　レーザ計測やフォトグラメトリによる3Dデジタル化技術の発達により，写真や映像だけでなく，3Dデジタルデータによる文化遺産の記録が一般的に行われるようになっている[1]。特にレーザレンジセンサ（或いはLiDAR）の発達により都市や遺跡といった非常に大規模な構造物も数ミリからサブミリ精度で3Dデジタル化することが可能となっている。そのため，世界中で貴重な文化遺産が3次元的にアーカイブされる例も多くみられる。またアーカイブだけでなく，3Dデータの様々な形で利活用することも広く行われている。

　我々は3Dデジタル化技術によって得られたデータをe-Heritageと名付け，アーカイブから解析，展示まで幅広い研究を進めている。バイヨンデジタルアーカイブプロジェクト[2]では，5年の年月をかけてセンサやデータ処理技術を開発，実地計測を行い，Fig. 3.10.1のようなバイヨン全体の3Dデータを取得した。このプロジェクトでは，後述するように特殊なセンサシステムを開発し，寺院全体，浅浮彫，ペディメントの精細な3D計測を行った。また考古，建築，美術史といった異なる分野の研究者と連携して，得られた3Dデータの利活用も進めてきた。

　本項では，このプロジェクトを中心として大規模文化遺産の3Dデジタル技術と，得られた3Dデータを利用して新たな知見を得ることを目的としたサイバー考古学について紹介する。

2. バイヨン3Dデジタル化

　ここではレーザレンジセンサを用いて，バイヨンのよ

1. Introduction

　The advancement of three-dimensional digitization technologies, such as laser measurement and photogrammetry, has enhanced the recording of cultural heritage in 3D digital form, not just photographs and videos ［Ding X, W Lan, Y Li, et al. 2021］. In particular, the development of laser range sensors (or LiDAR) has enabled digitizing massive structures like cities and archaeological sites with millimeter to sub-millimeter precision. As a result, many instances worldwide exist where valuable cultural heritage is archived in three dimensions. Additionally, using 3D data in various forms, beyond mere archiving, is now widely practiced.

　We have named the data obtained through 3D digitization technology "e-Heritage" and are conducting extensive research ranging from archiving to analysis and exhibition. In the Bayon Digital Archive Project, we developed sensors and data processing technologies over five years, conducted field measurements, and acquired comprehensive 3D data of the entire Bayon, as depicted in Fig. 3.10.1. In this project, we developed a particular sensor system for detailed 3D measurements of the entire temple, bas-relief, and pediments, as will be discussed later. We have also collaborated with researchers from various fields, such as archaeology, architecture, and art history, to further utilize the 3D data obtained.

　This paper focuses on the Bayon Digital Archive Project, introducing 3D digital technology for large-scale cultural heritage and cyber-archaeology to gain new insights using the acquired 3D data.

2. Bayon 3D Digitization

　This section introduces the technology for 3D digitization of large and complex structures like the Bayon using laser

Fig. 3.10.1 3D Model of Bayon from Laser Scanning

うな大規模かつ複雑な構造物を3Dデジタル化する技術について紹介する。バイヨンは150m四方の敷地に建てられた石造りの巨大な建造物である。二重の回廊や52本の塔など，建築学的にも非常に複雑な構造物とされている。そのため，センサの制限により計測困難な箇所が多く，また得られた多数の部分データをどのように処理して完全な3Dモデルを生成するかというデータ処理技術も必要となる。

本節では，プロジェクトを通して開発したセンサやデータ処理手法について解説する。レーザレンジセンサを用いた物体の形状取得は，おおまかに(1)データ取得，(2)位置あわせ，(3)統合の3つの処理からなる。以下，各処理について順に説明していく。

(1) データ取得

実物体の形状を得るためにはレーザレンジセンサを用いて複数回にわたって異なる方向，位置から計測する必要がある。一般的にレンジセンサは可視領域つまりセンサから見える領域しか計測できないため，対象全体の形状を得るために，異なる位置から複数回の計測を行う。多くの従来型レンジセンサは，三脚で地面に設置して計測するため，計測距離やレーザの入射角，遮蔽によって不可視となる高所や狭い場所での計測は困難となる。そ

range sensors. Bayon is a massive stone structure built on a 150 meter square site. It is architecturally complex, featuring a double Galleries and 52 towers. Due to the sensor's limitations, many areas are difficult to measure, and the technology to process the numerous partial data to create a complete 3D model is also required.

This section will explain the sensors and data processing methods developed throughout the project. The shape acquisition of objects using laser range sensors generally involves three processes: (1) data acquisition, (2) alignment, and (3) integration. Below, we will explain each procedure.

(1) Data Acquisition

In capturing the shape of an object, it is necessary to measure the entire target object at multiple positions using a laser range sensor. Generally, range sensors can only measure the visible area from the sensor, so multiple measurements from different positions are required to capture the entire shape of the object. Many traditional range sensors, mounted on tripods and placed on the ground, have difficulties measuring high or narrow places due to limited measuring distance, laser incident angles, and occlusions.

Therefore, we developed new sensor systems to measure areas that are difficult to capture with conventional sensors.

・Ground-Based Moving Sensor

Galleries usually surround the temples in Cambodia, and

こで，このような従来型センサでは難しい領域を計測するために新たなセンサシステムを開発した。

・地上移動型センサ

カンボジアの寺院の多くは回廊に囲まれており，この回廊に精密に刻まれた浅浮彫を高精度・高密度で計測する必要がある。一般に寺院は回廊とその内側の中央祠堂などの建物によって構成されている。この回廊に神話や当時の人々の様子などが浅浮彫として刻まれており，これらの浅浮彫は神話や歴史を伝える貴重な文化遺産となっている。一方で，石で造られた寺院は風化，劣化が著しく，デジタル化して保存することは急務であると考えられている。

長い回廊の浅浮彫を計測する場合，既存センサでは様々な問題がある。固定型レーザレンジセンサを用いた場合，レーザは放射状に広がるため，センサから遠くなるほどデータ解像度は低くなる。つまり浅浮彫を均一に計測することは難しい。一方，光切断法，構造化光法による近距離センサを用いた場合は，計測範囲が狭いことから，多量のデータを取得する必要があるため，計測時間・データ処理時間が膨大になるという問題もある。

そこで我々は広い範囲を効率的，均一にレーザ計測するための地上移動型センサを開発した。レールセンサ[3]は，回廊上に敷いたレールの上を移動しながら計測を行う。ローバ型センサ[4]（Fig. 3.10.2）はホイールタイプの移動機構によって不整地でも移動が可能である。これらのセンサシステムはいずれもレーザプロファイラ（ラインスキャン）と全方位カメラによって構成されており，前者が表面形状を計測し，後者を併用することでスキャンラインごとのセンサシステムの位置姿勢推定を行っている。カメラは色彩情報も同時に取得する。このような移動型センサによって，これまで数年かけて計測していた浅浮彫を，数日間で計測できるようになった。

・気球センサ

地上からの計測では，バイヨンのような大規模構造物の上部まで計測することは不可能である。大型のクレーンや足場は，設置場所に制限があり，安定性や景観の問題もあるため現実的ではない。

そこで我々は空中から計測を行うため気球搭載型レーザレンジセンサを開発した（バルーンセンサ）。このセンサは気球の下に高精度なレーザレンジセンサを吊り下げて，上空から計測を行うものである（Fig. 3.10.3）。レーザレンジセンサは1スキャンに数分を必要とするため，計測中の気球の揺れによるセンサの移動にともなって，得られる距離データには歪みが生じてしまう。この歪み

Fig. 3.10.2 Rover-type Laser Scanning System

measuring the bas-relief carved into these corridors with high precision and density is difficult but crucial. Generally, a temple consists of a gallery and buildings, such as a central shrine. The bas-relief depicting myths and scenes from people's lives at the time are valuable and convey mythology and history. However, many temples made of stone are severely weathered and degraded, making digital preservation an urgent matter.

Measuring the bas-relief in a long gallery with existing sensors poses various problems. When using fixed laser range sensors, the data resolution decreases with distance from the sensor as the laser emission spreads radially, making it difficult to measure the bas-relief uniformly. On the other hand, using close-range sensors based on light-sectioning or structured light methods requires capturing many frames due to their limited measurement range, resulting in extensive measurement and data processing time.

Thus, we developed a ground-based moving sensor with a laser sensor to measure a wide area efficiently and uniformly. The rail sensor[3] measures while moving along rails laid on the gallery. The rover-type sensor[4] (Fig. 3.10.2) can move on uneven terrain as a result of its wheel-type moving mechanism. These sensor systems consist of a laser profiler (line scan) and an omnidirectional camera, with the former measuring surface shapes and the latter used for estimating the poses of the sensor system for each scan line. The camera also captures color information. With these mobile sensing systems, bas-relief that used to take years to measure can now be measured in just a few days.

・Balloon Sensor

Measuring only from the ground makes it impossible to cover the upper parts of large structures like Bayon. Using large cranes or scaffolds is impractical due to their limited placement options, stability issues, and impact on the scenery.

Therefore, we developed a balloon-mounted laser range sensor (Balloon Sensor) for aerial measurement. This sensor suspends a high-precision laser range sensor beneath a balloon to conduct measurements from the air (Fig. 3.10.3). Since the laser range sensor requires several minutes for a single scan,

を補正するために，センサにカメラを搭載して，映像と距離画像からセンサの動きを推定して距離画像の歪みを補正するアルゴリズムや[5)6)]，地上データとラインのデータを合わせることによって，高精度に位置姿勢を推定する手法を開発した[7)]．気球センサによって空中から得られたデータと，地上から得られたデータを統合することによって，巨大な構造物の完全な3Dモデルを生成することが可能となった．

(2) 位置合わせ

レンジセンサによって様々な方向から得られた部分形状データはそれぞれ異なる座標系で記述されているため，相対位置姿勢を求めて一つの座標系で記述する必要がある．この処理は位置合わせと呼ばれる．位置合わせ手法としては，各部分形状モデルに含まれる頂点間で対応点を探索し，得られた対応点間の距離の総和が最小となるような相対位置姿勢を繰り返し求めるIterative Closest Point（ICP）が最も広く知られている．しかし，大規模な建造物の場合，非常に多くの部分形状データを位置合わせするため，逐次位置合わせでは誤差の蓄積によって大きな誤差が生じてしまう．

そこで，我々は多数の部分モデルを高速に同時位置合わせする手法を開発した．この手法では，すべての部分データ間の誤差を同時に最小化している．さらに大規模なデータを扱うために，計算時間やメモリ使用量を考慮し，PCクラスタなどの分散メモリシステム上で並列に同時位置合わせする手法を開発した[8)9)]．これらの手法によって，多量のデータを高精度に位置合わせすることが可能になった．

(3) 統合

最後に，位置合わせされた複数の部分データを統合して，一つのメッシュモデルを生成する．複数の部分モデル間には重なりや解像度のばらつきがあるため，重なりを取り除いて，正則化された一つのメッシュデータに変換する．正則なメッシュモデルを得るためには，空間を均等なボクセルに区切って表現するボリュメトリックな手法が適している．この手法では，複数の部分メッシュデータを互いの整合性を取りながら一つのボクセル空間に投影し，ボクセルからの符号付距離による陰関数表現によって統合を行う．複数の異なるセンサから得られたデータを統合するためには，各センサの信頼度を用いて重みづけすることで，選択的により高精度なデータを生成することができる．得られたボリュームデータはボクセルの格子間をつなぐマーチングキューブ法を用いて再びメッシュデータに変換される．大規模データを扱

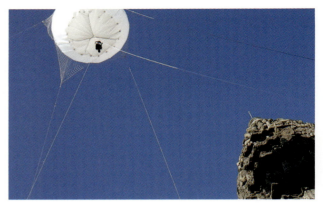

Fig. 3.10.3 Balloon Sensor

the movement of the sensor due to the swaying of the balloon during measurement distorts the scanned data. To rectify the distortion, we equipped a camera and developed algorithms to estimate the sensor's motion from the video and depth images and correct the distortion in the depth images[5)6)]. We also developed a method for accurately estimating the sensor poses by combining the data taken from the ground with the scanned profiler data[7)]. Integrating data from the balloon sensor with that obtained from the ground made it possible to create a complete 3D model of the massive structure.

(2) Alignment

Partial shape data obtained from various directions using range sensors are described in different coordinate systems, so it is necessary to determine their relative poses to represent them in a unified coordinate system. This process is known as alignment. Iterative Closest Point (ICP) is the most widely known alignment method, which repeatedly finds the relative poses that minimize the total distance between corresponding points found among vertices in each partial shape model. However, in the case of large structures, sequentially aligning a vast number of partial shape data can result in significant errors due to the accumulation of local errors.

Therefore, we developed a method to align multiple partial data rapidly and simultaneously. This method minimizes errors across all partial data simultaneously. Furthermore, to handle large-scale data, we developed a method for parallel simultaneous alignment working on distributed memory systems such as PC clusters, considering computation time and memory usage[8)9)]. These methods enable high-precision alignment of large volumes of data.

(3) Integration

Finally, we integrate multiple aligned partial data sets to generate a unified mesh model. Since there are overlaps and inconsistencies in resolution between multiple partial data, we need to remove the overlaps and convert the data into a regularized single mesh. Volumetric methods, representing space as evenly divided voxels, are suitable for obtaining a regular mesh model. This method projects multiple partial

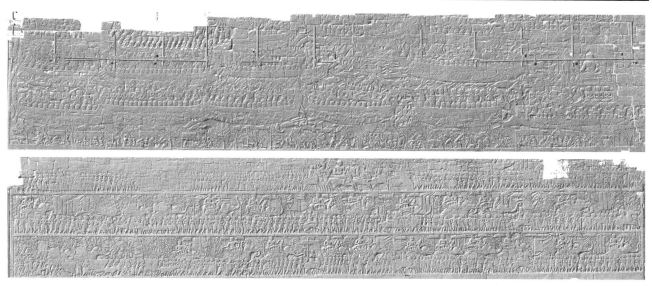

Fig. 3.10.4 3D Models of the Bas-Reliefs
(Top: South Side of the Outer Gallery's East Wing, Bottom: South Side of the Outer Gallery's East Face)

Fig. 3.10.5 3D Model of the Hidden Pediment

う際には位置合わせと同様に計算時間，メモリ使用量が大きくなるため，並列化したボリュームトリックな統合手法を開発した。

⑷ デジタル化結果

Fig. 3.10.1は前述のセンサ及びデータ処理手法を用いてバイヨン全体を3Dモデル化した結果である。上記の開発したセンサだけでなく，固定型センサ（Cyrax 2500, HDS3000, Imager5003）を用いて計測したデータも含まれている。統合時のデータ解像度＝ボクセルサイズは約2cmである。センサの計測精度が1cm程度であるため十分な解像度のデータが得られていると考えられる。Fig. 3.10.4は光切断法を採用しているVIVID910で計測した浅浮彫データの一部を示している。外回廊，内回廊すべての浅浮彫を精細に計測している。Fig. 3.10.5は鏡を用

mesh data into a single voxel space while maintaining consistency with each other. It integrates them using an implicit function representation based on signed distances from the voxels. We can generate selective high-precision data by weighting each sensor's reliability to integrate data from different types of sensors. Finally, we convert the resulting volumetric data into mesh data using the marching cubes method, which connects grids between voxels. Similar to alignment, handling large-scale data requires the development of parallelized volumetric integration methods due to increased computation time and memory usage.

⑷ **Digitalization Results**

Fig. 3.10.1 shows the results of 3D digitization of the entire Bayon using the sensors mentioned above and data processing methods. The data include those obtained from the developed sensors and fixed sensors (Cyrax2500, HDS3000, Imager5003).

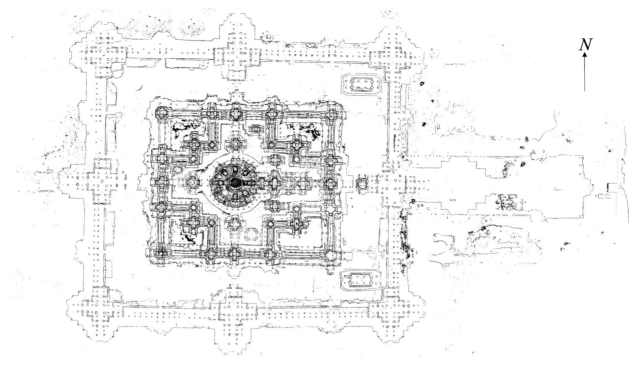

Fig. 3.10.6 Plan View Automatically Generated from 3D Data

いて計測した狭隘部にあるペディメントのデータである。特に通常の可視光下では見ることができない形状を見ることができる。またもとの浅浮彫が削られており，宗教の変遷を示す貴重なデータであると言える。Fig. 3.10.6 は，得られた3Dモデルから高さ方向に複数階層の断面図を生成し，重畳することによって取得した平面図である。これらの取得した3Dデータは，展示だけでなく，考古学的な解析や，寺院の保存修復のための様々な基礎資料として利活用することが可能である。

3. サイバー考古学

計測3DデータはXR（Extended Reality）やビデオコンテンツの製作に有用であるが，それ以上に様々な研究データとしての利用価値が高い。本章では，3Dデータを活用して新たな知見が得られた事例について紹介する。

(1) 類似度推定と分類

バイヨンには52の塔があり，合計で173の尊顔が刻まれているとされている。これらの尊顔は，仏の顔を模しているとされることもあるが，ヒンドゥー教に由来するとも言われている[10]。朴らによるとこれらの尊顔はデーヴァ，デヴァター，アスラの3種類に分類される。しかし，これまでの分類は主観評価に基づいているため，より客観的に評価するため計測3Dデータを用いて数値

The data resolution at the time of integration, i.e., the voxel size, is approximately 2 cm. Considering that the measurement accuracy of the sensors is about 1 cm, we believe that the data obtained are of sufficient resolution. Fig. 3.10.4 shows a part of the bas-relief data measured with the VIVID910, which employs the light-sectioning method. We have measured all bas-relief of the Outer and Inner Galleries in detail. Fig. 3.10.5 presents data from a pediment in a narrow area measured using VIVID910 and a front surface mirror. In particular, it reveals invisible shapes under normal light conditions, also providing valuable data indicative of religious changes as the original bas-relief have been eroded. Fig. 3.10.6 is a plan view obtained by generating multiple cross-sectional views in the vertical direction from the acquired 3D model and superimposing them. These acquired 3D data can be utilized not only for exhibition purposes but also as various foundational materials for archaeological analysis and for the preservation and restoration of the temple.

3. Cyber-Archaeology

Measured 3D data is useful for XR (Extended Reality) and video content production but are even more valuable as various research data. This chapter introduces cases where we gained new insights through the use of 3D data.

(1) Similarity Estimation and Classification

The Bayon has 52 towers and 173 faces carved on them. Some works of literature describe these faces as modeled

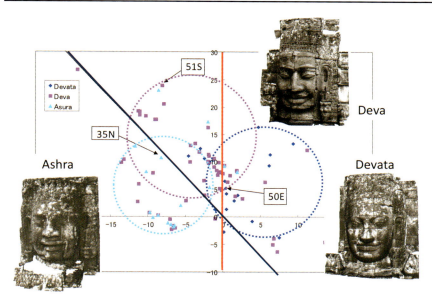

Fig. 3.10.7 Results of Linear Discriminant Analysis

解析による分類を行った[11]。

朴らの分類から標準的な尊顔を選び，線形判別分析（教師あり）を行ったところ，Fig. 3.10.7に示すようにすべての尊顔をおおまかに分類する超平面が得られた。この超平面による分類の多くは Meng H, L Luo, HW Chan, Y Katayama, et al.（2022）と一致するが，異なる種別に分類される尊顔も多いことが分かった。一方，階層クラスタ分析（教師なし）を行ったところ，実空間中で距離が近い尊顔が似た形状を持つことも判明した。これは複数の彫り師のグループがそれぞれの範囲を担当して作成したためではないかと予想されている。

⑵ 3Dプリンタを利用した中央塔構造解析

バイヨンの中央塔は石材の劣化や構造の経年変化によって倒壊の危機にさらされている。そのため構造の安定化が急務の一つとなっている。特に石材の崩落は風による物理的な力による場合も多いため，風荷重の解析が重要である。しかし，バイヨンのように大規模で複雑な形状をもつ構造物のシミュレーションは一般に困難である。そこで計測3Dデータから3Dプリンタを用いて模型を製作し，この模型を用いて風洞実験を行った[12]。この風洞実験により，風向きや風速に応じた風荷重や空気の流れが可視化され，風向きによっては凹部で渦が発生し，大きな負圧が生じることなども明らかになった。解析の詳細については，3.11を参照されたい。

⑶ 時系列データを用いた壁面劣化状況の把握

バイヨンの内回廊，外回廊には貴重な浅浮彫が残されているが，近年劣化が著しいため，時系列3Dデータを用いて劣化状況の解析を行った。バイヨンの浅浮彫は自

after the Buddha but are also said to be derived from Hinduism[10]. According to Park et al., we can classify these faces into three types: Deva, Devata, and Asura. However, since previous classifications were based on subjective evaluations, we conducted numerical analysis-based classifications using measured 3D data for a more objective assessment[11].

Choosing standard faces from Park et al.'s classification and performing linear discriminant analysis (supervised), we obtained a hyperplane that roughly classifies all faces into the above three gods, as shown in Fig. 3.10.7. While most of the classifications by this hyperplane are consistent Meng H, L Luo, HW Chan, Y Katayama, et al. (2022), we also found that we can classify many faces into different types. On the other hand, hierarchical cluster analysis (unsupervised) revealed that faces close to each other in real space tend to have similar shapes. This finding suggests that multiple groups of sculptors may have been responsible for carving different areas.

⑵ Structural Analysis of the Central Tower Using 3D Printer

The Central Tower of Bayon is at risk of collapse due to the deterioration of the stone materials and the structural changes over time. Therefore, stabilizing the structure is an urgent matter. In particular, the collapse of stone materials is often caused by physical forces due to wind, making the wind load analysis crucial. However, simulating structures with large and complex shapes like the Bayon is generally complex. Therefore, we made a tower model using a 3D printer from the measured 3D data and used this model for wind tunnel experiments12). These wind tunnel experiments visualized the wind load and airflow patterns according to wind direction and speed. We revealed that vortices could form in concave areas depending on the direction of the wind, causing significant negative pressure. For detailed analysis, please refer to 3.11.

⑶ Understanding Wall Deterioration Using Time-Series Data

Bayon's Inner and Outer Galleries have valuable bas-relief, which have been deteriorating significantly in recent years. Therefore, we analyzed the deterioration using time-series 3D data. The bas-reliefs at Bayon undergo significant surface changes over months and years due to natural or human-induced damage. JASA's research team identified 13 wall locations for monitoring, and we have measured regularly over seven years to visualize the differences and understand the deterioration quantitatively.

然或いは人的な要因による損傷によって数ヶ月から数年の間に表面形状が大きく変化する。そこで，壁面の13ヶ所を研究グループ内で設定し，7年間に渡って定期的に3D計測を行い，差異を量的に可視化することによって劣化状況を把握することとした。

異なる時期に計測した壁面の表面形状データを位置合わせし，最近傍点間距離を計算することによって，差異つまり劣化度合いを求めることができる。Fig. 3.10.8の各画像は上から，計測箇所の写真，2020年3月の形状データ，2014年と2016年の形状変化，2016年と2020年の形状変化である。形状変化は距離を色で示してあり，緑色部分はほとんど差がなく，赤色部分は変化が大きい，つまりこの期間で欠けた部分を意味している。最大誤差は5mmに設定してあり，5mm以上の誤差は赤色で示されている。

対象箇所では剥離によって失われた部分が少なからずあることが分かる。また2016年からさらに剥離が進んでおり，早急な対応が必要であると考えられる。全体を場所別にみると，外回廊の特に低い位置において劣化が他の箇所よりも早く進んでいることが分かる。これは石材の剥離現象が，浸透した水に起因するものであり，回廊の下部では水分が長時間残留しやすいことが理由であると考えられる。浅浮彫保存の詳細については3.8を参照されたい。

4. まとめ

本項では，バイヨンを対象として，文化財の3Dデジタル化技術，解析技術について紹介した。レーザレンジセンサによる大規模構造物の3Dデータ取得方法として，回廊を計測するレールセンサやローバ型センサシステム，高所を計測するためのバルーンセンサ，多量の距離画像を処理して最終的な3Dデータを得る手法について解説した。さらに3Dデータを用いた多数の尊顔の分類や，3Dプリンタを用いて製作した模型を用いた風洞実験，浅浮彫の経年劣化の可視化について紹介した。

これまで我々は，バイヨンだけでなく，アンコール・ワットやプレア・ヴィヘア[13]，サンボー・プレイ・クック遺跡群など様々な遺跡の3Dデジタル化を手掛けてきた。これらのデータは，カンボジア政府機関APSARAやJASAによって今後も広く活用されていくことが予想される。また考古，建築，美術史といった分野と連携して3Dデータを解析することによって，これまで明らかにされなかった新たな知見を得ることが可能となってきている。今後も技術開発に加えて，様々な分野との連携

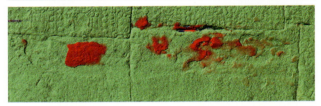
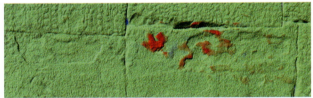

Fig. 3.10.8 Visualization of Bas-Reliefs' Ablation Conditions

By aligning the surface shape data of the walls measured at different times and calculating the nearest neighbor point distances, it is possible to determine the differences, i.e., the degree of deterioration. The images in Fig. 3.10.8 show, from top to bottom, photographs of the measurement locations, the shape data from March 2020, the shape changes between 2014 and 2016, and the shape changes between 2016 and 2020. The color indicates the shape changes, where green areas show little difference, and the red regions indicate significant change, meaning these parts have eroded during the period. We set the maximum error at 5mm, with errors exceeding 5mm indicated in red.

We can see areas where some pieces are missing due to abrasion. The deterioration has progressed further since 2016, suggesting an urgent need for action. A site-wide comparison reveals that the lower areas of the Outer Gallery deteriorate faster than other parts. We think it is due to the stone abrasion phenomenon caused by water infiltration, with moisture tending to remain longer in the lower parts of the gallery. For more details on bas-relief preservation, please refer to 3.8.

4. Conclusion

This paper introduced the 3D digitalization and analysis technologies for cultural heritage, focusing on the Bayon. We described methods for acquiring 3D data of large structures

を深めることで学際的な研究を推進していくことが重要であると考えられる。さらに，得られた技術や知見，データが観光や教育に役立てられることを期待したい。

using laser range sensors, including the rail sensor and rover-type sensor systems for measuring corridors, balloon sensors for measuring high areas, and methods for processing numerous depth images to obtain final 3D data. Additionally, we introduced the classification of multiple faces using 3D data, wind tunnel experiments using a model made with a 3D printer, and visualization of the age-related deterioration of bas-relief.

We have conducted the 3D digitization of various sites, including the Bayon, Angkor Wat, Preah Vihear[13], and the Sambor Prei Kuk Monuments. We expect the Cambodian and Japanese government agencies APSARA and JASA to use this data effectively in the future. Furthermore, by collaborating with other research fields such as archaeology, architecture, and art history to analyze 3D data, it has become possible to gain new insights that were not previously evident. It is essential to continue technological development and deepen collaboration with various research fields to promote interdisciplinary research. Additionally, we know that the acquired technologies, insights, and data will benefit future conservation efforts as well as tourism and education.

References

1) 池内克史，大石岳史 (編著), 3次元デジタルアーカイブ，東京大学出版会，2010.11.

2) K. Ikeuchi, K. Hasegawa, A. Nakazawa, J. Takamatsu, T. Oishi and T. Masuda, "Bayon Digital Archival Project," Proc. the Tenth Int'l Conf. Virtual System and Multimedia, pages 334-343, November 2004.

3) B. Zheng, T. Oishi, K. Ikeuchi, "Rail Sensor: A Moving Lidar System for 3D Archiving the Bas-reliefs in Angkor Wat," IPSJ Trans. Computer Vision and Applications, Vol. 7, pp. 59-63, July 27, 2015.

4) R. Ishikawa, M. Roxas, Y. Sato, T. Oishi, T. Masuda, K. Ikeuchi, "A 3D Reconstruction with High Density and Accuracy using Laser Profiler and Camera Fusion System on a Rover," International Conference on 3D Vision (3DV), pp. 620-628, Oct 27, 2016.

5) A. Banno, T. Masuda, T. Oishi and K. Ikeuchi, "Flying laser range sensor for large-scale site-modeling and its applications in Bayon digital Archival project," Int. J. Computer Vision, (78):207-222, 2008.

6) B. Zheng, X. Huang, R. Ishikawa, T. Oishi, K. Ikeuchi, "A New Flying Range Sensor: Aerial Scan in Omini-directions," 3DV, 2015.

7) R. Ishikawa, B. Zheng, T. Oishi, K. Ikeuchi, "Rectification of Aerial 3D Laser Scans via Line-based Registration to Ground Model," IPSJ Trans. Computer Vision and Applications, Vol. 7, pp. 89-93, July 27, 2015.

8) T. Oishi, R. Sagawa, A. Nakazawa, R. Kurazume and K. Ikeuchi, "Parallel alignment of a large number of range images on PC cluster," 3DIM, 2003.

9) T. Oishi, A. Nakazawa and R. Kurazume, K. Ikeuchi, "Fast simultaneous alignment of multiple range images using index images," 3DIM, 2005.

10) 朴亨國，浅井和春："バイヨンの四面塔に関する二・三の考察－彫刻史的アプローチによる－,"アンコール遺跡調査報告書1998, 中川武 (監修)，pp.275-306,（財）日本国際協力センター，1998.

11) M. Kamakura, T. Oishi, J. Takamatsu and K. Ikeuchi, "Classification of Bayon faces using 3D models," VSMM, 2005.

12) S. Yamada, M. Araya, A. Yoshida, T. Oishi, "Structural stability evaluation study applying wind tunnel test and monitoring of Bayon main tower, Angkor Thom in Cambodia," Structural Studies, Repairs and Maintenance of Heritage Architecture XV, WIT Transactions on The Built Environment, 171, 287-296, 2017.

13) M. Kamakura, H. Ikuta, B. Zheng, Y. Sato, M. Kagesawa, T. Oishi, K. Sezaki, T. Nakagawa, K. Ikeuchi, "Preah Vihear Project: Obtaining 3D point-cloud data and its application to spatial distribution analysis of Khmer temples," In 3rd ACM SIGSPATIAL International Workshop on Geospatial Humanities (GeoHumanities'19), Article No. 5, pp. 1–9, November 5, 2019.

3.11 バイヨンの建築構造学
Structural Mechanic Research of Bayon

山田 俊亮　　　橋本 涼太　　　小山 倫史
YAMADA Shunsuke　　HASHIMOTO Ryota　　KOYAMA Tomofumi

1. アンコール地域と空積み構造

　バイヨンの上部構造は，砂岩の空積みによる構造である。空積みの塔の建造過程では，石を積み安定性を確認しながら建造することとなる。石材間には，接合材等は用いないので，組積した状態が建物の安定性となる。現代建築で用いられる鉄筋コンクリート造は，鉄筋の引張強度に依存した構造形式であり，鉄筋が錆びて引張応力を負担できなくなると強度が失われる。空積みでは，石を積み重力だけで安定化させているので，永久性のある構造形式であるとも言える。

　一般的に，構造形式に応じて，不同沈下による傾斜角の許容量があり，許容量を超えると亀裂が生じ，場合によっては塔体の崩壊の原因となる。空積みは，水平目地間の開閉および鉛直目地間のズレで不同沈下による応力を分散する。この石材を積んだだけなので弱いと思われる構造は，砂と石材で造られた基礎の上に長い歴史にわたって建造物を存続させることを考えると耐久性が高いとも言える。

　空積みの最大の弱点は，地震に弱いことであろう。重さに比例して慣性力として作用する地震力に対しては，空積みのみで抵抗することは難しい。アンコール遺跡のある地域は地震リスクが低い地域である。バイヨンの構造形式は，クメールの長い歴史の中で，地震が無い環境であることにも大きく起因して育まれた構造形式であると捉えている。バイヨンの保存修復設計においては，上述のように地震リスクは低く，想定される水平力は風である。風圧力は風を受ける受圧面積に応じて大きくなるが，形態に応じて風圧力は変動する。また，重量が大きいことは風に対しては安定性が高くなる。6.2で後述するが，バイヨン中央塔を対象とした風洞試験を実施した。その結果からは，複雑な形状を有する主塔上部の風圧力

1. Angkor Area and Dry Masonry

The superstructure of the Bayon is a dry masonry structure. In the process of building a dry masonry tower, the stones are stacked and checked for stability. Since no joint materials are used between the stones, the stability of the building is determined by the state of the stacked stones. Reinforced concrete construction used in modern buildings is a structural form that relies on the tensile strength of the steel bars, and if the bars rust and are unable to bear tensile stress, strength is lost. In dry masonry, stones are stacked and stabilized by gravity alone, and it can be said to be a permanent structural form.

Generally, there is an allowable amount of inclination due to unequal settlement depending on the structural type, and if the allowable amount is exceeded, cracks will occur, possibly causing collapse. By unequal settlement, dry masonry distributes the stresses by opening and closing the horizontal and vertical joints. This structure, which seems weak because it is only stacked with stones, can be said to be durable considering the long history of the building's existence on a foundation made of sandy soil with minimum stone support.

Perhaps the most significant weakness of dry masonry is its lack of resistance to earthquakes. It is difficult for dry masonry to resist seismic forces, which act as inertial forces in proportion to its weight. The area of the Angkor Monuments is a region with a low seismic risk. The structure of the Bayon is considered to be a structural form that was developed in the long history of the Khmer culture, in large part due to the earthquake-free environment. In the conservation and restoration design of Bayon, the seismic risk is low as described above, and the assumed horizontal force is wind. The wind pressure force increases with the pressure-receiving area of the structure, but it is variable depending on the form of the structure. In addition, high weight means high stability against wind. As described later in chapter 6.2, wind tunnel

は，一般的な四角形平面や円形平面よりも風圧力は低い結果であることが示された。加えて，風圧力が大きくなりやすい主塔の隅角部は既に崩落して失われている。このことは，高層ビル等で風圧力を低減するための隅角部の隅切のような効果を生じていることも分かった。今の主塔の形態というのは，風工学的に見ても興味深いものである。

2．構造研究と修復

　修復においては，当初のクメール遺構としての構造分析，そしてそれらが数百年の時を経て，現在に至るまでに生じた変状の分析，EFEO（フランス極東学院）を中心とする過去の修復の分析，といった複合的な分析が必要となる。さらには，バイヨンは，改変による複雑な建造過程を有している。JASAでは，緻密な分析を通じて，修復を行う。鉄骨材や木材で，応急的に補強を行うこともあるが，それらは材料の耐久年数の観点からも仮設のものである。バイヨンの変状においては，長い年月の間，忘れられた密林に埋もれた遺跡であった，という点が大きな事象である。樹木が遺跡を覆い，崩落や目地開きなど様々な変状を生じている。石材間の目地開きを生じると，石材同士の接触により伝達していた力が伝達されなくなり，不安定化の原因となりうる。こうした変状においては，積み直しや新材での補填を行いながら，時間をかけて丁寧に修復することが求められる。数百年を経て生じた変状を巻き戻すような長い年月を要する修復作業である。

　空積みは構造解析の点からは，不連続体を扱う工学となり，鉄やコンクリートを用いて一体化した連続体として扱われる現代建築よりも，工学的には高度な解析技術が求められる。石材間の圧縮力は石材間の接触により伝達され，せん断強度は摩擦力に依存するという非線形現象を扱うこととなる。これまでJASAではそれら構造解析に関する研究開発もはじめ，構造分野においても様々な研究がなされてきた。代表的なものを列挙すると，岩崎・福田らは，前述の地盤系の各種実験・対策手法の開発に加え，遺跡の挙動のモニタリングと併せて環境・地盤系のモニタリングを実施し遺跡の挙動観測手法について展開してきた。前田らは，遺跡の微動測定からの遺跡の振動特性の分析や不連続変形法などの離散体力学の適用についての研究を展開してきた。小山・橋本らは，地盤と上部構造の連成解析手法を中心に，不連続変形法などの離散体力学手法の高度化を中心に進めてきた。新谷・山田らは，各種モニタリングや実験，不連続変形法

tests were conducted on the Central Tower of the Bayon. The results showed that wind forces at the top of the main tower, which has a complex shape, resulted in lower wind forces than for a typical square or circular plane. In addition, the corners of the Central Tower, where wind pressure forces tend to be higher, have already collapsed and been lost. This was also found to produce an effect similar to that of corner cutting at corner angles to reduce wind pressure forces in high-rise buildings. The current form of the main tower is interesting from a wind engineering point of view.

2. Structural Research and Restoration

　Restoration requires complex analysis such as structural analysis of the original Khmer monuments, analysis of the deformations that occurred over several hundred years up to the present, and analysis of past restorations led by EFEO. Furthermore, the Bayon has a complex construction process due to alterations and addition. JASA carries out restoration through detailed analysis. Although some temporary reinforcement using steel or timber may be used, these are temporary from the standpoint of the durability of the materials. The main reason for the deterioration of the Bayon is that the ruins were buried in the jungle for a long period of time. Trees covered the ruins, causing various deformations such as collapses and joint openings. When joints open between stones, the force transmitted by the contact between stones is no longer transmitted, and this will cause unstable conditions. Such deformations must be carefully repaired over time, either by restacking the stones or replacing them with new materials. This restoration work requires a long time, as if the deformation that has occurred over several hundred years is being rolled back.

　From the standpoint of structural analysis, dry masonry is an engineering process that deals with discontinuities, and requires a more advanced engineering analysis technique than modern architecture, which is treated as a continuous structure made of steel and concrete. The compressive force between stones is transmitted by the contact between stones, and the shear strength depends on the frictional force, which is a nonlinear phenomenon. JASA has conducted various studies in the structural engineering field, including research and development related to structural analysis. Representative examples are: Iwasaki and Fukuda et al. have developed methods of conducting environmental and geotechnical monitoring in addition to the development of various experimental and countermeasure methods for geotechnical systems mentioned above. Maeda et al. have analyzed the vibration characteristics of ruins based on microtremor measurements and applied discrete mechanics, such as the discontinuous deformation analysis method. Koyama and Hashimoto et al. have focused on the advancement of discrete

3.11　バイヨンの建築構造学　135

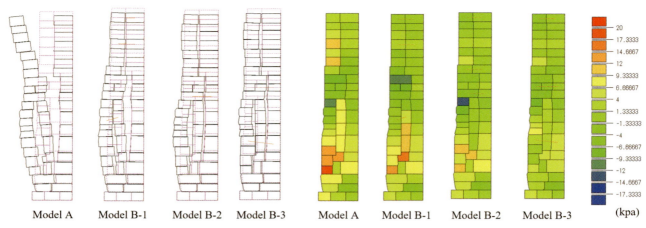

Fig. 3.11.1 Deformation diagram and shear stress diagram

の補強設計手法への応用を進め，具体的な補強手法の開発などを進めてきた。

　離散体力学の一種である不連続変形法（Discontinuous Deformation Analysis，以下DDA）を修復設計へと応用した構造解析の例として以下に記述する。バイヨン中央塔の中層のギャラリーレベルの石積みを対象に強風を想定した水平力載荷の解析により補強設計について検討した例である。この検証では，主に石材の崩壊前の水平耐力，補強材に作用する応力，石材の応力を評価し補強方法の検討を行った。空積みの石積みを要素ごとに弾性ブロックの離散体としてモデル化し，補強部材は要素間を接続するバネ要素としてモデル化している。強風時の風荷重を想定して石積みの片側に水平荷重を徐々に増加し解析を行う条件である。Model Aは補強なしの現状を想定した解析モデルとし，Model B-1，Model B-2，Model B-3にはいずれも異なる3ヶ所の補強箇所を想定した解析モデルである。この補強材については鎹やロックボルトを想定したものである。最終荷重後の各モデルの変位図およびせん断応力図をFig. 3.11.1に示す。補強材が無い解析モデルでは，全体が崩れ下部の石材に高い応力が発生する変形が見られる。その他の補強を想定した解析モデルでは，全体が崩れる変形が抑制され，補強位置の違いにより，異なる変形モードと応力分布を示している。このように，石積みの構造解析手法や補強設計手法の研究開発も進められた。

　バイヨンをはじめアンコール遺跡の修復においては，上部構造と地盤・基礎構造の連生問題が重要な因子となる。プラサート・スープラN1塔は，基壇の変形に伴う上部構造の傾斜が大きな課題となり，修復が成された例であるが，バイヨンの修復においても，地盤・基礎構造の状態が上部構造にもたらす影響については，重要な事項である。空積みの上部構造と基礎構造の相互作用下での安定性を検討したものとして，NMM-DDAによる安

mechanics methods such as the discontinuous deformation analysis method, focusing on the coupled analysis method of ground and superstructure. Araya and Yamada et al. have advanced the application of the discontinuous deformation analysis method to reinforcement design methods, and have developed monitoring method, experiments and reinforcement methods.

　The following is an example of structural analysis in which Discontinuous Deformation Analysis (DDA), a type of discrete mechanics, is applied to reinforcement design. This is an example of a study on the reinforcement design of a mid-level gallery-level masonry of the Central Tower of the Bayon by analyzing the horizontal force loading under the assumption of strong winds. In this verification, the horizontal bearing capacity of the masonry before collapse, the stress acting on the reinforcement, and the stress of the masonry were mainly evaluated and the reinforcement method was studied. The dry masonry is modeled as a discrete body of elastic blocks for each element, and the reinforcement members are modeled as connecting spring elements that connect the elements. Model A is an analytical model assuming the existing condition without reinforcement, and Model B-1, Model B-2, and Model B-3 are analytical models assuming three different reinforcement locations. For these reinforcements, clamps and rock bolts were assumed. The displacement and shear stress diagrams for each model after final load are shown in Fig. 3.11.1. The result with no reinforcement, shows deformation that results in total collapse and high stresses in the lower stone. The others, which are assumed to be reinforced, show different deformation modes and stress distributions depending on the reinforcement location. Thus, the actual restoration has been carried out while research and development of structural analysis methods and reinforcement design methods for masonry have also been carried out.

　In the restoration of Angkor Monuments, including Bayon, the coupling of the superstructure and the ground and foundation structures is an important factor. The Prasat Suor Prat N1 Tower is an example of a restoration that was

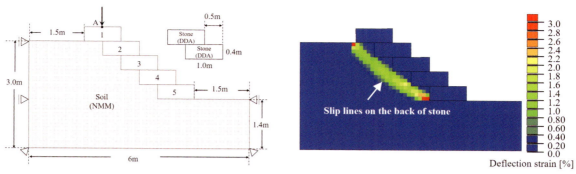

Fig. 3.11.2 Analysis of deformation and destruction loading from the upper structure on the platform (Hashimoto et.al)

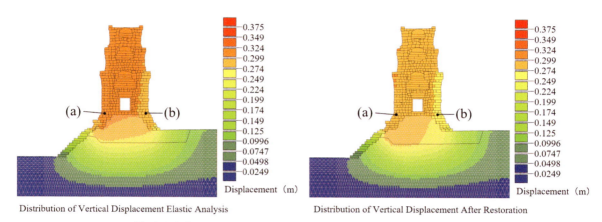

Fig. 3.11.3 Coupled analysis of upper structure and ground for Prasat Sour Prat N1 Tower (Hashimoto et.al)

定解析について以下に記す。DDAとNMM (Numerical Manifold Method) は，不連続体の力学解析手法であり，NMM-DDAはDDAとNMMの連成解析を可能にした手法である。上部構造の空積みの不連続性に加え，版築土および基礎地盤の変形・破壊，そして石材と地盤の相互作用を評価するには，石材の挙動を適切に再現できる離散体モデルと地盤材料の応力―ひずみ特性を反映できる連続体モデルの連成解析手法が求められる。その要件を満足し得る手法としてNMM-DDAの適用が試みられた。

Fig. 3.11.2は，DDAで石材，NMMで盛土を表すことでアンコール遺跡の基壇構造を模擬したモデルにて，上部荷重 (点Aに作用) の影響により生じる基壇への影響を評価した例である。上段の石材の角を起点として地盤内部に滑りを生じて破壊する様子が見て取れる。バイヨンにおいても同様な基壇構造が見られるが，このような数値解析を通じて，基壇が土の強度と石材の摩擦によって耐力を発揮していることや，雨水の浸透が変状の進行の一因となり，遮水などの対策が必要であることが示唆されている。

Fig. 3.11.3は，プラサート・スープラN1塔を対象として上部構造と基礎・地盤構造を連成解析により評価した例であり，基壇および基礎地盤の変形の影響で塔体の傾斜を生じる原因について解析的に検証している。また

carried out due to the inclination of the superstructure caused by the deformation of the foundation. DDA (Discontinuous Deformation Analysis) and NMM (Numerical Manifold Method) are two methods of mechanical analysis of discontinuous bodies. NMM-DDA is a method that enables coupled analysis of DDA and NMM. In order to evaluate the deformation and failure of the soil and foundation structures, as well as the interaction between the stone and the ground, in addition to the discontinuity of the dry masonry of the superstructure, a coupled analysis method of a discrete model that can appropriately simulate the behavior of the stone and a continuum model that can reflect the stress-strain characteristics of the ground materials is required. NMM-DDA was applied to satisfy this requirement.

Fig. 3.11.2 shows an example of evaluating the effect of the upper load (acting on point A) on the platform structure of the Angkor site, which is simulated by using DDA to represent the stone material and NMM to represent the soil. It can be seen that the upper stone slides into the ground starting from the corner of the upper stone and destroys it. This kind of numerical analysis suggests that the platform is resistant to the soil strength and the friction of the stones, and that rainwater infiltration is a factor in the progression of deformation, necessitating measures such as interception of water.

Fig. 3.11.3 shows an example of a coupled analysis of the superstructure and ground and foundation structures of a Prasat Suor Prat N1 tower, and analytically verifies the

Fig. 3.11.4 View of experiment
(Left: Stone friction test at Siem Reap office, Right: Anchor strength test at Waseda University laboratory)

Fig. 3.11.5 Strength test of reinforced beam (left) and repaired beam (right)

基壇内部の盛土の消石灰改良の有無による強度の違いが塔体の沈下を抑制する結果となっている。岩崎らが3.12でも述べているように，アンコール遺跡においては，この基礎・地盤構造と上部構造の関係性は修復において重要な事項である。そのためJASAでは，建築構造および地盤構造の専門家らが共同で研究を進めながら，修復は進められている。

　構造解析手法について前述したが，強度等に関する各種の実験も行いながら修復は進められてきた。現地事務所での簡易的な試験から，日本の実験室での試験など様々な実験を行ってきた (Fig. 3.11.4)。例として，57塔周辺の修復の際に行った実験について記述する。57塔開口部窓枠の梁の多くは，割れ，亀裂などを有し，20世紀前半にEFEOによるコンクリート補強が施されるなどの対策がなされていたが，修復が必要な状態であった。57塔を中心とするエリアが整備される経緯となり，損傷箇所の強化，EFEOのコンクリート補強を外す，ことなどを目的に梁にステンレス材を挿入し補強する方針となった。そこで，補強による砂岩材の梁の性能確認，な

cause of the tower tilting due to deformation of the base and foundation structures. The analysis also shows that the improvement of the strength of the embankment inside the base by slaked lime suppressed the settlement of the tower. As Iwasaki et al. stated in this book, Chapter 3.12, the relationship between the ground and foundation structures and the superstructure is an important issue in the restoration of Angkor Monuments. Therefore, JASA is proceeding with the restoration while specialists in architectural and geotechnical structures are collaborating in the research.

　As mentioned above for the structural analysis method, the restoration has been carried out while also conducting various experiments on strength and other aspects of the restoration. Various tests were conducted, ranging from simple tests at the local office to laboratory tests in Japan (Fig. 3.11.4). The beams of the window frames of Tower 57 of Bayon had cracks and splits, and although concrete reinforcement by EFEO was applied in the first half of the 20th century, they were in need of restoration. The plan was to reinforce the damaged areas and remove EFEO concrete reinforcement by inserting stainless steel in the beams. Therefore, bending tests of the reinforced beams were conducted to confirm the performance

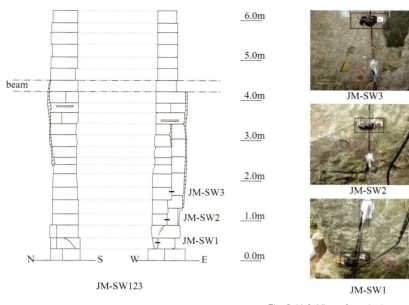

Fig. 3.11.6 View of crack observation

of the reinforced sandstone beams and to compare the results with the calculated results based on the design formula (Fig. 3.11.5). Since the tests generally confirmed the performance of the beams and confirmed the consistency with the design formula, the repair of Tower 57 openings by reinforcing the beams with stainless steel was carried out.

Monuments are constantly in motion, though invisibly, in response to natural phenomena such as rainfall and solar radiation. There are two types of behaviors: reversible and non-reversible. In the case of daily natural phenomena, the behavior is basically reversible, but heavy rains and strong winds occurring within several decades can cause non-reversible behavior, i.e., displacement spreading, cracking, etc. These behaviors are accumulated, and the present deformation is the result of the accumulation of such deformations. Iwasaki and Fukuda et al. have conducted observation and evaluation of the behavior of Prasat Suor Prat N1 tower, which was restored by JASA in the early stages of the project, as well as of measures to be taken at other Angkor Monuments. Various observation evaluations have been conducted at the Bayon, and the Middle Gallery level of the Central Tower has been continuously observed (Fig. 3.11.6). Using the environmental factor data, the analytical model was extended by clarifying the relationship between air temperature and surface temperature, and rainfall and surface moisture content, to examine the degree of influence of the environmental factors at the measured locations where monitoring was conducted. Thus, restoration is proceeded by analyzing the causes of deformation from the observations and analyzing appropriate countermeasures.

3. Superstructure of the Central Tower

In restoration design, it is necessary to analyze the original design concept and structural form. In the case of the Central Tower, the structural technology and design concept of the time remain to be clarified. One part of this is described below, using 3D laser scan data (Ikeuchi and Oishi Laboratory, University of Tokyo) and 3D photogrammetry data (Architectural History Laboratory, Waseda University) of the Central Tower, which has a complex shape.

Fig. 3.11.7 shows the exterior view of the Central Tower, Fig. 3.11.8 shows the composition of the Central Tower and upper stories, and Fig. 3.11.9 shows the composition of the walls extracted at representative heights. The Central

らびに設計式にもとづく計算値との比較を目的として，補強された梁の曲げ試験を行った（Fig. 3.11.5）。試験により概ね性能が確認され，設計式との整合も確認できたことから，57塔開口部の梁のステンレス材の補強による修復は実施された。

　遺跡は降雨や日射などの自然現象に応じて，目には見えないほどではあるが常に動いている。挙動には，可逆的な挙動と非可逆的な挙動がある。日常的な自然現象であれば，基本的には可逆的な挙動であるが，数十年に一度というような豪雨や強風が生じれば，非可逆的な挙動，すなわち変位の進展や亀裂の発生等を生じうる。それらの挙動が蓄積されて，現在の変状を生じている。岩崎・福田らは，JASAが初期に修復を行ったプラサート・スープラ等での挙動観測をはじめ，アンコール遺跡群における対策を講じるにあたり，観測による評価を実施してきた。バイヨンにおいても様々な観測による評価を実施しているが，バイヨン中央塔の中段のギャラリーレベルにおいては，継続的に観測を実施してきた（Fig. 3.11.6）。山田らもバイヨン中央塔のギャラリーレベルの観測や分析手法の研究などを実施し，環境因子データを用いて，気温と表面温度，降雨と表面含水率の関係を明示することで分析モデルの拡張を行い，モニタリングを実施した計測箇所においての環境因子の影響度の検討なども進められた。観測から変状の原因を分析し，適切な対策を分析しながら修復は進められている。

3. 中央塔の上部構造について

修復設計においては，本来の設計思想や構造形式の分析を通じた設計が求められる。中央塔においては，未だ解明しきれていない当時の構造技術や設計思想が背景にある。その一端について，複雑な形態を有する中央塔の3Dレーザースキャンデータ（東京大学池内・大石研究室）および3Dフォトグラメトリーデータ（早稲田大学建築史研究室）を用いて以下に記述する。

Fig. 3.11.7に中央塔の外観図，Fig. 3.11.8に中央塔および上層部の構成，Fig. 3.11.9に代表的な高さで抽出した壁体の構成，を示す。中央塔は主塔とその周囲を取り囲む8つの副塔から構成されている。主塔の最も内側の壁は垂直に頂上まで約30m程，空積みにより立ち上がっている。最も高い主塔の下部の石材にかかる圧縮応力は1〜2N/㎟程度と推定され，砂岩の圧縮強度に対しては十分な余裕度である。空積みは，建造過程においても石材間の引張強度には期待することができない，石材間の圧縮力のみで力を伝達し安定する構造である。この構造形式は，材料劣化等による引張強度の低下の影響を受けにくい構造形式であり，遺跡の永続性にこの空積みの構造形式が寄与している。主塔低層部の仏陀像が置かれた中心部の内壁は東西に長い扁平な楕円状の平面であり，高層部になると内壁は四角形状の平面となる。これは，中層部で迫り出し構造により幅を狭めながら四角形状の平面となるよう組積されている。また，東西方向の開口部の柱梁には，応力を低減するよう迫り出し構造を用いて南北の壁体に力が流れるよう組積されている（Fig. 3.11.10）。このように東西南北で対称な構造ではなく，複雑な構成を実現する組積は，極めて緻密に立体的に計画されている。低層部は主塔と副塔とが複雑に一体化されており，平面的に放射状に配置された8つの副塔は主塔の安定に寄与している。この形式により放射状に配置された壁は，石と土で構成される基壇の上に，高い塔を建造する上では，合理的である。

8つの副塔は，東西南北の4つの副塔と，その間に配置された4つの副塔とで構成が異なる。東西南北の4つの副塔は，低層部において通路としての開口を有する構成であり，北東・南東・南西・北西に配置された4つの副塔とは構成が異なる。更に，この8つの副塔間の低層部には，副塔同士を連結する8つの小空間がある。また，副塔の頂部は，中央塔の中層部にて空中回廊とよばれる柱・梁を円周上に配置した構造により主塔および副塔同士が連結されている。中央塔は以上の様な主塔と副塔の

Tower consists of a main tower and eight sub-towers around it. The inner wall of the main tower rises vertically to the top by dry masonry for about 30 meters. The compressive stress on the stones at the bottom of the tallest main tower is estimated to be about 1~2 N/mm², which is adequate compared to the compressive strength of the sandstone. Dry masonry is a structure in which forces are transmitted and stabilized only by compressive forces between stones, with no expectation of tensile strength between stones during the construction process. This type of structure is less susceptible to deterioration of tensile strength due to material degradation, etc., and this dry masonry type of structure contributes to the durability of the ruins. The inner wall of the central part where the Great Buddha was placed in the lower part of the main tower is a long, flat, oval-shaped plan from east to west, and in the upper part, the inner wall becomes a square-shaped plan. This is assembled to become a square-shaped plane while narrowing its width with the use of corbel arches in the middle section. The columns and beams of the east-west openings are constructed with corbel arches to reduce stresses so that the forces flow to the north-south walls (Fig. 3.11.10). The structure is not symmetrical in cardinal directions, but the masonry is carefully planned three-dimensionally to achieve a complex configuration. In the lower section, the Central Tower and sub-towers are complexly united, and the eight sub-towers, arranged radially in plan, contribute to the stability of the Central Tower. This form of radially arranged walls is reasonable for building a tall tower on a base composed of stone and sandy soil.

The eight sub-towers differ in configuration, with the four sub-towers located in cardinal directions and the sub-towers located between them. The configuration of the four sub-towers which they have openings as passageways at the lower levels in cardinal directions are different from the others between them. Furthermore, there are eight small spaces connecting the sub-towers at the lower level. The tops of the sub-towers are connected to the Central Tower and the sub-towers by a structure called an Aerial gallery, which consists of columns and beams arranged in a circle in the middle of the Central Tower. The Central Tower is composed of a group of main and secondary towers as described above, and the stability is enhanced by connecting the towers together.

As described above, the complex structure of the Central Tower was outlined by shape analysis using 3D laser scan data. This complex shape has a significant relationship with structural stability, and without analysis of this point, the conservation and restoration of the Central Tower will not be possible. A detailed structural engineering analysis and specific policies for the conservation and restoration of the Central Tower are described in Chapter 6.2 below.

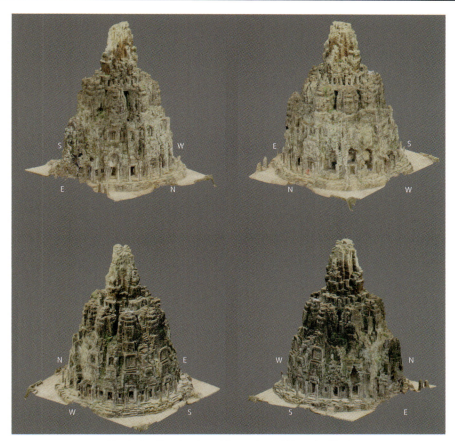

Fig. 3.11.7 Exterior view of Bayon Central Tower by 3D photogrammetry

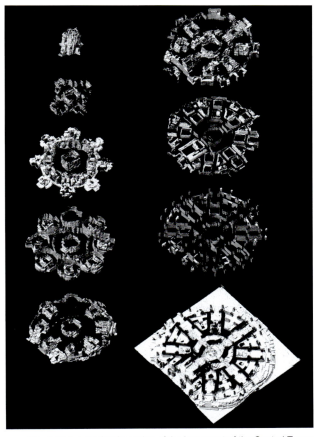

Fig. 3.11.8 Left: Configuration of the lower part of the Central Tower, Right: Configuration of the upper part of the Central Tower

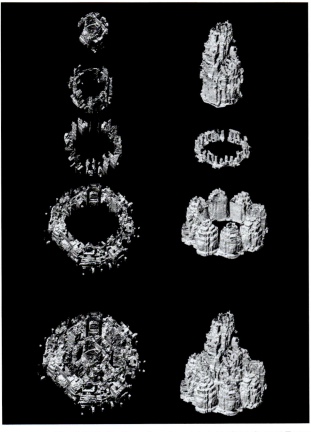

Fig. 3.11.9 Configuration at each height of the Central Tower

3.11 バイヨンの建築構造学 141

塔群で構成されており，塔同士を連結することで安定性を高める構成となっている。

　以上のように，3Dレーザースキャンデータを用いた形状分析により，複雑な中央塔の構造について概説した。この複雑な形状は，構造的な安定性とも大きく関係しており，これらの分析を基に，中央塔の保存修復計画は進められている。中央塔の保存修復の具体的な方針などについては，後の6.2にて記述している。

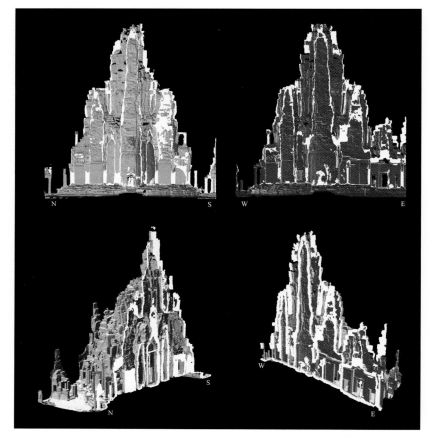

Fig. 3.11.10 Cross section of the Central Tower

References

1) S.Yamada, M..Araya, A.Yoshida, T.Oishi, "Structural stability evaluation study applying a wind tunnel test and monitoring of Bayon main tower, Angkor Thom, Cambodia", WIT Transactions on the Built Environment , vol.171, pp.287-296, 2017
2) Y.Honda, S.Yamada, A.Yoshida, T.Oishi, M.Araya, Y.Tamura, "New Manufacturing Method of Wind Pressure Model for Complicated-Shape Architectural Heritage Applying 3D Scanning Data and 3D Printer", Journal of Wind Engineering, 2016, Volume 41, Issue 1, pp.24-27, 2016
3) R.Hashimoto, K.Kawakami, M.Mimura, "Development of Soil-Water coupled NMM-DDA considering Unsaturated Seepage", Journal of Japan Society of Civil Engineers, Japan Society of Civil Engineers, vol.73, pp199-21-2017
4) R.Hashimoto, T.Koyama, M.Kikumoto, S.Yamada, M.Araya, Y.Iwasaki, Y.Ohnishi, Application of coupled elasto-plastic NMM–DDA procedure for the stability analysis of Prasat Suor Prat N1 Tower, Geosystem Engineering, vol.16(1), pp.62-74, 2013
5) T.Maeda, "Vibration Observations", Report on the Conservation Research of the Bayon, JASA, Tokyo pp.90-101, 2011
6) S.Yamada, R.Hashimoto, T.Koyama, M.Fukuda, Y.Iwasaki. "Study on evaluation method of reinforcement effect of dry masonry in historical monuments applying DDA", International conference of structural analysis of historical construction, 2023
7) Y.Iwasaki, M.Fukuda, T.Fujiwara, "Geotechnical Study during Dismantling of Southern Library, Bayon temple and Structural Monitoring", Annual Technical Report on the Survey of Angkor Monument 2007, JASA, Tokyo pp.101-116, 2007
8) Y.Iwasaki, I.Yamamoto, M.Araya, "Stabilization of the Central Tower and Countermeasures for Long Term", The Bayon Master Plan, JASA, Tokyo pp.206-222, 2005
9) A. Banno, T. Masuda, T. Oishi and K. Ikeuchi, "Flying Laser Range Sensor for Large-Scale Site-Modeling and Its Applications in Bayon Digital Archival Project," International Journal of Computer Vision, Vol. 78, No. 2-3, pp. 207-222, Jul. 2008.
10) K. Ikeuchi, K. Hasegawa, A. Nakazawa, J. Takamatsu, T. Oishi and T.Masuda, "Bayon Digital Archival Project," Proc. the Tenth Int'l Conf. Virtual System and Multimedia (VSMM), pages 334-343, November 2004.

3.12 バイヨンの地盤工学
Geotechnical Engineering of Bayon

岩崎 好規　　福田 光治　　ロバート・マッカーシー
IWASAKI Yoshinori　FUKUDA Mitsuharu　Robert McCarthy

1. 地盤特性と基礎構造

Fig. 3.12.1にバイヨンの平面図と概略断面，ボーリング位置，および内回廊から外回廊に至る基壇表面を外回廊の外側の地盤に至るまで伸ばしてのロングトレンチ掘削調査位置を示した。Fig. 3.12.2にボーリングを含む断面図を示した。バイヨンの北ヤードにおけるボーリング結果によれば，地表面から約35mまでシルト質～粘土質砂層で，以深は風化凝灰岩層が続いている。

地下水位は，表層水と深層水とに分かれているが，双方ともに雨季の終期にはほぼ地表面近くまでとなり，乾季には表層水は蒸発により，深層水は飲料用，農業用などの人工的な揚水により水面低下となっている。

雨季には標準貫入試験によるN値は，深度と共に増加するが，乾季には地表付近のN値はN＝20程度まで増大する。これは，含水比低下による強度の増加によるものである。

1. Geotechnical Characteristics and Foundation Structure

Geological boring and long trench excavation from the Inner Gallery to outside of the Outer Gallery at the northern area in the Bayon are shown in Fig. 3.12.1. Vertical section is shown in Fig. 3.12.2 with the results of boring, which revealed the ground consists of silty to clayey sand down to GL-35m followed by weathered tuff.

Underground water consists of the surface and deeper water with different levels; however, both show the water levels extend to the ground surface at the end of the rainy season. In the dry season, both water levels decrease by evaporation for the surface and by pumping the deeper water respectively.

SPT, N-values increases with depth in the rainy season. The N-values at the top surface increase from N=0(rainy season) to N=20(dry season). This is caused by the increase of the strength by decreasing water contents by drying.

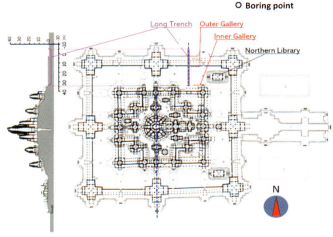

Fig. 3.12.1 Plan of Bayon

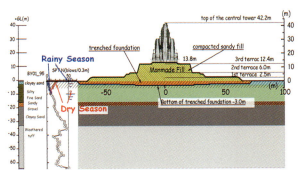

Fig. 3.12.2 Vertical section of foundation of Bayon

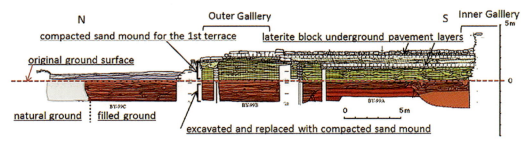

Fig. 3.12.3 Archaeological Study of Long Trench

Fig. 3.12.4 Southern side of Northern Library, Bayon

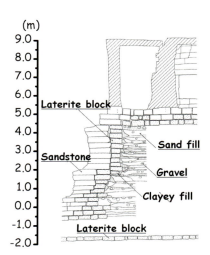

Fig. 3.12.5 Trenched West Porch

2. 掘り込み基礎と基壇盛土構造

Fig. 3.12.3にロングトレンチ[1]の断面図を示した。外回廊より約10mまで外側を，当時の自然地盤表面（赤点線）より2〜3m掘削し，版築状に締固めて，いわゆる掘り込み基礎としている。外回廊より内側では，そのうえに，砂質土で版築盛土を構築し，ラテライトブロック及び砂岩の敷石を表面に設置し，高さ約2.5mの第1基壇テラスとしている。内回廊の内側は，高さ約6.0mの第2基壇テラス，さらにバイヨン主塔の基礎となる高さ約12.4mの第3基壇テラスがあり，各テラスの基壇盛土の外側は，積石擁壁構造で支えられている。

3. 北経蔵の基壇盛土

バイヨンの修復でJSAが最初に手がけたのが，北経蔵である。Fig. 3.12.4に示した北経蔵の両端部のポーチ部分と主室の間に縦の目地開きが見える。西側ポーチ部分の考古学調査のトレンチ断面をFig. 3.12.5に示した。断面は，ほぼ均質な砂質土の版築層となっており，ポーチの外面を形成する砂岩の内側のラテライトブロックと

2. Trenched Foundation and Foundation Mound

As shown in Fig. 3.12.3, the long trench[1] revealed the trenched foundation was extended outwards from the Outer Gallery with the depth of 2-3 meters with layered compaction. Inside of the Outer Gallery, an additional compacted sand layer is identified with thickness of about 2.5m. This is the first terrace covered by laterite blocks and sand stone. Inside the Inner Gallery, the second terrace with 6.0m in height and the top third terrace with 12.4m in height where the main tower is constructed. The vertical sides of each terrace are covered by a masonry retaining structure.

3. Foundation mound of Northern Library

JSA started to work with the Northen Library of Bayon. As shown in Fig. 3.12.4, vertical openings were recognized between the main hall and the porches at both ends. Trenched section by the archaeological study is shown in Fig. 3.12.5. The section was found as a uniform mound with layered compacted sandy soil. Clayey compacted soil is recognized between the layered mound and laterite blocks to prevent rainwater infiltration into the mound. The openings of the vertical gap (δw) of the mound and horizontal gap(δc) at

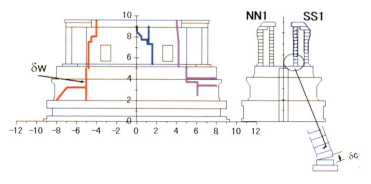

Fig. 3.12.6 Openings of porch and base of column
δw:vertical opening , δc:base opening at the base of column

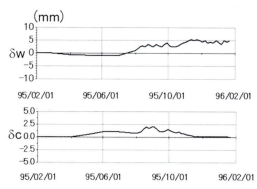

Fig. 3.12.7 monitoring of δw and δc

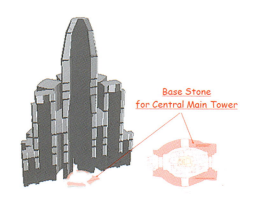

Fig. 3.12.8 Base Stone for Central Tower

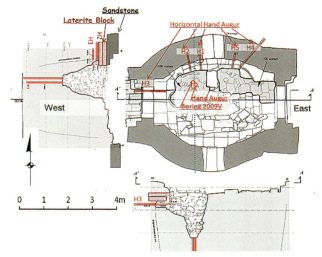

Fig. 3.12.9 Hand auger survey under base stone

砂の版築層との境界には粘性土質がおかれ基壇内部への遮水を目指していることが分かる。Fig.3.12.6に示したが，ポーチと主室の間にある縦目地の開き（δw）と石柱底部の上下開き（δc）の季節変化の観測結果（1995/2～1996/2）をFig. 3.12.7に示した。縦目地開き（δw）は雨季の間に増大し，乾季においての減少は観測されていない。石柱底部の上下開き（δc）は雨季に大きくなったが，乾季でもとに戻っている。

Fig. 3.12.5のトレンチを見ると，縦目地のあった場所の版築層の境界の水平は連続している。最上部の敷石はやや落ちこんでいる。これらのことは，雨水による盛土内への浸水によって水平に膨張し，乾季には戻ることは無かったものであろうと思われる。

4. 主塔における基礎構造

バイヨン主塔および基礎石をFig. 3.12.8に示したが，この基礎石の下部構造の調査のためにFig. 3.12.9に示したように，基礎石の下部の内側から外側に向けてハンドオーガー探査を実施した[2]。実施した5点すべてにおいて，得られたのは版築土で石材は確認されなかった。このことは，バイヨン中央主塔は，浅い直接基礎で構築され700年以上の間，特に問題なく支持されていたこと

the base of the inclined pillar were monitored as shown in Fig. 3.12.6. The monitored result of one year from 1995/2 to 1996/2 is shown in Fig. 3.12.7. The vertical gap (δw) increased during the rainy season and kept the deformation in the dry season. The vertical gap (δw) also showed opening during rainy season but returned to the original position in the dry season.

Both sides of the vertical gap in Fig. 3.12.5 continues horizontally but the stones at the top surface settled compared to both sides. This implies that the infiltrated rain water had caused the horizontal expansion during rainy season and stayed as deformed.

4. Foundation Structure of the Main Tower

The Main Tower is supported by base stones as shown in Fig. 3.12.8. Archaeological survey[2] was performed in 2008. Hand auger was inserted below the base stones at 5 points as shown in Fig. 3.12.9. No stone was found beneath the base stones. It was only densely compacted sandy soil. This implies the Main Tower has been supported by shallow and direct foundation for more than 700 years without any special

になる。クメール方式とでも呼べる砂質系の高い版築盛土を基礎として、砂上の楼閣の奇跡としか言いようがない。

5. 中央塔の基檀構造

EFEO（フランス極東学院）は、1933年に中央塔の基礎中心に直径約2.5mの立坑を掘り、仏座像を発見している。その後埋め戻されているが、埋め戻しの状態を調査するために、2009年にボーリング調査（BYV 2009）を実施した。さらに2010年には主塔・副塔の基壇より外側の第3テラスから基壇の調査ボーリング（BYV 2010）[3][4]を実施し、これらの結果のうち、標準貫入試験および採取試料の含水比をFig. 3.12.10に示した。

中央塔立坑の埋め戻しは、基礎面から14mまでの深度まで標準貫入試験のN値はN≦4という小さい値であることから、締固めなしで埋め戻し、非常に緩い状態であることが判明した。

第3テラスからのボーリング結果を見ると、テラス表面の砂岩とラテライトの敷石の下に約6mの厚さのラテライトブロックが確認され、版築盛土層が続いている。版築層の標準貫入試験のN値が非常に大きな値が得られている。通常の砂質土の締固め土のN値は30＜N＜40程度であるのに対して、N＞100〜200という非常に大きな値が得られている。

このラテライトブロックの探索のための水平および斜めボーリングが、Fig. 3.12.11に示したように、2012年にかけて実施された。電気探査も実施して総合的に検討した結果、Fig. 3.12.12に示したように、第2テラスの完成のあと、ラテライトブロックを設置し、第3テラスを構築したと思われる。ラテライトブロックの存在で、主塔・副塔の安定性が大きく増大した。主塔の荷重をラテライトブロックで直接受けることではなく、基礎の直下地盤の水平移動を規制することで安定化を図るという特徴が見られ、基礎構造の真正性（オーセンティシティ）の特徴決定要素の一つとみられる。

6. 版築土特性

2つのボーリング結果から得られたN値と含水比の関係をFig. 3.12.13に示した。単純な埋め戻しの立坑の場合、含水比の変化に対してN値の関係は見られないが、第3テラスのオリジナルの版築土においては、含水比が小さいと大きなN値で、含水比の増大によりN値は減

problems. It is amazing that the direct foundation on sandy ground without any damage survived for such a long period.

5. The basement structure of the Central Tower

EFEO excavated a vertical shaft with diameter of about 2.5m in 1933 and found a fragmented Buddha statue and other stone remnants. Backfilled soil was studied by geotechnical boring in 2009[3]. Another boring was performed at the top terrace in 2010[4]. Among the results, Standard Penetration Test and water content of the samples are shown in Fig. 3.12.10.

Very small SPT, N values of N<=4 at the central shaft shows the backfilled soil is very loose state without any compaction. The boring at the top terrace shows a layer of laterite block of about 6 m in thickness beneath the paved sandstone and laterite blocks followed by compacted sandy soil layer with extra ordinary large SPT, N-values larger than N>100, compared to the common values of N=20~40 for compacted sand.

Additional study of horizontal as well inclined boring and electric survey was performed in 2011 and 2012 and the results are shown in Fig. 3.12.11. After the construction of the second terrace mound, the laterite blocks were installed for the construction of the top terrace, which was designed for the stability of the Main and sub-Towers. The blocks do not support the load of the towers, but prevent the horizontal displacement of the foundation soil beneath the direct base stones. This in one of the character defining elements of the authenticity of the foundation.

6. Characteristics of Foundation Mound

The relationship between SPT, N-values and water content is shown in Fig. 3.12.13. A strong relationship between SPT-N and water content is shown for the original compacted soil at the top terrace, but not for the soil without compaction at the vertical shaft. The Fig. 3.12.14 shows the collapse of the sampled stiff sandy soil after the infiltration by water within 10 min. The characteristic of strength and water content was confirmed by laboratory test. The original sand was arranged as a saturated state with about a water content =15% and compacted in more than 20 plastic containers. These containers were put outside, and the bearing strength of the soil was tested by Yamanaka Cone Stiffness tester after every few days and the results are shown in Figure-16. As shown in Fig. 3.12.17, the cone bearing capacity is increased with the decrease of the water content. Qbc=50-100 (kN/m2) at w/c=15% had increased to 60-100 times at w/c=4~5%.

The grain size distributions of the sampled soils for the original soils at various sites of the libraries and foundation

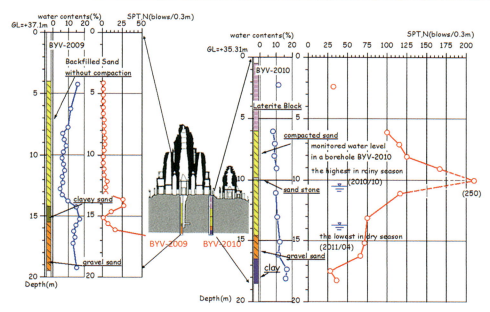

Fig. 3.12.10 Borings at the vertical shaft and at the top terrace for foundation of Main Tower

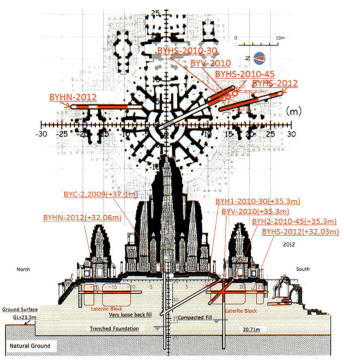

Fig. 3.12.11 Additional borings to confirm the laterite block in the foundation

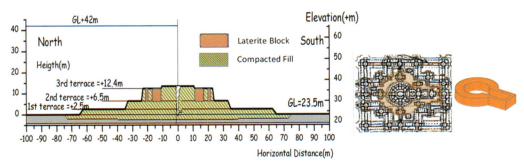

Fig. 3.12.12 Laterite block in the foundation of Bayon

3.12　バイヨンの地盤工学　　147

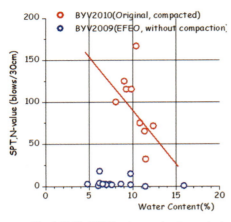

Fig. 3.12.13 SPT-N-values and water contents

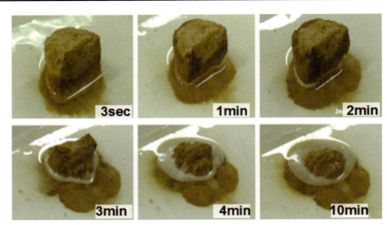

Fig. 3.12.14 Collapse stiff filled sand in water

Fig. 3.12.15 Yamanaka Cone test

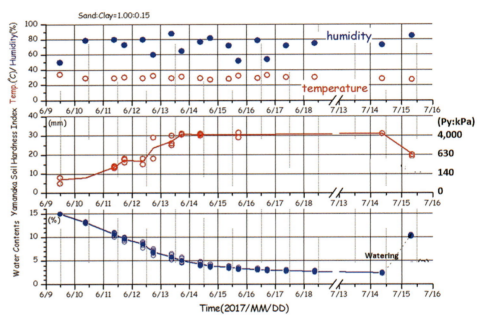

Fig. 3.12.16 The effects of drying and wetting on the cone bearing capacity by Yamanaka Cone

少することが分かる。

　含水比の影響を直接確認するために，サンプルを水浸してその挙動をFig. 3.12.14したが，水浸後，水が試料に浸潤し，約10分後には崩壊している。室内試験で確認するために，オリジナル版築土の材料をほぼ飽和状態となる含水比15％に調整し，Fig. 3.12.15に示したポリ容器に締固め，20個以上の試験体を用意した。これらの試験体を屋外に置き，数日ごとに山中式硬度計による支持力の変化を求め，試験体の含水比を測定し，Fig. 3.12.16に示した。

　時間の経過とともに蒸発による含水比の減少につれて，山中式による硬度指数が大きく増大していることが分かる。Fig. 3.12.17に含水比とコーン支持力の関係を示した。含水比15％時のコーン支持力 $Qcb = 50 〜 100$ （kN/m²）に比べて，含水比4〜5％となると60〜100倍に増大している。

mound of the Main Tower of Bayon, and the mound of Prasat Suor Prat are shown in Fig. 3.12.18. Sandy soil shows about 10-20(%) of fine soil (less than d<0.06mm) and clayey soil shows about 30-40(%) of higher contents. The uniform shape of the distribution curve is specially recognized. The microphoto and the X-ray diffraction analysis are shown in Fig. 3.12.19 and 20. X-ray diffraction analysis shows the Quartz and Halloysite which belongs to clayey mineral of Kaolinite. The photo shows clear particle of rounded ball shape of Quartz with clayey material surrounding the ball.

The mechanism of the increase of the strength is considered as the stronger negative pressure inside of the water membranes. When the soil becomes dry, the radius of water membrane becomes smaller which induces stronger tension as well as stronger negative suction pressure as shown in Fig. 3.12.21. Compared to the chemical reaction, the water membrane is much easier and faster to be dissolved.

版築土の試料の粒度試験結果を，バイヨンの南北経蔵，主塔基壇，プラサートスープラ，さらにバプーオンなども含めてFig. 3.12.18に示した。一般的な砂質土は，細粒土分（粒子径d＜0.06mm）が，ほぼ10〜20%を示しており，北経蔵で見られた遮水ゾーンとしての粘土質の盛土材は，細粒分が30〜40%と高い値を示している。非常に均一性のある粒度特性を示している。オリジナル版築土のマイクロ写真およびX線回折解析結果をFig. 3.12.19およびFig. 3.12.20に示した。X線解析結果からは，石英（Quartz）およびカオリナイト系の粘土Halloysiteが示されている。Fig. 3.12.19には，透明で球形の石英砂と周囲を埋めている粘土が観察できる。

　乾燥によりなぜ大きな強度を示すのかについては，Fig. 3.12.21でしめしているように水幕の有する引っ張り張力，水幕内の負の水圧の増大によるものであると考えられる。水幕の径が小さくなればなるほど，吸引力が大きくなり，粒子間の結合が大きくなる。化学的結合の解消に比べて，水幕の消滅は容易であるからFig. 3.12.14のように短時間で弱化する。

7．熱帯性モンスーン気候下における版築土の含水比変化

　アンコール地域は，熱帯性モンスーン気候で，雨季による雨水浸透による影響をみるために，Fig. 3.12.22に示したように水分センサーを敷石直下に数個設置した[5]。Fig. 3.12.23に観測結果の一部を示したが，降雨が2回観測されていて，最初の降雨は2時間内で5〜7mm程度の降雨であるが，GL−0.5m，−1.0mの含水量は増加しているが，GL−1.5mの含水量には変化が見られない。浸透水が1.5mまで到達していないことが分かる。次の降雨は総雨量20mm程度の降雨であるが，この降雨では先行降雨で浸透していたこともあり，1.5mまで到達している。浸透速度は，1.0〜1.5m/hour程度で，降雨が終了すると，含水量は減少に転じていることが分かる。熱帯性モンスーン気候での降雨は，スコール（Squall）と呼ばれ，突然に降り始め，数時間の後晴天となり，浸透水は蒸発に転じるために，降雨の浸透が制限されている。しかしながら，温暖化により，スコールから長時間降雨へと降雨タイプが変化しつつあることを考えると対応策が必要であろう。

8．叩き（消石灰混合土）の導入

　JSAが，最初に手掛けたバイヨン北経蔵の変状の様子

7. Water Contents under Tropical Monsoon Climate

Angkor belongs to tropical monsoon climate zone. Moisture sensors were installed at several depths beneath the paved stone[5] in the top terrace as shown in Fig. 3.12.22. Two cases of rainfalls are shown in Fig. 3.12.23. The first case is small rain fall of 5-7mm in two hours. The sensors responded to an increase at upper levels at GL-0.5m and -1.0m but did not respond at GL-1.5m. The seepage did not reach to the depth of GL-1.5m. The second case is about 20mm in total rainfall. The rainwater infiltrated into GL-1.5m with seepage rate of around 1.0-1.5(m/hour).

After the rainfall, the water contents return to decreasing the moisture in the ground.

Rainfall in the tropical monsoon zone is known as a "Squall," which causes a sudden rainfall of rather strong intensity for a few hours and returns to normal good weather. Under the rain fall of the Squall type rain, the infiltrated rainwater in the ground shall turn to dry after the end of the rain and the water content in the foundation mound shall keep the dry condition with strong strength. However, in the anticipated warmer climate conditions, the rainfall changes from the strong but short duration to long duration. To prevent the weakening of the strength of the foundation mound for the Main Tower, some countermeasures are necessary to safeguard the Bayon.

8. Introduction of mixed soil with slaked lime

The deformation of the Northern Library was caused by weakened original compacted mound soil by infiltration of rainwater. "Tataki(tamping)" is a traditional method to improve soil in Japan and was further developed as "Jinko-Ishi (artificial stone)" by "Chohichi Hattori" in the early Meiji-period of 1870'. JSA introduced this technique with technical advice from the Research Institute of INAX who had been conducting research on "Jinko-Ishi(manmade-stone)".

Slaked lime ($Ca(OH)_2$) is produced from quicklime (CaO) adding with water.

$CaO + H_2O = Ca(OH)_2$

Slaked lime becomes limestone of calcium carbonite by adding carbonic acid gas.

$Ca(OH)_2 + CO_2 = CaCO_3 + H_2O$

The slaked lime mixed with the original soil can keep the basic characteristics of the soil, and prevent seepage of water by mixing the slaked lime of 5-10%. Fig. 3.12.24 shows an example of the increase of strength and Young's modulus with time of aging effects. The comparison of the results of plate loading tests on the compacted original soil and the

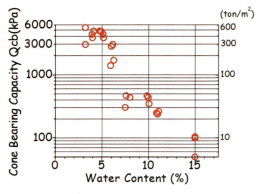

Fig. 3.12.17 Yamanaka Cone vs. Water Contents

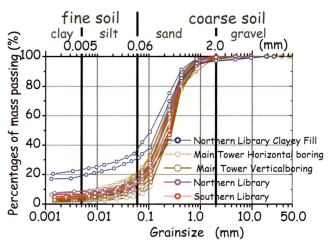

Fig. 3.12.18 Grain size Distribution of the original filled soils

Fig. 3.12.19 Micro photo of the sandy fill

Fig. 3.12.21 Vacuum suction of water within meniscus
Large radius for large water contents
Small radius for small water contents in dry state

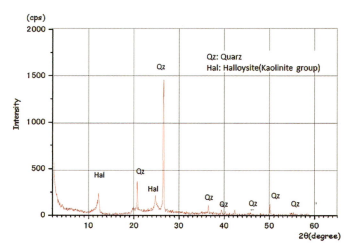

Fig. 3.12.20 X-ray diffraction analysis

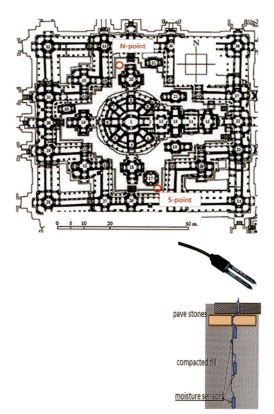

Fig. 3.12.22 Installation of moisture sensor

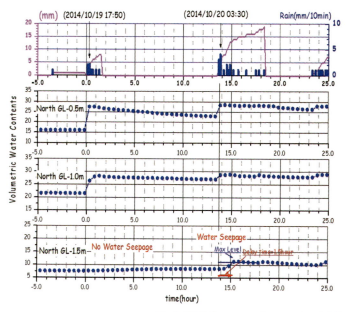

Fig. 3.12.23 Response of sensors to rainfall

150　第3章　JSA/JASAの調査研究

は，降雨浸透によって弱化するオリジナル版築土による
ものであった。乾燥時には大きな強度であるが，浸水に
よる弱化を防ぐための方策として，日本に伝わる叩きを
導入した。叩きを基礎に服部長七によって人工石として
明治初期に水門や海岸岸壁などの構築に使用され現在も
日本各地に現存している。2000年当時長七叩きを研究
していた㈱INAX基礎研究所の協力を得た。

　叩きは，石灰岩を1,000℃の高温で焼成して出来る酸
化カルシウム：生石灰（CaO）に水を加えることで得ら
れる水酸化カルシウム：消石灰（Ca(OH)₂）を用いる。

$$CaO + H_2O = Ca(OH)_2$$

　消石灰は空気中の炭酸ガスとの化学反応により炭酸カ
ルシウム：石灰岩（CaCO₃）を生成する。

$$Ca(OH)_2 + CO_2 = CaCO_3 + H_2O$$

　叩き工法による消石灰混合工法は，オリジナルの版築
土の特性を保持し，消石灰を5〜10%程度混合すること
で，雨水浸透による基壇盛土の弱化を改良することが出
来る。Fig. 3.12.24に，オリジナルの砂に消石灰10%混
合土の強度・変形特性のエイジング（続成効果）による
増加特性の一例を示した。Fig. 3.12.25には，南経蔵基
壇におけるオリジナルの締固められた地盤と消石灰混合
土地盤との平板載荷試験の比較を示した。散水により，
オリジナルは強度が大きく低下するが，混合土では見ら
れない。

9．北および南経蔵の基壇盛土修復施工

　基壇盛土の構築については，次のような手法を用いて
盛土に使用されていた土の特性を粒度試験によって確認
し，新規に用いる消石灰混合土を調整した。消石灰混合
土による盛土材の設計は，①盛土に作用する上部構造荷
重の推定，②推定荷重に対する十分な地耐力および想定
荷重による沈下量を許容値以内に収めるための一軸圧縮
荷重およびヤング率を決定する。このような盛土特性を
達成するために，事前に締固め試験，突固め試料の一軸
圧縮試験をして，①消石灰混合比率，②混合時の含水比
を決定する。さらに，盛土の締固めには，巻きだし厚，
各層における突固め方法，突固め回数などを検討し，山
中硬度計などによる施工管理を実施した。

10．バイヨン基壇における水位

　バイヨンの基壇は締固められた地盤で構成されており，
強度は水浸により弱化する。基壇内の水位は，基壇の安

slaked lime mixed with the original soil is shown in Fig.
3.12.25. Water content causes the weakening strength for the
compacted original soil, but not for the slaked lime mixed
with the original soil.

9. Reconstruction of foundation mound for Northern and Southern Libraries

For the reconstruction of the foundation mound, the
grainsize distribution was adjusted based upon the original
soil mixed with slaked lime based upon the following several
tests.

The design procedures for 1) the mixing ratio of the slaked
lime with soil, and 2) the water contents of the soil consist
of 1 to estimate vertical load from the upper structures, 2 to
estimate the compression strength and Young's modulus of the
compacted ground to withstand the estimated load and within
allowable settlements. The compaction step was designed
by the thickness of soil distribution, ramming compaction
method with how many times for one layer and controlled by
Yamanaka-cone tests.

10. Water level in foundation mound Bayon

Foundation mound of Bayon consists of very dense sandy
soil. The strength of the soil becomes weaken in water. The
water level in the foundation mound is one of the key factors
for the stability of the foundation structure.

The change of water levels of Lucky Well and the boring
of BAV2010 on the third terrace of the foundation mound is
shown in Figure 26 with that of boring point of BA1994.

Compared to the change of water level in natural ground
from +17~+23m, those in the foundation ground are
+22m~+25m, which are always higher than the natural level.
Infiltration of rainwater into the foundation mound is the main
reason for the water in the mound higher than those in natural
ground. The ancient drainage system within the Bayon must
also be considered

11. Reconstruction of stone masonry retaining wall in Angkor

Restoration methods for the stone masonry retaining wall in
Angkor are shown in Fig. 3.12.27.

The retaining wall of Baphuon, which had failed in 1943
during a heavy rain, was tried to be reconstruct as the same
structure before the failure. When the compacted mound
reached around 5m in height, it failed. It was retried, but
in vain. Reinforced concrete structure was introduced in
Baphuon as a substitute. Comparison of reconstruction

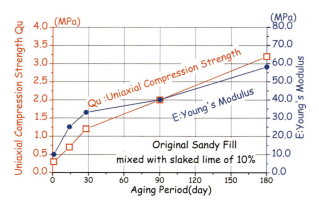
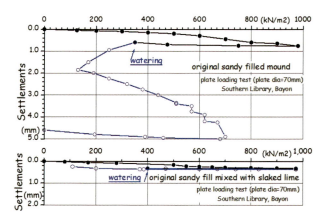

Fig. 3.12.24 Aging of fill mixed with slaked lime

Fig. 3.12.25 Plate loading tests

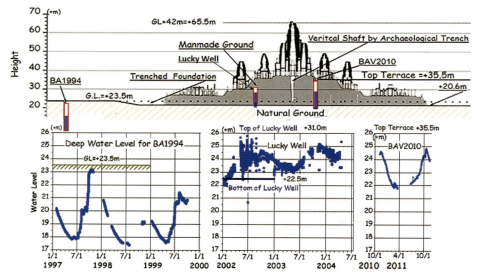

Fig. 3.12.26 Seasonal change of water level in BA1994, Lucky well, and BAV2010

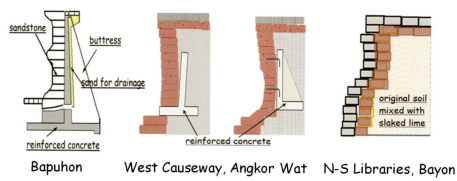

Fig. 3.12.27 Conservation of retaining stone walls in Angkor

Table 3.12.1 Comparison of conservation of retaining stone wall in Angkor

Authenticity and Integrity		Baphuon	West Causeway	N・S Library, Bayon
Fill material silty sand	Character of Authenticity	No discussion	No discussion	Grain Size Distribution
	Integrity	—	—	preserved
Structure	Retaining structure	RC wall	RC wall	Retaining stone wall
Retaining stone wall	Integrity	lost	lost	preserved

152 第3章　JSA/JASAの調査研究

定にとって重要な要素の一つである。

第2テラスの東側基壇内に，ラッキーウエルと称されている井戸がある。ラッキーウエルの井戸内水位，第3テラスにおけるボーリング孔BAV2010，バイヨンの北側のボーリング地点BA1994の水位変化をFig. 3.12.26に示した。

自然地盤における水位の変動＋17～＋23ｍに比較して，基壇内水位は＋22～＋25ｍ程度で，常に自然地盤よりは高い水位となっている。降雨による浸透水が基壇内水位を保持する要因となっていることが理解できる。

11．アンコールにおける石積擁壁盛土修復

Fig. 3.12.27にアンコール遺構の積石擁壁の既存および現在における修復手法を示した。1943年の豪雨で崩壊したバプーオンの修復では，擁壁背面の盛土が5ｍ盛り上げた時点で崩壊し，再度試みたが同様な結果となったので，コンクリートRC擁壁構造が採用された。バプーオン石積擁壁[6]，アンコール西参道石積擁壁[7]，バイヨン北・南経蔵の石積擁壁における真正性などの比較をTable 3.12.1に示したように，バイヨンの北・南経蔵以外の石積擁壁の修復においては，盛土材の真正性の特徴についての議論は見られず，擁壁構造については，石積構造から鉄筋コンクリートによる擁壁として修復したために，構造としての真正性は保全されず，完全性（インテグリティ）は喪失している。鉄筋コンクリートの寿命はせいぜい100年程度であることに対して，消石灰混合によれば，ほぼ永久的であることを考慮すると，材料および構造の真正性の保全の観点から消石灰混合土による修復がすぐれていることが理解できる。

methods of the masonry stone retaining wall for Baphuon, the west causeway of Angkor Wat, and Northern and Southern Library of Bayon is shown in Table 3.12.1. No discussion of the authenticity of the soils for compacted filled mound is recognized except for the Northen and Southern Libraries of Bayon. When the design of the retaining structure had been changed from the masonry stone retaining to a reinforced structure, failed to keep the authenticity of the structural design and lost the integrity. As in the case of the Northern and Southern Libraries, the life of the slaked lime mixed filled mound is almost permanent compared to around 100 years for reinforced concrete, the slaked lime mixed with filled soil is much better than the reinforced concrete in terms of the authenticity and the integrity of the material as well as structural design.

References

1) Narita, T., Nishimoto, S., Shimizu N., Akazawa Y.: Trench Excavation of Outer Gallery, Bayon, Annual Report on the Technical Survey of Angkor Monument 2000, pp.3-18 ,317 (2001)

2) Shimoda I., Yamamoto N., Iwasaki Y., Fukuda M.:" Excavation Survey of the Central Tower Chamber," Annual Technical Report on the Survey of Angkor Monument 2008, JASA, Tokyo pp.67-88 (2009)

3) Iwasaki Y., Fukuda M.," FY2009 Report-Geoengineering/Environment Unit-," Annual Technical Report on the Survey of Angkor Monument 2008, JASA, Tokyo pp.323-356 (2009)

4) A Iwasaki Y., Fukuda M., Haraguchi T., Kitamura A. Ide Y., Tokunaga T., Mogi K., "Structural of Platform Mound of Central Tower Based upon Boring Information, Annual Technical Report on the Survey of Angkor Monument 2012-2013, JASA, Tokyo pp.93-113 (2014)

5) Koyama T., Yamada S., Iwasaki Y., Fukuda M., Shimoda I., Ishizuka M.: "Installation of Moisture Sensor," Annual Technical Report on the Survey of Angkor Monument 2014-2015, JASA, Tokyo pp132-137 (2016)

6) Jean Launay(1994) "Angkor temples: A geotechnical and structural engineering approach", XIII ICSMFE, 1994, New Delhi, India,

7) Nao Ishizu et al.(1999) "A Study on the Restoration over the Western Causeway of Angkor Wat, Conservation Activities by EFEO at "Rapport d'Angkor"", Proc. AIJ_1999,(in Japanese)

3.13 バイヨンマスタープラン・JSA の挑戦宣言
Bayon Master Plan and JSA's Declaration of Challenge

中川　武
NAKAGAWA Takeshi

2005 年 6 月 JSA により発刊された『バイヨン全域の保存修復のためのマスタープラン』(The Master Plan for the Conservation & Restoration of the Bayon Complex) に記述された内容がバイヨンマスタープランの全てであると言ってもよい。以下に目次を記す。

バイヨン寺院全域の保存修復のためのマスタープラン
目次
巻頭写真
寄稿

Foreword for The Master Plan for the Conservation & Restoration of the Bayon Complex　（ブン・ナリット）
Foreword for The Master Plan for the Conservation and Restoration of the Bayon Complex　（松浦晃一郎）
The significance of the faces of the Bayon
（ジャック・デュマルセ）
The ruins of Angkor, Cambodia　（平山郁夫）
Angkor : Success and Toward the New Era（近藤誠一）

目次
　執筆者一覧
　バイヨン憲章

序論
第 1 章　目的，方法，構成
　1.1　目的
　1.2　方法と構成
第 2 章　バイヨン寺院の現況と保存修復への課題
　2.1　バイヨン寺院での既往の保存修復活動
　2.2　建築インベントリー調査の概要と保存修復への課題
　2.3　美術史調査の概要と保存修復への課題
　2.4　考古学調査の概要と保存修復への課題

"The Master Plan for the Conservation & Restoration of the Bayon Complex", published by JSA in June 2005, is the entire Bayon Master Plan. The following is a table of contents.

The Master Plan for the Conservation & Restoration of the Bayon Complex
Table of Contents
Photographs
Foreword and Contributions
　Foreword for The Master Plan for the Conservation & Restoration of the Bayon Complex　（Bun Narith）
　Foreword for The Master Plan for the Conservation and Restoration of the Bayon Complex　（Koichiro Matsuura）
　The significance of the faces of the Bayon
（Jacques Dumarset）
　The ruins of Angkor, Cambodia　（Ikuo Hirayama）
　Angkor : Success and Toward the New Era　（Seiichi Kondo）

Table of Contents
　Authors
　Abbreviations
　The Bayon Charter

Introduction
　Chapter 1　The Purpose, Method and Composition
　　1.1　The Purpose
　　1.2　Method and Composition
　Chapter 2　The Present Situation of the Bayon temple and Themes for Conservation and Restoration
　　2.1　Previous Conservation and Restoration Activities at the Bayon temple
　　2.2　Outline of Architectural Inventory and Theme for Conservation and Restoration
　　2.3　Outline of Art History Investigation and Theme for Conservation and Restoration
　　2.4　Outline of Archaeology Investigation and Theme for Conservation and Restoration
　　2.5　Outline of Building Structure, Geo-technological

2.5 建築構造および地盤調査の概要と保存修復への課題

2.6 岩石学調査の概要と保存修復への課題

2.7 保存科学調査の概要と保存修復への課題

2.8 バイヨン寺院の排水システムの概要と保存修復への課題

2.9 生きた寺院としてのバイヨン——バイヨンに描かれた浅浮彫りの一場面から——

第3章　バイヨン寺院の破損と劣化

本論

第1章　バイヨン寺院の保存修復と活用のための基本理念

1.1 バイヨン寺院の特質

1.2 環境保全

1.3 バイヨン寺院の寸法計画——バイヨン北経蔵と南経蔵の比較を中心に——

1.4 修復技術

1.4.1 バイヨン期の伝統構法と保存修復技術

1.4.2 カンボジア人修復技能士，技術者，研究者の養成

1.5 国際協調によるアンコール遺跡の保存とカンボジアの地域，民族，国家への影響

第2章　バイヨン寺院の修復計画

2.1 修復前調査項目の決定

2.2 修復計画の概要

2.3 修復計画の各論

2.3.1 中央塔安定化と恒久的保存

2.3.2 浮彫り彫刻の精密記録と修復

2.3.2.1 浮彫り彫刻の精密記録

2.3.2.2 浮彫り彫刻の修復

2.3.3 南経蔵修復計画

2.3.4 APSARAとの協調と開かれた組織

2.3.5 修復工事の安全性の確保とツーリズムの調和

第3章　バイヨン寺院の保存活用計画

3.1 記録の保存・公開と説明責任

3.2 世界遺産保護に資する記録・教育のための国際的ネットワークの構築と参加

3.3 バイヨン寺院の将来像とアンコール地域の持続的発展

3.4 保存活動を支える組織体制の提言

結論

Investigation and Theme for Conservation and Restoration

2.6 Outline of Petrology Investigation and Theme for Conservation and Restoration

2.7 Outline of Conservation Science Investigation and Theme for Conservation and Restoration

2.8 Outline of the Drainage System of the Bayon temple and Theme for Conservation and Restoration

2.9 Bayon, As a Living Temple - Message from the Scene of the Bas-relief of the Bayon temple -

Chapter 3 Destruction and Degradation Phenomenon in the Bayon temple

Main Discourse

Chapter 1 Fundamental Idea for the Conservation and Restoration, and the Utilization of the Bayon temple

1.1 Characteristics of the Bayon temple

1.2 Environmental Preservation

1.3 The Dimensional Plan of the Bayon temple -A Comparison between the Bayon Northern Library and Southern Library-

1.4 Restoration Techniques

1.4.1 Traditional Construction and Structural Method of the Bayon Period and the Techniques of Conservation and Restoration

1.4.2 The Cultivation of Cambodian Restoration Workers, Engineers, and Researchers

1.5 International Partnership for the Conservation of the Angkor Monuments and its Influence on the Region, People, and Country of Cambodia

Chapter 2 Restoration Plan of the Bayon temple

2.1 Establishing Survey Items for Pre-Restoration Surveys

2.2 Overview of the Restoration Plan

2.3 The Theory for the Restoration Plan

2.3.1 Stabilization of the Central Tower and Countermeasures for Long Term

2.3.2 Precision Documentation and the Restoration of the Bas-relief

2.3.2.1 Precision Documentation of the Bas-relief

2.3.2.2 Restoration of the Bas-relief

2.3.3 Restoration Plan of the Southern Library

2.3.4 Cooperation with APSARA and an Open Restoration Organization

2.3.5 Securing Safety of the Restoration work and the Harmonization of Tourism

Chapter 3 The Conservation and Utilization of the Bayon temple

3.1 Keeping and Opening Records to the Public and the Accountability

3.2 Establishment and Participation to the International Network for Record-keeping and Education

3.13　バイヨンマスタープラン・JSAの挑戦宣言　155

付録

1 バイヨンシンポジウム

2 バイヨン寺院の3次元デジタル保存調査報告

3 バイヨン寺院の美術史調査報告

  3.1 バイヨン寺院における調査活動とその成果

  3.2 バイヨン寺院の図像および尊顔に関する考察

    3.2.1 バイヨン寺院に関する図像学的考察

    3.2.2 バイヨン寺院の尊顔をめぐる諸問題

4 バイヨン寺院の考古学調査報告

5 バイヨン寺院とアンコール・トムの都市計画調査報告

  5.1 アンコール・トム中央寺院バイヨンの都市計画的背景の調査報告

  5.2 アンコール・トムにおける利用実態と周辺地域の居住環境調査

    5.2.1 アンコール・トム王宮前広場とバイヨン寺院周域の利用実態

    5.2.2 バイヨン寺院とその周辺での人々の動向

    5.2.3 アンコール遺跡周辺の農村地域の生活実態と住居形態，アンコールクラウ村中心部集落を事例にして

    5.2.4 アンコールクラウ村での住民ワークショップの実践

6 バイヨンの建築構造調査報告

  6.1 バイヨン寺院などの建築構造調査報告——バイヨン北経蔵，プラサート・スープラ，およびアンコール・ワット北経蔵——

  6.2 バイヨン寺院の微振動測定調査

7 バイヨン寺院の岩石学調査報告

8 バイヨン寺院の保存科学調査報告

9 バイヨン北経蔵修復工事の評価

10 バイヨン寺院修復のための各専門工事標準仕様

  10.1 修復技法のマニュアル化

  10.2 崩落部材の原位置同定調査

  10.3 解体工事

  10.4 基礎・基壇版築層の工事

  10.5 部材修理の判定

  10.6 砂岩材の修復

  10.7 ラテライト材の修復

11 バイヨン寺院のメンテナンス活動

12 バイヨン寺院の崩落石材調査

13 バイヨン寺院の危険箇所のモニタリングと応急処置

カラー図版
クメール語抄訳

Contributing to the Protection of the World Heritage

  3.3 Future Image of the Bayon temple and Sustainable Development of the Angkor Region

  3.4 Proposal of Organizational Structure for Supporting the Preservation Activities

Final Conclusion

Appendices

1 The Bayon Symposium

2 3D Digital Archive Survey Report of the Bayon temple

3 Art History Survey Report of the Bayon temple

  3.1 Investigation Activities and its Results of the Bayon temple

  3.2 Examination of the Iconography and Deity Faces of the Bayon temple

    3.2.1 Iconographical Examination of the Bayon temple

    3.2.2 Subjects Concerning Deity Faces of the Bayon temple

4 Archaeology Survey Report of the Bayon temple

5 City Planning Survey Report of the Bayon temple and Angkor Thom

  5.1 Survey on the City Planning Background at Bayon, the Central Temple of Angkor Thom

  5.2 The Usage Status of the Angkor Thom Royal Plaza and the Residential Environment Survey of the Surrounding Area

    5.2.1 Usage Status of the Royal Plaza of Angkor Thom and the Bayon temple Area

    5.2.2 Human Trends in the Bayon temple and Environs

    5.2.3 The Life Style and Housing Style in the Rural Villages at the Angkor Monumental Area, A Case Study of Angkor Krau Village

    5.2.4 A Villagers' Workshop in Angkor Krau Village

6 Building Structural Survey Report of the Bayon temple

  6.1 Building Structural Survey of the Bayon temple - Bayon Northern Library, Prasat Suor Prat, and Angkor Wat Northern Library -

  6.2 Bayon temple Micro-Tremor Measurement Survey

7 Petrology Survey Report of the Bayon temple

8 Conservation Science Survey Report of the Bayon temple

9 Evaluation of the Restoration of Bayon Northern Library

10 Standard Specifications for Specialty Works in the Restoration of the Bayon temple

  10.1 Compiling a Manual of Restoration Techniques

  10.2 Survey for the Settlement of the Original Position of the Fallen Stone Elements

  10.3 Dismantlement Work Specification

  10.4 Construction Specification for Foundation and Platform Compacted Layers

  10.5 Judgment on Repairing Elements

目次・バイヨン憲章・結論

しかし重要な問題は，それらの記述にこめられなかった前後の事情にあるかもしれない。その発端から問い直すべきであろう。

1. バイヨンマスタープランの発端

1992年10月，初めてバイヨンを見た。驚いた。まだ難民生活の名残や，繁茂する植物も，半壊状態の遺跡，散乱石材等々もほぼ放置のままであったことも影響していたかもしれない。巨大な石仏の顔の表面に，苔，黴，汚れが至る所に附着していたせいかもしれない。興福寺北円堂にある2体の僧形像（鎌倉期の木造無著・世親立像）の無音の笑いが波のように押し寄せてくる。私にはそのように感じられた。この不穏さは何だ。これは一筋縄ではいかない。1970年代末，私にとって初めての外国であったエジプト，ギザのクフ王のピラミッドを見て，あらゆる感受と考想の力を一瞬のうちに石の塊に吸引された時，はたまた1980年代中頃，ロサンゼルス下町の闇の中で，ワッツタワーを見て，この世界には恐ろしいものがあると感じた時，驚きの強度という意味で，バイヨンの，私にとっての初見は，それらの体験に並ぶものであった。バイヨンの秘密を解き明かしたい。キチンと修復してカンボジアの未来に手渡したい。そして世界の建築の夢と力の列に，バイヨンを並べたい。でもどこから手をかけるべきか。

1992年の10月から予備調査を，1994年の11月から正式にプロジェクトがスタートした。「アンコール・ワット最外周壁内北経蔵の部分解体再構築修復工事」，「アンコール・トム王宮前広場プラサート・スープラ塔群の整備」，「バイヨン寺院の整備」の3項目を我々のミッションとしたが，当初，木造や紙の修理はさておき，石造建築の修復に未経験の日本がなぜアンコールか，と公然と批判する人々がいた。勿論私は日本にも，高度な石垣の技術や石橋の美学があることは知っていたし，文化遺産の保存修復にとって体験は大切だが，それ以上に遺構の劣化原因を科学的に究明し，伝統工法と調和した修復技術をリバーシブルかつサスティナブルに適用することが第一義であることを私は確信していた。それに，内戦で疲弊していたカンボジア社会の復興を，世界的に関心の高いアンコール遺跡の国際的救済協力をテコに進めようとした日本政府の主導を高く評価していたので，JSAチームはその先頭に立つ決意であった。それにしても，

10.6 Sandstone Repair

10.7 Laterite Block Repair

11 Maintenance Activities of the Bayon temple

12 Survey on Fallen Stone Elements of the Bayon temple

13 Monitoring and Emergency Measures of the Bayon temple

Color Figures
Summary in Khmer
Table of Contents, The Bayon Charter, Final Conclusion

However, the important issue may lie in the circumstances that preceded and followed those statements. We should reexamine the Bayon Master Plan from its proposal.

1. Origin of the Bayon Master Plan

In October 1992, I saw Bayon for the first time. I was surprised. This may have been due to the fact that there were still remnants of refugee life, overgrown vegetation, half-destroyed remains, scattered stones, and other things that had almost been left unattended. It may have also been due to the moss, mold, and dirt that were attached to the face of the huge Buddha sculpture everywhere. The silent laughter of the two monk-shaped statues in the Hokuendo hall of Kofukuji Temple (the Kamakura-period wooden statue of Mujaku and Seshin Bosatsu) comes in waves. It felt that way to me. What is this disquiet? This is not a simple question. When I saw the Pyramid of Khufu in Giza Egypt at the time of my first foreign country visit in the late 1970s, and all my powers of perception and contemplation were sucked into the mass of stone in that moment. When I saw Watts Tower in the darkness of downtown Los Angeles in the mid-1980s, I felt that there was something terrifying in this world In terms of intensity of surprise. My first sighting of Bayon, for me, was on par with those experiences. I want to unlock the secrets of Bayon. I want to restore it properly and hand it over to the future generations of Cambodia. I want to put the Bayon in the line of the dreams and power of architecture in the world. But where should we start?

A preliminary survey began in October 1992, and the project officially started in November 1994. We had set three missions: "Partial dismantling and reconstruction of the Northern Library inside the Outermost Enclosure of Angkor Wat", "Maintenance of Prasat Suor Prat Tower in front of the Royal Palace of Angkor Thom", and "Maintenance of the Bayon temple". There were those who openly criticized us, asking why Japan, which had no experience in the restoration of stone architecture should be involved in Angkor. Of course, I knew that Japan had advanced stone wall techniques and the aesthetics of stone bridges, and experience was

どうやってバイヨンを！　しかし，途方に暮れてばかりはいられない。マスタープランの策定自体に時間がかかりそうなことを覚悟しながら，ともかくプロジェクトのスタートを切らなければならなかった。

　プラサート・スープラ塔群のテラスの考古学調査を続ける一方，毎日のようにバイヨン伽藍を見続けた。アンコール遺跡の継続的な保存協力問題を考える時大切なことは沢山ある。人材育成の基礎は社会的なものであって外国チームにとっては困難が多いが，現場実務訓練は必要である。また気象条件などの環境データの収集は当事国の責任であろうが，まだできないからこそその国際協力なのである。そんな中で雨水，地下水脈を含めた水環境調査は，永続的かつ，すぐにでも必要となる。JSAは地盤班の強い意欲もあり，岩盤まで達する（約80〜100ｍ）ボーリングコアサンプリング調査をバイヨン境内やシェムレアップ街中を含めたアンコール地域で初めて1994年に9ヶ所で実施した。このころカンボジアにはボーリング調査を実施できる組織はなく，日本・タイ合弁会社のチームにバンコクから来ていただいた。当然大型車輌で大型の機材を積んで運んでいただいたのであるが，当時のカンボジア国内の道なき道は通行が困難であったばかりでなく，ところどころ交通税を私的に撤収するために私兵を雇っていたらしい。とくに大型車輌の方も一々支払っていたのではたまらないので，私兵を雇い，払え，払わないと空砲を撃ち合いながら運んできたとのことであった。こともなげにその話を打ち明けたタイ人技術者にも驚いたが，そんな危険を犯してまで調査することはないと気付いたが，後の祭りであった。戦争の中の，国際関係における日常性の問題の一つを垣間見た思いであり，以後東南アジアにおける隣国の複雑な国民感情にも気を配ることになった。

2.　バイヨンマスタープランの目的

　JSAの修復プロジェクトは，傷んだところを直して終わり，というのではなく，調査，修復，保存活用の全てのプロセスにおいて知識，技術のオープンな共有化を果たすことであった。そのためには，まず，遺跡の意義と価値を広範な学術調査により明らかにし，遺跡の劣化，崩壊要因を極力科学的に解明し，それらを解決するための，オリジナリティを重視した修復方法を構築する必要がある。これは言うは易く，行うに難しなので，継続的議論のための枠組として必要になるのがマスタープランである。水環境の他に大気環境データ，気象データ，アンコール遺跡全般の岩石調査，主な遺跡建物の実測図の

important for the conservation and restoration of cultural heritage. However, I was more convinced that the first priority was to scientifically investigate and determine the causes of deterioration of the remains and to apply restoration techniques in harmony with traditional construction methods in a reversible and sustainable manner. Moreover, I highly appreciated the Japanese government's initiative to promote the recovery of Cambodian society, exhausted by the civil war, by leveraging international relief cooperation for the Angkor Monuments, which were of global interest. The JSA team was determined to take the lead in this endeavor. But still, how to progress the restoration in Bayon! We had to start the project, while preparing for the fact that the Master Plan itself was going to take time.

While continuing the archaeological research on the terraces of the Prasat Suor Prat Towers, I continued to see the complex of the Bayon every day. There are many important things to consider when thinking about the issue of continued cooperation in the conservation of Angkor Monuments. The basis for human resource development is social issues, which is often difficult for foreign teams, but on-the-job training is necessary. The collection of environmental data, such as weather conditions, is the responsibility of the countries concerned, but it is precisely because they are not yet able to do so that international cooperation is necessary. In this situation, the survey about the water environment including rainwater and groundwater veins is needed permanently and immediately based on the highly recommended by geotechnical team. The JSA conducted the first nine borehole core sampling surveys in the Angkor area in 1994, including the Bayon and the Siem Reap township, reaching down to bedrock (about 80 to 100 m). At that time, there was no organization in Cambodia capable of conducting borehole surveys, and a team from a Japanese-Thai joint venture came from Bangkok. Naturally, the team was transported by large vehicles carrying large equipment, but at that time, not only were the roadless roads in Cambodia difficult to navigate, but it was said that private soldiers were hired in some places to privately collect traffic tax. In particular, large vehicles could not afford to pay the tax one by one, so they hired private soldiers to bring them in, firing blanks at each other to tell them to pay or not to pay. I was also surprised at the Thai engineer who candidly told me this story, and I realized that there was no need to take such a risk to investigate, but it was too late to stop the investigation. It was a momentous experience for me, as I glimpsed one of the problems of everyday life in international relations in the context of war, and I have since become attentive to the complex national sentiments of neighboring countries in Southeast Asia.

作成と設計方法の分析方法も公開した。アンコール遺跡の基壇基礎の版築土層は，地盤工学，建築構造学，土質工学，材料施工学全般にわたる重要な学問的課題であることが想定されたため，日本の非焼成煉瓦の研究者をはじめ，多くの専門家の参加をいただいた。またバイヨン上部構造の複雑な動きと強度の判定はアンコール遺跡全般の参考になると思われた。浅浮彫の保存科学研究はオリジナルな石材と微気象条件が重要なため，試験体のバイヨンサイトでの長期的，曝露試験と遺構の保存活用実態を徹底的にフォローする計画がたてられた。3Dと写真測量によるバイヨン全域，尊顔像，内・外回廊浅浮彫等の画像の作成，特に内回廊浅浮彫装飾は画像と視認によるチェックを繰り返し，手描き線描画展開図を完成させた。文字資料が限定されるアンコール遺跡では，浅浮彫で描かれる内容が重要な歴史研究資料となり，アンコール時代の人々の生活を卒業論文研究で取り上げるカンボジア人学生にも重宝されている。遺跡の特質から学ぶ人材育成の課題でもあった。

このようにバイヨンマスタープランの大まかな目的を勘案しながら実際の各分野の調査研究を開始したが，個々の具体的な課題に取り組みながら，より切実に，よりふさわしい方向に各担当者の創意と全体の目的のフィードバックのもとに展開しながら進められ，1994年から2005年までのJSA11年の活動成果のまとめが実際のバイヨンマスタープランだといえよう。そして，もう一つ言及しておかなければならないのは，1996年からJSAの主催で行ったバイヨンシンポジウムである。直接の目的を，バイヨンマスタープランのフレームワークの形成としつつ，実際にはバイヨンのみならずアンコール遺跡の全体に関して，今後どのように調査研究，保存修復していくかをテーマとして，アンコールで働く全ての外国人チームとカンボジアの若い世代に呼びかけ，オープンな議論の場を目指したものである。アンコール遺跡の保存修復協力のための正式な国際調整会議（ICC Angkor）は1993年末より既にスタートしていた。しかし，これは約30の各国政府，国際機関等のフォーマルな協議のためのものであって，当時も現在も議題が多く，各個別修復問題に対して十分な時間をかけての議論がなかなか困難な状況も一方にはあった。そこで実際の修復プロジェクトを担当する各国の専門家同志の自由な議論を通じて，とりわけカンボジアの若い世代にアンコール遺跡の重要性に関心を寄せてもらうことを目的とした。

バイヨンの朝の光の中で，伝説的なアンコール遺跡スペシャリストの懇切な話を聞き，午後はシェムレアップ市の会議室で心ゆくまで議論し合ったことが忘れられない。2004年の第9回バイヨンシンポジウムまでの議論

2. Purpose of the Bayon Master Plan

JSA's restoration project was not to simply restore the damaged parts and be done with it, but to achieve open sharing of knowledge and technology in all phases of research, restoration, conservation and utilization. To this end, it was first necessary to clarify the significance and value of archaeological sites through extensive academic research, to elucidate the factors that cause deterioration and collapse of archaeological sites scientifically as much as possible, and to construct restoration methods that emphasize originality and authenticity of construction. It is easier said than done. Therefore a Master Plan was necessary as a framework for continuous discussion and forward progress. In addition to the water environment, atmospheric environment, meteorological data, rock survey of Angkor Monuments in general, and the preparation of measured drawings of the main monument buildings and analysis methods of design methods were made public. As with all construction, the foundation mound of the Angkor Monuments is an important academic issue covering geotechnical engineering, building structure science, soil engineering, and material construction science in general. Many experts, including Japanese researchers on unfired bricks, participated in the project. In addition, the complex movement and strength determination of the Bayon upper structure was thought to be a useful reference for Angkor Monuments in general. Since original stone composition and microclimatic conditions are important for the conservation science research of Bas-reliefs, a plan was made to conduct long-term exposure tests at the Bayon and to thoroughly follow up the actual conservation and utilization of the Bas-reliefs. The hand drawings of the Inner and Outer Galleries, in particular, were completed through repeated visual checks of images that were created using by 3D modeling and photogrammetry. The entire Bayon, including the face towers, and Bas-relief of Inner and Outer Galleries were subjected to analysis. At the Angkor Monuments, where written materials are limited, the content depicted in the reliefs is an important historical research source, and is also useful for Cambodian and international academics and students who are studying the life of people during the Angkor period for thesis research. It was also an issue of human resource development to learn from the characteristics of the monuments.

In this way, the actual research and study in each field was initiated while taking into consideration the general purpose of the Bayon Master Plan. The actual Bayon Master Plan is a summary of the results of 11 years of JSA activities from 1994 to 2005. With considering individual specific issues, it proceeded in a more earnest and appropriate direction, developing under the creativity of each person in charge and feedback from the overall objectives. Another thing that

とそれまでのJSAの成果をもとにバイヨンマスタープランはまとめられた。2009年6月にアンコール遺跡の各国隊，調達，修復活動を紹介し，自由な討議，発表の場であるJSAバイヨンインフォメーションセンターを開所した。バイヨンシンポジウムに参加していた主なコアメンバーはそのまま重複して2002年よりアンコール憲章の起草作業に入った。2009年からはバイヨンインフォメーションセンターにてその作業を続行した。即ち，バイヨンを中心に，古代クメール文明の価値を保護しようとするバイヨン憲章に対し，アンコール遺跡の保護の理念と修復の指針に特化しているアンコール憲章という違いがあるが，同様な環境と人材によって担われたという共通性もある。近い将来，バイヨン中央塔の修復が終了し，その評価が定まった時点で，両憲章はあらためて再検証される必要があるだろう。

must be mentioned is the Bayon Symposium, that has been organized by JSA since 1996. While the major purpose of the Bayon Symposium was to form a framework for the Bayon Master Plan, the actual theme of the symposium aimed to provide a forum for open discussion on the theme of how to conduct research, conservation, and restoration with young Cambodian experts and foreign teams not only in the Bayon, but of the entire Angkor Monuments. The International Coordinating Committee for Safeguarding and Development of Historical Site of Angkor (ICC Angkor) had already started at the end of 1993. However, ICC Angkor is for formal discussions among about 30 governments, international organizations, and others, and there were, and still are, many issues on the agenda, making it difficult to spend sufficient time discussing each individual restoration issue. Therefore, the purpose of the Bayon Symposium was to raise awareness of the importance of the Angkor Monuments, especially among the younger generation in Cambodia, through free discussions among experts from each country who are in charge of actual restoration projects.

I will never forget the morning light of Bayon, listening to the talks by specialists of the legendary Angkor, and in the afternoon discussing to our heart's content in the conference room in Siem Reap. The Bayon Master Plan was summarized based on the discussion of the Bayon Symposium and other aspects and achivement of JSA research. In June 2009, the JSA Bayon Information Center was opened as a place to introduce, freely discuss, and present the activities of cooperation between each team, and restoration of the Angkor Monuments. The main core members who participated in the Bayon Symposium began drafting the Angkor Charter in 2002. This work was continued at the Bayon Information Center from 2009. The Bayon Charter aimed to protect the values of the ancient Khmer civilization with a focus on the Bayon, while the Angkor Charter specializes in the principles and guidelines of protection and restoration for Angkor Monuments. The Angkor Charter and Bayon Charter are similar in that they were drafted by members of the Bayon Symposium. In the near future, when the restoration of the Bayon Central Tower is completed and its evaluation is finalized, both charters will need to be reexamined.

第 4 章　JSA/JASA の保存修復事業

Chapter 4　JSA/JASA Restoration and Conservation Project

4.1 アンコール・トム王宮前広場プラサート・スープラの保存修復
The Conservation and Restoration of the Prasat Suor Prat on Royal Palace, Angkor Thom

赤澤　泰
AKAZAWA Yasushi

1. 王宮前広場とプラサート・スープラ

　アンコール・トムの中央には，アジアの都市には稀な壮大かつ壮麗な王宮前広場が存在する。その広場を挟んで西側には王宮跡，東側に配置されているのがプラサート・スープラ（Prasat Suor Prat 以下PSP）と呼ばれる12基の塔状建築物とテラスから成る遺構である。広場と王宮に面する配置から，PSPが何らかの儀式的な目的に使用されたことを想像させるが，その建立目的などは未だ明確にはされていない[1]。

　このPSPについて，JSAは1994年から開始された考古班によるテラスの発掘調査をはじめとして，保存修復に必要と考えられる様々な分野の調査を実施した。基本的な考え方としては，短期間で全ての対象を保存修復するのではなく，12基の塔とテラスの劣化状態に対応しながら長期的な修復を目指すという展望で臨んだ。従って2001年から2005年に渡るN2塔ポーチおよびN1塔

1. Prasat Suor Prat on the Royal Palace

　In the center of Angkor Thom, there is a magnificent Royal Palace Plaza, which is rare in Asian cities. On the west side of the plaza is the ruins of the royal palace, and on the east side is the remains of 12 towers and terraces called Prasat Suor Prat (here after PSP). The placement facing the plaza and the royal palace suggests that the PSP was used for some kind of ceremonial purpose, but the purpose of its construction has not yet been clarified[1].

　Regarding PSP, the JSA carried out a variety of surveys, including the excavation of the terraces by the archaeological team, which was started in 1994, and considered necessary for conservation and restoration. As for the basic concept of preservation and restoration, instead of carrying out all the objects in a short period of time, we approached the project with the vision of aiming for long-term restoration while dealing with the deteriorated state of the 12 towers and terraces. Therefore, the preservation and restoration work of

Fig. 4.1.1 Panoramic view of PSP and Royal Plaza (from north-west) Photo by JSA

163

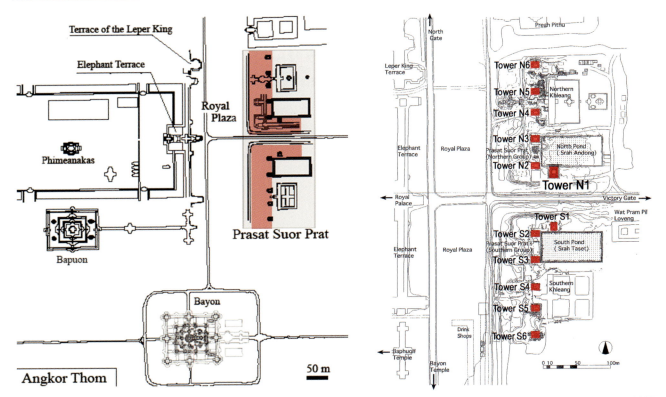

Fig. 4.1.2 Site Map on Center of Angkor Thom

Fig. 4.1.3 Site Map of PSP

の保存修復工事は，その先導的な役割を果たすパイロットプランとして位置づけ実施されたものである[2]。

2．PSPのテラスおよび建物の概要

　PSPは，南北に長いテラス，さらに12基の塔から成る複合構築物である。王宮側から勝利の門（Gate of Victory）に向かって東に延びる道路は，PSPの南北の中央を貫き，2つのエリアに区分する。南北群それぞれに6基の塔を有し，その5基は広場に向かって正面を構える配置（西向き）であるが，道路に最も近い南北の各1基は，それぞれこの道路に正対する配置となっている。

　塔の東側には，南北群とも沐浴池が存在する。この南北の池は，ラテライトの加工痕跡等から塔よりも前に構築されたものと考えられる（Fig. 4.1.1, 4.1.2, 4.1.3）。

　12基はほとんど同一の規模・形状を有し，しかも，ほぼ全部の塔が未完成と思われる状態であり，王宮前の重要な配置を鑑みると何かしら不自然さを感じる建造物群である。この塔状の建物は，テラスの上に基壇を載せ，上部が3層と見える壁体を持ち，正面と背面に飾り破風を有する屋根が載る形状である。平面形状は正面幅に対し奥行きが少し長い長方形を基本としている。その基本形を上層ではそれぞれ同率で低減し3層構成としている。12基とも基本的には同様の建築構成をとる。

the N2 tower antechamber and N1 tower from 2001 to 2005 was positioned as a pilot plan to play a leading role. The plan was implemented[2].

2. Summary of PSP

　PSP is a complex structure consisting of a long north-south terrace and 12 towers. The road extending east to the Gate of Victory passes through the north and south center of PSP, dividing it into two areas. Each of the north and south groups has six towers, five of which face the plaza (facing west), while the north and south, which are closest to the road, are each facing the road.

　There are ponds on both the north and south areas of the tower on the east side. These north and south ponds are thought to have been built before the towers, based on traces of laterite processing (Fig.4.1.1, 4.1.2 and 4.1.3).

　The 12 towers have almost the same size and shape, and almost all of them appear to be unfinished. Considering the important arrangement in front of the royal palace, it is a group of buildings that is somewhat mysterious.

　This group of towers has a platform on top of the terrace, the upper part has a wall body that can be seen as three layers, and the roof with decorative pediment on the front and back. The plane shape is basically a rectangle with a slightly longer depth than the width of the front. The basic shape is reduced at the same rate in the upper layer to form a three-layer

Fig. 4.1.4 N1 West elevation (after restoration)

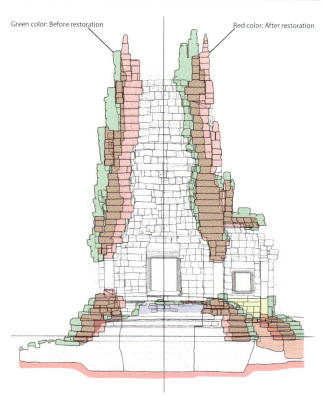

Fig. 4.1.5 Section of N1 tower (North-South)

塔の劣化状況は，各塔とも傾斜が確認され，そのことに起因したと思われる頂部屋根の崩落，ポーチの部分的な崩壊，飾り破風などの装飾部材の落下等が見られた。中でもN1塔は傾斜が最も大きいことが調査によって明らかにされた。

3．保存修復工事の特徴

PSP塔の保存修復工事の特徴は，対象がこれまでアンコール遺跡群では修復事例の非常に少ないラテライトブロックの組積造構築物であるとともに，建築学的に塔状建築として特殊な形式を持つ構築物であり，さらに結果的に全解体を伴う保存修復工事であったことが挙げられる。PSPは，1950年から1960年代にEFEO（フランス極東学院）によって解体修復工事が実施されたが，対象となった塔（JSAによる呼称はN3塔）では基壇・基礎への介入が行なわれなかった。また，この時の工事においては，目地接着剤としてセメントモルタルが使用されたほか，RC造の大梁を挿入するなどの処理がとられた。

そのため，N1塔の解体工事では，ラテライトブロックの建立当初の組積方法に関する調査研究から，再構築に際して必要となる破損したラテライト部材の修復方法やそのための材料の選定まで，多様な課題に対してあらたに調査が必要になり，研究開発すべき多くの項目に対

structure. All 12 towers have basically the same architectural composition.

As for the deterioration of the towers, it was confirmed that each tower was tilted, and the top roof collapsed due to this tilt, the antechamber partially collapsed, and decorations such as sandstone gables fell down. The survey revealed that the N1 tower has the biggest incline.

3. The Features of the conservation and restoration work

The features of the conservation and restoration work on the PSP towers in question are that they are laterite block masonry structures, which has rarely been restored in the Angkor Monuments, furthermore, it can be pointed out that the preservation and restoration work involved complete dismantling as a result.

The PSP was dismantled and restored by EFEO in the 1950s and 1960s, but no intervention was made to the foundation and platform of the target tower. In addition, during the construction work, cement mortar was used as a joint adhesive and measures were taken such as inserting reinforced concrete beams.

For this reason, JSA is conducting new research on a variety of issues, from research and research on the masonry methods used when laterite blocks were first erected, to methods for repairing damaged laterite members and the selection of materials needed for reconstruction. It became necessary,

応する必要があった。このことが，今回の修復工事の重要な目標の一つであった。

第2の特徴は，基礎・基壇の詳細発掘調査を実施し，塔の傾斜要因の解析に努めたことである（Fig. 4.1.3, 4.1.4, 4.1.5）。アンコールの遺構における基壇・基礎に関する知見は極めて少ない。1996年から1999年にかけてJSAが実施したバイヨン北経蔵保存修復工事においても，部分的ではあるが基壇部の解体調査が実施され，一定の成果を得た。しかしバイヨン北経蔵は，バイヨン伽藍の下部テラス上に設置された遺構であるため，基壇の下部はPSPのように独立した建築に用いられる通常の基礎と異なる構成を採っている。また，これまでアンコール地域で実施された基礎・基壇に関わる保存修復工事は，主に現代建築の工法と材料を取り入れて安定化を図っている。例えば，基壇内部にコンクリート壁を巡らし，適宜排水管を導入する等の手法である。1999年から開始されたプレ・ルプにおける基礎の修復工事（イタリア隊によって実施）は，煉瓦造の遺構であるため，上部構造体の解体を実施せずに床下を発掘して鉄筋コンクリートの箱形の基礎を設置し，ここから周囲のラテライトブロックに鉄筋を挿入することで基礎の強度を回復しようとした。これらの手法の導入については，修復工事が進められた当時，相応に適切な調査研究がなされ計画されたものと考えられるが，JSAは創建時の工法の保存について真摯に検討する必要があると考えてきた。このような背景から，徹底した調査・劣化要因の解析に臨み，各種の試行と実験を経て実際の修復方法を策定した。

4. 修復方法の検討

文化財の保存修復であるから，極力現状保存が望ましいことは言うまでもない。しかし，前述したようにN3塔において実施された解体修復工事は，修復後50年ほど経過した現在，塔の様相は再度傾斜し，開口部材などが破断し危険な状態にある。このN3塔の傾斜はおそらく修復工事直後，もしくは修復工事中にも始まっていた可能性がある。基礎・基壇の修復を実施せずに上部構造を固化した結果，塔は再び傾斜してしまったのであろう。このような事例もあり，JSAでは基礎・基壇部の修復の必要性を認め，当初ハンドオーガーなどを使用した調査を繰り返し実施した。また，全解体せず部分的な解体での修復可否の検討やピサの斜塔における保存修復工事に用いられた手法など，さまざまな可能性を検討した。しかし，基礎・基壇部の構成を理解し，その劣化損傷要因を把握するためには十分とはいえない状況であった。

and it was necessary to respond to many items that should be researched and developed. This was one of the important goals of this restoration work.

The second feature is that detailed excavation surveys of the foundations and platform were carried out, and efforts were made to analyze the causes of the tilting of the tower (Fig. 4.1.3, 4.1.4 and 4.1.5). There is extremely little knowledge about the platform and foundations of the remains of Angkor. During the conservation and restoration work of the Bayon Northern Library carried out by the JSA from 1996 to 1999, the podium was partially dismantled and investigated, and some results were achieved. However, since the Bayon Northern Library is a remains that was built on the lower terrace of the Bayon complex, the lower part of the platform has a different structure from the usual foundations used for independent buildings like PSP. In addition, the conservation and restoration work related to foundations and foundations that has been carried out in the Angkor region to date has mainly incorporated modern architectural methods and materials in an effort to stabilize them. For example, a concrete wall is laid around the inside of the platform, and drainage pipes are introduced as appropriate. Restoration work on the foundations of the Pre Rup (carried out by an Italian team) that began in 1999 did not involve dismantling the superstructure, as it was a brick structure, but excavated the area beneath the floor and replaced it with a box-shaped reinforced concrete structure. An attempt was made to restore the strength of the foundation by installing a foundation and inserting reinforcing bars into the surrounding laterite blocks. It is believed that the introduction of these methods was planned after appropriate research and research was conducted at the time the restoration work was underway, but JSA believes that it is necessary to seriously consider preserving the original construction methods. I've been thinking about it. Against this background, we conducted a thorough investigation and analyzed the causes of deterioration, and after conducting various trials and experiments, we formulated an actual repair method.

4. Consideration of conservation and restoration methods

Since we are preserving and restoring cultural properties, it goes without saying that it is desirable to preserve them in their current state as much as possible. However, about 50 years after the restoration, the N3 tower is now in a dangerous state as it has tilted again and the opening members have broken. This tilting of the N3 tower probably began immediately after or even during the restoration work. The tower probably tilted again as a result of solidifying the superstructure without repairing the foundation and platform. In such cases, JSA recognized the need for detailed

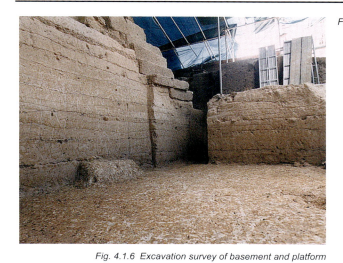

Fig. 4.1.6 Excavation survey of basement and platform

Fig. 4.1.7 Section of platform North part (west face) (from north-west)

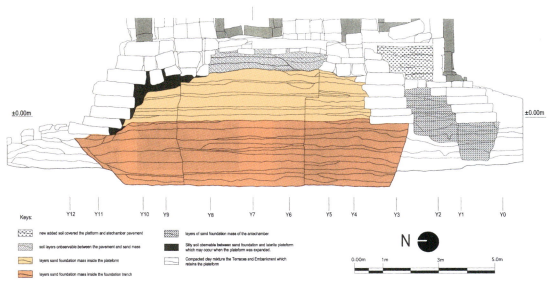

Keys:
- new added soil covered the platform and atechamber pavement
- soil layers onbservable between the pavement and sand mass
- layers sand foundation mass inside the plateform
- layers sand foundation mass inside the foundation trench
- layers of sand foundation mass of the antechamber
- Silty soil obervable between sand foundation and laterite plateform which may occur when the plateform was expanded.
- Compacted clay mixture the Terraces and Embankment which retains the plateform

Fig. 4.1.8 Section of basement and platform (South-North)

Fig. 4.1.9 N2 antichanber (after restoration)

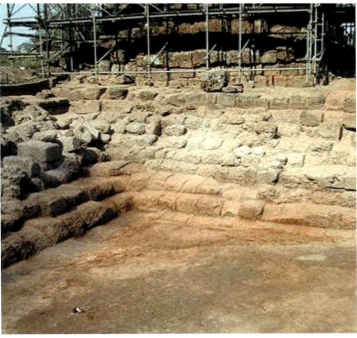

Fig. 4.1.10 Excavation survey of North pond (south-west corner)

4.1　アンコール・トム王宮前広場プラサート・スープラの保存修復

Fig. 4.1.11 Using a rammed earth construction method (rod tamping)

Fig. 4.1.12 Using a rammed earth construction method (elephant foot tamping)

Fig. 4.1.13 After restoration of PSP N1 (South-West View)

Fig. 4.1.14 After restoration of PSP N1 and North Pond embankment (North-East View)

そのため，まずN1塔と同等に危険な状態であったN2塔のポーチ部での解体・再構築工事を先行し，調査方法や修復方法の深度を深め，また，傾斜の要因の一つと考えられる北池についても発掘調査を実施し，池の護岸構成を明らかにしたうえで，N1塔の保存修復工事に着手することとした。

N1塔の保存修復工事は，近い将来に保存修復工事が必要とされるであろう他の11の塔や，これに加えて，アンコール遺跡の保存修復における基礎・基壇の保存修復方法の新たな可能性を模索して，全解体という方法の採択に至っている。多面的な各種調査と研究結果を受けて，基礎を含む全てを解体の対象とし，塔の安定化のために独自に開発した消石灰改良土を使用し，オリジナル工法に近似する版築工法によって再構築を行なった（Fig. 4.1.11, 4.1.12）。

基礎部の詳細調査および全解体・再構築は，これまでのアンコール地域での保存修復事業では先例を見ないもので，今回の保存修復工事を通して得られた調査研究結果や経験は，今後のアンコール地域での遺構の保存修復事業にとって，大きな収穫であったと思われる。

investigation and repair of foundations and foundations, and at first conducted repeated investigations using hand augers. We also examined various possibilities, including whether it would be possible to restore the structure by partial demolition rather than complete dismantling, and the method used for conservation and restoration work on the Leaning Tower of Pisa. However, the situation was not sufficient to understand the composition of the foundation and platform and to understand the causes of its deterioration and damage.

For this reason, first, the dismantling and reconstruction work of the antechamber of the N2 tower, which was in a dangerous state equivalent to that of the N1 tower, was carried out in advance. After excavation surveys were also carried out on the North Pond, which is currently being built, and the structure of the pond's embankment was clarified, it was decided to begin conservation and restoration work on the N1 Tower.

The reason why we decided to dismantle the entire N1 Tower during the conservation and restoration work was to explore new possibilities for preserving and restoring the foundations and platforms of the Angkor ruins, including the other 11 PSP towers. In response to the results of various multifaceted surveys and research, the conservation and restoration work on the N1 Tower included the complete dismantling of all parts, including the foundation, and improvements using a mixture of slaked lime, which was originally developed to stabilize the tower. Reconstruction was carried out using a rammed earth construction method that approximates the original construction method (Fig.4.1.11, and 4.1.12).

The detailed investigation of the foundation and the complete dismantle and reconstruction are unprecedented in conservation and restoration projects in the Angkor region. The research results and experiences gained through this conservation and restoration work are believed to be of great benefit for future conservation and restoration projects of ruins in the Angkor region.

References
1) Nakagawa Takeshi. (Supervisor) 1996-2005. Annual Report on the Technical Survey of Angkor Monument 1995-2004, Japanese Government Team for Safeguarding Angkor (JSA), Japan International Cooperation Center
2) Nakagawa Takeshi. (Supervisor). 2005. Report on the Conservation and Restoration Work of the Prasat Suor Prat Tower, Royal Plaza of Angkor Thom, Kingdom of Cambodia, Japanese Government Team for Safeguarding Angkor (JSA), Japan International Cooperation Center.

4.2 バイヨン北経蔵
──アンコールにおける新たな修復モデルの提示
Northern Library of Bayon:
Presenting a New Model for Restoration in Angkor

友田 正彦
TOMODA Masahiko

1. アンコール修復史上の位置付け

バイヨン北経蔵はJSAチームが最初に手掛けた修復対象であると同時に，アンコールの遺跡修復史上においては，EFEO（フランス極東学院）以外が計画・実施した最初の本格的修復事業のひとつでもあった。発足間もないJSAチームとしては，以前からクメールの石造建造物を研究対象としてきたメンバーこそいたものの，その修復という作業は全く未知の経験であり，あらゆる面でゼロからの模索に近い，相当にハードルの高い取り組みであったと言える。そして，そうであるからこそ，それまでのEFEOによる長年にわたる実践の結果として半ばルーチン化していた手法を抜本的に見直すとともに，国際的な文化遺産修復理念に照らしても十分に説明可能な，実施時点における技術的最適解を改めて提示することがわれわれに課せられた責務でもあった。

2. バイヨン全体の保存に向けて

アンコール・ワットとともにアンコール遺跡群を代表するバイヨンは，日本政府による修復支援事業のターゲットとして当初から認識されていたが，アンコール・ワットと比較したとき，建築作品として不可解な要素が多いだけでなく，構造物としての安定性や石材の保存状態といった様々な観点からもはるかに多くの問題が内在していることは一見して明らかであった。バイヨンの重要性が，中央塔をはじめ，巨大な人面彫刻を施した奇怪な塔群にあることは衆目の一致するところであったとしても，それらを修復対象として扱うには解決すべき難問があまりにも多いと思われた。そこでわれわれが着目したのが，伽藍の一角に独立して建つ，南北2つの経蔵の

1. Significance in the history of restoration in Angkor

Northern Library of Bayon became the first target of restoration in which JSA team engaged. At the same time, its restoration was one of the first full-scale restoration projects completed through planning and execution by the team other than Ecole francaise d'Extreme Orient (EFEO) in the history of restoration in Angkor. This must be a rather difficult task starting from almost zero in every aspect for the JSA team, just after its establishment, which had no previous experience in the restoration of Khmer stone architecture, even though some members of the team had engaged in its academic study. And, for this very reason, it became a clear mission for us to present a renewed answer which was technically most appropriate at that moment and accountable enough in the light of contemporary international norms of heritage conservation, by fundamentally reexamining the conventionalized methodologies resulted from long practices by EFEO.

2. For the conservation of Bayon as a whole

Bayon is the representative monument in Angkor, together with Angkor Wat, and therefore the Japanese government recognized Bayon as a target of its aid project for safeguarding Angkor from the beginning. However, when compared with Angkor Wat, Bayon obviously contains more enigmatic elements as an architectural work, and much greater problems in various viewpoints including structural stability and preservation status of stone materials. It can be widely agreed that the significance of Bayon depends mainly on the strange towers carved with giant human faces, but we found that too many difficult questions must be solved before dealing with these towers as restoration targets. Then, we noticed two libraries which stood in the north and south corners of the temple complex.

Fig. 4.2.1 Overall view of Bayon during the restoration of the Northern Library

存在であった。

　似通った構造と残存状態を示す両経蔵のうちでも，壁体の傾斜が進行して倒壊の切迫度がより高かった北経蔵をまず対象として，その調査研究と修復計画策定，施工，記録といった一連のプロセスを経験することを通じ，バイヨンを含むアンコールの石造建築に関して大きく以下3つの課題への取り組みを推進することを当面の目標として定めた。

・アンコール時代の建築技術の解明
・最適な修復手法の研究と開発
・それを高い水準で実施できる作業体制の構築ならびにカンボジア人技術人材の育成

　このような基本的考えを，当時の新生カンボジア政府においてアンコール遺跡保存を一手に所管していたヴァン・モリヴァン上級国務大臣に説明したところ，最初の反応は決して芳しいものではなかったと記憶している。内戦前のカンボジアにおいて既に国を代表する建築家だった彼にとってもバイヨンは特別な存在であり，その片隅に建つささやかな経蔵にだけ手を付けるという計画はにわかに受け入れ難いものだったようである。あくまで伽藍全体の恒久的保存に道筋を付けることが彼にシハヌーク国王から託された使命であって，そのためのマスタープラン策定を確約しない限りはバイヨンに指一本触れさせることはできないとの気迫を強く感じた。JSAではこのリクエストに応えるべく，以後約10年をかけて「バイヨン寺院全域の保存修復のためのマスタープラン」を策定するとともに，とくに中央塔の恒久的保存を目標に掲げつつバイヨンでの調査ならびに修復活動を今日まで継続することとなったのである。

Among the two libraries having similar composition and preservation status, we selected the northern one as the initial target because it demonstrated more risk of collapse with progressive leaning of the wall structures. By experiencing, with this building, a thorough process of research studies, restoration plan formation, construction work and documentation, we aimed to achieve the three main objectives regarding stone monuments in Angkor including Bayon as follows:

i) Explication of construction techniques from the Angkor period

ii) Study and development of the most appropriate methodologies for restoration

iii) Establishment of work system and cultivation of Cambodian technical personnel for the implementation at a high level

When we explained this basic work plan of JSA to H.E. Senior Minister Van Molyvann who was exclusively responsible for the conservation of Angkor Monuments at the newborn government of Cambodia, his first response seemed reluctant, I remember. As a representative architect of the nation since even before the civil war, he also felt special devotion to Bayon and thus the idea to work on only with such tiny library at a small corner of the temple might not be acceptable. His mission entrusted by His Majesty the King Sihanouk was to pave the way for permanent preservation of the whole complex of Bayon, and he urged us to make a definite promise to formulate a comprehensive masterplan for that purpose. In response to this request, JSA then started to develop the "Masterplan for the Conservation & Restoration of the Bayon Complex" spending nearly 10 years and has continued working till today on the investigation and restoration activities at Bayon aiming for the permanent conservation of its central tower, especially.

Fig. 4.2.2 Degrading status before the restoration
a) Southeast corner of the upper structure

Fig. 4.2.3 Degrading status before the restoration
b) Interior view from the west

3. もう一つの時代的背景

バイヨン北経蔵の修復作業に本格的に着手したのは1995年の夏であるが，奇しくも前年の11月に日本の奈良で開催された専門家会合の成果文書として，「オーセンティシティに関する奈良ドキュメント」が採択されている。

建築遺産の保存修理をめぐっては1964年のベネチア憲章において価値に関する本質的評価要素としてのオーセンティシティという概念が確認され，1972年の世界遺産条約において制度化された。しかし，主としてヨーロッパの組積造建築の文脈において生み出されたオーセンティシティ概念が世界における文化遺産の多様性を十分に反映していないとの問題意識をうけて，これをより包摂的な概念へと拡張しようとする試みが日本の主導による奈良ドキュメントであった。従って，JSAがこのタイミングで世界遺産アンコールにおける修復活動を開始するにあたっては，必然的に，非ヨーロッパ的文脈における今後の建築遺産修復の手本となることが求められていたといえよう。

4. 保存状態と劣化メカニズム

バイヨン北経蔵は基底部で南北11m×東西18mの平面規模を有する石造建築で，三重の高い基壇上に長方形平面の主室が載り，東西両面にポーチが取りつくという，クメール建築でもあまり類例のない構成からなる。コー

3. Another historical background

Restoration project of the Northern Library of Bayon substantially started in the summer of 1995. In November of the previous year coincidently, an experts conference organized in Nara, Japan adopted as the outcome document "The Nara Document on Authenticity".

Concerning the conservation of architectural heritage, The Venice Charter in 1964 confirmed the concept of authenticity as a fundamental element in evaluation of heritage value, and The World Heritage Convention in 1972 integrate this concept into the operational system. But concerns arose later that this concept of authenticity that was created mainly in the context of European masonry architectural culture did not fully reflect diversity of cultural heritage in the world. The Nara Document under Japanese initiative was an answer to this trying to widen the concept of authenticity to become more inclusive. Consequently, when JSA started its restoration activity in Angkor at this moment, it was inevitably expected to show a paragon of architectural heritage restoration in a non-European context.

4. Conservation status and degradation mechanism

The Northern Library of Bayon is a stone masonry building measuring 11 m north-south by 18 m in an east-west directions. It has a rather unique composition even among Khmer architecture that a quadrangular room, attached with open-sided porches in the east and west ends, stands on top of three-tiered platform. The corbel-vaulted roof already

Fig. 4.2.4 Degrading status before the restoration
c) Southwest corner of the platform

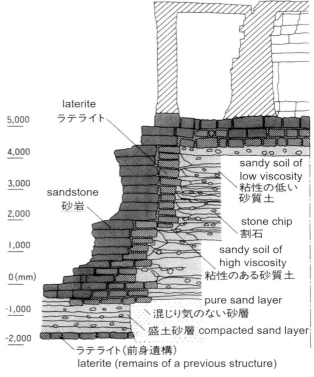

Fig. 4.2.5 Inner composition of the platform

ベル・アーチの屋根は既に失われており，破損や変形は上部躯体と基壇の東西両端部に集中していた。上部砂岩材の一部に応力集中による破断等が見られたものの，基壇を構成する大半の材は概ね健全であり，建物が載る人工地盤である中庭石敷面にも顕著な不同沈下等は認められなかった。

これに対して，基壇上面では最大で150mm前後に及ぶ沈下が生じており，基壇端部では外装材が外方に大きく押し出されている状況であった。このため，建物を構造的に健全にし，本来の形状に復するためには基壇の安定化こそが必要な作業であった。クメール石造建築の定石として，基壇は彫刻を施す外装にだけ砂岩材を用い，その背後にはラテライトブロック，さらに内部は突き固めた盛土層で構成される。基壇上面についても同様の構成となる。石材の変位によって生じた空隙から雨水等が浸入し，盛土材が流失することが不同沈下の原因であり，植物の生育等がこうした劣化・変形をさらに促進する。

5. 修復の理念と手法

EFEOによってアンコールで従来行われてきた修復では基壇基底部までを全解体し，RC造の耐圧版を新設し

had disappeared. Damage and deformation concentrated in the areas of the upper structure and the end sections of the platform. Although breakage caused by concentrated stress appeared with some sandstone members in the upper section, majority of the materials composing the platform remained in a sound condition, and no remarkable uneven subsidence was observed at the paved yard level on which the building stood. In contrary, subsidence of about 150 mm maximum occurred on the top surface of the platform, and sandstone finishing blocks were largely pushed out at the end sections of the platform. Therefore, the very necessary work was to stabilize the platform so that the building becomes structurally sound and the original appearance is recovered. As a standard formula of Khmer architecture, the platform wall consists of sandstone blocks for the outer finishing with carvings, laterite blocks behind, and compacted soil layers in the core part. If displacement of stones occurs rainwater penetrates into the open gaps and washes inner soil out of the foundation. This is the typical mechanism that causes uneven subsidence, adding to which the growth of vegetation accelerates the deterioration and deformation.

5. Concept and methodology for restoration

In the general way restoration was previously conducted

た上にオリジナルの外装材と転用・整形したラテライト,新設盛土によって再構築を行うという手法が一般に行われてきた。バプーオンのように基壇が高い場合は外装背後ラテライトの内側にRC擁壁を新設して内部盛土の土留めとする例もある。これによって構造的安定化と外観保存は両立するが,当初技法のオーセンティシティ保持という観点からは大いに問題を孕んでいた。

バイヨン北経蔵の基壇は高さ5mに達することから当初は何らかの補強策が必要とも思われたが,中・下層基壇の中央部では目立った孕み出し等が認められず,構造計算上も問題がなかったことから,最小限介入の考え方に沿ってこの部分には手を触れず,変形範囲のみを部分解体する方針で修復を行うこととなった。さらに,改修部分においても創建当初と同様の構法に極力近い伝統的技法を採用することも検討した。しかし,この場合,建造から800年を経て圧密した存置部分と新規に突き固める改修部分の盛土層相互を同等の強度と安定性をもって一体化することは不可能と結論せざるを得なかっ

by EFEO at Angkor, after totally dismantling the existing structure up to the bottom of the platform, an RC slab is constructed, on which rebuilding is made with the original sandstone finishing blocks, remodeled laterite blocks, and newly compacted soil layers. In case the platform is very high like Baphuon, additional retaining RC walls were built behind the laterite layers to keep the inner soil stable. This method can realize both structural stabilization and preservation of external appearance, but it involves fundamental problems in terms of preserving authenticity of the original building technique.

Since height of the platform of the Northern Library of Bayon reaches to 5m, we initially thought that some reinforcing measure might be required. But no remarkable deformation was observed at the middle section of the lower and middle platform, on which structural calculation also confirmed the stability. Then, we decided to keep this stable section untouched and conduct restoration by partially dismantling the deformed sections, following the conservation principle of minimum intervention. Furthermore, we considered to apply traditional building techniques as closer as possible to the original even at the section to be restored. However, we concluded that it was impossible to unify soil layers of the existing section after experiencing 800 years of consolidation and the restored section of new compaction into perfectly equivalent in strength and stability. It was also inacceptable from viewpoints of economy and safety to take a risk of inviting such degradation as before for a short span of time after the restoration. We finally decided to apply a compacted mixture of fine sand, clay and slaked lime for inner filling of the platform, and for the area bearing much of the upper weight make structural improvement by replacing the original sand layer with a new laterite block. External sandstone blocks and laterite blocks behind them

Fig. 4.2.6 Dismantling work
a) Upper structure

Fig. 4.2.7 Dismantling work
b) Northwest corner of the platform

Fig. 4.2.8 Compaction of improved soil filling

た。また，修復後に短期間で再度同様の劣化を招くリスクを冒すことは経済的にも安全面からも受け容れ難かった。種々検討の結果，再構築部分の内部盛土には細砂と粘土に消石灰を混和した材料を突き固めて用い，特に荷重のかかる位置では砂層をラテライトブロックに置換するなどの改良を行うこととなった。外装砂岩とその背後のラテライトは基本的に当初材を空積みにて再構築したが，劣化の著しい内部ラテライトの一部は新材に交換した。また，当初砂岩材が欠失していた箇所で構造上不可欠な部位については新材砂岩で部材を制作して補った。これらの砂岩およびラテライト新材の入手も当初構法保存のカギであったが，カンボジア政府機関と共同で全国にわたる調査を行った末，オリジナル材に極めて近い材質の石材を新たに切り出して供給することに成功した。

6. 残された課題

本工事で解体した石材は1,500点余りで，そのおよそ3分の1について何らかの補修を行った。エポキシ樹脂やポリマーセメントといった近代材料も用いつつ，特に彫刻部材については相当に劣化程度が激しい材であっても補修して再用することに努めた。これにより，オリジナルの砂岩材を新材に置き換えたのは3点のみにとどめることができた。一方で，屋根周りを中心に大量の部材が行方不明のままに終わった。北経蔵の周囲には膨大な数の石材が集積されており，その中から欠失部材を発見して屋根を復原することも当初は期待していた。しかし，7,000点に及ぶ石材を移動し，平場に広げて整理・探索するという地道な作業を行ったにもかかわらず，北経蔵の部材として特定できたのは結局わずか57点にとどまった。西面ポーチのペディメントは回収材から過半を

were basically put back to the original position without using joint mortars, but some severely decayed inner laterite blocks were replaced with new materials. Also, for the area where the original sandstone blocks were missing but structurally indispensable, the blocks were supplemented by making with new sandstone blocks. Supply of such new sandstone and laterite material was a key factor to preserve the original way of construction. After a thorough investigation jointly undertaken with a relevant Cambodian governmental authority, we succeeded to find sources and develop new quarries to provide materials of the quality very close to the original.

6. Remaining issues

More than 1500 pieces of stone blocks were dismantled during the restoration, about one third of which repair works of various kinds were performed. Using modern materials including epoxy resin and polymer cement, we tried to reuse the original stone block as much as possible even if it showed substantial decay, particularly for the one with carvings. Consequently, only three pieces of the original sandstone blocks were replaced with new material. On the other hand, a large number of stone members mainly in the roof section remained missing. Since plenty of stone blocks were piled up in the vicinity of the Northern Library, we initially expected to find missing members of this building and recover the roof part. However, such time-consuming work of moving, spreading on the ground, sorting and identifying up to 7000 pieces of sandstone blocks resulted in finding out only 57 pieces identified as members from the Library. More than half of the front pediment on the west porch could be rebuilt with the recovered members, but we gave up the idea to put it back to the original position on the building for the safety concern. None of the main roof above the nave could be

Fig. 4.2.9 West pediment constituted with recovered stone blocks

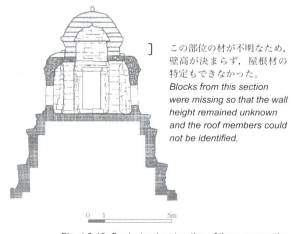

この部位の材が不明なため，壁高が決まらず，屋根材の特定もできなかった。
Blocks from this section were missing so that the wall height remained unknown and the roof members could not be identified.

Fig. 4.2.10 Conjectural restoration of the cross section including the roof

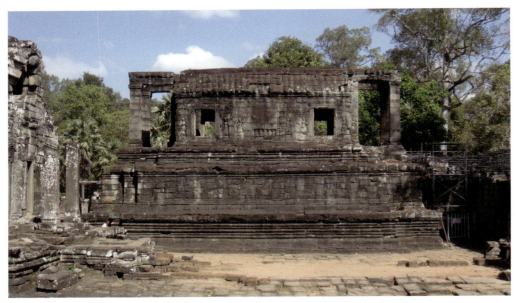

Fig. 4.2.11 Northern Library 20 years after restoration

復原できたが，建物上の原位置に復することは安全面から断念せざるを得なかった。とくに身舎屋根が全く特定できなかった理由は，この屋根に続く小壁部分の部材が100年ほど前に行われた整理清掃作業によって完全に失われていたためである。もしこれらの材が発見されていたら，巨大なコーベル・アーチの屋根をいかに安全に再構築するかというもう一つの難題に取り組まねばならなかった筈である。

7. 結語

バイヨン北経蔵修復工事は約4年の工期をかけ，1999年9月に無事竣工した。それから既に四半世紀が経つ。バイヨン北経蔵修復工事においてJSAが開発・採用した技法の多くは，その後も様々な改良を加えられつつ，APSARAや他の国際チームによるアンコールでの修復においても事実上のスタンダードとなりつつあるが，品質管理や記録作成・公開といった面ではまだまだ課題が多いのが実情である。日本から優秀な技術と人材を投入し，潤沢な予算にも恵まれた本工事と同等の水準での事業は実現困難な場合がほとんどであろうし，改良土の使用は技法のオーセンティシティ維持に抵触するのではといった批判があることも事実である。しかし，膨大な修復需要を抱えるカンボジアにおける遺産保全の持続可能性にも鑑みてベストな解を追求した結果がバイヨン北経蔵修復であったし，以後のモデルを提示するという当初の目的は十分以上に達成できたものと今日でも自負している。

identified because the original members which composed the side walls supporting the roof were totally missing due to the past clearance work about one hundred years ago. If these members were recovered, we had to tackle another difficult task of how to safely rebuild this corbel-vaulted roof.

7. Conclusion

Restoration work of the Northern Library of Bayon completed in September 1999 after about four years without accident. Since then, it has passed a quarter of a century. Many of the methodologies which JSA developed for and applied to the restoration work of the Bayon Northern Library has become, with added various improvements, becomes standard for restoration in Angkor even by APSARA and other international teams. But there remain many challenges in such areas as quality control and thorough documentation including its dissemination during the project. In most cases, it would be difficult to achieve such high level of work as the Bayon project without excellent technical resources as well as ample budget from Japan. It is also true that there is a criticism that use of the improved soil filling conflicts with the principle of technical authenticity. Nevertheless, the restoration of the Northern Library of Bayon was a result of our pursuing the best answer in view of the sustainable heritage conservation in Cambodia having an enormous needs of monument restoration. We are proud of our accomplishments in presenting a model for the future more than we first intended.

4.3　アンコール・ワット最外周壁内北経蔵
Northern Library Inside the Outermost Enclosure of Angkor Wat

土屋　武
TSUCHIYA Takeshi

1.　遺構の概要

　アンコール・ワットはスールヤヴァルマンⅡによって12世紀中頃に建造されたヒンドゥー教の大規模寺院であり，他の多くのクメール王達がその祭祀寺院にシヴァ神を祀ってきたのに反してヴィシュヌ神を本尊としていた。近世以降では仏教寺院として使用されている。当寺院はカンボジアにインドの宗教建築が伝わってから1,000年近くに及ぶクメール建築の発展の集大成と云えるものであり，規模，伽藍構成，建築様式，建築技術，美術様式の全般において極めて高い完成度を見せている。修復対象はアンコール・ワット内にある回廊に接続しない建物の一つで，西大門から中央のピラミッドへ続く大舗道の北側に位置している。現在，一般的に北経蔵と呼ばれているが，これはフランスの考古学分野で同様の配置にある建物をBibliothèqueと呼んでいるものをそのまま仏教建築の経蔵に翻訳したのであり，本来のヒンドゥー教寺院としての建物の名称と役割はわかっていない。建物の規模は東西約42 m，南北約25 m，高さ約11 m。二重の基壇の上に，十字形平面の主室と矩形平面の東西側室と四方のポーチから構成される。構造の基本は版築とラテライトによる基礎部を作り，その上に砂岩のブロックを整層に空積みすることで躯体を作る。屋根架構は空積みの尖頭形ヴォールトによる。

2.　事業の概要

　本保存修復工事はプロジェクトの第2フェーズの一部として行われた。事前調査は1998年から2001年に掛けて，建築学，考古学，岩石学，地盤地質工学等の分野において行われた。それらの成果に基づき修復計画が策定

1. Overview of the remains

　Angkor Wat is a large Hindu temple built in the mid-12th century by Suryavarman II, who worshiped Lord Vishnu as his principal deity, contrary to many other Khmer kings who worshiped Lord Shiva in their ritual temples. In modern times, it has been used as a Buddhist temple. The temple represents the culmination of nearly 1,000 years of Khmer architectural development since the introduction of Indian religious architecture to Cambodia, and is extremely complete in terms of scale, temple architecture, architectural style, building techniques, and art style. The building to be restored is one of the buildings in Angkor Wat that is not connected to the Gallery, and is located on the north side of the main causeway leading from the Western Gate to the central pyramid. It is now commonly referred to as the Northern Library, but this is a direct translation of the French archaeological term "Bibliothèque" for a building in a similar arrangement, and the original name and role of the building as a Hindu temple are not known. The building measures approximately 42 m east to west, 25 m north to south, and 11 m high, and consists of a cross-shaped main chamber, rectangular east-west side chambers, and four porches on a double base. The basic structure consists of a foundation made of slabs and laterite, on which sandstone blocks are piled in layers to form a frame. The roof structure is based on lancet vaults.

2. Project overview

　This conservation and restoration work was part of the second phase of the JSA project. Preliminary investigations were conducted from 1998 to 2001 in the fields of architecture, archaeology, petrology, and geotechnical engineering. Based on the results, a restoration plan was developed and presented to the International Coordinating Committee (ICC)

177

Fig. 4.3.1 Northern Library inside the Outermost Enclosure of Angkor Wat

され，2000年12月の国際調整委員会（ICC）に提起された。工事は2001年12月に開始され，2005年4月に竣工した。当遺構がプロジェクトの対象の一つに選ばれた理由についてはここでは言及しない。詳細は工事報告書を参照されたい。

3．修復工事前の遺構の状態

当経蔵の構造は断面を下から見ていくと，版築地業，ラテライトブロックを積んだ基礎，内部をラテライトブロックで側面と上面を砂岩ブロックで積んだ二重の基壇，砂岩ブロックを積んだ身廊の柱と側廊と妻の壁，砂岩ブロックを積んだ側廊の半ヴォールト屋根，柱上を繋ぐ砂岩ブロックを積んだ身廊の肩壁，砂岩ブロックを積んだ身廊のヴォールト屋根，となる。事前調査及び修復工事では地上に見える基壇最下層から順に石積み層毎にアルファベットを振り，各層では数字を振ることで各部材のナンバリングをした。

この構造の特徴は，同時期の他のクメール建築にも共通することであるが，柱上の大梁の連結に鉄製の鎹を用いる以外は，石材の空積みで構築されていることである。カンボジアは地震がほとんど無い地域であるため，構造としてはそれで問題が無いが，基礎部の不同沈下や樹木の浸食には砂岩材を用いることもあって一際弱い。また空積みのヴォールトという屋根構造もその構造の釣り合いが上下ブロック間の摩擦力に寄っているために，やはり躯体の変形に弱い。

当経蔵の基礎地業は砂を主体とした版築が深さ約2 mで広範囲になされていることがボーリング調査で分かっている。不同沈下の調査は建造時一律の高さで作られている下部基壇の壁沿いのレベルを計測する方法をとった。最高部と最低部の差は約15cmになる。当経蔵で最も上部荷重が大きいのは主室の四方の妻壁部と中央の交差

in December 2000. Work began in December 2001 and was completed in April 2005. The reasons why this site was chosen as one of the project targets are not discussed here. For more details, please refer to the construction report.

3. Condition of the remains before restoration work

The structure of the perceived sutra repository, viewed from the bottom in cross-section, consists of the following elements: a foundation built of laterite blocks, a double platform built of laterite blocks on the interior, sandstone blocks on the sides and top, pillars and side and gable walls of the nave built of sandstone blocks, a half-vaulted roof of the side nave built of sandstone blocks, shoulder walls of the nave built of sandstone blocks connecting the pillars, and a vaulted roof of the nave built of sandstone blocks. The restoration work was carried out on the ground level. During the preliminary survey and restoration work, each layer of masonry was numbered by assigning a letter to each layer of masonry, beginning with the lowest level of the base, which is visible from the ground level, and then assigning a number to each layer.

This structure is characterized by the fact that it is constructed with stone piles, except for the use of iron clamps to connect the large beams above the pillars, which is common to other Khmer monuments of the same period. Since Cambodia is an earthquake-free area, there is no structural problem with this method, but the use of sandstone makes the structure more vulnerable to unequal settlement of the foundation and intrusion by trees. The roof structure, called a vault, is also vulnerable to deformation because the balance of the structure is based on the frictional force between the upper and lower blocks.

Boring investigations have revealed that the foundations of the perceived sutra storehouse were extensively covered with sand layers at a depth of approximately 2 m. The unequal settlement investigation was conducted at the time of restoration. The unequal settlement was investigated by measuring the level along the wall of the lower platform, which was built at a uniform height at the time of construction. The difference between the highest and lowest parts is approximately 15 cm. The highest upper load in this storehouse is on the four gable walls of the main room and on the columns supporting the cross-vaulted roof in the center, where irregular settling was observed from the porch to the main room. The north porch is also generally sinking, but the reason for this is unknown. These unequal settlements are thought to have resulted in the distortion of the building. This distortion caused unbalanced loads to be applied to each member of the building frame, resulting in deterioration and damage to each member, especially in cases where damage

ヴォールト屋根を支える柱部であり，ポーチから主室に向かって不規則に沈下している状態が観測された。また北ポーチは全般的に沈んでいるが理由が不明である。これらの不同沈下はそのまま建物の歪みになったと考えられる。この歪みによって躯体の各部材に偏った荷重が掛かった結果，各部材の劣化と破損が生じ，特に破損が著しい場合にはそれが建物の部位の崩落に繋がっている。

各部材の劣化は特に圧縮応力と引張応力の掛かる部分に著しく見られる。石材の表面の風化は全般的なものであるが，応力の掛かる部分では部分のウエハース化とそれによる痩せ，ひび割れや破断が発生している。ウエハース化が顕著なのは大梁材や窓枠と扉枠の框材の下面，肩壁の内側面である。ポーチの柱材は特に破損が著しくその半数以上が破断を発生し，修復において鉄ベルトで補強されるか，鉄筋コンクリートで置き換えられている。

当遺構は，アンコール朝時代の補修やその後の王国時代の補修や改築は別として，20世紀前半のフランス保護国時代にアンコール保存修理局とEFEO（フランス極東学院）による調査と整備と補修を受けている。また1986年から1993年にかけて行われたインド考古局ASIによるアンコール・ワット全体の保存修復工事の一部として，鉄筋コンクリートによる基礎の補強，柱材の復元，欠損部の補充などが行われている。

4. 修復の方針

本修復工事において最も難しかったのはこの北経蔵をどのような方針で修復するのかという決断であったと思う。

文化財の保存においての基本は対象物を可能な限り良い状態で長い時間残すことである。建造物の修復の場合，修復の方法は大まかに言って3つになる。一つは現状をそのまま保存することであり，破損が進まないように構造的な補強を加え，細かい劣化部分に補修を加える。場合によっては覆い屋を架けることも検討される。一つは完全解体・再構築である。建造物の破損の主な原因は基礎部の不同沈下と雨漏りによる部材の劣化であり，またアンコールのような遺跡の場合は樹木の浸食が加わる。これらを根本的に解決するためには建物を完全に解体して圧縮された地盤を復帰させる必要がある。実際に本プロジェクトにおいてはプラサート・スープラ北第2塔において完全解体・再構築が実施された。しかし完全解体の作業は同時に弱体化した遺構の部材の劣化をかえって進めてしまう可能性もある。一つは部分解体・再構築である。これは前二者の間をとる妥協ではあるが，実際の

was significant, which led to the collapse of parts of the building.

Deterioration of each member is particularly noticeable in areas subjected to compressive and tensile stress. While weathering of stone surfaces is generalized, wafer thinning, cracking, and rupture occur in areas subject to stress. Wafer-sizing is most noticeable on the large beam members, the underside of the stile and rail members of the window and door frames, and the interior surfaces of the shoulder walls. The porch columns are particularly damaged, with more than half of them having been broken and either reinforced with iron belts or replaced with reinforced concrete during a previous restoration.

Apart from the Angkorian repairs and the subsequent repairs and reconstructions, the remains were surveyed, maintained, and repaired by the Angkor Conservatory and EFEO during the Protectorate period in the first half of the 20th century. In addition, as part of the conservation and restoration of the entire Angkor Wat by the Indian Department of Archaeology ASI between 1986 and 1993, the foundation was fortified with reinforced concrete, pillar materials were restored, and missing parts were replaced with ne material.

4. Restoration policy

The most difficult part of the restoration work was deciding what policy to adopt for the restoration of the Northern Library.

The basic principle in the conservation of cultural properties is to preserve the object for as long as possible in good condition. In the case of restoration of buildings, there are roughly three methods of restoration. The first is to preserve the building as it is now, and to add structural reinforcement to prevent further damage, and to repair minor deterioration. In some cases, a cladding may be considered. The second is complete demolition and reconstruction. The main causes of damage to buildings are unequal settlement of foundations and

Fig. 4.3.2 Restoration work scenery of Northern Library

保存修復の選択肢としては実効的なものでもある。

当経蔵の修復では方針の基本は部分解体・再構築として，どの範囲にどの程度の作業を行うのかが策定の中心となった。当経蔵の現状は，基礎部の不同沈下が周辺から中央部に向かって10㎝以上発生していて，建物全体の崩壊はないものの，ACO-EFEOが着手する以前には屋根部の半分とポーチの大部分が崩落していた。またASIによる修復後も，側室とポーチの屋根部はほとんど残っていなかった。一方，建物周辺には大量の崩落部材が残存していた。それらの崩落部材は原位置同定調査によっておおよそ半分は原位置に復帰させられる可能性があった。

崩落部材の原位置同定は散乱している部材の記録と仮組みによって行われた。その結果として原位置が判明した部材についてどこまで復帰させるのかも問題の一つであった。判明した部材はそのまま原位置に設置できる訳ではなく，それを支える範囲の構造の中で欠落している部分を別に埋めなければならない。本工事においては新たな砂岩材を用いて不足する部分の部材を製作・補充することになるが，その新部材が多くなりすぎれば，遺構のオリジナリティを超えて建物を復元してしまうことにもなる。そこで復帰させる原部材と加入させる新部材の割合を変えてシミュレーション画像を作成し検討した。遺構の各部分では原位置の同定された割合が異なることから必ずしも遺構全体では同じ割合で新部材が加入させることにはならないが，新部材1個が最低限現原部材1個以上の復帰に寄与することを条件とし，約440個の崩落部材を復帰させることになった。

また，既往の修復において鉄筋コンクリートを用いて補充されたポーチの柱と基壇を主とした鉄筋コンクリートが補充された部分については，過去の修復が行われた当時としては一般的な選択であったかもしれないが，現在の修復作業としては鉄筋コンクリートの耐用年数に不安があり，また外観上違和感が大きいため，新しい砂岩を加工した新部材に置換することにした。

部材の補修については第1フェーズのバイヨン北経蔵で用いられた方法を踏襲している。現存建物の部材の劣化破損部分については，ウエハース化した部材表面へのポリマーセメントモルタルによる補強と破損部分への新しい砂岩材の補充を行う。復帰させる崩落した部材はそのほとんどが劣化破損しているため，現存する部材と同様の処置を施す。破断している部材についてはステンレス鋼ボルトとエポキシ樹脂接着剤による接着を行うが，構造的に負担が大きい部材についてはステンレス鋼バーの埋め込みなどの構造補強措置をとることにした。

deterioration of components due to rain leaks, and in the case of monuments such as Angkor, tree invation is also a factor. To solve these problems fundamentally, it is necessary to completely dismantle the buildings and restore the compacted ground. In fact, in this project, complete dismantling and reconstruction of the second northern tower of Prasat Suor Prat were carried out. However, the complete dismantling of the structure may cause deterioration of the weakened components at the same time. The third is partial dismantling and reconstruction. This is a compromise between the two, but it is also an effective option for actual conservation and restoration.

In the case of the restoration of Northern Library, the basic policy is partial dismantling and reconstruction, and the main focus is on the extent and degree of the work to be done. The previous condition of the library was that the unequal settlement of the foundation occurred more than 10 cm from the periphery to the center, and although the entire building had not collapsed, half of the roof and most of the porch had collapsed before ACO-EFEO began work. Even after restoration by ASI, very little remained of the roof sections of the side rooms and porch. On the other hand, a large number of collapsed elements remained scattered around the building. Approximately half of these collapsed elements could be restored to their original positions by in-situ identification.

The in-situ identification of the collapsed elements was done by recording and temporarily assembling the scattered elements. One of the issues was the extent to which the resulting in-situ materials could be returned to their original locations. The identified components could not be placed in situ as they were, and the missing parts had to be filled in separately within the structure that supported them. In this project, new sandstone materials was used to make and fill in the missing parts, but if too many new parts are used, the building will be restored beyond the originality of the monuments. Therefore, we created simulation images by changing the ratio of the original parts to be restored and the new parts to be added. The proportion of the original location identified in each part of the remains is different, and therefore, the same proportion of new members will not necessarily be added to the entire remains.

As for the portions of the porch that were replenished with reinforced concrete, mainly the columns and base of the porch that were replenished with reinforced concrete in the previous restorations, this may have been a common choice at the time the past restorations were done, but there are concerns about the service life of the reinforced concrete for the current restoration work, However, the service life of reinforced concrete is uncertain and the appearance of the building is not pleasing, so it was decided to replace the concrete with new elements made from new sandstone.

The repair of the components followed the method used for the Northern Library of Bayon in the first phase of the project.

5．工事の概要

　現場は北経蔵の北60ｍほどにある現代の仏教寺院から離れの建物を一つ借り受け，現場の資材倉庫や作業車両の駐車場として用いた。パワージェネレーターとエアコンプレッサーなどの機器もそこに設置された。建物の解体・再構築には重量のある石材の上げ下ろしが必要なため，25ｔラフテレーンクレーンを建物周囲に近づけて運用する必要があるため，建物の周囲を菱形に囲むような形で砂利を敷いたランプウェイを設置した。

　本工事の全体的な流れは，部分解体→部材の補修→再構築となるが，当経蔵の修復対象部位はその十字形平面のそれぞれ四方に分かれている。そこで各作業段階を四方毎にずらしてスケジュールを組むことで，現場はクレーンを使った解体・再構築作業班と部材補修作業班の2つが並行作業をする形になった。

　各作業の手法と用いた材料や工具，クレーン作業の手順，カンボジア人エキスパートや作業員の雇用と現場体制などについては，バイヨン北経蔵と同じであるので割愛し，ここではアンコール・ワット北経蔵に特徴的だった部分を紹介する。

6．崩落部材の原位置同定作業

　当経蔵の周囲に当時散乱していた部材と部材片はアンコール保存修理局がアンコール・ワットの整備を行った際に，建物の室内と基壇周りに積み重なっていたものを整理したものである。ACOはアンコール・ワット本体の崩落部材の再構築作業を行っているが，その時に彼らがどのような手法で原位置同定を行ったのかは不明であるが，基本，本工事の事前調査で行った手法と大差は無いと思われる。つまり現物を使った3Dジグソーパズルである。

　パズルの手掛かりになるものは幾つかある。第一に部材の断面形状で，それによってどの層の部材であるかはほぼ断定される。特に屋根部材の場合，屋根表面の傾きと断面幅によって何層目かがおおよそ判明する。第二に部材表面の彫刻で，その繋がり具合が凡そ確認できる。特に屋根部材は瓦筋の凹凸が明確なことで部材相互の組み合わせが容易になり，また浅浮彫彫刻の完成度の違いがどの側室かポーチかの判断基準にもなる。

　このパズルは最初に各部位毎に地上でミニクレーンを用いて行われ，次に遺構上で25ｔクレーンを用いて行わ

For the deteriorated and damaged parts of the existing building members, polymer cement mortar was used to reinforce the wafer-formed member surfaces, and new sandstone materials were added to the damaged parts. Most of the collapsed members to be restored are deteriorated and damaged, and will be treated in the same manner as the existing members. Fractured members will be bonded with stainless steel bolts and epoxy resin adhesive, while structurally stressed members will be reinforced with stainless steel bars or other structural reinforcement measures.

5. Construction Overview

The construction site was a detached building rented from a modern Buddhist temple located about 60 m north of the Northern Library, and which was used as the site's materials warehouse and parking area for work vehicles. A power generator and air compressor and other equipment were also installed there. Since the dismantling and reconstruction of the building required the lifting and lowering of heavy stone materials, a 25-ton rough terrain crane had to be operated close to the perimeter of the building, therefore, a gravel rampway was installed in a diamond shape around the building.

The overall flow of this project was partial dismantling, repair of components, and reconstruction. Therefore, the schedule was set up by staggering the work stages on each of the four sides, so that two teams worked in parallel on the site: a crane-based dismantling/reconstruction team and a component repair team.

The methods and materials used, tools, crane operation procedures, employment of Cambodian experts and workers, and on-site organization were the same as those used for the Bayon Northern Library, therefore, I will skip these details and introduce some of the features of the Angkor Wat Northern Library.

6. Identification of the collapsed stones

The materials and fragments scattered around the repository were sorted out from the piles inside the building and around the base when Angkor Wat was restored by the Angkor Conservation and Restoration Office. It is not known what method they used for in-situ identification at that time, but it does not seem to be very different from the method used for the preliminary survey of the main construction work. In other words, it was a three-dimensional puzzle using actual materials.

There are several clues to the puzzle. The first is the cross-sectional shape of the member, which will almost certainly determine which layer the member belongs. In the case of a

4.3　アンコール・ワット最外周壁内北経蔵　181

Fig. 4.3.3 Replace the New Sandstone Process

れた。各部材の位置を物理的に調整するためには単管足場組と木片の楔と鉛板を使った繰り返し作業が必要とされた。成果は担当した下田一太氏とヒム・ダラ氏の苦労によるところが大である。

7. 部材の欠損部分への新材補填

本工事で復帰させた崩落部材のほとんどはひび割れや部分欠損があり，復帰させるためには構造部材として荷重を担う強度を持たなくてはならない。ひび割れについてはポリマーセメントモルタルの注入と，状況によってステンレス鋼ボルトの埋め込みを行ったが，欠損部の補填には基本的に新しい砂岩材を埋め込むことを選択した。欠損部の補填に新石材を用いるかバイヨン北経蔵修復工事に倣ってポリマーセメントモルタル（エチレンブタジエンラバー樹脂）を用いるかは悩んだ所であった。結論として新石材の補充を決断した要因には，日本の古建築修復の手法があったとは思うが，可能な限りオリジナルに近い状態に修復するという方針がある。石材加工主任の山本成則氏と検討した末，新材補填においては破損部分を圧縮応力に対する垂直面に削り取って新材を接着する方法を選択した。

また新規の柱材を製作するためには断面が1m以上の石材を切断する必要があり，中国チームの運用するものを参考にさせて頂いて新規の大型カッターを製作した。特に直径1mのダイヤモンドブレードは日本から手配するのが困難であったところを中国チームの伝手で上海から安価に調達することが出来た。このブレードがなければ本工事の工程は大幅に遅れていた。

加えて，変則的な補修事例としては破損柱材の柱身の新材への置換には柱頭と柱座の位置関係を正確に保持するために単管で装置を組み上げた。

roof member in particular, the slope of the roof surface and the width of the cross section will give a rough idea of the number of layers. Secondly, the surface engravings of the members allow us to determine the degree to which they are connected to each other. In the case of the roofing members in particular, the clear irregularities of the roof tile striations make it easy to combine the members, and the difference in the degree of perfection of the relief carvings can be used as a criterion to determine which side room or porch is the best.

The puzzle was first solved for each section on the ground with a mini-crane and then on the remainder with a 25-ton crane. The physical alignment of each component required repetitive work using single-tube scaffolding, wedges of wood, and lead plates. The results are largely due to the hard work of Mr. Ichita Shimoda and Mr. Him Dara, who were in charge of the project.

7. Replacing missing parts with new materials

Most of the collapsed members that were restored in this project had cracks or partial defects, and in order to restore them, they had to be strong enough to carry the load as a structural member. For the cracks, polymer cement mortar was injected and stainless-steel bolts were embedded depending on the situation, while new sandstone material was basically chosen to fill in the missing parts. The decision to use new stone or polymer cement mortar (ethylene-butadiene rubber resin), as was used in the restoration of the Northern Library of Bayon, was a difficult one. In conclusion, the decision to use new stones was based on the policy of restoring the building as close as possible to the original state, which I believe was the method used in the restoration of ancient Japanese architecture. After discussions with Mr. Shigenori Yamamoto, the chief stone fabricator, the decision was made to cut the damaged area into a plane perpendicular to the compressive stress and glue the new material to it.

In order to fabricate new columns, it was necessary to cut stones with a cross section of more than 1 m, so a new large cutter was fabricated based on the one used by the Chinese team. The Chinese team was able to procure a diamond blade with a diameter of 1 m from Shanghai. Without these blades, the construction process would have been significantly delayed.

In addition, as an anomalous repair case, a single pipe was used to replace the damaged column body with a new one in order to maintain the exact positional relationship between the column head and the column seat.

8. ポーチ柱材とポーチ大梁材と扉枠上框材の補修

　本工事では多量の砂岩部材の補修を行ったが，その中でもポーチ柱材，ポーチ大梁材，妻壁上框材の補修はその構造的な重要性から個別に検討を要した。

　ポーチの柱材は，基礎の変異がその荷重分布偏移に直結することと雨風に晒されていることから，劣化が最も進みやすい部材である。実際にポーチ柱材は現存するものも倒壊して遺構周囲に放棄されているものも，砂岩の層理面方向に縦斜めに断裂しているものが多数であった。これらの柱材について本工事では3つの手法を用いた。現状で再用に耐えると判断されたものは縦斜めに断裂した2つの石材の補強接着を行った。この接着には柱のせん断強度を補強するために細いステンレス鋼ボルトを断裂面に沿って斜め網状に挿入した。この手法の検証の為に，プノンペンの試験場において斜めにピン接合された砂岩材の圧縮強度試験を行っている。また，柱身部の破断と劣化の状況が著しい部材については，柱身そのものを新材に交換する処置も行った。それらの接合部も垂直の圧縮応力に対応するために水平に面を取るように加工している。再利用が不可能と判断された柱材については，新しい砂岩材を加工して代替した。

　ポーチの大梁材の一部は中央で縦に破断していた。これは崩壊による破損ではなく，屋根の上部荷重による曲げ応力による破断であると想定された。この例ではバイヨン北経蔵の部材補修に倣って大梁材の下面に溝を掘りステンレス鋼バーを宛がうことで補強した。

　主室北翼妻壁の扉枠上の框材は，3個に破断していた。この部材は上部の妻壁の荷重を扉枠の両脇に受け流す役割を持つ重要な構造材であり，その補修と再利用は悩みどころであった。オリジナル部材を可能な限り再利用することが修復の基本方針であったため，その部材に掛かる荷重とたわみを計算し，3個の破片をステンレス鋼ボルトで接合するのと同時に，欠損部を新材で補填し，三角形に抉れている下面にテンションバーを施すことで補強を図った。この部材は再構築後にはペディメントの裏に隠れて外観からは隠されている。

9. 砂岩材の調達と運搬

　本工事では欠損部の補充の為に大量の新砂岩材を必要とした。砂岩はバイヨン北経蔵の修復工事に引き続き，カンボジア政府の許可を得て，クーレン山の麓から切り

8. Repair of porch columns, porch large beams, and upper stile and rail of door frames

Among the many sandstone members repaired in this project, the porch columns, porch beams, and upper stile and rail members of the gable wall required individual consideration due to their structural importance.

The porch columns are the most vulnerable to deterioration because the variation of the foundation directly affects the load distribution and because they are exposed to rain. In fact, many of the existing porch columns and those that had collapsed and been abandoned around the ruins were found to be broken longitudinally and obliquely in the direction of the sandstone stratigraphic plane. Three methods were used in this project to examine these post materials. For the columns that were determined to be reusable in their present condition, the two stones that were broken longitudinally and obliquely were reinforced by gluing them together. To reinforce the shear strength of the columns, thin stainless-steel bolts were inserted along the fracture surface in a diagonal mesh pattern. To verify this technique, compressive strength tests of diagonally pin-jointed sandstone materials were conducted at a test site in Phnom Penh. In addition, the column bodies themselves were replaced with new materials for members that showed significant fracture and deterioration. These joints were also machined to be horizontally faced to accommodate vertical compressive stresses. New sandstone was processed to replace the columns that were determined not to be reusable.

A portion of the large beam material on the porch was broken vertically in the center. It was assumed that this was not a failure due to collapse, but rather a rupture due to bending stress caused by the upper load of the roof. In this case, a groove was dug on the underside of the large beam and stainless steel bars were used to reinforce it, following the method used to repair members of the Bayon's north storehouse.

The stile and rail material above the door frame on the gable wall of the north wing of the main chamber was broken in three pieces. Since this member is an important structural member that carries the load of the upper gable wall to both sides of the door frame, its repair and reuse was an important issue. Since the basic policy of the restoration was to reuse the original member as much as possible, the loads and deflections on the member were calculated, and the three pieces were joined with stainless steel bolts, and at the same time, the missing parts were replaced with new material and reinforced with tension bars on the triangular gouged bottom surface. This component was hidden behind the pediment after the reconstruction and is concealed from the exterior.

出して現場まで運搬した。石材の切り出しにあたっては担当者が何度も石切り場に赴き対象箇所の確認を行ったが，それにも関わらず，切り出した大型石材にはしばしば層理面を横断するひび割れとそこに結晶化した石英系鉱物の面が確認された。本工事では欠損したポーチ柱材を過去の修復で鉄筋コンクリートにより補塡されたものと置換するために品質の良い大型石材を複数必要としていたが，石材は切り出すまでその状態を正確に確認することは出来ず，使用に耐えないと判断された石材については再度切り出しを行うことになった。柱材に使えない石材も他の部材には転用出来るために最終的には切り出した石材の無駄は出ることがなかったが，この工事で最も悩まされた件の一つである。

　ポーチの柱を新たに製作するに当たって，柱そのものの重量は2tに満たないが，それを加工する前段階に必要とされる石材の重量は10tを上回った。これは柱頭や柱座と上下端のホゾを作るための削りシロを必要としたためである。これは石切り場から工事現場へのダンプ車による運搬も労力を要したが，現場での取り扱いが特に難儀した。結局は石材上面の四隅にドリルで穴を掘り，U字形の鉄筋をアンカーとしてエポキシ樹脂接着剤で埋め込むことによって解決した。この石材移動の問題はアンコール・ワット建造時の現場でも最大の問題となったことであり，実際バイヨン外回廊西面の浅浮彫にも，石材上面にアンカーを埋め込み，大きな天秤で石材を移動する様子が描かれている。

10. 新部材及び新材補塡部分の表面加工

　文化財の修復においてオリジナルの欠損部分に新材を補塡することは建造物のみならず絵画彫刻でも普通に行われていることである。本工事では多数の新材を補塡することになったが，それをどれだけ違和感の生じないように加工できるかが検討された。現存部材の表面は建物の部位によって浅浮彫の完成度が異なっている。新材の表面形状は周辺の現存部材に合わせるようにして，同時に地肌のマチエールは新材であることが判りながら周辺の現存部材に新材であることを主張しないような穏やかなものであることが求められた。このマチエールを決めるために加工に用いるブッシュハンマー（たたき）の目数とたたき具合を変えたサンプルを屋根先瓦部位と柱座について作成し検討した。このサンプルについてはICCの現場見学会でも各国の修復チームに披露しご意見を頂いた。

9. Procurement and transportation of sandstone material

This project required a large amount of new sandstone material to fill in the missing sections. Following the restoration of Northern Library of Bayon, sandstone was quarried from the foot of Phnom Kulen and transported to the site with the permission of the Cambodian government. The person in charge of the quarrying visited the quarry several times to check the quarry site. Nevertheless, cracks crossing the stratigraphic plane and quartz mineral surfaces crystallized on the cracks were often found on the large quarried stones. The project required several large stones of good quality to replace the missing porch pillars that had been replaced by reinforced concrete in the past restorations, but the condition of the stones could not be accurately confirmed until they were quarried. The stones that could not be used for the pillars had to be quarried again. The stone that could not be used for the columns could be used for other elements, so in the end, there was no waste of quarried stone, but this was one of the most difficult aspects of the project.

Although the weight of the porch columns themselves was less than 2 tons, the weight of the stone required for the preliminary stage of processing them exceeded 10 tons. This was due to the need for shavings for the pillar head and base, as well as the top and bottom edges. The transportation of the stone from the quarry to the construction site by dump truck was labor-intensive, but the handling of the stone at the site was particularly difficult. In the end, the problem was solved by drilling holes in the four corners of the top surface of the stone and embedding U-shaped reinforcing bars as anchors using epoxy resin adhesive. In fact, the bas-relief on the west side of the Bayon Outer Gallery depicts how anchors were embedded in the upper surface of the stone and the stone was moved using a large balance.

10. Surface Treatment of new Materials and new Replaced parts

In the restoration of cultural properties, it is common practice not only for buildings but also for paintings and sculptures to fill in missing parts of the original work with new materials. In this project, a large number of new materials were used to fill in the missing parts, and we considered how much we could process them so that they would not look out of place. The surfaces of the existing members have different degrees of relief depending on the part of the building. The surface of the new material was to match the surrounding existing members, and at the same time, the surface was to be gentle enough so that the new material would be recognizable,

11. 再構築における層間嵩上げ

崩落石材の再構築において最大の問題は，建物全体の躯体が基礎部の不同沈下によって歪んでいることであり，崩落部材をそのまま積み直せば収まる訳ではないことだった。さらには崩落部材そのものが経年の劣化によって接合面に痩せや剥離が生じていることであった。よって，再構築においては，部材相互の位置関係を微妙に調整する為に，バイヨン北経蔵での手法を踏襲して，部材の上下間の四隅に鉛板を噛ませた。部材間の位置関係は鉛板で調整されるが，荷重の伝達を上下面全体に延べるために鉛板によって生じる間隙にはライムモルタルにセメントとポリマーを加えたものを充填した。理想的にはローマ帝国以来の永続性に確証のある純粋なライムモルタルで補填をしたかったが，薄い間隙にライムモルタルを強度が保てるように施工することは難しく，セメントとポリマーを調合することで強度と施工性の向上を図った。この配合を決める為にプノンペンの試験場で3ヶ月ほど通ってサンプルの強度試験を繰り返した。また，特に不同沈下による歪みが多く多量の嵩上げを必要とした東側室については新材の薄板を加工して補填することで対処した。

12. 屋根部再構築の構造補強

本工事において最も気を使ったのは屋根部の再構築である。アンコール・ワットの石造屋根は整層空積みのコーベル・ヴォールトで作られている。つまり，上下部材間の摩擦力が確実でなければ屋根部の崩落の危険性が残ってしまうということである。この屋根をセメントモルタルでがちがちに固めるというのでなければ，何らかの補強が保険として必要と考えた。そこで本工事で再構築した屋根部については部材の上下間にステンレス鋼ピンを噛ませて横ズレを防ぐ細工をした。

13. 最後に

修復事業の手法の是非はその時代時代で認識が変化するし，その時代の最新技術が次の時代に否定されることも多い。当時の方針策定に関わった方々の方向性を述べるならば，日本における古建築の保存修復事業の水準に相当する，遺構のオリジナリティを最大限保存する方法

but not so gentle that it would dominate the surrounding existing members. In order to determine this surface condition, samples were prepared for the roof tiles and the columns by changing the number of hammers and the degree of hammering. These samples were presented to the restoration teams in each country at the ICC site visit and received their comments.

11. Interlaminar raising in reconstruction

The biggest problem in the reconstruction of the collapsed stones was that the entire building frame was distorted due to unequal settlement of the foundation, and it was not possible to fit the collapsed elements by re-stacking them as they were. Furthermore, the collapsed members themselves had become thin and peeled off at the joint surfaces due to deterioration over time. Therefore, in order to adjust the positional relationship between the members slightly, lead plates were inserted at the four corners between the upper and lower members, following the method used at the Northern Library of Bayon. While the positional relationship between the members was adjusted by the lead plates, the gaps created by the lead plates were filled with lime mortar with cement and polymers in order to extend the load transmission to the entire upper and lower surfaces. Ideally, we would have used pure lime mortar, which has proven its durability since the Roman Empire. However, it is difficult to apply lime mortar in a thin gap, therefore, that its strength is maintained, so a mixture of cement and polymers was used to improve strength and workability. In order to determine the mix, we repeated strength tests on samples at a testing facility in Phnom Penh over a period of three months. In addition, the east side room, which was distorted due to unequal settlement and required a large amount of raising, was supplemented by processing a thin plate of new material.

Fig. 4.3.4 After Reconstruct Process of Northern Library

の模索だったと思う。アンコール・ワットは現代のカンボジア王国の象徴であり，その表玄関の脇に位置する北経蔵は日本が保存修復の専門分野においてどの様な有様を見せるのかのプレゼンテーションの場所ともなってしまった。バイヨン北経蔵の修復工事は，日本の古建築修復の蓄積を応用した成果として堅実な仕上がりになっていると思う。当経蔵の保存修復工事はフランス政府とEFEOによる整備事業とインド政府とASIによる既往修復事業の成果の上に我々の修復事業があることを記して感謝申し上げたい。

12. Structural reinforcement for roof reconstruction

One of the most important part of this project was the reconstruction of the roof. The stone roof of Angkor Wat was constructed as corbel vaults, which are stacked in layers. This means that if the frictional force between the upper and lower members is not assured, there is a risk of the roof section collapsing. Unless this roof was to be solidified with cement mortar, some kind of reinforcement was considered necessary as insurance. Therefore, stainless steel pins were inserted between the top and bottom of the reconstructed roof to prevent lateral displacement.

Finally

The pros and cons of restoration methods change with the times, and the latest technology of a particular era is often rejected by the next era. If I were to describe the direction taken by those involved in the formulation of the policy at that time, I would say that it was a search for a method to preserve the originality of the remains to the maximum extent possible, equivalent to the level of conservation and restoration projects for ancient buildings in Japan. Angkor Wat is a symbol of the modern Kingdom of Cambodia, and the Northern Library, located by the front gate of Angkor Wat, has become a presentation site to show what JSA can do in the field of conservation and restoration expertise. Additionally the restoration of the Northern Library of the Bayon is a solid result of the application of Japan's accumulated experience in the restoration of ancient buildings. We would like to express our gratitude for the fact that our restoration work on this library is built upon the achievements of the arrangement project by the French government and EFEO, and the previous restoration project by the Indian government and ASI.

4.4 バイヨン南経蔵の修復工事

──持続的な遺産保護への試行と基壇内からの新知見

Restoration of the Southern Library of Bayon:
Attempting Sustainable Heritage Conservation and New Insights from within the Platform

下田 一太
SHIMODA Ichita

1. 持続的な修復活動のための試み

　バイヨン南経蔵の修復工事は2006年4月から2011年8月にかけて実施された。1994年に開始された日本国政府による修復事業は，バイヨン北経蔵，プラサート・スープラ，アンコール・ワット北経蔵の修復工事を通じて，古代クメールの組積造建築に対する修復方針を検討し，修復のための技術開発に取り組んだ。各分野の専門家が産学連携体制で取り組んだ結果，歴史的工法と構造をできるかぎり尊重したそれまでとは異なる修復理念と技術を実現するに至った。2006年に開始された第3フェーズは，それらの蓄積の上に対象遺構に最適化した修復仕様の改良を図り，先端的な技術導入を試みると同時に，永続的な修理サイクルを必要とするアンコール遺跡群において，持続的な修復活動の在り方を検討することを目的とした。

　そのために，第3フェーズからはユネスコ，在カンボジア日本国大使館，カンボジア政府アプサラ機構，日本人専門家，日本政府外務省のオブザーバーという，複数のステークホルダーが参加する運営会議によって事業方針や計画が決定される仕組みとし，また日本人専門家である中川武とアプサラ機構の副総裁が共同事業団長として事業運営の責任を担う体制へと移行した。それまでの国際的な支援事業から，協働事業へと更新されたのである。事業予算についても，アプサラ機構がカンボジア人専門家と技能員への給与の一部，カンボジア国内で調達される資機材の購入費を負担することとなった。こうした事業体制の変更は，事業名称をそれまでのJSA（Japanese Government Team for Safeguarding Angkor）からJASA（Japan APSARA Safeguarding Angkor）へ更新することによって対外的にもアピールされた。

　ユネスコも事業運営により直接的に関与することとな

1. Attempts towards Sustainable Restoration Activities

　The restoration work of the Southern Library of Bayon was carried out from April 2006 to August 2011. The restoration project, initiated by the Japanese government in 1994, aimed to explore restoration strategies for the unique masonry structure of ancient Khmer architecture and develop the necessary techniques through restoration works on the Northern Library of Bayon, Prasat Suor Prat, and Northern Library of Angkor Wat. Collaborating experts from various fields achieved a restoration philosophy and techniques that significantly respected historical methods and structures. The third phase, which began in 2006, aimed to further optimize the restoration specifications for the target structure, attempt the introduction of cutting-edge technology, and explore the approach to sustainable restoration activities required for the Angkor Monuments, which demands an ongoing repair cycle.

　To achieve this goal, a management committee involving multiple stakeholders, including UNESCO, the Embassy of Japan in Cambodia, the Cambodian APSARA National Authority, Japanese experts, and observers from the Japanese Ministry of Foreign Affairs, was established to determine project policies and plans. Additionally, Takeshi Nakagawa, a Japanese expert, and the Deputy General Secretary of APSARA took on the roles of co-project leaders responsible for project operation. This shift transformed the initiative from an international support project to a collaborative project, and the project's name was updated from JSA (Japanese Government Team for Safeguarding Angkor) to JASA (Japan APSARA Safeguarding Angkor) to enhance its external appeal. The APSARA National Authority took on the responsibility of covering part of the salaries for Cambodian experts and skilled workers, as well as the procurement cost of materials and equipment sourced locally. These changes in the project structure aimed to establish appropriate relationships and division of roles while endeavoring to construct an

187

り，現地の事業事務所や重機，車両の管理，日本からの資機材の搬送にかかる免税手続き，カンボジア政府との各種連絡業務を担当した。こうして日本－カンボジア－ユネスコの三者がそれまで以上に密接に連携して事業を運営する中で，適切な関係性や役割分担を検討し，国際的な協働事業モデルの構築に努めた。

遺跡の修復事業を通じた地域教育や国内外の来訪者への発信も第3フェーズにおける重要な目的とされた。2009年にはシェムレアップ事業オフィスの敷地内にガイダンス施設「バイヨン・インフォメーション・センター」を，またバイヨンの近傍には「バイヨン・ハット」を開設し，日本国政府による修復事業を始めとする国際的な修復や研究事業を国内外からの来訪者に広く紹介した。また，これらの施設はカンボジア人学生の教育の場としても活用し，遺跡での修復現場見学と合わせた学外学習の機会を設けた。その他，旅行会社とタイアップした遺跡修復の体験学習を提供するツアーの実施や，日本ユネスコ協会連盟と連携した修復工事への企業や個人からの支援事業の仕組みを構築し，持続的な修復活動に寄与する可能性がある様々な事業を実施した。

加えて，カンボジア国内NGOである「アンコール人材養成支援機構」と連携することで，遺跡保全と地域の生活環境の改善を両立し，それらの相乗効果をもたらすためのプログラムに取り組んだ。バイヨンの修復事業という遺跡への直接的な関与を一つの資源や機会として，関係者が多様な形で関与し，それぞれに学び，豊かになることで，持続的な遺跡保全を実現する方法を模索した。

2. 南経蔵における技術的継承と挑戦

南経蔵は第1フェーズに修復工事の対象となった北経蔵とほぼ同形式の遺構である。南経蔵の修復工事は，一連の修復工事の工程をカンボジア人専門家と技能員が中心となって進められた（Fig. 4.4.1）。5名の建築と情報学分野の専門家と3名の考古学分野の専門家により，工事計画の立案・資機材調達・現場管理・記録報告が取り組まれた。

南経蔵は東西に18.5m，南北に11m，現存する遺構の高さは9.6mの石積み建築である。3段の基壇の上に上部構造体を載せ，中央の一室の東西には吹き放ちのポーチが接続する。東西の基壇面には急勾配の階段が削り込まれており，東側の階段は外回廊の扉と位置を合わせて配置されている。基壇の外壁と上部構造体は砂岩積みよりなる。現存する砂岩部材数は2,658個であるが，柱上の梁材よりも上方は全て崩落していることから，当

international collaborative project model.

UNESCO also became directly involved in project management, overseeing tasks such as managing the local project office, heavy machinery, and vehicles, as well as handling tax exemption procedures for transporting equipment from Japan and various communications with the Cambodian government. Through this close collaboration between Japan, Cambodia, and UNESCO, the three parties strived to develop an international cooperative project model.

Promoting regional education and disseminating information to domestic and international visitors became important objectives during the third phase of the restoration project. In 2009, the "Bayon Information Center" was established within the premises of the Siem Reap Project Office, and the "Bayon Hut" was set up near Bayon to widely introduce international restoration and research efforts, including those conducted by the Japanese government, to visitors. These facilities also served as educational venues for Cambodian students, providing opportunities for extracurricular learning through site visits to restoration sites. Additionally, various programs were implemented, such as experiential learning tours in collaboration with travel agencies, and the establishment of support mechanisms for restoration projects by corporations and individuals through cooperation with the Japan National Commission for UNESCO, all contributing to sustainable restoration activities.

Furthermore, cooperation with the Cambodian NGO "Joint Support Team for Angkor Community Development" allowed for programs that balanced the preservation of the site with the improvement of the local living environment, resulting in synergistic effects. Viewing the restoration of Bayon as a valuable resource and opportunity for direct involvement in a heritage site, stakeholders explored ways to contribute to sustainable site conservation while engaging in diverse forms of participation and learning.

2. Technical Continuity and Challenges in the Restoration of the Southern Library

The Southern Library of Bayon is a structure that closely resembles the Northern Library, which underwent restoration during the first phase. The restoration work of the Southern Library was primarily carried out by Cambodian experts and skilled workers (Fig. 4.4.1). A team of five specialists in architecture and informatics, as well as three experts in archaeology, were involved in planning the construction, procuring materials and equipment, managing the site, and documenting the progress.

The Southern Library measures 18.5 meters east-west and 11 meters north-south, and its existing structure stands at a height of 9.6 meters. It is a stone construction comprising three tiers of platform with an upper superstructure. A

Fig. 4.4.1 Cambodian experts and skilled workers on the Southern Library

初は3,000以上の砂岩材よりなる構造であった。基壇の砂岩外装材の内部にはラテライト積みが内部擁壁となり，さらにその内部は版築土が充填される。アンコールにおける寺院の一般的な構造である。

　一見して北経蔵と同形式であるが，平面規模や壁体の窓の開閉の点でやや異なる（北経蔵は一部が疑似窓である）。また南経蔵の室内中央には台座が設置されていた痕跡があり，両経蔵では室内の利用方法が異なっていたものと推測される。バイヨン以外のアンコール時代の複合寺院においても，参道の両側に配置された経蔵では，装飾や窓開口，平面形式，換気孔の有無等に違いがみられることが多く，北側の施設室内がより実利的な目的と有していたものと推測されるケースが多い。

　修復工事の基本的な方針は，バイヨン北経蔵やアンコール・ワット最外周壁内北経蔵で培われてきた考え方を踏襲した。つまり，1）石積みの変形を解消し構造的安定性を向上するために有効な範囲での部分解体再構築を行う，2）基壇内部の脆弱化した版築土を改良土によって安定化する，3）破損部材を修復し最大限の再利用を図る，4）原位置が同定された石材を復帰しそれらを支持するために最小限の新材を追加する，5）改良土により目地を充填処置し基壇内部への雨水浸透を防止する，といった考え方である。また，これらを実現するための修復技術についても，それまでの技術や材料，仕様に基づいて計画，施工した。ただし，砂岩材の修復仕様は材料の配合等を改め，また基壇内部の盛土と変形解消のための石材間の嵩上げ土，そして石目地間の充填土といった各種の土材料についても南経蔵の特性に基づいて粒度分布を変えるなどの改良を加えた。修復に利用する機材においても無振動ドリルを導入するなど，各作業において改善できる点を検討した。

　また，修復前後の形状記録にあたっては，レーザレンジセンサを利用した3D計測による幾何モデルでの記録

projecting porch connects to the central chamber in the east-west direction. Steep stairs are carved into the eastern and western faces of the platform, and the stairs on the east side are aligned with the doorways of the Outer Gallery. The outer walls of the platform and upper superstructure are made of sandstone. While 2,658 sandstone elements are still preserved, all the elements above the upper beam on pillars level have collapsed, suggesting that the original structure comprised over 3,000 sandstone elements. The internal filling of the sandstone cladding on the platform consists of laterite masonry, and it is further filled with earth filling. This general structure is typical of temples in Angkor.

Although the Southern Library appears similar to the Northern Library, there are slight differences in its plan size and the openings of its wall windows (some windows in the Northern Library are false windows). Additionally, part of a pedestal remained at the center of the interior of the Southern Library, suggesting that the use of the chambers in the two libraries might have been different. Not only in the Bayon but also in other compound temples of the Angkor period with libraries located on both sides of the approach, significant variations are often observed in terms of decorations, window openings, floor plans, and the presence of ventilation holes. It is likely that the facilities on the northern side served more practical purposes.

The fundamental principles of restoration were derived from the methods employed in the restoration of the Northern Library of Bayon and the Northern Library within the Outer Enclosure wall of Angkor Wat. These principles included; 1) implementing partial disassembly and reconstruction within a range where it is effective in eliminating deformation and improving structural stability; 2) stabilizing the vulnerable earthen filling inside the platform by improving it with suitable soil; 3) restoring damaged elements and maximizing their reuse; 4) reintegrating identified original stone elements and adding a minimal amount of new materials to support them; and 5) preventing rainwater infiltration into the platform interior by using improved soil to fill the joints. The restoration techniques based on these principles were planned and executed, considering the previous techniques, materials, and specifications. However, the restoration specifications for sandy filling material was revised, and improvements were made, such as adjusting the particle size distribution for the earth filling used to raise the soil level between stones to mitigate deformation and for the soil filling between the stone joints, based on the characteristics of the Southern Library. The introduction of new tools such as non-vibrating drills was also considered to improve the equipment used for restoration.

In addition, new methods were employed for recording the shapes before and after restoration. Three-dimensional measurements using laser range scanners were conducted to record the geometric models. While point measurements with conventional surveying instruments were used for routine on-

を新たに実施した。従来の測量機器による点的な計測によって，変形分析や修理設計，現場管理といった日常的な現場作業は継続したが，3D計測による計測によって，修復前後の各種図面作成や基壇内部の土量計算といった作業労力を大幅に軽減し，また立体形状での変形分析や修復後の挙動観測を行った。

　石材記録においてもデジタル技術を積極的に活用した。南経蔵の南側，外回廊との間には20世紀前半に移動された石材が山積みにされており，修復作業現場の確保と，それらの石材中からの南経蔵の遺失石材を同定することを目的に，石材を移動し記録する作業を行った。こうして移動した計1,726個の石材はMicrosoft Accessによってデータベース化して管理した。南経蔵に同定された石材は数個に限られたが，こうして散乱石材の記録は将来的な修復工事においても有用である。また，南経蔵の部分解体再構築によって修復処置を施した砂岩材は，個別にデータシートを作成しHTML形式で記録を行った。修復した計857材の石材に対して，使用した修復材料や挿入した補強材の位置や数を個別の図化し，また修復前後の石材写真記録等を備えたものである。これらの修復記録はインターネット上で閲覧することができるものとした（http://archives.bayon-project.org/rwsl/stone-repair-db/index.html）。

　また，解体再構築を通じた変形の矯正結果を確認できるように，全ての石材層の図面を作成し，各石材四隅の平面位置と高さ情報を記録し，図化した。この図面によって部材単位でどのように遺構の変状を矯正したのか確認することができるものとした。

　こうした各種のデジタル記録は，修復工事の現場作業に加えて大きな負担になるものであるが，バイヨンのように大規模な遺構で長期にわたって断続的な関与が必要となる対象においては将来的に重要な資料となる。これらのデジタルベースでの部材記録と図面記録は，カンボジア人専門家が担当した。修復記録の重要性が必ずしも浸透していないアンコール遺跡群の修復事業において，こうした記録の有用性と実現可能性を示すことに寄与することを願うものである。

3．南経蔵の修復工事に伴う新事実

　南経蔵の修復工事に伴う基壇内部の調査からは，いくつかの重要な発見があったので一部を紹介する。

⑴鎮壇具の発見
　南経蔵の室内中央には，二層の石積みよりなる台座の

site work such as deformation analysis, repair design, and site management, three-dimensional measurements substantially reduced the workload for tasks such as creating various drawings before and after restoration and calculating the volume of soil inside the platform. The three-dimensional data also allowed for the analysis of deformation and observation of the post-restoration behavior in three dimensions.

Digital technology was actively used for stone records. Stones that had been moved to form a mound between the southern side of the Southern Library and the Outer Gallery were moved and recorded to secure the restoration work site and identify the missing stones of the Southern Library. The data for these 1,726 stones were entered into a Microsoft Access database. Although only a few stones were identified as belonging to the Southern Library, these scattered stone records are expected to be useful for future restoration projects. For the sandstone elements restored by partial disassembly and reconstruction, individual data sheets were created, containing graphical representations of the position and number of repair materials used, as well as reinforcing materials inserted in each of the 857 stones repaired. These records also included photographs of the stones before and after restoration. The restoration records are available for public access on the internet (http://archives.bayon-project.org/rwsl/stone-repair-db/index.html).

Moreover, drawings of all stone layers were created to confirm the results of the correction of deformation through disassembly and reconstruction. The positions and heights of all four corners of each stone were recorded and graphically represented. These drawings allow us to verify how the deformation of the structure was corrected on a member-by-member basis.

Although various digital records added a significant burden to the on-site restoration work, they are crucial resources for large-scale structures like the Bayon, where intermittent involvement is required over a long period. These digital-based stone and drawing records were managed by Cambodian experts. In the context of restoration works at the Angkor Monuments, where the importance of restoration records is not yet fully recognized, these records demonstrate the usefulness and feasibility of such documentation.

3. New Discoveries Accompanying the Restoration of the Southern Library

During the investigation of the platform's interior as part of the restoration work on the Southern Library, several significant discoveries were made, and some of them are presented here.

⑴Discovery of Foundation Deposits
At the center of the Southern Library's interior, part of a

一部が残存し，その内側には盗掘孔が穿たれていた。この台座の四隅には柱穴が残されているため，かつては木造の天蓋が設置されていたことが推測される。基壇内部構造を確認することを目的に，この盗掘孔をさらに掘り下げる調査を行ったところ，二層の深さより鎮壇具が出土した。上位鎮壇具は基壇上面から50cm下，下位鎮壇具は基壇上面から1m下で当初の土壌底部から出土した。これらは鎮壇具を奉納する際に掘り込まれた土壌の北西隅に埋納されていたため，幸運にも盗掘を免れたものであった。

上位鎮壇具は金属板計10枚よりなる（Fig. 4.4.2）。直径19.0cm前後の皿形銅板1枚，鏨打ちで牛の線刻が描かれた8.6×8.3cmの金属板1枚，銅板を裁断して成形した約7.5cm角の方形銅板5枚，幅6〜7cm，高さ10〜11.5cmの馬耳形銅板3枚，そしてそれらの板に挟み込まれた不規則な形態の鉛化合物塊3点で構成される。牛の線刻が施された板は，金・銀合金製あるいは銅板に金か銀の鍍金製品であった。

下位鎮壇具は直径11.0cm前後の銅板製亀甲と腹部の二材よりなる亀形容器状のものである。内部には木綿布と銅板で包み込んだ水晶が納められていた。容器直下には縒りをかけた銅線が確認され，亀甲と腹部の左右と下部にある円穴を銅線が結束していたものと考えられる。亀形の鎮壇具は過去に王宮前広場の象のテラスから複数発見されているほか，バイヨンの南池の発掘調査でも亀形石彫品が確認された。近年実施されたスラ・スラン中央の小島内でも大型亀形石彫品が出土した。アンコール時代に好まれたインド神話である乳海攪拌の攪拌棒が亀上に設置されたように，亀は大地や地盤を安定し，繁栄の基盤を象徴し，広く地鎮のために用いられたものと推測される。

⑵基壇内部の方形ラテライト構造体

基壇内部の版築土内からは，2基のラテライト構造体が確認された。それぞれ一辺3.4mの方形平面でラテライト材を6〜7層積み上げた，高さ1.6mの構造であった（Fig. 4.4.3, 4.4.4）。平面関係からみると，これら2つの構造体の四隅は上部構造体の柱と妻壁の直下に位置するため，上部構造を支持するために設置されたと考えられるが，直接に上部構造を石積みが連続して支持するものではない。北経蔵では同様の構造体は基壇内部に確認されなかったが，南経蔵の基壇の解体範囲はやや広かったため，同様の構造体が北経蔵の基壇内にも内包されていた可能性はある。版築作業を行う上でも，小区画に分けることは盛土の締固めに有効であったと推測される。

バイヨン中央塔群を支える中央テラスの基壇内部の

Fig. 4.4.2 Foundation deposits found in the platform

two-tier stone pedestal remained, with evidence of looting holes pierced inside. Given that pillar holes are preserved at the four corners of the pedestal, it is presumed that a wooden canopy was once installed. To examine the internal structure of the platform, the looting holes were further excavated, resulting in the discovery of foundation deposits.

The upper foundation deposits consisted of ten metal plates (Fig. 4.4.2). They consist of a copper plate with a dish-like shape with a diameter of around 19.0 cm, a copper plate measuring about 8.6 × 8.3 cm with a carved line representing a cow, five square copper plates measuring approximately 7.5 cm on each side, and three horse-ear-shaped copper plates measuring 6-7 cm in width and 10-11.5 cm in height. These plates were sandwiched between irregularly shaped lead compounds. The plate with the cow carving was either made of a gold-silver alloy or copper plated with gold or silver.

The lower foundation deposits consist of a copper plate turtle shell and two materials for the abdomen, forming a container in the shape of a turtle with a diameter of about 11.0 cm. Inside the container was a quartz crystal wrapped in cotton cloth and copper plates. Copper wires with twists were found beneath the container, suggesting that the copper wires were secured to the holes on the left and right sides and bottom of the turtle shell. Similar turtle-shaped foundation deposits have been found in the past, including multiple discoveries from the Elephant Terrace in front of the Royal Palace in Angkor Thom and during excavations in the southern pond of Bayon. Recently, large turtle-shaped stone sculptures were also unearthed on a small island in the central area of Srah Srang. In Hindu mythology, which was favored during the Angkor period, the churning staff used during the Churning of the Ocean of Milk was placed on a turtle. The turtle symbolizes the stability of the earth and the foundation of prosperity, and

調査においても，塔直下の周辺部をラテライト擁壁で囲繞し，塔直下は版築土とする内部構造が確認されており，南経蔵の基壇内部と共通している。基礎としての石積みは，直接の支持体というよりも盛土の拘束体としての利用する意識が高かったものと考えられる。こうした発見は，アンコール王朝の最成熟期に築かれたバイヨン築造の思想背景を窺い知る上で重要である。

it might be widely used for land consecrations.

(2) Laterite Structures Inside the Platform

During the investigation of the platform's interior, two laterite structures were identified. These structures were constructed with laterite blocks, forming square planes with sides measuring 3.4 meters and reaching a height of 1.6 meters (Fig. 4.4.3, 4.4.4). From the plan view, the four corners of these two structures were positioned directly under the pillars and the gables of the upper superstructure, suggesting that they were installed to support the upper structure. However, they were not directly connected to the stone masonry continuously supporting the upper structure. Although similar structures were not identified within the interior of the platform in the Northern Library, the dismantling scope of the platform in the Southern Library was slightly larger, leaving a possibility that similar structures might have been present within the platform of the Northern Library as well. Dividing the area into smaller plots was likely effective for compacting the earth filling.

During the investigation of the central terrace, which supports the central tower complex of Bayon, a structure similar to the one found in the interior of the platform of the Southern Library was estimated. The area immediately below the tower was enclosed by laterite retaining walls, while the space directly beneath the tower was filled with earth, and these internal structures were surrounded by laterite retaining walls. This configuration suggests that the stone masonry used as the foundation was likely intended more as a restraint for earth filling rather than a direct supporting structure. These discoveries provide valuable insights into the philosophical background behind the construction of Bayon during the peak period of the Angkor civilization.

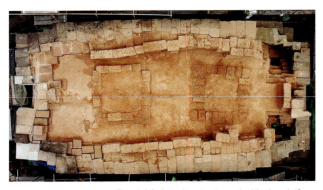

Fig. 4.4.3 Laterite structures inside the platform during partial dismantling, Southern Library of Bayon

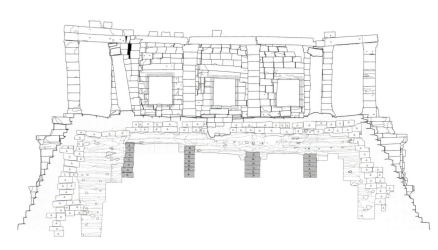

Fig. 4.4.4 East-West cross section, location of the laterite structures inside the platform

4.5 バイヨン外回廊東面景観整備
Landscape Improvement of the East Outer Gallery of Bayon

石塚 充雅
ISHIZUKA Mitsumasa

1. はじめに

　バイヨンには2つの回廊がある。バイヨン以前の寺院の壁面においては基本的にはヒンドゥー教の神話や伝説を基にした絵物語の浅浮彫が彫られていることがほとんどであるが，バイヨンの2つの回廊のうち，バイヨン外回廊の壁面にはジャヤヴァルマンⅦの大きな偉業であるチャンパ軍を撃破し，アンコールを再平定した戦いとなるクメール軍とチャンパ軍との戦いを主題とした当時の様子が浅浮彫で描かれている。そしてその中には戦いの様子のみならず，漁や狩り，調理や遊戯の風景といった当時の生き生きとした民衆生活の様子も含まれている。カンボジアにおいて現在当時の事を知ることができる資料が石碑や建物に刻まれた碑文，中国人による当時の渡航記，そして壁面に描かれる浅浮彫に限られることから，バイヨン外回廊に描かれている浅浮彫のカンボジアにおける歴史的な意義は非常に大きい。

　またその外回廊の四辺中央および四錐には同一平面形状，そして残存している箇所で確認できる限りでは基本的に同一の装飾が施されている建物が配されている。ア

1. Introduction

　Bayon has two principal galleries. The bas-reliefs of the walls of the temples before the Bayon period were basically carved with stories based on Hindu myths and legends. However on the bas-reliefs of the walls of the Outer Gallery of Bayon, the main theme is the battle between the Khmer and the Champa army. This was the great battle of King Jayavarman VII, who defeated the Champa army and re-pacified Angkor. It includes not only scenes of battle, but also vivid scenes of people's life at the time, such as scenes of fishing, hunting, cooking, and games. In the present Cambodia, the materials available to know about the situation of ancient time is limited to inscriptions carved on the steles and buildings, travelogues written by Chinese people at the time, and bas-reliefs carved on walls. Therefore, the bas-reliefs carved on the walls of Outer Gallery of Bayon have great historical significance for Cambodia.

　In addition, in the centers of the four sides and the four corners of the Outer Gallery, there are buildings with the same plan and basically the same decorations as far as can be seen from the remaining elements. In Angkor, it is very rare to find buildings with the same characteristics in the center of each

Fig. 4.5.1 East Façade of Bayon

Fig. 4.5.2 South wing of the East Outer Gallery

Fig. 4.5.3 Naval battle between Khmers and Chams(upper part) and daily life(lower part)

ンコールでは同一回廊において四辺中央と四錐に同一の特徴を有する建物が配される例は非常にまれである。バイヨンのこれらすべての建物の柱および柱・入口上部の小壁部にはダンシング・アプサラの彫刻が施され，すべての方位からの来訪者を歓迎する意図を想起させる形式をとっている。

バイヨンにおいては20世紀前半にEFEO（フランス極東学院）によって整備がすすめられたが，それから100年近く立ち，現在危険な状態にある箇所も多くなっている。

その中でも観光客の多くが利用し，かつバイヨンにとっての顔として重要な意味を持つバイヨン外回廊を中心とした東正面の整備作業を日本国政府アンコール遺跡救済チーム（JASA）第4フェーズより開始した。

2. 作業方針

本作業はこれまでのJSA/JASAによる修復の経験を生かしつつ，今回の目的が景観整備であることを念頭に置き作業を進めた。

部分解体・再構築は構造的に危険が高い箇所のみに限定して行った。

side and in the four corners in the same gallery. The pillars and small walls above the pillars and the entrances of all these buildings in Bayon are carved with dancing Apsaras, a form that evokes the intention of welcoming visitors from all directions.

Bayon was maintained in the first half of the 20th century by École française d'Extrême-Orient (EFEO), but nearly 100 years have passed since then, and many parts of the Bayon are now in a dangerous state.

Under the situation, the Landscape Improvement of East Façade centered on the Outer Gallery of Bayon, which is accessed by many tourists and has an important meaning as the face for Bayon, started in the 4th phase of the Japan-APSARA Safeguarding Angkor (JASA) Project.

2. Work Policy

This work has been carried out based on the understanding that the aim has been landscape improvement by taking advantage of the experience of restoration by JSA/JASA.

Partial dismantling and reconstruction work was limited to places with high structural risk.

Scattered sandstones were recorded, removed, assembled and identified as to their original position. Identified sandstone elements were reassembled in the case that structural stability

Fig. 4.5.4 Cockfight

Fig. 4.5.5 Inside of East Gate (T55)

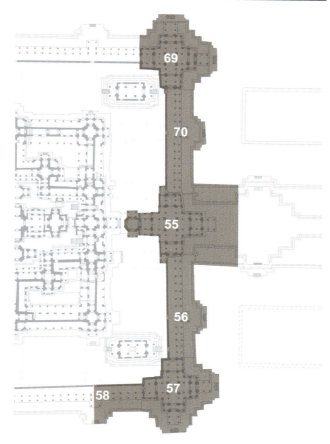

Fig. 4.5.6 Target area

　散乱石材は記録した後，移動し，同定作業を行った。同定された砂岩材のうち構造的な安定性も確保された場合には再構築作業を行っている。同定できなかった，あるいは今回再構築が難しかった砂岩材に関しては近傍に整理して配置している。

　基壇部と床石については変位が大きい箇所の部分解体再構築のほか，目地開きのある箇所については，雨水の浸入による内部版築層への浸食のリスクを避けるため，目地開きを調整する。

　鎹による結合，モルタルの充填，コンクリートによるサポート等過去の修復によって施された処置のうち，機能を失っているものについてはいずれも取り除き，再処置を行う。

　また今回の修復では部分解体に留めたため，多くの部材は原位置に設置されたままで基本的には移動を控えた。しかし，劣化が進行している箇所に関しては原位置のままの状態で強化処置を行っている。

　そして今回の方針では解体－非解体部材間に微妙なずれは残る。そのため再設置の前に同定作業を慎重に行い，可能な限りずれを最小化し，安定した状態に調整した。

　この整備作業はJASA第3フェーズに引き続き，カンボジア人スタッフの主体的取り組みを促進する体制で行った。

can be ensured. For sandstone elements not identified or not possible for reassembling at this time, we collected and rearranged nearby in the form of a depository or exhibition. For platform and pavement, in addition of partial dismantling and reconstruction at large deformation parts, we readjusted gap opening parts in order to stop the risk of erosion of the inner soil caused by rain water infiltration.

Among the measures taken by previous interventions such as reattachment by iron crump, mortar filling, concrete support, all the lost functions were removed and retreated.

As we conducted only a partial treatment, many elements remained in their original locations. However, the deteriorated parts were reconsolidated while in their original position.

Using a limited intervention policy, subtle distortion of the un-dismantled and dismantled parts remained. Therefore, before actually reassembling, we carefully performed trial assembling work to minimize gaps as much as possible and make adjustments to ensure a stable condition.

This maintenance work was carried out under a system that encouraged the Cambodian staff to take the initiative, continuing from Phase 3 of the JASA project.

3. 作業経過

・外回廊南東隅塔（塔57）およびその周辺

2011年11月より整備作業を開始した。整備前には屋根の大半が崩壊し，一部残存している北西部についても壁体が傾いており，非常に危険な状態であった。これらの屋根及び壁体部は過去の修復にて設置されたコンクリート支持材によって保持されていたが，このコンクリート支持材自体も弱体化していた。また北面ペディメントに対しては，崩壊した際のリスクを鑑み，アプサラ機構によって木製のサポートが設置されていた。ペディメントの修復に際してはJASA構造班と共にペディメント下端部梁材に関する強度試験を行い，その後の整備の方針にも繋がる補強方針を検討した。

基壇部についても部分解体の間に地盤構造調査を行い，基壇整備の基本指針を検討した。

散乱石材については同定作業の結果，塔57の上部装飾箇所については多くの部材が同定された。しかし元位置にすべて戻すのは現時点では難しかったため塔57近くに展示保存した。

またあわせて周辺部である外回廊東面南翼（回廊56）南辺および外回廊南面東翼（回廊58）東辺の整備作業を進めた。

各種整備が完了した後，2014年3月に一般開放した。

・外回廊東門（塔55）およびその周辺

2014年4月より作業を開始した。整備前にはバイヨンの正面入口にもかかわらず，屋根部は完全に崩壊して，内外に多くの石材が散乱しているため，観光客の訪問を阻害していた。

東参道についても同参道内の塔55周辺部において変形箇所があったことから，整備のために床面を部分解体

3. Work Progress

· Southeast Corner Pavilion (T57) in the Outer Gallery and its Surroundings

We started the work from November 2011. Before improvement, large parts of the roof collapsed and the small remaining part that is in the northwest corner was in danger of collapse as the wall had inclined. The remaining roof part and wall was supported by concrete beams and poles installed by the past intervention, but the concrete support itself was weakened due to age. A wooden structure was by APSARA installed for supporting the northern high pediment in order to prevent the risk of collapse. When repairing the pediment, a strength test for beam parts at the bottom of pediment was conducted with a JASA structural team to examine the reinforcement policy that have led to subsequent maintenance policies.

A geotechnical survey was also conducted for the platform during partial dismantling, and based on the results, future basic guidelines for the improvement of the platform were considered.

From scattered stones, many elements for the upper decoration part of T57 were identified. However, since it was difficult at this time to return every stone to its original position, the stones were exhibited near T57.

We also proceeded with the maintenance of the bas-reliefs and some floor areas around the south part of the south wing of the East Outer Gallery (G56) and the east part of the east wing of the South Outer Gallery (G58).

The site was opened to the public in March 2014 after the completion of the various improvement work.

· East Gate of the Outer Gallery (T55) and its Surroundings

The work began in April 2014. Before improvement of T55, the roof was completely collapsed and many stones were scattered inside and around T55. Therefore, these conditions

Fig. 4.5.7 T57 (before improvement)

Fig. 4.5.8 T57 (after improvement)

Fig. 4.5.9 T55 (before improvement)

Fig. 4.5.10 T55 (after improvement)

したところ，塔55前身基壇と思われる痕跡が出現した。また参道床面上には多数の柱穴痕も確認されていたことから，該当箇所の整備とあわせて，建造過程の検討のための調査を行う必要もあった。上記の中で，塔55，そして東参道の一部を含む塔55周辺部の調査ならびに整備作業が行われた。加えて塔55東正面の2体の守護神像の部分修復および設置位置の調整，整備前に参道周辺に散乱していた仏座像の破材の整理，そして塔55に西面する塔52の部分整備ならびに暫定支保工設置作業も行った。これらの整備後，2016年4月に一般開放した。

本整備作業とあわせて外回廊東面北翼（回廊70）南辺および外回廊東面南翼（回廊56）北辺の整備作業もあわせて進めた。回廊70南辺の整備は2016年3月末に開始し，整備後2016年12月に一般開放し，回廊56北辺の整備は2016年6月中旬に開始し，整備完了後12月に一般開放した。

・外回廊北東隅塔（塔69）およびその周辺

整備前は塔69の屋根部の大半は崩壊していた。また一部屋根が残存している南西部については壁体が傾いており，過去にはEFEOの修復によりコンクリートの支持材が設置されたが，後年劣化が進んでおり，その後アプサラ機構による木造の支保工が設置されている状態だった。また床面および基壇部については北および東入口部周辺部を中心に変状が進んでいた。

整備前の各種準備作業は2016年10月から進め，その後整備作業は2021年7月から開始している。本整備作業に関しては検討の結果，6つの区域に分けて整備を進めており，2023年8月時点でこれまでに2区域の整備作業を終えている。

また塔69の整備に先んじて外回廊東面北翼（回廊70）北辺の整備作業を進めた。本整備作業は2020年7月から整備作業を開始し，2021年10月に整備を完了した。

hindered tourist visits despite T55 being the main entrance of Bayon.

As for the East Causeway, there were deformed areas around Tower 55 that requierd attention. Therefore, when the floor was partially dismantled for maintenance, traces that were possible to be the former platform structure of T55 had been identified. In addition, since numerous posthole traces were confirmed on the floor of the causeway, it was also necessary to conduct a survey to consider the construction process as well as improvement work in this area. Survey and improvement work was carried out on T55 and its surrounding area, including the parts of East Causeway. Partial restoration of two guardian statues in front of T55 and adjustment of their positions was performed. Sorting the broken pieces of Buddha statues that were scattered around the causeway, and the partial improvement and temporary reinforcement by installing supports in the dangerous areas of T52 facing west of T55 were also implemented at that time. The site was opened to the public in April 2016 after completion of this work.

In addition of this work, improvement work on the south part of the north wing of the East Outer Gallery (G70) and the north part of the south wing of the East Outer Gallery (G56) were implemented. Improvement work on the south wing of G70 began at the end of March 2016, and it was opened to the public in December 2016 after completion of the work. Improvement work on the north wing of G56 began in mid-June 2016, and it was opened to the public in December after completion of the work.

・Northeast Corner Pavilion (T69) in the Outer Gallery and its Surroundings

Before improvement work, most of the roof of T69 had collapsed, and in the southwestern part where some of the roof remained, the wall was leaning dangerously. Although concrete supports were installed at this part in the past through restoration work by EFEO, their deterioration has progressed in later years, and wooden supports were subsequently constructed by APSARA. In addition, deformation of the

Fig. 4.5.11 Improvement work of T69

Fig. 4.5.12 Improvement work of North Part of G70

・その他

上記した作業区域におけるナーガ，ライオン彫像および欄干の修復に関しては日本ユネスコ協会連盟およびアンコール人材養成支援機構と協力して行った。

4．本整備作業を通して得られた新たな知見

整備に伴う考古調査によって，特に塔55周辺で多くの増改築の痕跡が確認された。東正面においては数次に渡る増改築を経た前身基壇の痕跡が確認されたほか，北側からも階段の痕跡が確認された。これまでのバイヨンの増改築過程に関する研究においては外回廊は基本的に同一の段階で建造されたとみる見解が多くを占めていたが，今回の調査により，外回廊東面においては正門となる塔55の位置に先んじて独立した建物ないしはテラスが存在し，その後両翼に回廊が拡張されたことが示唆された。加えて東正面においては度重なる増改築が行われたことが確認された。

塔55―参道接続部周辺の地盤基礎構造発掘調査の成果により，当初の基礎工事の段階において参道の区域は含まれておらず，参道は後年基礎部から増築された可能性を示唆する痕跡が確認された。

加えて外回廊基壇版築盛土内からはラテライト列の存在が確認された。類似した痕跡は本調査のみならず，1999～2000年のバイヨン北方でのバイヨン内回廊から周回道路までのロングトレンチ調査を行った際にも同様の痕跡が確認され，この際にはそれに加えて外回廊外中庭側にも類似したラテライト列が発見された。このラテライト列が施工時に必要とされた構造だったのか，増改築の痕跡を意味するものなのか，今後検討を進めていく必要がある。

さらに各建物で地盤構造調査を行っているが，その中で塔57および塔69基壇内部で使用されている版築盛土

pavement and platform was progressing mainly around the north and east entrances.

Various pre-improvement work was started in October 2016, and improvement was started in July 2021. This improvement work was divided into six areas, and as of August 2023, improvement work in two areas has been completed.

In addition, prior to the improvement work of T69, improvement work on the north part of the north wing of the East Outer Gallery (G70) was carried out. This work began in July 2020 and was completed in October 2021.

・**Others**

The restoration of the Naga and Lion Statues and Balustrade in the above-mentioned work area was carried out in cooperation with National Federation of UNESCO Association in JAPAN and Joint Support Team for Angkor Community Development.

4. New findings through the improvement work

Archaeological surveys accompanying the improvement work revealed many traces of expansions and renovations, especially around T55. On the East Façade, traces of former platforms, which had undergone multiple expansions and renovations, were confirmed, and trace of a stair with multiple steps was also confirmed on the north side. In the previous study on the Bayon's expansion and renovation process, the majority view was that the Outer Gallery was basically constructed at the same stage. However the result of this survey suggested that on the east side of the Outer Gallery there was an independent building or terrace that preceded the location of T55, which served as the main gate, and that the East Outer Gallery was later expanded to both wings. In addition, it was confirmed that the East Façade of T55 had been repeatedly expanded and renovated.

The results of the excavation survey of the ground foundation structure of the connection area between T55 and

Fig. 4.5.13 Traces of steps on east side of T55

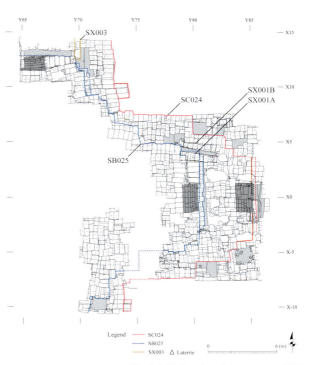

Fig. 4.5.14 Trace of step on north side of T55

において，その性質を見極める上で重要な尺度である粒度分布に違いが見られた。塔57において使用された版築土はバイヨン南北経蔵や中央塔のオリジナルの版築盛土に近いバイヨンで多く見られる粒度分布が確認されたが，塔69の版築盛土はそれよりも荒いものであった。これまで版築盛土を含む基礎の内部構造の性質に着目した建物の分類やその建造過程の研究は十分に進められてこなかったが，同一回廊内で違いが見られた状況を鑑みると今後この点に関しても検討を進めていく必要がある。

5．今後の課題

　東面の整備が完了した後，外回廊のその他の面もアプサラ機構と協力もしくはアプサラ機構主導の下で，これまでの手法を踏襲しつつ，順次整備していく必要がある。その際にはアンコールにおける修復の原則である部分解体・再構築という前提に準拠しつつ，大きな変形を起こしている箇所のみの局所的な整備に留まらず，回廊および各建物の連続性を考慮して各区域毎に順次整備していく。

　また今後もこれまでに発見された課題を留意した上で

Fig. 4.5.15 Drawing of traces around T55

causeway suggest that the causeway was not included at the initial foundation construction period, and that the causeway had been expanded from the foundation in a later period.

In addition, the presence of laterite rows was confirmed within the compaction soil structure inside the platform of the Outer Gallery. Similar traces were found not only in this survey but also in the survey of 1999-2000 when a long trench survey was conducted north of Bayon from the Inner Gallery to the circumferential road. At this time, similar laterite rows were also discovered on the side of the courtyard outside the Outer Gallery. Future research will need to be conducted to determine whether these laterite rows were structures required at the time of construction, or whether these represents traces of an extension or renovation.

Furthermore, in the results of the geotechnical survey conducted for each element, differences were found in the particle size distribution of the compaction soil used inside the platform of T57 and T69, and is an important measure for determining their character. The compaction soil used in T57 has a particle size distribution that are often seen in Bayon, which is close to the original compaction soil used in the Northern and Southern Libraries and the Central Tower of Bayon, but the compaction soil used in T69 is coarser. Until now, study on the classification of buildings and their construction processes has not focused on the characteristics of the internal structure of foundations, including compaction soil. However, considering the current situation where differences were observed within the same gallery, it is necessary to further consider this point in the future.

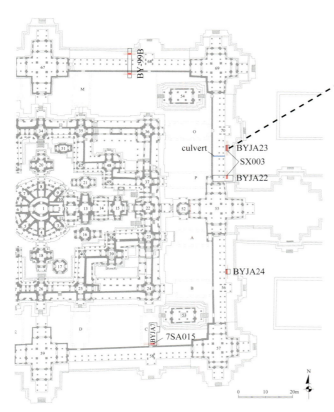

Fig. 4.5.16 The map detected lower laterite row in the Outer Gallery

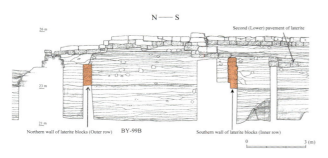

Fig. 4.5.17 The Lower laterite row in the Outer Gallery, The 6th survey(BY-99B)

整備作業に伴う各種調査を進めることになるが，その際にはバイヨン外回廊の各区域の特徴並びに建造過程に関して研究を継続していく必要がある。

そして大半の箇所で壁体・柱部以上の構造が欠損しているため，これらの部分を再構築できる可能性を探るための大規模な散乱石材同定作業，その上での再構築作業が必要とされる。特に外回廊の四辺中央および四錐の建物に関しては塔状であった可能性を示唆する見解もあるが，その論拠として示される散乱石材はかなり限られたものであり，壁体部以上の構造全容を散乱石材から具体的に再構築できた例は現時点までにないことから，今後バイヨン内外に存在する膨大な散乱石材の整理・原位置同定作業を通じて実際の形状を具体的に検証していく必要がある。

Fig. 4.5.18 The Lower laterite row in the Outer Gallery, The 23rd survey(BYJA23)

5. Future Tasks

After the improvement work of the East Façade is completed, it will be necessary to gradually continue to improve the other sides of the Outer Gallery while following the methods used in cooperation with or under the leadership of APSARA. For this work, it is necessary not to limit to improve the partial parts where major deformations have occurred, but to improve each area in turn, taking into account the continuity of the gallery and each element by following the principle of partial dismantling and reconstruction, which is the principle of restoration in Angkor.

Various surveys related to improvement work will be continued while keeping in mind the issues that have been discovered until now. In these surveys, it is necessary to continue study about the character of each area of the Bayon Outer Gallery and its construction process.

In most places, structures above the wall and pillar parts are missing. It is necessary to implement large scale identification work of the scattered stones in order to consider the possibility of reconstructing these areas, and to implement subsequent reconstruction work. In particular, there are some opinions suggesting the possibility that the centers of the four sides and the four corners of the Outer Gallery may have been tower-shaped, but until now the number of scattered stones shown as evidence for this is quite limited, and there has been no example in which the entire structure above the wall part has been concretely reconstructed from scattered stones. Therefore, in the future, it will be necessary to verify the actual shape of these parts through sorting and identification of the huge number of scattered stones that exist inside and outside Bayon.

第 5 章　人材育成及び協力関連事業

Chapter 5　Human Resource Development and Collaborative Project

5.1 保存修復現場での研修とカンボジア人専門家の育成
On-the-Job Training at Restoration Site and Cambodian Expert Development

中川　武　　　ソ・ソクンテリー
NAKAGAWA Takeshi　So Sokuntheary

チュン・メンホン
Chhum Menghong

1. アンコール遺跡救済のための国際協力と人材育成

　世界的文化遺産の保存に関する国際協調活動で特質されるのは①70年代のアブ・シンベル神殿を中心としたエジプト，ヌビア，②80年代のインドネシア・ボロブドゥール寺院，③90年代のカンボジア・アンコール遺跡である。それぞれ，保存修復活動の方法や国際機関の役割が異なっているが，①，②に比べて③の特異点は，内戦からの社会復興と文化遺産の国際協調による救済活動の連携が強く意識されたことであろう。

　戦争もしくは紛争の当事者が和平協議のためのテーブルに着き，停戦調印に漕ぎつけることと，社会復興を実現するための長い道程は全く別のことであることは，中東紛争の歴史と現状を見るまでもなく了解されるであろう。しかし，文化遺産の保存修復のために国際協力することとそのための人材育成とは，連関しつつも，両者の間にはかなりの距離があり，プロジェクトによりその内容が異なっていることが改めて認識される機会になった。

　文化遺産が危機に瀕していて，当該国に，技術的，経済的，社会体制的困難があって十分に対応ができない時，当該国からの要請による外国や国際機関からの支援は，個別物件の解決に留まらず，それをきっかけとして，その分野の教育の始動に結びつく可能性がある。しかしそれはあくまでも可能性であって，技術面に限定した向上はまだしも，一般的な学力や倫理・情操面の成長はその社会の自律的，内部的努力による以外にないことをつい見失いがちになる。外国からの支援がかえってその分野の人材養成の妨げになることさえある。ではやらない方が良いのか，ということではなく，やり方が問題だということになろう。私たちJSA（日本国政府アンコール遺跡救済チーム）の人材育成の方針はこの問題を巡る試行の連続であった。

1. International Cooperation and Human Resource Development for the Rescue of Angkor Monuments

The international cooperative activities for the conservation of world cultural heritage are characterized by (1) the Abu Simbel in Egypt and Nubia in the 1970s, (2) the Borobudur Temple in Indonesia in the 1980s, and (3) the Angkor Monuments in Cambodia in the 1990s. Although the methods of conservation and restoration activities and the roles of international organizations differ in each case, what is unique about (3) compared to (1) and (2) is that there was a strong awareness of the need to coordinate social reconstruction due to civil wars and international cooperation for the restoration of cultural heritage.

It is clear that the parties to a war or conflict reaching a table for peace talks and signing a ceasefire and the long process of social reconstruction are two completely different things. However, while international cooperation for the conservation and restoration of cultural heritage and human resource development for this purpose are interrelated, there is a considerable distance between the two, and the contents of the two are recognized as difference depending on the project.

When cultural heritage is in danger and the country concerned is unable to respond adequately due to technical, economic, or social difficulties, support from foreign countries or international organizations at the request of the country concerned may not be limited to solving individual properties, but may lead to the start of education in that field. However, this is just a possibility, and the autonomous and internal efforts of the society is necessary to improve the technical aspect, general academic ability and ethical and emotional growth. Foreign assistance may even hinder the development of human resources in that field. So, it is not a question of whether it is better not to do it, but rather how to do it. The human resource development policy of the Japanese

2. JSAにおける人材育成の基本方針

文化遺産の保存修復は基本的にはオリジナルな伝統技術の再現が必要となる。アンコール遺跡では特にその比重が高く，厳密で，環境的にも，歴史的にも広範な理解が必要となる。従来は，理論的には伝統技術の完全な再現は不可能であり，遺跡には，それ以上の劣化崩壊の防止対策以外は手をつけないで，そのオリジナリティをそのまま保存するという考え方が主流であった。しかし文化遺産といえども修復しながら使い続けることの保存面での有効性，崩壊箇所の原位置復帰の重要性，そして，歴史的環境や文化的伝統にも連関する遺跡景観としてのオーセンティシティ（真正性）の確保への努力が注目されつつある。その中で，かろうじて伝来したオリジナルの保存の意義もさることながら，多くのものが失われ，その意味が風前の灯火のような状況で，それを理解し，その広がりが持つ意味をイメージするためにこそ失われた伝統技術の再現が求められよう。JSAのミッションは，アンコール遺跡の保存修復のための技術協力である。これを，どのように，どこまで行うのか，と考えた時，カンボジア人を含めたJSA全体で，上記の基本命題をどのようにして，どこまで共有するのか，がJSAの人材育成の基本方針として意識されてきたと思う。どのような方法でそれは可能であっただろうか。

3. JSA10年間の人材育成システムと 現在までの現場研修

文化遺産の保存修復事業の進展によって，その人材育成の方法も変化する。JSAが正式に修復事業を始めたのは1994年11月，アンコール・トム王宮前広場の，プラサート・スープラの12塔とテラス群の，測量と考古学発掘調査であった。遺跡の保存修復事業は多分野の連携によって進められる。しかし私たちの事業開始当初は，長年の修復事業の中断のためEFEO（フランス極東学院）チームも，離散していた以前のスタッフを中心に再出発したとのことであったが，JSAでも，かつてのEFEOのスタッフで，内戦終結後自力で遺跡の整理などを行っていた3人の修復体験者（後のJSA棟梁と副棟梁）を中心に，ほぼアンコール・トムに隣接するノコール・クラウ村の農民達によってチームを組んでもらい，日本人専門家と日本からの職人による現場実務訓練で修復技能工として育てるべく進めることになった。修復事業は各種調査，

Government Team for Safeguarding Angkor (JSA) has been a series of trials, tribulations, and successes concerning this issue.

2. Basic Policy of Human Resource Development in JSA

The conservation and restoration of cultural heritage requires the reproduction of original traditional techniques. The Angkor Monuments are particularly important, and requires a rigorous and extensive understanding of the environment and history. Traditionally, it has been theoretically impossible to completely reproduce traditional techniques, and the prevailing view has been to preserve the originality of the monuments as they are, without intervention them except to prevent them from further deterioration and collapse. However, the effectiveness in terms of conservation of cultural heritage of continuing to use them while restoring them, the importance of restoring collapsed areas to their original locations, and efforts to secure authenticity as archaeological landscapes related to the historical environment and cultural traditions are attracting more and more attention. JSA's mission is to provide technical cooperation for the conservation and restoration of the Angkor Monuments. When considering how and to what extent to do this, how and to what extent to share the above basic propositions with the entire JSA team, including Cambodians, has been a basic policy of human resource development of the JSA. How is this basic proposition achieved ?

3. JSA's 10-year human resource development system and on-site training

As the conservation and restoration projects of cultural heritage have progressed, the methods of human resource development have also changed. JSA officially started its restoration project in November 1994 with the survey and archaeological excavation of 12 towers and terraces of Prasat Suor Prat in the square in front of the Royal Palace of Angkor Thom. The conservation and restoration of archaeological sites is a multidisciplinary project. Our team was as a organized the development team for restoration technician led by three former EFEO staff who had been carried the conserve the monuments themselves after civil war, with the residents of Nokor Krau Village near from Angkor Thom. In this team, Japanese experts and technicians provided them the skills and technique through On-the-Job-Training. Restoration projects require various surveys, planning, analysis, on-site guidance, reporting, etc., and it is inevitably necessary to have highly trained and skilled personnel. Educated people as restoration technicians or specialists through further specialized

計画，分析，現地指導，レポーティングなどの必要があり，どうしても高度教育を受けた者を，さらに専門教育して，修復技術者，あるいは専門家として育成する必要がある。当時は王立プノンペン芸術大学に，考古学と建築学科があった。ユネスコ／日本信託基金による両学科への講師派遣やJSA専門家による出張授業など，大学との連携を強め，年に2回（夏期と冬期あるいは春期の長期休暇中，1回2週間）のJSA現場研習生を募集し，ペーパーと面接試験の結果，平均して，考古学＋修復学の2コースで12〜14名の研修を10年間継続してきた。これは㈶文化財保護振興財団の絶大な支援によって可能となったものであるが，JSAの専門家以外にも，毎回様々な分野からの日本人専門家の参集があったことが忘れられない。若きカンボジア人学生研修生達が多くの，この分野の日本人専門家に出会うことができたと思う。また毎回はできなかったが機会をとらえて，奈良文化財研究所やイコモスのローマ，ベネチア研修にも選抜メンバーを派遣した。そしてこれらの研修を通して，通常のレポート以外に自分のテーマを発見し，外部に研究成果を発表すること，自分の卒論研究や博士号取得論文に発展させる事を奨励した。

　JSA研修は，学生だけでなく卒業生にも門戸を開いており，毎回応募テストに合格が条件だが，5回の参加経験者は，希望によりJSA社会人研修生の試験に応募することができ，合格すればJSAのオフィスに常駐するアシスタント・エキスパートのメンバーとなる。さらに2年間の実績が評価されれば，試験の結果，晴れてJSAエキスパートとなる道を用意した。これらのプロセスで，いずれも試験での選別を行ってきたが，教育の社会的制度がまだ十分でなかった当時のカンボジアでは個人の専門的学力と意欲が重要と考えられたからである。現場作業員は，通常の勤務実績により，上級技能工への登用を行って意欲の向上を期待した。その後，現在までカンボジア人エキスパート，現場スタッフとも体験を蓄積し，各々の分野においてアンコール遺跡の保存に貢献している。またJSAの人材育成を経て，他チームや他分野で活躍した人も多い。

4. 文化遺産の保存修復における技術移転と技術者あるいは研究者の理念

　伝統技術の解明にとって，建物の解体調査に立ち会うことは極めて特権的なことである。それだけに記録を後世に残すことは義務であって，必要な比較調査を加えるなどして，オリジナルな技法を解明することが研究者の

education was required. At that time, the Royal University of Fine Arts in Phnom Penh had departments of archaeology and architecture. The instructors and JSA experts supported by the UNESCO/Japan Trust Fund were dispatched, and the cooperation with the university was strengthened. For 10 years the average number of trainees has been between 12 to 14 in the two courses of archaeology and restoration. This was made possible by the generous support of the Foundation for Cultural Heritage and Art Research. The young Cambodian student trainees were able to meet many Japanese experts in this field. Although it was not possible every time, we took the opportunity to dispatch selected members to the Nara National Research Institute for Cultural Properties, and Rome and Venice for training by ICOMOS. Through these training programs, students were encouraged to discover their own themes in addition to the usual reports, to present the results of their research to the outside world, and to develop them into their research or doctoral thesis.

The JSA training program was open to graduates as well as students, and although they must pass an application test, those who have participated in the program five times can apply for the JSA trainee exam. When they pass the exam, they become a member as a JSA assistant expert stationed in the JSA office. Based on 2 years performance and result of an exam, they could become a JSA expert member stationed in the JSA office. In these processes, selection has been done by examination, as the professional academic ability and motivation of the individual were considered important in Cambodia when the social system of education was not yet entirely adequate. The site workers who exhibited proficiency in their regular work performance were promoted to senior skilled tradesmen. Since then, both Cambodian experts and site worker have accumulated experience and are contributing to the conservation of Angkor Monuments in their respective fields. Many of them have been active in other teams or in other fields through JSA's human resource development program.

4. Technology Transfer and the Philosophy of the Engineer or Researcher in the Conservation and Restoration of Cultural Heritage

It is exciting to be present at the dismantling of a building in order to investigate traditional techniques. It is therefore an obligation to preserve records for posterity, and it is the role of the researcher to elucidate the original techniques by conducting the necessary comparative studies. When it is necessary to insert and support new wood to restore a surviving original member to its original position, it is the duty of the restoration technician to design a working drawing for the production of new wood based on the dimensional

5.1　保存修復現場での研修とカンボジア人専門家の育成　　205

役割となる。残存したオリジナル部材を原位置に復帰させるために新材を挿入して支持する必要がある場合，復原考察により導き出された寸法情報をもとに，新材製作のための加工図を設計するのは修復技術者の任務であり，その加工図をもとにオリジナルな技術の理解と修復理念を調和させて新材を製作する仕事は修復技能工の役割である。このような仕事内容の分節と役割分担は，浅浮彫の保存修復工事など他の業務についてもほぼ同様である。勿論，一人が研究，技術，技能の役割を有機的，総合的に果たすこともあり得ないことではないが，多くは各々の担当者の連携によって対応することが多い，要は，各自の役割と相互の連関をよく認識して，現場での訓練とデスクワークを有効に組み立て，短・中・長期の各養成システムの課題に適応することが求められる。とりわけ，他の遺跡や他チームとの交流そして公的機会での発表，できれば外国留学なども養成システムに取り入れる必要があろう。さらに人材養成にとって，資格の認定制度と職場の確保は最も肝要な事項である。この問題は，外国チームには限界もあるが，考え方の重要性は積極的に発言し，できるだけの協力をすべきであろう。いずれにしても，文化遺産の保存修復に対する国際協力の主眼は人材養成にあることは疑いないので，バランスの良い修復技能工─技術者─研究者の養成に努めなければならない。その時の鍵になるのは，アンコール遺跡の伝統技術の再生がなぜ必要であり，それを私たちはどのようにして"わがもの"とするかということに対する，理念とイメージと方法をチームとして一貫して追求することであろう。

　以上は，JSA第1フェーズ及び第2フェーズの10年間を通して実践してきた人材養成プログラムの概要である。それまでの実践を経て，JSA/JASAの基本的な人材育成の考えが作られ，その後現場の状況に対応しながら，続けられている。ラオスのワット・プーの修復現場での国際サイト・トレーニングのプログラムにはJASAのカンボジア人専門家スー・ソティおよび現場作業員ダオイ・チュライ，コーン・プレン，ボーン・ブンの計4名が参加した。彼らはその場で，我らのチームが国際的水準にあることを示した。一方，学生時代にJSAの現場トレーニングの実習生として参加した経験を基に，卒業後，社会人実習生，専門家としてのトレーニングコースを歩み，外国の大学で関連する学問を学び，博士号を取得し，カンボジアのこの分野で現在めざましい活躍をしている専門家もいる。アセアンのみならず，ヨーロッパ諸国における文化遺産の保存に関わるコンペティションを通して交流を広げている。またユネスコ世界遺産リスト登録を通してカンボジアにおける文化遺産保護活動を積極的

information derived from the restoration study. It is equally important to produce new wood based on the working drawing by harmonizing the understanding of the original technique with the restoration philosophy. This division of work and the assignment of roles are similar for other work, such as the conservation and restoration of bas-relief. Of course, it is not impossible for one person to organically and comprehensively fulfill the roles of research, technology, and skills, but in most cases, the roles are handled in cooperation with each other, and in short, each person must be well aware of his or her own role and the interrelationship between them, and effectively combine on-site training and desk work to meet the challenges of short, medium, and long term training systems. The key is to be well aware of their roles and their interconnections. In particular, exchanges with other sites and teams, presentations at official occasions, and, if possible, study abroad, should be incorporated into the training system. In addition, the most important issues for the human resource development are the certification system for qualifications and the availability of workplaces. There is no doubt that the main focus of international cooperation in the conservation and restoration of cultural heritage is the development of human resources, so we must strive to archive a good balance of restoration technicians, expert, and researchers. The key to this is to consistently pursue as a team the philosophy, image, and methods of why the revival of the traditional techniques of the Angkor Monuments is necessary and how we can make them "our own".

The above is an overview of the human resource development program that has been practiced throughout the 10 years of JSA Phases 1 and 2. Through the practice, the basic idea of human resource development of JSA/JASA was established, and it has been continued while responding to the situations in the field ever since. The international site training program at the Vat Phu Temple restoration site in Laos was attended by JASA's Cambodian expert SEUR Sothy and site workers DOY Chrach, KONG Pleng, and BON Bun. They demonstrated on the spot that our team is of international standard. On the other hand, there are professionals who, based on their experience as trainees in JSA field training as students, have followed training courses as interns and professionals after graduation, studied related subjects at foreign universities, obtained doctoral degrees, and are active in their chosen field in Cambodia. They are expanding their contacts through competitions related to the preservation of cultural heritage not only in ASEAN but also in European countries. There are also experts who are actively promoting the protection of cultural heritage in Cambodia through the inscription of sites on the UNESCO World Heritage List. They are expected to continue to play an active role as leaders in this field in the country, because they are aware that the study, preservation, and education of cultural heritage nurture their pride and solidarity for peace.

に推進している専門家もいる。彼等は今後もこの国のこの分野のリーダーとして活躍していくことが期待される。それは何よりも，かれらが文化遺産の研究，保存，教育が自らの誇りと平和への連帯を育むことを自覚しているからである。これらの成果を基に第3フェーズ以降は必要に応じ，可能な範囲でアドホックにトレーニング・プログラムを実施してきたが，文化遺産保存の裾野を広げることや公教育と連動した専門基礎教育と，より高度な専門家育成に向けての継続的な教育の連携は，まだまだ必要であると考えている。

Based on these results, ad-hoc training programs have been conducted in the third and subsequent phases as needed and to the extent possible, but there is still a need to broaden the base of cultural heritage conservation and to link basic professional education with public education and continuing education for the development of more highly skilled professionals.

5.2 バイヨン本尊仏のレプリカ作製と修復による再安置プロジェクト
Bayon Great Buddha Project: Making Replica, Restoration, Reconstitution and Reinstallation of the Original Bayon Buddha Image

矢野 健一郎　　中川　武　　重松 優志　　石塚 充雅
YANO Kenichiro　　NAKAGAWA Takeshi　　SHIGEMATSU Yushi　　ISHIZUKA Mitsumasa

1. はじめに

　バイヨン本尊仏彫像については諸説あるが[1]，私たちはジャヤヴァルマンⅦの治世期に中央塔に安置されたものと考えている。本彫像は大きく7つに破断され，中央塔直下の穴に投げ棄てられていたものを1930年代にEFEO（フランス極東学院）による発掘調査後，修復・再構築し，王室の指導の下，アンコール・トム内のプレアヴィヘア・プランピー・ロヴェンに奉納された。我々は本彫像に対して，これまでのEFEO，王室，現地機構，周辺住民によるこれまでの処置に敬意を払ってきた。現在私たちは往時のバイヨン本尊の姿の復原考察の一環としてレプリカの作成を進めている。これは現在バイヨン中央に安置されている本尊仏は，アユタヤ侵攻時に安置されたもので，明らかに中央塔主室の空間と彫像との釣り合いが取れていない。そこで中央塔の修復完了時にはこのレプリカを再安置したいと申請したところ，前アプサラ機構総裁よりオリジナル仏を修復して再安置してほしい，ついてはアプサラ機構が責任を持って関係者と調整したい，とのことであった[2]。その後，バイヨン中央塔直下抗の埋め戻しがルーズなため，この補強がまず必要であることが判明した。

　現在私たちはJSA/JASAの協力事業としてバイヨン本尊レプリカ模刻作業をアプサラ機構と協調して進めており，これが完了した時点で改めて関係者と協議し，各方面から理解が得られれば，レプリカを現在のアンコール・トム内プレアヴィヘア・プランピー・ロヴェンに安置した上で，バイヨン本尊の修復処置及び中央塔の構造安定化事業が完了した後に，その本物の本尊仏をバイヨン内の原位置への再安置を強く望んでいる。

1. Introduction

　Although there are various theories[1], we think great Buddha image of the Bayon was originally installed in the Central Tower during the reign of Jayavarman VII. After the discovery of great Buddha image by the excavation survey of EFEO, which was broken into mainly seven pieces and thrown away directly into a hole beneath the Central Tower, it was restored, reconstituted, and dedicated on the platform of Preah Vihear Pram Pi Lveng in Angkor Thom under the mentorship of the Royal Household in the 1930's. We have respected all contributions by EFEO, the Royal Household, and local organizations and residents in order to maintain this image. Now, we are making a replica of Bayon Great Buddha as a part of consideration to restore the original form. The current Buddha image in the center of Bayon, was enshrined during the invasion of Ayutthaya, and the space of the main room of the Central Tower of Bayon is clearly not in balance with this current image. Therefore, when we applied to re-enshrine this replica when the restoration of the Central Tower will be completed, the former President of APSARA National Authority proposed that the original Buddha be restored and re-enshrined and that APSARA National Authority would be responsible for coordinating with relevant parties[2]. Later, it became clear that reinforcement was necessary because the backfilling soil beneath Central Tower of Bayon was uncompacted.

　Currently, we are proceeding with replica making as cooperation project of JSA/JASA in cooperation with APSARA National Authority. When this work will be completed, we will discuss plans with the concerned parties again. If understanding will be obtained from all sides, the replica is Planned to be enshrined to Preah Vihear Pram Pi Lveng in Angkor Thom. After enshrining the replica, we strongly hope the original Buddha statue will be conserved, and re-installed to the original position in the Bayon after the stabilizing construction work of the Central Tower.

Fig. 5.2.1 Present situation of original Bayon Great Buddha

Fig. 5.2.2 Original Bayon Great Buddha assembled after excavation on 1933 (EFEO)

2. バイヨン本尊レプリカ模刻事業について

　本事業はJSA/JASAの協力事業として関わっており，予算はNPO法人GREEN WIND ASIA（GWA）の管理の下，各種寄付金によって実施している。

　本作業にあたり，重要な点としてJASAカンボジア人スタッフへの技術移転があった。これまで彼らは浅浮彫を修理するために，一部を模刻した経験はあったが，3次元の丸彫り彫刻を御した経験はなかった。その中で正しくオリジナルの本尊を復原するためには，彼らの技術向上が必須であった。そしてそれは往時のクメール帝国の彫刻技術の中核を理解し，未来に継承することの一助とするためにも必要であると考えた。

　本事業においては日本人仏師の指導のもと，往時のクメール帝国の彫刻技術の非常に優れた技術を尊重した上で，日本の仏像修理・制作に関する保存技術，保存哲学を踏まえた「技術の移転」を行っている。加えて本レプリカ模刻作業を通して，出来る限り当時の姿や考えを復元することを目的として作業・研究を進めている。

　このような目的の元，本レプリカ作成作業はただ単に日本人専門家がカンボジア人スタッフに指示をする

2. Details of the project of making the replica of Bayon Great Buddha Project

This project is a cooperative project of JSA/JASA and is financed by various donations under the management of NPO GREEN WIND ASIA (GWA).

An important aspect of this work was the transfer of carving techniques to JASA's Cambodian staff. They had experience in shallow relief carving in restoration work, but they had no experience in carving a three-dimensional round carved statue of the image. In order to correctly restore the original statue, it was essential for them to improve their skills. This was also necessary in order to understand the core of the Khmer Empire's sculpture techniques of the past and to help pass them on to future generations.

In this project, under the guidance of a Japanese master sculptor, while respecting the excellent carving techniques of the Khmer Empire in the past, we are conducting a "technology transfer" based on the preservation techniques and philosophy for repairing and producing Buddhist statues in Japan. In addition, through this replica carving work, we aim to restore as much as possible the appearance and ideas of the original situation of Bayon Great Buddha.

With these objectives, this replica creation work has not been simply the Japanese master sculptor has given instructions

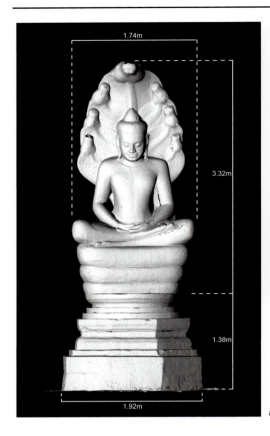

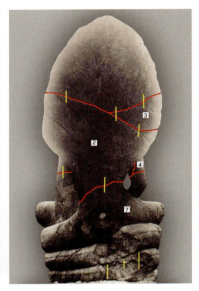

Fig. 5.2.4 Breakage and pinning (Front and back)

Fig. 5.2.3 3D scanning image of the original Buddha and its size

のではなく，3次元の形状を理解するための各種ワークショップ，度重なるカンボジア人スタッフとオリジナルの本尊の実地確認を行い，カンボジアの環境や思想に寄り添った方針を検討しながら，模刻作業を慎重に進めてきた。その結果少しずつカンボジア人スタッフの技術にも向上が見られている。

3．本尊について

本彫像は1.5 mの高さの台座を有する総高4.7 mの白色砂岩の丸彫の彫像である。本彫像はクメール帝国で知られているブッタ彫像の中で最も大きな彫像の一つである。像姿は坐像，七頭蛇神ナーガに座る。右脚上の吉祥座。御手は左手掌に右手掌上に重ねる禅定印とする。頭部には螺髪・肉髻・白毫を表す。耳朶は環状。これらは日本における如来像と同様の特徴を示している。また螺髪や髪際の彫り込みは浅く，白毫は額中央に線刻で現わす。服制は裙を付け，左上腕から大腿にかけて僧祇支あるいは袈裟らしき布端が表現されているが，体部には見当たらない。瞑想した表情には平和的で慈悲深く，親和的な雰囲気が漂い，他には見られない傑出した印象を与える。

この仏陀像は1933年のEFEOによるバイヨン中央塔直下における発掘調査時に発掘された。発見時には損

to Cambodian staff, but has been carried out carefully while considering policies that are close to Cambodia's environment and ideology through various workshops to understand three-dimensional shapes and repeated on-site inspections of the original image with Cambodian staff. As a result, the skills of the Cambodian staff have gradually improved.

3. Description of the Great Buddha statue

This statue is a white sandstone round carved statue with a total height of 4.7 m with a 1.5 m high pedestal. This is one of the largest known seated Buddha images in the ancient Khmer Empire. The figure is seated on the seven-headed serpent Naga. The sitting style is on his right leg known as Kichijo-za. The hands are placed in a meditative sign, with the right palm placed over the left palm. The head has spiral hair, knots in the hair, and a whorl of white hair. The earlobes are ring-shaped. These exhibit similar characteristics to the Tathagata statues in Japan. The spiral hair and the hairline are shallowly carved, and a whorl of white hair is indicated by line engravings in the center of the forehead. A piece of cloth can be seen like Sougishi (Underwear of Kesa) or Kesa (Buddhist stole) is visible from the left upper arm to the thigh, but it is not visible on the body. The meditation face is gentle with a peaceful, merciful and friendly disposition. It gives an outstanding impression that we cannot find anywhere else. This Buddha image was found at the time of excavation survey beneath the Central

傷が激しく，多数の部材に分かれていた。EFEOエキスパートが再構築し，アンコール・トム内のプレアヴィヘア・プランピー・ロヴェンに安置された。

一方，現状のバイヨンには，13，14世紀以後に安置されたと考えられるアユタヤ仏が祀られている。しかし本堂と本アユタヤ仏では懸隔が大きく，本来バイヨンが有していた本尊と本堂が調和した空間性とは乖離した状況となっている。

4. 本尊に関する予備調査

許可が得られるのであれば，我々としては今後本尊に対する過去の保存処置を評価した上で，現在入手できる最新の技術を用いて処置の改良を行っていく予定である。

この仏陀像は中央塔から発見された際には，少なくとも大きく7個程度のピースに分かれており，非破壊調査によって，本彫像におけるピン接合箇所の位置を特定した。また，モルタルは欠損した箇所に対して広い範囲で用いられていた。

修理の許可が得られた場合，我々の計画としてはまずはこれらのモルタル及びピンを取り除き，各部材を取り外す予定である。その後，適切な処理のもと清掃し，オリジナル部材の復原を基本方針とした再構築作業を行う予定である。

5. レプリカの作成プロセス

バイヨン本尊の往時の姿の復原，そして将来的に各所に理解が得られるのであればオリジナルの本尊の代わりにプレアヴィヘア・プランピー・ロヴェン内に安置することも念頭においた本尊レプリカの作成を2011年末より開始した。

本尊レプリカを作成するためにプレア・ヴィヘア地域から砂岩塊を入手した。2011年12月の終わりに，この砂岩はJASAオフィスに移動した後，アンコール・トム内に移動された。この砂岩塊（21 t）はバイヨン北方の修復サイトにあるコンクリートスラブの上に配され，2012年2月より，彫刻作業が開始された。また2013年3月には，砂岩塊は30 tクレーンによって吊り上げられ起こされた。そこからは立たせた状態での彫刻作業を行うことにした。

本レプリカを作成するにあたり，まず本尊の3D計測を行い，そのデータを基に彫刻を進めてきた。その後細部に関しては本尊から各所の型紙を作成し，形を写して

Tower of Bayon by EFEO in 1933. This image was severely damaged and separated into multiple pieces when discovered. EFEO experts reconstituted the image and installed it on the platform of Preah Vihear Pram Pi Lveng in Angkor Thom.

On the other hand, the current Bayon enshrines an Ayutthaya style Buddha, which is thought to have been placed after the 13th or 14th centuries. However, there is a large gap between the main hall and this Ayutthaya style Buddha, so it seems the situation has diverged from the spatial quality that Bayon originally had, where the original image and the main hall were in harmony.

4. Preliminary survey of the main sanctuary

If we can get the agreement, based on the examination of the previous conservation work of the original Great Buddha image, we plan to improve on that works using the latest technology available.

The Buddha image was separated into at least mainly seven large pieces when it was discovered in the excavated pit of the Central Tower. By a non-destructive survey, we confirmed the position of the connecting pins at several places in this image. Mortar was applied to large areas for filling the missing parts.

If we can get the agreement for conservation of the Original Great Buddha, we plan to remove the old mortar and pins, and dismantle the pieces. After clean and treatment by approved methods, these pieces will be reconstructed based on the basic policy of restoring original parts.

5. The process of creating a replica

We started to create the replica from the end of 2011 with the aim of restoring Bayon original Great Buddha's former appearance and also had the possibility to be enshrined in the Preah Vihear Pram Pi Lveng instead of the original one if we can get the agreement from related local and international representatives in the future.

We ordered the sandstone block for making the replica of the Great Buddha Image from Preah Vihear province. At the end of December 2011, this stone was delivered to the JASA office and transported into Angkor Thom. We installed this large stone (21t) on the concrete stage at the restoration area at the north side of the Bayon. We started the curving work of this stone from February 2012. In March 2013, the stone block was up-righted by the 30t crane and we started the curving work in the standing condition.

For creating this replica, at first, we performed 3D measurement of original Buddha and curved based on that data. After that, for details, we created various paper templates from the original Buddha and copied detail shapes.

Fig. 5.2.5 Transportation of sandstone on March 2012

Fig. 5.2.6 Workshop for making the face on March 2012

Fig. 5.2.7 Measurement of 3D data on March 2012

Fig. 5.2.8 Check using pattern paper on September 2015

いる。さらに欠損し，EFEOによって修復された箇所に関しては，本尊の確認のほか，古写真の検証や他の仏像と比較を進めながら，オリジナルの形状を慎重に検討している。加えて，最終的な表面仕上げの方法も類例と比較しながら検討を進めている。またこれらの検討の際にはアプサラ機構によるカンボジア人専門家ワーキンググループと定期的に話し合いの場を設け，カンボジア側の意見も伺いながら，作業を進めている。

　途中，世界規模のCovid-19の蔓延により長らく中断を余儀なくされたが，猛威が落ち着いた2022年11月から作業を再開した。これまでに主に全体の造形・量感の

In addition, regarding the missing part repaired by EFEO, the original shape has been carefully examined by checking old photographs and comparing with other Buddha statues. The final surface finishing method is also being studied in comparison with similar examples. In these studies, we have also been holding regular meetings with a working group of Cambodian experts from APSARA National Authority. We are proceeding with the work while listening to the opinions of the Cambodian representatives.

During the process, the work had to be suspended for a long time due to Covid-19, but resumed in November 2022 after the outbreak had subsided. So far, we have mainly worked

Fig. 5.2.9 Check using pattern paper on August 2019

調整や手足などの細部の彫刻，型紙や写真資料を用いた表情の調整を進めてきたが，2022年の作業としては形状・量感が決定しつつある頭部の螺髪や面部の彫刻を進めたほか，造形を終えた肉身部を用いて，最終的な仕上げに向けた検討を進めた。

6. 今後について

本尊レプリカについては少しずつ完成に近づいている。今後の課題としては以下の点がある。

・全体の形状の最終調整ならび細部線刻作業

今後本尊およびナーガ部の形状の最終調整，本尊部については頭部の螺髪線刻の残部および肉髻部（頭頂部の三角錐状の部分），そして衣装表現に関する線刻作業，ナーガ部に関しては各頭部，体部の鱗，そして背面の円型文様等の線刻作業を行っていく必要がある。これらの作業の中で，本尊部の形状の最終調整おいては特に尊顔及び頭部は微細な表現によって表情が変化するため，今後より慎重な作業を要する。ナーガ部の形状においては各頭部に関してより完成度を高めていく必要がある。

他方，線刻作業においては特に本尊部における螺髪表現や衣装表現，ナーガ部における背面の円型文様に関しては美術史の専門家も含め，詳細を検討した上で，最終的な方針を検討していく必要がある。

・最終表面仕上げ

今後仕上げとして磨き仕上げを行っていく必要がある。
またそれに加え，表面の着色の有無や時期についても検討していく必要がある。P. バティスト[3]によると，コー・ケー遺跡群（10世紀）において着色された石像破

Fig. 5.2.10 Replica on December 2022

on adjusting the overall shape and volume, sculpting details such as hands and feet, and adjusting facial expressions using paper patterns and photographic materials. In 2022, we proceeded with sculpting the spiral hair of the head and face, whose shape and volume are being determined, and we also proceeded with consideration for the final surface finish way at the body part that had been finished modeling.

6. Future plans

The replica of the original image is gradually nearing completion. The following issues need to be addressed in the future.

- Final adjustment of the overall shape and detail line engraving

In the future, we will make final adjustments to the shape of the main image and the Naga element. Regarding the main image, it is necessary to carry out line engraving work on the remaining part of the spiral carvings on the head, the beard part (the triangular pyramid-shaped part at the top of the head), and the costume. Regarding the Naga component, it is necessary to perform line engraving work on each head, scales on the body, and circular patterns on the back. During these steps, more careful work will be required in the final adjustment of the shape of the main image, especially as the facial expressions of the face and head will change depending

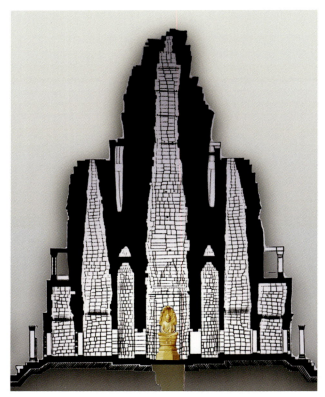

Fig. 5.2.11 Section image of Bayon Great Buddha seated in the main chamber of Bayon

片が発見されており，彫像が作られた当時の着色の可能性が高いと考えられている。バイヨン本尊に関しても類似彫像とあわせて塗料の残存する箇所を美術史の専門家と共に確認・研究することにより，造像時に着色された可能性も視野に入れながら，造像当時の像容について考え，その上で最終表面仕上げ方針を検討していく必要がある。

・その他

最終的な設置方針を検討していく上で，台座等に関してもどのようにすべきか検討していく必要がある。

また現在までに本尊レプリカ作製のための復原研究および模刻作業を進めているが，各所の理解が得られれば，将来的にはバイヨン本尊修復再安置計画を進めていきたいと考えている。

7．さいごに

本事業の重要な点として，本尊レプリカ作製に関する復元研究や実際の作業を通じて，当時の本尊の状況をできる限り，学問的，そして実践的に理解することに努めることにある。

また類似した文化を有する国のチームとして，寺院が

on the minute expression variations. Regarding the shape of the Naga component, it is necessary to improve the degree of perfection for each head.

In the line engraving work, it is necessary to discuss the final policy after detailed examination by art history experts, especially with regard to the expression of the spiral hair and costume on the main image and the circular pattern on the back of the Naga component.

- Final surface finish

In the future, it will be necessary to perform a polishing finish on the surface.

In addition to this, it is also necessary to consider whether and when the surface was colored. According to P. Baptiste[3], colored stone statue fragments were discovered in Koh Ker Monuments (10th century), and it is thought that it is highly likely that the statues were colored at the time they were made. By confirming and researching the remaining parts of the Bayon statue along with similar statues together with art history experts, we will consider the appearance of the statue at the time it was created, taking into account the possibility that it may have been colored at the time of its creation. Based on the result of these studies, it is necessary to consider the final surface finishing policy.

- Others

In considering the final installation policy, it is necessary to consider how the pedestal and other parts of the statue should be done.

In addition, although we are currently proceeding with restoration research of original Bayon Great Buddha and creating its replica, if we can gain the understanding of all parties, we would like to move forward with a plan to restore and re-enshrine the original Great Buddha image of Bayon in the future.

7. Conclusion

One of the important points of this project is to understand as much as possible about the conditions of the original Bayon Great Buddha at that time, both academically and practically, through restoration research and actual work on the replica of this image.

As a team from a country with a similar culture, we understand that a temple is not just a building, but that the original function of a temple is restored when the main image is enshrined in the center and a space in which the temple and the main image are united is expressed. In order to truly restore the spatiality of the Bayon, we think it is necessary to finally re-install the main image in the center of the temple.

Through this work and study process, we would like to think together with the Cambodian people about what is

単なる建物ではなく，中心部に本尊が安置され，寺院と本尊が一体となった空間が表現されることにより，寺院本来の機能を取り戻すことを理解していることから，バイヨンの空間性を本当の意味で修復するためには最終的に本尊を中心部に再安置する必要があると考えている。

　これらの作業や検討過程を通して，カンボジアの方々と共にバイヨン，そしてカンボジアの未来にとって何が重要なのかを一緒に考えていきたい。また何よりこの事業がカンボジアの人々が自国の文化財により一層誇りを持ち，後世に伝えていくことの意義を再確認する機会になれば幸いである。

important for the future of Bayon and Cambodia. Above all, we hope that through this project, the Cambodian people will take more pride in their cultural heritage and reaffirm the significance of passing it on to future generations.

References
1) MARTIN POLKINGHORNE, CHRISTOPHE POTTIER, CHRISTIAN FISCHER, "ONE BUDDHA CAN HIDE ANOTHER", Journal Asiatique 301.2 (2013): 575-624 etc
2) Remarks at the Restoration Executive Committee in 2008
3) PIERRE BAPTISTE, " La polychromie dans l'ancient Cambodge : statuaire et décor architectural (viie – xiiie siècle)", p249-266, Voir et concevoir la couleur en Asie, 2015

5.3　民間組織協力による，バイヨン東参道，外回廊ナーガ欄干およびライオン彫像修復事業

Restoration Project of Naga Balustrade and Lion Statues at the Outer Gallery and the Eastern Causeway of Bayon in Cooperation with a Non-Governmental Organization

下田　麻里子
SHIMODA Mariko

1．事業の概要

　本事業は，これまでのJSA/JASAによるプロジェクトの既存の枠組みとは異なり，長期的なスパンでの今後の修復事業の形を見据え，民間組織との協力体制で実施されたものである。また，これまで日本人専門家らによって育成されたJSA/JASAのカンボジア人スタッフの知識と技術を次世代につなげるための，次なるステージの人材育成事業であることも特徴である。

　外回廊および東参道のナーガ欄干，ライオン彫像は，20世紀初頭にEFEO（フランス極東学院）による修復処置が施されたものの，経年劣化に人為的自然的要因が加わり，再び破損し，多くの石材が遺跡周辺に散乱する状態にあった。これらの欄干や彫像を修復，再整備することは，バイヨンの景観整備に欠かすことのできない最重要項目の一つであり，近年急務となっている急増する観光客への安全性確保にも寄与するものであったが，JASAの枠組みの中では外回廊全域の欄干，彫像の修復，整備には手が回らない状態であった。こうした状況の中，日本ユネスコ協会連盟（NFUAJ）にご賛同いただき，NFUAJが主に広報，資金調達を担当，現地ローカルNGOであるアンコール人材養成支援機構（JST）が修復業務の実施・管理や作業員の雇用管理を担い，JASAが技術技能支援および機材協力を行うという形で，2012年9月より2020年8月までの8年間にわたり，三者合同事業という新たな民間組織協力による事業が実施された。本事業予算は，NFUAJの積極的な広報活動を通じて本事業に賛同してくださった一般企業や個人の寄付により賄われた。企業においては遺跡修復事業への協賛を社会貢献活動の一貫として位置付け企業広報に活用してもらい，また，個人寄付者に向けて返礼品や現地での寄付者銘板台設置を行うなどの新たな取り組みを行ってきた。

1. Overview of the Project

This project differs from the existing framework of JSA/JASA projects in that it was implemented in cooperation with a private organization with a view to the future shape of restoration projects over the long term. It is also characterized by its next stage of human resource development, which aims to transfer the skills of JSA/JASA's Cambodian staff, which have been developed by Japanese experts, to the next Cambodian generation.

The Naga balustrades and Lion statues in the Outer Gallery and the eastern causeway were restored by EFEO in the early 20th century, they were again damaged due to the deterioration caused by time-related deterioration as well as man-made and natural factors, and numerous stone elements were scattered in the surrounding sites. The restoration and maintenance of these balustrades and statues were one of the most important tasks in the maintenance of the Bayon's landscape, and would also contribute to the safety of the rapidly increasing number of tourists, which has become an urgent issue in recent years. However, within the framework of JASA, it was not possible to undertake the restoration and maintenance of the balustrades and statues in the entire Outer Gallery and causeway. In this situation, we were able to get the support of the National Federation of UNESCO Associations in Japan(NFUAJ), NFUAJ is mainly responsible for public relations and fundraising, while the local NGO, Joint Support Team for Angkor Human Resources Development (JST), is responsible for implementing and organizing the restoration work and managing the employment of the workers, and JASA provided technical support and equipment cooperation. In this way, a new project in collaboration with a non-governmental organization, the Tripartite Project, was implemented over an eight-year period from September 2012 to August 2020. The budget for this project was funded by donations from general companies and individuals who sponsored this project through NFUAJ's active publicity activities. The companies

2. 修復前の様相

バイヨン外回廊及び東参道には，ナーガの姿をした欄干がめぐらされており，各入口や角にはバイヨン期の特徴であるナーガ上にガルーダがのるモチーフを有する彫像が設置されている。欄干は，ナーガ彫像と胴体部分からなる架木，それを支える斗束と，さらに基礎となる地覆で構成されている。また，外回廊各塔への入口と，東参道の入口を合わせて18ヶ所の入口の両脇にはライオン彫像が立つ。

推定される当初のナーガ像，ライオン像の数はそれぞれ98体，36体と考えられるが，事前調査ではそれぞれ86体，28体のみ確認された。また欄干部材は，寺院の倒壊による石材の散乱や後世の石材再利用などにより，架木は全体の4分の1程度，斗束は全体の半数以上が失われていることが判明した。EFEOによる既往修復では代用材を活用しつつ，景観を重視した景観修復的な方法が一部とられたようで，特に保存・残存状態の良い彫像を，原位置とは異なる景観的に目立つ位置に設置している事例も散見された。また，安定性と景観上の目的から，明らかに本来同一部材ではない架木部材同士を接合し，接合部の矛盾をコンクリートで補っているケースも見られた。これら既往修復で用いられた材料は半世紀以上を経て劣化が進みその機能を失いつつあった。さらに近年の人為的自然的要因，外回廊基壇の不同沈下といった要因が重なり，大部分がすでに崩落，あるいは崩落の危機に瀕していることが確認された。事前調査では，これら現存する彫像及び部材の破損状況などを確認し，現状を示したハザードマップを作成。これらをもとに，本事業の修復方針と対象を，JASAの専門家の意見を交えて議論，策定した。

3. 修復，整備の方針と成果

本事業はJASAの第4フェーズ以降の外回廊東面景観整備事業と並行して進められた。JASAにより基壇の整備が行われた外回廊東面においては，欄干全体を解体修復対象とした。それ以外の東参道，外回廊北・西・南面では，前述のハザードマップに基づき，すでに崩落，破損，あるいはその危険性の高い箇所を対象とし，部分的解体，修復，再構築を行った。東面以外のエリアでも基壇の不同沈下が崩落，破損の原因であると確認された箇所については，基壇の表層石材を外し，基壇内部の版築

have positioned their sponsorship of the restoration project as a part of their social contribution activities and have used it for corporate publicity, while new efforts have been made for individual donors, such as offering gifts in return and installing donor name plates at the site.

2. Situation before the Restoration Project

The Outer Gallery and the eastern causeway of the Bayon were surrounded by a balustrade in the shape of a Naga-Garuda body, a motif that is unique to the Bayon period. The balustrade consists of three elements: handrail, post and base. Also, Lion statues stand at each of the 18 entrances, including the entrances to the towers in the Outer Gallery and the eastern causeway.

The estimated original number of Naga and lion statues is 98 and 36, respectively, but only 86 and 28 statues were identified in the preliminary survey. As for the balustrade elements, it was revealed that about one-fourth of the handrails, and more than half of the posts were lost due to the scattering of stones caused by the temple's collapse and the reuse of stones by later periods. In the previous restorations by EFEO, it seems that some landscape restoration methods were used while utilizing substitute materials, there were some cases where statues in particularly good preservation and remaining condition were installed in prominent positions in the landscape different from their original locations. In some cases, for stability and landscaping purposes, obviously not originally identical handrail were joined together, and the inconsistencies in the joints were filled in with concrete. The materials used in these previous restorations had deteriorated over the past half century and were losing their functionality. In addition, a combination of human and natural factors, as well as the uneven subsidence of the Outer Gallery platform, have caused most of the materials to collapse or to be in danger of collapsing. In the preliminary survey, the damage to these existing statues and balustrade elements was confirmed, and a hazard map showing the current situation was prepared. Based on these map, the restoration policy and target of this project were discussed and formulated with the opinions of JASA experts.

3. Restoration and maintenance policies and results Outer Gallery

This project was carried out in parallel with the landscape improvement project on the east side of the Outer Gallery from the 4th phase of the JASA project onward. On the east side of the Outer Gallery, where JASA had conducted the maintenance of the platform, the entire balustrade was targeted for dismantling and restoration. In other areas, such

5.3　民間組織協力による，バイヨン東参道，外回廊ナーガ欄干およびライオン彫像修復事業　217

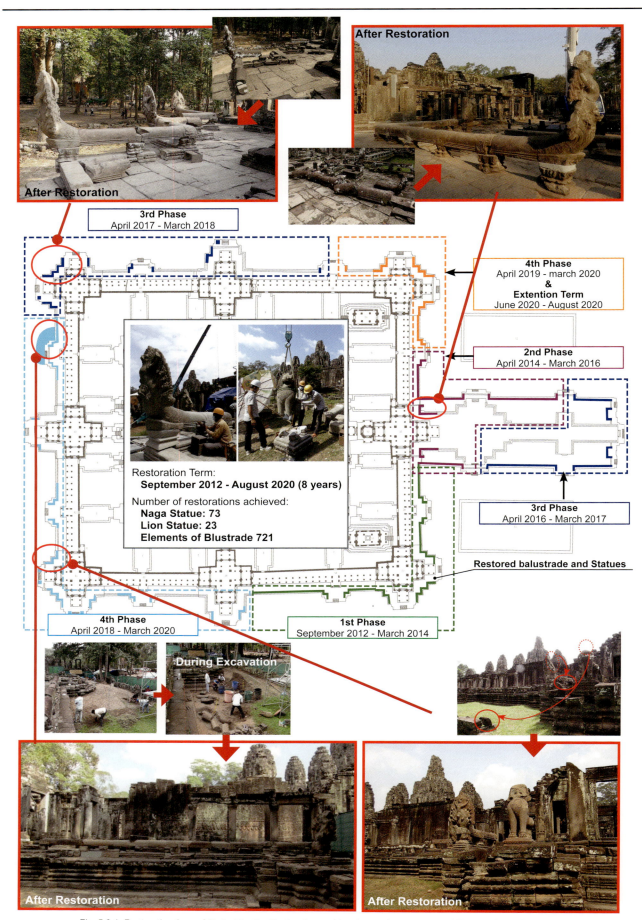

Fig. 5.3.1 Restoration Area of Project for the Restoration and Landscape Improvement of Naga and Lion Statues and Balustrade, and Photos before and after restoration

218　第5章　人材育成及び協力関連事業

土を再構築することで，床面の歪みや隙間を最小限にする処置も行われた。また，部分解体の対象とならない箇所でも，不安定な状況から将来的に崩落の危険性がある箇所については，安定性を高める「予防的保存処置」がとられ，必要に応じて，欄干，彫像と基壇との間に鉛板や砂岩板を挿入し調整を行った。

石材の修復処置や新材補填はJASAの方針，処置方法，材料を踏襲して行われた。そのほか，バイヨン北西基壇脇での土砂の除去作業や，JASAによるバイヨン周辺での散乱石材整理や土砂の除去作業でも多くの欄干石材や彫像部材が発見されたことから，各エリアの修復時においてはこれら散乱部材の同定作業が注意深く行われた。また，既往修復において原位置とは異なる場所に設置されていた欄干，彫像の原位置が特定された際は，原位置への移動や入れ替えを行った。最終的に当事業により部分解体，修理が施された部材は，ナーガ彫像73体，欄干部材721部材，ライオン彫像23体となり，8年間で東参道を含む外回廊全エリアでの欄干，彫像に対する処置を完了した（Fig. 5.3.1）。

4. 新たなステージの人材育成

本事業のもう一つの重要な目的として掲げたのが，JSA/JASAによりこれまで養成されたカンボジア人の人材を次の世代へと繋げるための，カンボジア人同士の技術継承であった。本プロジェクトの現場スタッフとして，新たに1名のカンボジア人専門家を，そして近隣の村に在住している若者を技能員として8名雇用し，JASAカンボジア人専門家，熟練作業員から日々現場での指導やアドバイスを受け成長した。JASAの修復理念や方針だけでなく，石材の修理方法や設置方法，修復材料となる充填剤の準備や配合，図面記録方法，機材操作やメンテナンス方法といった修復工事に必要な知識全般と技術を短期間で身に着けることができたのは，カンボジア人同士による円滑な育成によるところが大きい（Fig. 5.3.2）。現在このプロジェクトによって育成されたスタッフはJASAのスタッフとして再雇用されて活躍しており，本事業の修復成果だけではない，大きな人材育成成果といえるだろう。

as the eastern causeway and the north, west, and south sides of the Outer Gallery, based on the aforementioned hazard map, partial dismantling, repair, and reconstruction were carried out for areas that had already collapsed, been damaged, or were at high risk of such damage. In areas aside from the east side, where uneven settlement of the platform was identified as the cause of collapse and damage, the surface stones of the platform were removed and the inner foundation soil of the platform was reformed to minimize distortion and gaps in the floor surface. Even in areas not targeted for partial dismantling, "preventive conservation methods" were taken to improve stability in areas where there was a risk of collapse in the future due to unstable conditions, and lead or sandstone slabs were inserted between the balustrade, statues, and platform as necessary.

The restoration treatment of the stones and the new material filling were done following JASA's policy, treatment methods, and materials. Since many balustrades and statues elements were found during the removal of mound soil next to the northwest platform in this project and during the sorting of scattered stones and removal of mound soil around the Bayon by JASA, the identification of these scattered elements was carefully carried out during the restoration of each area. When the original locations of balustrades and statues were identified, which were installed in different places during the previous restoration, they were moved to their original locations or replaced. In the end, 73 Naga statues, 721 balustrade elements, and 23 Lion statues were partially dismantled and repaired as a result of this project, completing the treatment of balustrades and statues in all areas of the Outer Gallery, including the eastern causeway, in eight years (Fig. 5.3.1).

4. New Stage of Human Resource Development

Another important purpose of the project was to pass on

Fig. 5.3.2 Exchange the Tecniques between Cambodian Workers of JSA/JASA and this project

skills from Cambodians to Cambodians, in order to pass on the Cambodian human resources trained by JSA/JASA to the next generation. A Cambodian expert and a eight young villagers from a neighboring were newly hired as technical staff for this project, and they received daily on-site training and advice from JASA Cambodian experts and skilled technical staff. In addition to JASA's restoration policies and philosophy, overall knowledge and skills necessary for restoration work, such as repair and installation methods of stones, preparation and mixing of fillers for restoration materials, drawing recording methods, equipment operation and maintenance methods, were acquired in a short period of time. This was largely due to the smooth training provided by Cambodian staff members (Fig. 5.3.2). The staff trained through this project are now working as JASA staff, which is a significant achievement that is not only the result of this project's restoration.

5.4 アンコールの子供たちと石工村
Children of Angkor and the Stone Carpenter Village

中川　武
NAKAGAWA Takeshi

　なんどもふれてきたように，私たちのプロジェクトは日本とカンボジアの政府間協力であり，国際機関を含めたフォーマルな協議と専門家によって進められている。私がこのプロジェクトの担当を依頼された時，外務省の責任者から，このプロジェクトは両国の友好のために関係者の等身大の交流によって進められるべきものです，と言われた。この等身大という言葉とともに印象に残っているいくつかの出来事がある。環濠を介したアンコール・ワット西側正面からアンコール・トムの南大門へと向かう，いわゆるアンコールのメインストリートがある。この通りの西側に，プノム（丘）・バケン（アンコール三聖山の一つ）という，アンコール・ワット中央塔と同じ高さの小高い丘がある。当初お客さんが来るとまずここに案内していた。木々の間からアンコール・ワットが見えること，今でも夕陽の名所であるが，西方に拡がる一面に西バライ（灌漑貯水池），そしてこんもりと茂ったアンコール・トムの森，今では大都会の一つになったシェムレアップの街が，当時は大きな村そのものであって，昼時など幾筋かの炊事の煙が立つのが見えた。プノム・バケンはピラミッド型寺院の古いタイプの一つで，丘の上に基壇をピラミッド型に重ね，中央塔がかろうじて一層目だけを残していた。この脇にアンテナ塔が，これも残骸のように建っていた。ある時上の方から声がしたので登ってみると，西北方向に大砲が据えられ（どうやって運んだのだろう），数人の兵士に上官が訓辞を垂れていた。そういえば，北の方から，機関銃の連射音が近づいてくるように聞こえたり，時に遠くで大砲の響きがしたりしていた。一方では「竈の煙，立つが見ゆ」である。1995年頃までこんな情景はアチコチであったし，エッ！　そんな!!　ということばかりで，その度に戦争と平和の混在併存のようなことを感じていた。しかし確実に時代は安定（？）の方向に進んでいくのも感じていた。

　文化遺産の保存修復プロジェクトは広範な専門領域か

As I have mentioned many times, our project is an intergovernmental cooperation between Japan and Cambodia, and is being carried out through formal consultations and experts, including international organizations. When I was offered to take charge of this project, the head of the Ministry of Foreign Affairs told me that this project should be carried out through life-size exchanges between the concerned parties for the sake of friendship between the two countries. Along with the word "life-size", there are several events that have left a lasting impression on me. There is the main throughfare of Angkor, which runs from the western front of Angkor Wat via the moat encircling it to the Southern Gate of Angkor Thom. On the west side of this throughfare, there is a small hill called Phnom Bakheng that is one of the three sacred mountains of Angkor. It is the same height as the Central Tower of Angkor Wat. At first, when visitors came to Angkor Wat, I guided them to this hill. At sunset you can see, Angkor Wat through the trees, the West Baray (irrigation reservoir) spreading to the west, the thick forest of Angkor Thom, and the city of Siem Reap. Siem Reap was a big village at that time, and some smoke from cooking could be seen at lunch time. Phnom Bakheng is one of the older types of pyramid shaped temples, which put the foundation on the hill, and at the time only the first layer of the central tower remained. An antenna tower stood beside it like a wreck. One day, I heard voices from above, so I climbed up and then I found a cannon mounted in the northwest direction (I wondered how it had been transported), and a superior officer giving a few soldiers an instruction. I remenbered that I sometimes heard the sound of a series of machine gun shots approaching from north side, and sound of cannon in the distance. Until around 1995, such scenes were everywhere and I was surprised at this kind of mixed existence of war and peace occured. However, I also felt that the times were moving in the direction of stability or at least normalcy year by year.

A conservation of cultural heritage and restoration project consists of a wide range of specialized areas. Moreover, most of the counterparts were inexperienced. We had dispatched many experts, artisans, and students from Japan to the site,

らなる。しかもカウンターパートはほとんど未経験の人たちである。日本から多くの専門家や職人指導者，そして学生たちに，常駐者として，あるいはスポット的な短期滞在者として現場に来ていただいた。特に長期滞在者にとっては，現場で共に働き，教え，教わるカンボジア人スタッフとの間に，ごく自然に交流が生まれ，多くのスタッフの村，ノコール・クラウ村との間に，お祝いやお祭りの際の休日訪問等で，それこそ等身大の交流が生まれていったのである。

アンコール遺跡の修復プロジェクトに現場スタッフとして働きに来ている人は近隣の農村から農閑期に来ている人がかなりいる。また，遺跡でお土産や飲みものを立ち売りしている子供たちは，当初は農村の子供たちで，観光客から話を盗み聞きして言葉を覚えたり，そのためだけに親が子供を語学スクールに通わせたりしていることがあった。彼等はセールストークは達者だが，他は何も分からない，とよく言っていた。アンコール・トムの近隣に住みながら，ワットもバイヨンも一度も見たことが無いという子供たちが多くいた。

長期滞在の日本人専門家が帰国する前に，彼等自身の休日労働で，村にコンクリート橋や集会所を作り，寄贈していった。かつて村から現場に働きに来る人は，仕事が無いから現金稼ぎに，という人が多かったが，中には古い遺跡が好きだからという人もいた。プノンペンの大学からJSAの研修に参加する学生は面接の時，確かにアンコール遺跡を見たいからという人が多かったが，中には将来保存の仕事がしたいと希望を述べる学生がいた。今は普通にアンコールの観光に来ているし，保存の仕事をしたいという学生はめったにいない。しかし，嘆くことはない。これは日本でも，世界でも，同じ事なのだ。

幕末，明治期に日本を訪れた探検家や旅行家の多くは，町や農村の隅々まで手が行き届いていて，美しいと書き残している。手工業段階の建築技術において，世界でも稀に見るほどの社会的な普及をもたらした日本建築技術と文化の担い手は，木工大工技術の高度で幅広い社会的発展にあった。支配層の第一級の建物と農村の民家が同じ質の大工技術によって作られ，それを担ったのが農村に居住し，農業と家作の両方に従事した半農半工の大工たちで，彼等の住む村を大工村といい，日本の多くの農村が大工村であったといっても過言ではないのである。カンボジア，ノコール・クラウ村がそのような意味での石工村にもしなっていく可能性があるとしたら，そのために何が必要なのであろうか，と考えてきた。

カンボジアの幼児・小学校教育では，当時も現在も情操教育にまで手が回っていない。今も外国NGOがカンボジア幼児教育のために協力しているのは，コンピュー

as permanent residents or short-term visitors. Especially for the permanent residents, interaction with the Cambodian staff through the work, and exchanging of the knowledge at the site came very naturally, and a "life-sized" relationship was born between many of the staff members and their village, Nokor Krau.

Many of the site staffs come to Angkor to work from neighboring farming villages during the off farming season. The children selling souvenirs and drinks around the site, were initially from farming villages, and they learned the language by eavesdropping on tourists, and sometimes their parents sent their children to language school just for that purpose. They often said that they were good at sales talk but knew nothing else. Many of the children had never seen Angkor Wat or the Bayon, even though they lived near Angkor Thom.

Before the resident Japanese experts returned to Japan, they built concrete bridges and meeting halls in villages and donated them as their own holiday work. In the past, many people from the village came to work at the site to earn cash because they had no work, but some came because they liked the old monuments. When we interviewed the students from universities in Phnom Penh for the JSA training program, many of them said that they came because they wanted to see Angkor Monuments, but some of them expressed their desire to work in conservation in the future. Nowadays, many of people usually come to Angkor for sightseeing, and rarely do they want to work in conservation. Unfortuneately, this is the same situation in Japan and in the world in general.

Many explorers and travelers who visited Japan at the end of the Edo period and during the Meiji period, wrote that every corner of towns and farming villages were well taken care of and beautiful. The bearers of Japanese building technology and culture, which led to a social diffusion of building technology at the handicraft manufacturing stage were the advanced and wide-ranging social development of woodworking and carpentry techniques. The first-class buildings of the ruling class and the houses of rural villages were built with the same quality of carpentry, and these were carried out by half-farmer, half-carpenter who lived in rural villages and were engaged in both agriculture and home production. Many of Japanese villages where they lived, are called "Daiku-Mura (Carpenter Village)". If Nokor Krau village in Cambodia has the potential to become a "mason village" in this sense, I thought about what is needed to make it happen.

Cambodian early childhood and elementary school education did not then, nor does it now, extend to social and emotional education. Even now, international NGOs are cooperating with Cambodian early childhood education mostly in the areas of computers and English conversation education. Such education is also necessary. However, will it help children to think that the Angkor Monuments are beautiful and to cherish them?

Aside from restoration project, we have established the

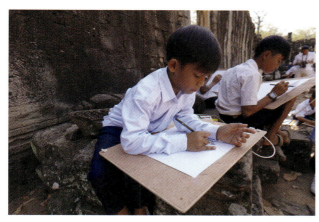

Fig. 5.4.1 Painting Competition Workshop with Nokor Krau School students in Bayon (December, 2023)

Fig. 5.4.2 Stone Carving Workshop with Nokor Krau School students in Bayon Information Center Organized by Tokyo University of the Arts, Department of Sculpture, Sculpture Studio 5 (November, 2023)

ターと英会話教育が大部分である。それも必要である。だが，アンコール遺跡が美しいと思い，それを大切に，と子供たちが思う手助けになるのだろうか。

　私たちは，私たちの遺跡修復のプロジェクトとまったく別に，想いを同じくする友人たちとともに私的なボランティアとしてNPO法人であるアンコールやまなみファンド，GREEN WIND ASIAをつくり，ノコール・クラウ村に開放的なフリースクールをつくり，年に一度，日本からおじさん，おばさんたちがやってきて，子どもたちと唄い，絵を描き，踊り，遊んできた。時にバイヨンで写生大会を開いたり，木造の小さな塔に昇り，雲の向こうを眺めたりした。あのヘンなおじさん，おばさん達は何だったのだろう，と将来子供たちがチラッとでも思い起こすことがあったとしたら，私たちが，アンコール遺跡が好きで，大切にしたい，という想いが共有されるかもしれないのである。

NPO organization "Angkor Yamanami Funds (AYF)" and "GREEN WIND ASIA" as a private volunteer effort with like-minded friends, and opened the free school in the Nokor Krau Village. Once a year, volunteer staff from Japan come to sing, draw, dance, and play with the children. Sometimes we have held a sketching contest at the Bayon, or climbed a small wooden tower to look beyond the clouds. If children in the future remember even a glimpse of what those strange "relatives" from far away were like, they may share our love of the Angkor Monuments and our desire to cherish them.

第6章　バイヨンの保存修復工事計画

Chapter 6 Restoration and Conservation Project of Bayon

6.1 中央塔群基礎地盤構造の恒久的安定化計画
Permanent Countermeasures for Foundation Structure of Central and Sub Towers

岩崎 好規　　　　福田 光治　　　　ロバート・マッカーシー
IWASAKI Yoshinori　　FUKUDA Mitsuharu　　Robert McCarthy

1．基礎の真正性（オーセンティシティ）とその保全

　遺産構造物の土や基礎の保全についての議論は殆どされてこなかった。例えば，1990年代に実施されたピサの斜塔の修復時には基礎の真正性についての議論はなされていないし，アンコール遺跡保存のガイドラインとされるAngkor Charter（2012）では，建設材料としては，煉瓦，砂岩，ラテライト，木材のみであって，土は含まれていない[1]。しかしながら，アンコール全域で確認されているわけではないが，バイヨンの遺跡の構造物は，細粒分を10〜20%程度含む均一な粒度特性の砂で，良く締固められた基礎地盤の上に直接基礎として支持されている。地盤は基礎の主要な構成要素であり，土はアンコールにおける重要な建設材料であると認識すべきである。

　国際規格ISO13822—現存建造物の評価（Bases of Structures- Assessment of existing structures）に2010年に付属文書Ⅰ遺産構造物が追加されたときに，次のように基礎の真正性が示されている。

　Ⅰ.5.3基礎の真正性
　保存の観点からすると，基礎も他の構造部分と同様，その遺産としての価値を考慮に加えた上で評価し，修復されるべきである。これは，基礎に関しても真正性（由緒正しさ）と特徴決定要素（遺産としての特徴を定義する要素）を特定することが必要であることを意味する。

　すでに，バイヨンの基礎の特徴については，3.12で詳述しているが，基礎の真正性の特徴は，

　1，掘り込み基礎

1. The Authenticity of soil and foundation and their conservation

　The authenticity of foundations of heritage structures has been never discussed in the past. As examples, the permanent restoration of the foundation of the leaning Pisa Tower was carried out in 1990' without discussion of the authenticity of the foundation, and Angkor Charter (2012) which was published by APSARA and UNESCO. The Charter describes the construction materials of brick, sandstone, laterite block, and wood for the heritage structures of Angkor while foundation structures of soil are not included[1]. Soil is one of the major construction materials which was used for the foundation mound. Every heritage structure of Angkor is supported by a direct foundation on manmade embankment of compacted uniform sandy soils with fine soils of 10-20%. The soil must be recognized as the important material for the construction and restoration of the heritage structures in Angkor.

　The Authenticity of foundation is introduced in the Annex I of ISO13822, Bases of Structures the Assessment of existing structures) as follows:

I.5.3 Authenticity of foundation
From the point of view of conservation, foundations are not different from the rest of the structure and should be assessed and rehabilitated taking into consideration their heritage value. This involves the requirement to identify their authenticity and character-defining elements.

　For the conservation of the foundation mound of Northern and Southern Libraries, the deformed parts of the edges of the retaining foundation were dismantled and reconstructed by compacted original soil mixed with slaked lime to keep the authenticity of the filled material. The foundation mound of the Central Tower of Bayon shows little damage or significant deformation. At present, proactive measures against the

Table 6.1.1 Estimated vertical load on base rock foundation for Bayon Towers

	unit	Central Tower	One Sub Tower
unit mass	kN/m³	23	23
volume	m³	967	156
total weight	kN	22,240	3,588
contact area	m²	15	7.64
contact load	kN/m²	1,482	470

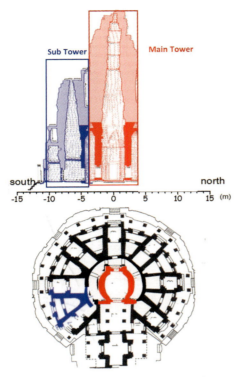

Fig. 6.1.1 Foundation bases of Tower

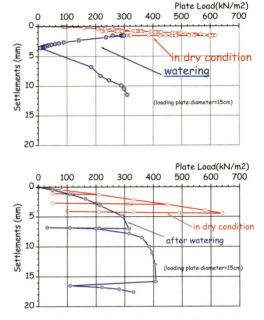

Fig. 6.1.2 Plate loading test for the original filled mound in dry and watering conditions
(Upper A: watering during unloading stage, Bottom B: watering before loading)

2，盛土材の粒度の均一性
3，締固めた盛土の土は乾燥時には強い強度を示すが水浸により弱化崩壊する
4，浅い直接基礎
5，主塔基壇周縁部に設置されたラテライトブロック

である。北・南経蔵の修復では，変状がみられる基礎端部は解体し，日本古来のタタキと称される消石灰をオリジナル土に混合する手法を導入して盛土の真正性を保全しつつ耐水強度を増加させる手法を採用した。バイヨン中央塔基礎の盛土には大きな変状が見られない。特定の箇所というより，温暖化による連続的降雨によって水浸弱化することに対応した対処法が求められよう。

基礎中央部には深さ14mの空洞が掘られており，埋め戻しはされているが，非常に緩い状態で，場合によっては，主塔及び副塔が倒壊に至る状態にあることが判明している。

2．バイヨン主塔の基礎の荷重

バイヨン主塔は，中央塔と副塔から構成されており，直接基礎底面に作用する平均荷重は，砂岩の単位堆積重量を23（kN/m³）と仮定し，Fig. 6.1.1に示したように主塔と副塔とのそれぞれの体積を求め，基礎面積で除することで平均的荷重強度を求めてTable 6.1.1に示した。

anticipated weakening effects of the infiltration of continuous rainwater to the compacted filled mound are under study and consideration.

At the center of the Central Tower of Bayon, there is a vertical hole of 14m in depth with a diameter of about 2.5 m, backfilled after an EFEO excavation, is of a very loose consistency and prone to lead to the eventual failure of the Central and Sub Towers structures.

2. Vertical load on the foundation from Central Tower of Bayon

The Main Tower consists of the Central and Sub Towers. The loads of these towers are estimated based upon the total volume of each tower assuming the unit weight of the sandstone as 23(kN/m³) as shown in Fig. 6.1.1 and in Table 6.1.1. The averaged load of the Central Tower is estimated at about 1,500(kN/m²).

中央塔基礎では 約1,500kN/m² (≒150ton/m²), 副塔では約500 (kN/m²) と中央塔基礎の約1/3程度と得られた。

3. 版築土の支持力

版築土に対する平板載荷試験として, バイヨン南経蔵において実施した結果をFig. 6.1.2に示した。オリジナル版築土の地盤で直径15cmの載荷版を用いてAおよびBの2つの載荷試験を実施した。Aの試験では, 自然状態で載荷し, 最大荷重まで達した後, 除荷過程の途中で載荷版下の版築土に散水した。散水直後から沈下が始まり, 除荷過程でも沈下は継続している。その後, 継続して含水比増加の状態で載荷試験を実施した。Bの試験では, 自然状態のままで, 載荷および除荷試験を実施した後, 載荷版直下の版築土に散水をした後に載荷試験を実施したものである。

乾燥状態では, AおよびBともに, 最大荷重の約650 (kN/m²) でも降伏していない。散水後の含水状態となると, Aでは300 (kN/m²), Bでは400 (kN/m²) 付近の荷重で終局耐力を示していることが分かる。Table 6.1.1に示されている基礎面に作用する荷重強度は約500〜1,500 (kN/m²) である。試験と実際の基礎形状が異なると形状効果のためさらなる検討を要するが, 荷重強度に比べると, 散水後の強度は小さいことが分かる。

この結果は, 熱帯性モンスーン気候のアンコールにおける既往の降雨形態であった数時間の豪雨のスコールでは, 降雨の浸透は限定的で, 降雨終了に伴い乾燥過程となっている現在の状況から, 温暖化が進展する中で, 長期的連続降雨となると, 降雨による基壇内浸透が基礎直下の基礎地盤まで及ぶ事態が想定され, 基壇盛土の浸水弱化となれば, 中央塔の基礎の安定性は損なわれることが予察できる。このような事態となれば, 実質上, バイヨンの全面的崩壊を意味する。

4. 載荷試験のFEMシミュレーションによる浸水時の強度特性の検討

載荷試験によって得られた支持力は直径15cmの円盤形状に対する場合であって, 基礎形状が異なる場合には適用できない。地盤のせん断強度を内部摩擦角および粘着力とし, モデルをFig. 6.1.3に示したFEMシミュレーションによって推定する。一般的な砂やシルト質砂の内部摩擦角は, $\phi = 27 \sim 34°$程度であるとされており, ここでは内部摩擦角として$\phi = 30°$と一定値とし, 粘着力

3. Bearing Capacity of the Foundation Mound

Two plate loading tests for the sandy filled mound of Bayon at the Southern Library are shown in A and B as shown in Fig. 6.1.2 These A and B tests were arranged to see the response of the compacted sandy filled soil to water infiltration into the tested ground.

Test A: The test started for dry condition for loading and unloading steps. Watering to the ground started at the middle of the unloading stage with increasing settlement with time.

Test B: Two independent test series for loading and unloading steps for dry and wet condition independently.

The maximum load for dry condition is obtained at about 600(kN/m²) without reaching at any yielding condition. The bearing capacity is larger than 600(kN/m²).

Watering to the filled ground is confirmed to cause softening the soil as well as weakening with the bearing capacity of about 300-400(kN/m²). The load of the Tower shown in Table 6.1.1 are about 500 and 1500 (kN/m²). The weakened strength of the filled mound is much less than the present load for the foundation stones.

The present rainfall of "squall type", which starts to rain suddenly and is sustained for a few hours and stops, which is anticipated to change to "continuous heavy rain", will cause the rainwater to infiltrate into the filled mound resulting in the weakening of the foundation ground beneath the base stones The coming anticipated warmer climate variance is predicted to result in the failure of the Main Tower. Substantial collateral damage to the Bayon is inevitable.

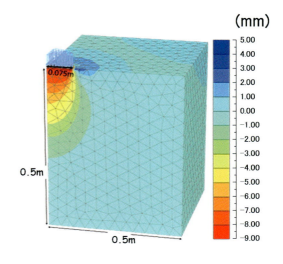

Fig. 6.1.3 FEM Model for Load test

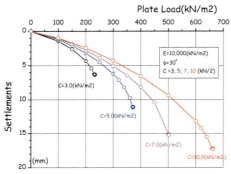

Fig. 6.1.4 Results of FEM Simulation of Load test

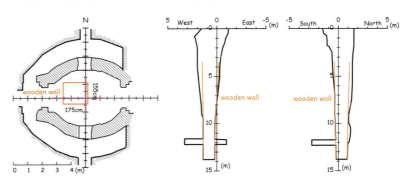

Fig. 6.1.5 Vertical shaft at the center of the basement of Bayon tower

を変化させて耐力の変化を求めた。

Fig. 6.1.4に示したように，終局耐力が300〜400（kN/㎡）程度を示す粘着力は，ほぼ，C＝5（kN/㎡）あたりの値であることがわかる。後述するように，現状の基礎が安定するための地盤強度とすると，f＝30°，粘着力C＝300（kN/㎡）以上が必要であることを考えると，浸水弱化による粘着力はほぼゼロになるといえよう。

5．中央塔竪坑

1933年にEFEO（フランス極東学院）のG．トルーヴェ保存官が，中央塔基礎部分の深掘りトレンチを実施し，仏座像を発見している。バイヨンが仏教寺院時代からヒンドゥー教寺院に変更された際に掘られたか，すでにあった盗掘坑に仏座像が埋め込まれたかであるが，さらにEFEOによる発掘を経て，非常に緩い埋め戻し状態のまま，数百年の長期にわたって立坑の形状が，奇蹟的に保持されていたと思われる。しかしながら，予想される温暖化により，現在は中央塔を保全している基盤盛土の支持力に影響が予見されている。

立坑はEFEOの記録によれば，Fig. 6.1.5に示した平面図と南北東西断面図のようである。土の立坑深度は14mに達しており，掘削時には，深度3〜4mまでは1辺2.5〜3mの土留め板無しで掘られているが，それ以深では土留め用に板材を使用し，南北155cm，東西175cmの方形の形状であると示されている。

この立坑は締固めすることなく埋め戻されていることが，JSAによるボーリング調査で判明している。

6．温暖化に伴う雨水の基盤内浸水による地盤弱化対策

バイヨン主塔群の基礎は，直接基礎形式であり，良く締固められて版築土による基壇によって支持されている。

4. FEM Simulation of the plate load test to estimate the weakened strength of the soil

The bearing strength of the weakened soil for the plate load test of plate diameter of 15 cm was simulated by the Model shown as Fig. 6.1.3. The strength of the soil is assumed to be the combination of friction and cohesion. The friction angle of sand and silty sand ranges from $\varphi=27°$ to $34°$ degrees and is assumed as $\varphi=30°$. As shown the results of the simulation in Fig. 6.1.4, the cohesion is about $C=5(kN/m^2)$ for the yielding strength of 300-400(kN/m2) which was obtained by plate loading with watering. As discussed later, the necessary strength of the foundation soil is obtained as $\varphi=30°$ and $C=300(kN/m^2)$. The cohesion strength of $5(kN/m^2)$ as estimated as above.

5. Vertical shaft at the center of the Main Tower

In 1933 G. Trouvé of the École française d'Extrême-Orient (EFEO) excavated a vertical hole with a diameter of about 2.5 m and found fragments of an enormous image of the Buddha. The vertical shaft was backfilled without any compaction. The vertical hole might have been dug to hide the Buddha statue when the temple was reformed from Buddha to Hindu style in 13th century or a result of looting.

Despite the uncompacted vertical shaft excavated by the iconoclasts or looters and later by EFEO, the Central Tower has maintained its basic shape for almost seven hundred years. However, climatic changes will most certainly affect the compacted and uncompacted soil elements that currently provide Central Tower stability.

The excavated depth was reached to 14 m in depth. When digging before reaching the depth of 3-4 m, no protection for the excavated wall was used. For further excavation, some wooden plate of width 155 cm in NS and 175 cm in EW direction were used to protect the excavated wall.

The backfill by EFEO was found very loose without any compaction by a boring study by JSA.

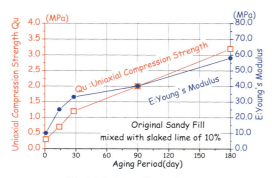

Fig. 6.1.6 Aging effects of mixed with slaked lime

温暖化に伴う連続長期降雨による雨水の基壇盛土層への浸透による版築土の支持力の弱化に対する対応策を検討する。

主塔群の雨水浸透の経路は，①主塔および副塔の頭頂部からの降雨，②副塔基壇周辺表面からの浸透，および③第3テラス敷石目地からの浸透に分けられる。最小の対策として，①には塔頂部の開口部を塞ぎ，②には目地部分にシーリングをすることが考えられる。

中央塔のリング状基礎の中心にある立坑については，①現状のまま，②緩い埋め土を掘削しオリジナル版築土で締固めて埋め戻す，③緩い埋め土を掘削し消石灰混合のオリジナル版築土で締固めて埋め戻すなどが考えられるが，比較検討する。オリジナル版築土という特性は，乾燥した状態では大きな強度を示すが，浸水状態となると崩壊するもので，物理的，化学的にもオリジナルと同一性能を有するものを指す。

消石灰を10％混合したオリジナル版築土の一軸圧縮強度特性をFig. 6.1.6に示した。消石灰は空気中の炭酸ガスとの化学反応によって固化していくが，Fig. 6.1.6に示されているように非常に緩い化学反応で，半年経過しても化学反応は継続している。

7．FEM有限要素法による浸透弱化の影響の解析

中央塔は南北が対称的となっているが，立坑の影響を解析するために，北西部分だけをモデル化してFig. 6.1.7に示した。Table 6.1.2および3に，設定した力学定数を示した。

版築土の雨水浸透による強度は，内部摩擦角と粘着力で表現されるとすると，雨水による劣化は内部摩擦角には影響せず，粘着力が弱化すると与えることが出来よう。

乾いた状態の初期モデルとして，内部摩擦角は一定の30°（$\phi=30°$），粘着力$C=300$（kN/m²）とし，Fig. 6.1.8に示したように現在の状態のモデルAとして中央

6. Countermeasures to the weakening foundation soils by infiltration of rainwater in the anticipate warmer climate weather modifications

Main Tower of Bayon is supported by a direct foundation on the densely compacted sandy soil. The infiltration of rainfall into the foundation mound is anticipated to cause weakening of the foundation soil in the coming warmer climate of continuous long heavy rain. Countermeasures to prevent the weakening of soil is a necessary discuss.

Possible routes of rainwater are 1) water flow from the top of the Main and Sub towers, 2) infiltration from the ground surface around the base stones of Sub Towers, and infiltration from gaps between pavement stones on the top terrace. Covering over the top open space of the towers for condition 1, and closing the gaps with sealing material for condition 2, are considered as the minimum countermeasures.

Another problem is the vertical shaft which is located in the center of the ring-shaped direct foundation of the Central Tower. Several choices for the vertical shaft are compared: 1) to keep the present state, 2) to replace the loose backfill with replicated original soil with compaction, and 3) to replace the loose backfill by replicated original soil mixed with slaked lime with compaction. Replicated original soil is defined as soil that has the exact same physical and chemical characteristics as the undisturbed foundation soil elements.

The uniaxial strength of the slake lime of 10% mixed with the replicated original soil is shown with aging time is shown in Fig. 6.1.6. Solidification of slaked lime is caused by the chemical reaction with carbon dioxide in air with a very slow rate as shown in Fig. 6.1.6.

7. FEM Analysis on the effects of the weakening foundation soil

The Central Tower was designed as the symmetry of the plane along the S-N direction. For the simplicity of the stability analysis of the stability of the foundation, the northwest section was modeled as shown in Fig. 6.1.7 with basic mechanical parameters in Tables 6.1.2 and 6.1.3.

When the strength of the original soil is assumed as an angle of internal friction and cohesion, the effect of the infiltrated rainwater may be assumed only to the decrease of the cohesion with the constant value of the friction angle.

The initial strength of the original filled soil in dry condition is assumed as the angle of the internal friction of $\varphi=30°$ and the cohesion strength $C=300(kN/m^2)$. Two models of A and B are considered. The model A is to simulate the present foundation mound with weakening of the filled mound beneath the foundation to the level of the top of the

塔群の基壇下第2テラスまでの版築土が浸水弱化した場合，また，立坑上部をキャッピングしたモデルBとして，立坑上端部から4m部分を消石灰混合のオリジナル版築土で置換した場合である。

消石灰混合土の力学特性は時間経過で強くなるが，Fig. 6.1.6に示されているように，ここでは，エイジング（続成効果）を1ケ月とし一軸圧縮強度として，Qu＝1,000（kN/㎡），ヤング率E＝35（MN/㎡）と設定した。

8．版築地盤弱化による塑性破壊領域

モデルAの主塔群基礎直下の7.5mが一様に弱化したという場合の内部摩擦角30°を保持し，粘着力を300から50（kN/㎡）まで減少させた場合の塑性破壊領域の進展をFig. 6.1.9に示した。粘着力がC＝300（kN/㎡）かC＝200（kN/㎡）に減少すると，塑性破壊域は基礎直下から基壇周縁に，C＝100（kN/㎡）でさらに副塔直下に塑性化領域が確認できる。C＝（50kN/㎡）まで弱化すると塑性破壊領域は下方にさらに伸びている。

9．立坑頂部固化による塑性破壊領域と変位特性の改良

粘着力がC＝50（kN/㎡）に弱化した場合の塑性領域と変位ベクトルを断面図としてFig. 6.1.10に示した。Fig. 6.1.10左側は無処理の場合のModel Aで，右側は立坑頂部を4mの深さまで消石灰混合土による固化処理した場合である。塑性域は，立坑の周囲および基壇の外周に深さ5m程度の深さまで広がっている。

Fig. 6.1.10右側に示したModel Bの立坑頂部を固化処理した場合は，基壇周縁部では変化は見られないが，立坑周縁では立坑周縁の塑性破壊領域が大きく減少している。

変位ベクトルを見ると，固化による変化が良く理解できる。無処理の場合，立坑周縁部は沈下とともに，中心方向に向けて水平に大きく変位し，最大で約17cmに達している。固化処理により水平変位はほぼ消失し，沈下だけとなり，最大値で7cm程度となっている。

以上のシミュレーション結果から，無処理の場合，粘着力の低下とともに，塑性破壊領域が深さ5m程度まで広がり，鉛直荷重による変位は，沈下と共に，立坑内部方向への水平変位が発生し，立坑の内部空間が縮小される変形モードである。立坑頭部の固化処理で立坑内部への水平変位を基礎の沈下を大きく減少させている。

2nd terrace. The model B is to cap the top of the vertical shaft with compacted original soil mixed with slaked lime of 4 m in thickness.

The strength and Youngs moduli of the original soil mixed with slaked lime increase with time as shown in Fig. 3.6.6 and assumed as Qu=1,000(kN/m2) and Youngs modulus E=35(MN/m2) at the aging time of 1month.

8. Plastic yielding region by the weaken foundation mound

Decreasing the cohesion strength from C=300 to 50(kN/m2) with the constant internal friction of φ=30°, the yielded plastic zone of the Model A is shown in Fig. 6.1.9. When the cohesion decreases from C=300 to 200(kN/m2), the yielded plastic zone appears beneath and surrounding the direct foundation and further expanding under the foundation of Sub Towers. When the weakening reaches to C=50(kN/m2), the plastic yielding region grows further downwards beneath the foundation.

9. Effect of capping the upper part of the vertical shaft

The plastic yielding region and displacement vector on the vertical section along the N-S center line was shown for the Model A with C=50(kN/m2) and Model B of capped by the soil mixed with slaked lime in the left and right sides of Fig. 6.1.10 respectively.

The plastic yielding region for Model A is found around the shaft and at the outer circumference of the foundation mound with 4 m in depth. Those for Model B shows a much decreased region of plastic yielding around the vertical shaft, but the same at the outer circumference.

The Model A shows very large vertical and inwards displacement of around 17cm. The Model B with capping of the top part of the vertical shaft shows little inwards displacement with vertical displacement of 7 cm.

Based upon the simulation, the Model A shows the plastic region of 5m in depth and the large horizontal displacement into the vertical shaft inducing vertical settlement and volume shrinkage of the shaft. The capping of the top of the shaft stops the inwards displacement resulting in small vertical settlement.

10. Countermeasures against rainwater infiltration to foundation ground

For conservation of the Central and Sub Towrs, the following countermeasures of water proofing to prevent the

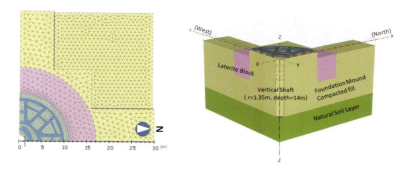

Fig. 6.1.7 FEM model

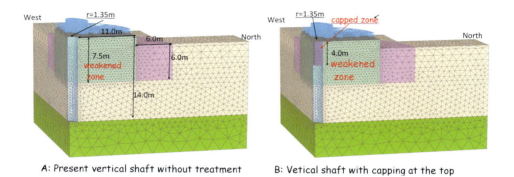

A: Present vertical shaft without treatment   B: Vetical shaft with capping at the top

Fig. 6.1.8 Simulation models of weakened foundation mound at present and with capping at the top

Table 6.1.2 Assumed Mechanical Properties of soil and foundation

	unit weight (kN/m^3)	Young's Moduli E(kN/m^2)	Poisson's Ratio v	Cohesion C(kN/m^2)	Friction angle ϕ (°)
Sandstone	23.0	55,000,000	0.3	Elastic	
Laterite Block	23.0	40,000,000	0.3	Elastic	
Compacted Fill	18.5	100,000	0.3	500	30
Natural Soil Layer	18.0	80,000	0.3	400	10

Table 6.1.3 Assumed parameters for weakened strength

	E	c	ϕ	v
1	60,000	300	30	0.3
2	40,000	200	30	0.3
3	20,000	100	30	0.3
4	10,000	50	30	0.3
5	6,000	30	30	0.3

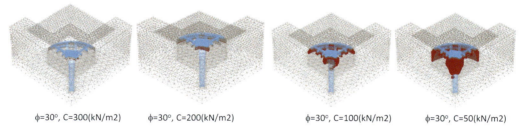

$\phi=30°$, C=300(kN/m2) $\phi=30°$, C=200(kN/m2) $\phi=30°$, C=100(kN/m2) $\phi=30°$, C=50(kN/m2)

Fig. 6.1.9 Development of plastic failure by decreasing cohesion by water penetration for Model A

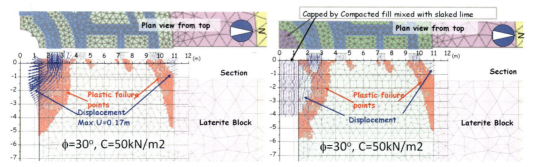

Fig. 6.1.10 Plastic failure zone and induced displacement for weakened foundation mound

6.1 中央塔群基礎地盤構造の恒久的安定化計画

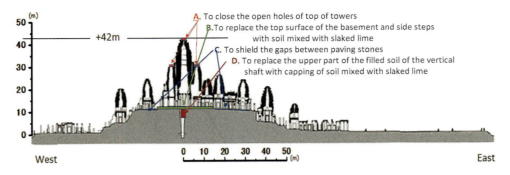

Fig. 6.1.11 Countermeasures against the penetration of rainwater into the foundation of top and Sub Towers

10．基壇盛土への雨水浸透防水対策

バイヨンの主塔副塔群の保存のため，雨水浸透による基壇版築盛土の弱化を防止するために，Fig. 6.1.11に示したように，次の対策を実施する予定である．

A，主塔および副塔の塔頂部空間を閉鎖遮水する．
B，主塔および副塔の基礎面および基壇側面の版築の表層部に消石灰混合土を用いて遮水し，それ以外の経路で流入する雨水に対する排水システムを，必要ならば，構築する．
C，第3テラスの敷石間の目地詰めに消石灰混合土を用いて遮水する．
D，主塔副塔群の基礎の安定化を目指し，立坑の上部の4～5mの埋め土を掘り出し，消石灰混合土で置換する．

11．観測体制

基壇保全に関する観測体制は，① 立坑掘削および埋め戻し時と②対策工事完了後の2段階に分けられる．
① 立坑掘削および埋め戻し時
非常に緩い状態の埋め土であるので，主塔基礎からの荷重は立坑周囲の地盤で支持されており，掘削による側壁の安定性への影響は少ないが，立坑周縁の基礎部に，精密傾斜計，水位式沈下計，さらに温度計などの観測を実施しつつ，掘削，埋戻し工を実施する．
② 対策工事完了時
目的とする降雨に対する遮水性を確認するために，適所に水分計を埋め込み，降雨量と共にモニタリングを実施し，温暖化による連続豪雨時の遮水性を確認する．

weakening of the foundation soil are being prepared as shown in Fig. 6.1.11.

A. To close the open space at the top of the Central and Sub-Towers preventing rainwater

B. To cover the top surface of the foundation mound with replicated original soil mixed with slaked lime to prevent infiltration of rainwater into the ground.

C. To close the gaps between paving stones on the surface of the top terrace.

D. To replace the loose filled soil of 4-5 m from the top of the vertical shaft with compacted replicated original soil mixed with slaked lime to strengthen the foundation.

11. Monitoring system

Monitoring of structures are performed in two stages of 1) the conservation step of excavation and back filling of the vertical shaft and 2) after the completion of conservation.

1, Excavation and backfilling stages

The vertical load of the central load is transferred to the hard soils of the surrounding the vertical shaft. The excavation of the vertical shaft is expected not to affect the stability of the foundation of the Central Tower. Monitoring is to monitor the settlement and the inclination of the foundation stones around the vertical shaft as well as temperature, and water content.

2, After the completion of the conservation work

Moisture sensors as well as rain gages would be installed in several points in the foundation mound to confirm the waterproofing in the coming heavy and continuous rain in the warmer climate.

12. Concluding Remarks

It was first realized that the soil in Angkor becomes stiff and strong in dry condition by geotechnical study of the first boring in dry ground in April 1994 and dynamic cone test in wet ground in September. Fifteen years later, it was

12. 結語に変えて

1994年春にアンコール地域で最初の地盤調査ボーリングを実施した際に，同年秋に地表面の地盤強度が減少し，含水比による地盤の強度変化を認識した。さらに，15年後の2010年，バイヨンの第3テラスからのボーリングによる結果は，驚愕的であった。通常，良く締固めた砂質土の標準貫入試験は，N＝30〜40程度であるのに対して，N＝100〜250というものであったからだ。採取された試料は軟岩のようであったが，浸水状態にすると，みるみる吸水し10分で崩壊した。盛土部の各深度の粒度試験結果から，均一な粒度分布で，カオリン粘土の細粒分が10〜20％のシルト質砂が，粒子間に形成された水幕内部の吸水圧によって形成された特殊な強度である。

バイヨンの近くにあるバプーオンは1943年に北東斜面が崩落したが，1960年当時修復に従事していた仏の地盤担当者のJean Launay氏とは，国際地盤工学会の遺産保存委員会活動を通じて友人となり，彼から提供された粒度分布特性は，バイヨンのそれと同一であった。このことは，バイヨンで発見された版築土の真正性（オーセンティシティ）の特性は，バプーオンにおいても適用され，さらには，アンコール・ワットを含むアンコール遺跡の基壇に適用される可能性が大きいと思われる。

今後予想される温暖化による長期にわたる連続豪雨に対して，バプーオンの悲劇を避けるための対応策として，バイヨンに限らず，アンコールの構造物の保存には，版築土の物質としての粒度特性による真正性，および直接基礎という構造上の真正性を保持しつつ，最小限度の対応策の原則を適用し，保全対策を考察する必要があろう。

astonishing when the standard penetration test at the third terrace showed extraordinarily high values of SPT. N>=100-250 for sandy filled soil. The common values for compacted dense sandy fill ranges SPT, N=30-40. The sampled soil looked like a soft rock but was easily collapsed under water within 10 minutes.

Grain size test on the filled soil at every depth showed a uniform distribution of silty sand with 10-20% of fine soils of kaolinite clay. Extraordinary strength comes from sucking pressure caused by the water membrane which covers the grain surface of each particle of sand.

Heavy rainfall on the Baphuon near Bayon in Angkor Thom had caused slope failure of northeastern side in June 1943. Through the activity of geotechnical engineering for heritage conservation in the Society of Soil Mechanics and Geotechnical Engineering, I encountered Mr. Jean Launay who was a geotechnical engineer and working in EFEO for the conservation of Baphuon Temple. He sent me a test result of grain size distribution of soil mound of Baphuon Temple responding to my request. The characteristics of the grain size distribution of Baphuon Temple was found to be the same as that of Bayon. The character defining elements of the authenticity of filled soil in Bayon is extended to the nearby Baphuon Temple and may be true for most of the foundations of the heritage structures including Angkor Wat.

In the proposed global warming climate, continuous long heavy rain is anticipated. To avoid the disaster of Baphuon Temple, every heritage structure in Angkor should include and be based on the study of the authenticity of the foundation soil, with the minimum countermeasures to the direct foundation system of the heritage structure analyzed, and implemented.

References
1) UNESCO, APSARA (2012), Angkor Charter-Guidelines for Safeguarding the World Heritage Site of Angkor, UNESCO
2) Y.Iwasaki and M.Fukuda(2018),"Preservation of the main tower of Bayon temple, Angkor, Cambodia," Geotechnics and Heritage-Historic Towers, CRC Press, pp191-227

6.2 バイヨン中央塔の上部構造の対策
Countermeasure for the Superstructure of the Central Tower, Bayon

山田 俊亮
YAMADA Shunsuke

バイヨン中央塔の上部構造の対策は，主塔の上部・中段のギャラリーレベル・副塔，といった対象範囲に応じて対策が求められる。それぞれの範囲の課題を分析により明らかにし，対策を講じる必要がある。早稲田大学新谷研究室では，解析や実験を通じてこれらの課題に取り組んできた。過去に実施した分析を中心に以下に記述する。

1. 主塔上部の現在の状況

バイヨン主塔上部の現在の形状の分析結果から，内壁は崩落箇所がなく健全であるものの，主塔の上部は，本来は円形状の平面形状であったが，十字平面の斜めの角部と位置付けている箇所は，GL+23m付近から上はほぼ全て失われていることが伺えた。過去の崩落状況を考察する上で，主塔上部の石積み方法に着目することは重要である。Fig. 6.2.1 にに現在の主塔上部の状況を示す。

EFEO（フランス極東学院）による1930年代のバイヨン主塔上部の工事においては，部分的な積み直し，目地

The Bayon Central Tower is in a precariously unsafe condition and countermeasures are required for the superstructure, depending on the areas, such as the top of the Central Tower, the Middle Gallery level, and the sub-towers. The plan is to clarify the issues in each area by scientific analysis for the countermeasures. The Araya Laboratory of Waseda University had been working on these issues through analysis and experiments. The following description focuses on analyses conducted in the past.

1. Present condition of the upper part of the Central Tower

The analysis of the present condition of the upper part of the Bayon Central Tower shows that although there are no collapsed sections on the inner wall, the upper part of the Central Tower, which was originally circular in plan on the outside, has lost almost all of its diagonal corners of the cross plane from around GL+23m and above. In considering the past collapse, it is important to focus on the masonry method of the upper part of the Central Tower. Fig. 6.2.1 shows the situations of detailed masonry constructions at the top area.

EFEO's work on the top of the Bayon Central Tower in the 1930's consisted of partial restacking, mortar filling in areas with large joint openings, installation of reinforcing members such as clamps to connect the stones, and partial reinforcement with reinforced concrete members. Currently, there are concerns about the deterioration of these past repair works, and has been ascertained that replacement and restoration efforts are necessary.

Fig. 6.2.1 View of masonry construction at the top area of Bayon Central Tower

開きが大きい箇所のモルタル充填，石材間を繋ぐ鎹工等の補強部材の設置，部分的な鉄筋コンクリート部材による補強，が主たる工事である。現在，これら過去の補修工事の劣化等が懸念される状況があり，更新が必要であると判断される状況である。

2. 主塔上部の風圧の評価

バイヨン主塔上部の強風に対する対策を講じるために，風洞試験により風の影響を評価することを試みた。しかし，バイヨンのような巨大かつ複雑な歴史的建造物の風洞試験は一般的に困難であった。その主な理由は，複雑な形状の風洞模型を製作することが技術的に困難であったためである。バイヨンの場合は，デジタルアーカイブとして保存し，修復工事に活用するために，東京大学池内・大石研究室により3Dレーザースキャンデータが取得されていた。そこで，2012年に3Dレーザースキャンデータと3Dプリンタを用いて風洞模型を製作する方法を開発し実施した。世界遺産建造物を対象に3Dレーザースキャンデータから3Dプリンタで風洞模型を作成し，風洞試験を実施したというのは，世界でも初めての技術だったと言われている。開発した手法は巨大かつ複雑な歴史的建造物に対して一般的な手法となり得るものであった。当時，3Dスキャニング技術や3Dプリント技術も非常に先駆的であったが，現在では一般的となった。このように先駆的な技術を取り入れながら保存修復は進められている。

3Dプリンタで出力した風洞模型を用いた風洞試験（Fig. 6.2.2）の試験結果から，日本の規準に基づき，各高さにおける試験による正風圧を，平面形状を一般的な円形または長方形とした場合と比較した。試験による正風圧は，一般的な円または長方形の平面形状の正風圧と

2. Evaluation of wind pressure at the top of the Central Tower

In order to take measures against strong winds at the top of the Bayon Central Tower, wind tunnel tests were conducted to evaluate the effects of wind. However, wind tunnel tests for a huge and complex historical structure such as the Bayon were generally difficult. The main reason for this is that it was technically difficult to fabricate a wind tunnel model with complex geometry. In the case of the Bayon, 3D laser scan data had been obtained by the Ikeuchi and Oishi Laboratory of the University of Tokyo in order to preserve it as a digital archive and utilize it for restoration work. Therefore, in 2012, a method was developed and implemented to produce a wind tunnel model using 3D laser scan data and a 3D printer. It is said that this was the first time in the world that a 3D printer was used to create a wind tunnel model from 3D laser scan data and conduct wind tunnel tests on a World Heritage Monument. The method developed could be a general method for large and complex historical buildings. At the time, 3D scanning and 3D printing technologies were also very pioneering, but are now commonplace. Thus, conservation and restoration are being carried out while incorporating pioneering technologies.

Wind tunnel tests were conducted using the wind tunnel model output by a 3D printer (Fig. 6.2.2). Based on the test results, the positive and negative pressures from the test at each height were compared with those from the case where the plane shape was a general circular or rectangular shape, in accordance with Japanese standards. The positive wind pressure from the test was almost consistent with the positive wind pressure of the general circular or rectangular planar shape. On the other hand, the negative wind pressure from the test is about 30% smaller than that of a typical circular or rectangular planform. This result suggests that the uneven shape of the current towers reduced the wind pressure.

Fig. 6.2.2 View of wind tunnel model and wind tunnel test

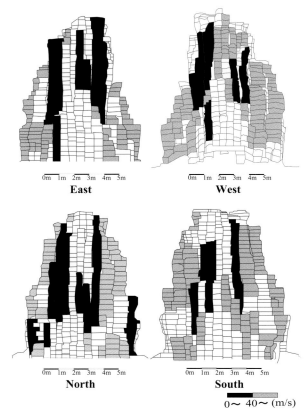

Fig. 6.2.3 Structural safety assessment of the upper part

ほぼ一致する結果であった。一方，試験による負の風圧は，一般的な円形や長方形の平面形状に比べて30％程度小さくなる。これは，現在の塔の凹凸形状が風圧を減少させていると考えられる結果であった。

3. 主塔上部の構造安全性の評価

石積みの水平載荷時の崩壊形式には，転倒形式と滑り形式の2つの形式がある。石積みの水平耐力の検証と風洞試験の結果に基づいて，暫定的にバイヨン主塔頂部の石積みの構造安全性の評価を実施した。石積みの形状図については，3Dレーザースキャンデータと精細画像を用いて分析を進めた。バイヨン主塔頂部の石積みの場合，転倒崩壊モードが支配的な要因となる。構造安定性を評価した結果をFig. 6.2.3に示している。過去のバイヨンでの風速の観測データをもとに，塔頂部の設計用風速を40（m/s）と設定している。

バイヨン主塔上部の石積みは部分的な崩落のリスクを有している。ただし，過去のEFEOによる補修により，主塔上部は目地にモルタル充塡等がなされており，これらにより石材間の安定化がなされていると考えられるものの，これらの劣化も危惧され，主塔上部においても部分的な崩落を防ぐ補修・補強が必要であると判断される。

3. Evaluation of Structural Safety of the Top of the Central Tower

There are two forms of collapse of masonry under horizontal loading: toppling and sliding. Based on the verification of the horizontal load capacity of the masonry and the results of the wind tunnel test, the structural safety of the masonry at the top of the Bayon Central Tower was provisionally evaluated. The geometry of the masonry was illustrated using 3D laser scan data and detailed images. In the case of the masonry at the top of the Bayon Central Tower, the toppling collapse mode is the dominant factor. The results of the structural stability evaluation are shown in Fig. 6.2.3. The design wind speed at the top of the tower was set to 40 (m/s), based on past wind speed observations at the Bayon.

The masonry above the Bayon Central Tower is at risk of partial collapse. However, the upper part of the Central Tower has been repaired by EFEO in the past, and the joints have been filled with mortar, etc., which are considered to have stabilized the masonry between the stones. However, there are concerns about the deterioration of these joints, and it has been determined that repairs and reinforcement are necessary to prevent partial collapse of the upper part of the Central Tower as well.

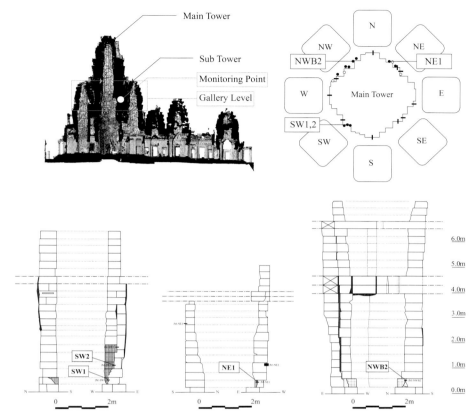

Fig. 6.2.4 Site of Crack Monitoring

4. 主塔中段（ギャラリーレベル）の現在の状況

バイヨン主塔中段の高さにあたるギャラリーレベルにおいて，部分的な崩落の対策が必要と判断される状況にある。JASAでは，1997年より，岩崎・福田らにより亀裂の観察が構造的に重要であると選定された箇所を中心に，観測が実施されてきた。これら亀裂の進展については，概ね安定しているという結果が報告されている。そのような観測結果も踏まえながら，対策について議論は進められている。

過去に観測された亀裂変動データから，バイヨン上部の亀裂幅の変動要因は，日射による石材の膨張・収縮，風による変動，降雨による変動の3つが考えられる。観測している箇所のSW1，SW2，NWB2，NE1（SWは南西，NWは北西，NEは北東を示す）の概要をFig. 6.2.4に示す。Fig. 6.2.5には4ヶ所の変位計の観測結果（1時間毎の変位を観測したデータ）を示す。本項では，例として2016年6月から2018年3月までの観測データを示している。Fig. 6.2.6には4ヶ所の表面温度の観測結果（1時間毎の表面温度を観測したデータ），Fig. 6.2.7にはバイヨンにて観測した気象観測結果（1時間毎の降雨量，平均風速，最大風速）を示す。観測結果からは，SW1，NE1に

4. Current Status of the Middle Level of the Central Tower (Gallery Level)

Since 1997, JASA has conducted observations at the gallery level, which is the middle level of the Bayon Central Tower, focusing on cracks selected by Iwasaki and Fukuda as structurally important. The results of these crack propagation observations have been reported to be generally stable. Based on such observation results, discussions on countermeasures are being conducted.

Based on the crack propagation data observed in the past, there are three possible causes of crack propagation in the upper part of the Bayon: expansion and contraction of the stone due to solar radiation, fluctuation due to wind, and fluctuation due to rainfall. An overview of the observed locations, SW1, SW2, NWB2, and NE1 (SW indicates southwest, NW indicates northwest, and NE indicates northeast) is shown in Fig. 6.2.4; Fig. 6.2.5 shows the results of the displacement meter observations (data from hourly displacements) at the four locations. As an example, the observation data from June 2016 to March 2018 is shown; Fig. 6.2.6 shows the observation results of surface temperature at the four locations (data of hourly observed surface temperature); and Fig. 6.2.7 shows the meteorological observation results (hourly rainfall, average wind speed, and maximum wind speed) observed at the Bayon. The observation

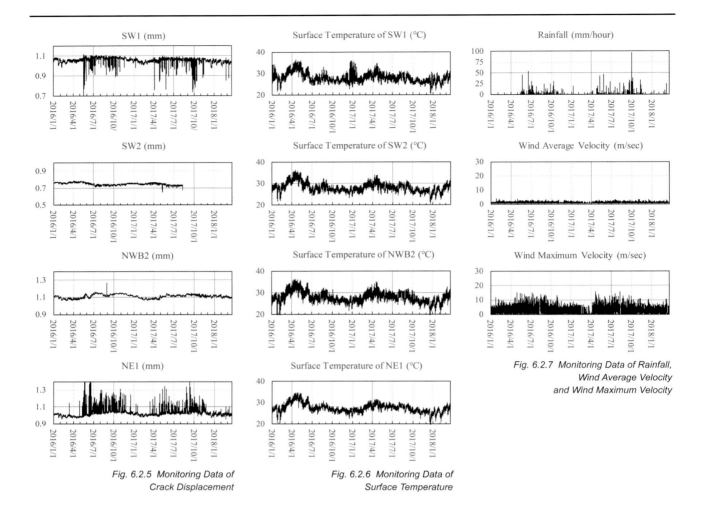

Fig. 6.2.5 Monitoring Data of Crack Displacement

Fig. 6.2.6 Monitoring Data of Surface Temperature

Fig. 6.2.7 Monitoring Data of Rainfall, Wind Average Velocity and Wind Maximum Velocity

おいては，降雨時に瞬間的な変動が生じているが，降雨後には変位値は回復しており，亀裂が大きくなっていると判断される挙動は示していない。SW2，NWB2については，年間を通じて安定した挙動を示している。以上のように，2016～2018年の観測データについても，概ね安定した変動であると判断される観測結果である。地盤・構造班としては，主塔上部の部分的な崩落は，強風及び豪雨によるリスクを危惧している。2016～2018年のバイヨンにおける気象観測データからは，最大降雨量は96（mm/h），最大風速は16（m/s）であった。よって，2016～2018年には，石材の崩落を起こすような強風は発生しなかったと判断される。

5. 主塔中段（ギャラリーレベル）の構造解析

バイヨン主塔中段のギャラリーレベルの対策について，離散体力学手法の一つであるNMM-DDAを用いて検証を行った。バイヨン主塔中段のギャラリーレベルの南西部の石積みを対象としている。まず，亀裂が存在していない状態を想定し，崩壊モード及び亀裂発生原因につい

results show that for SW1 and NE1, instantaneous fluctuations occur during rainfall, but the displacement values recover after rainfall and do not show any behavior that could be judged as crack growth; for SW2 and NWB2, the behavior is stable throughout the year. As described above, the observed data for the 2016-2018 period are also generally considered to be stable and variable. The Geotechnical and Structural Group is concerned about the risk of partial collapse of the upper part of the Central Tower due to strong winds and heavy rainfall; the meteorological observation data for 2016-2018 at the Bayon showed that the maximum rainfall was 96 (mm/h) and the maximum wind speed was 16 (m/s). Therefore, it is concluded that strong winds that could cause stone collapses did not occur in 2016-2018.

5. Structural analysis of the middle level of the Central Tower (Gallery Level)

The measures of the gallery level of the middle section of the Bayon Central Tower were verified using NMM-DDA, one of the discrete mechanics methods. The masonry in the southwestern part of the gallery level was targeted. First, assuming that no cracks existed, the failure mode and the

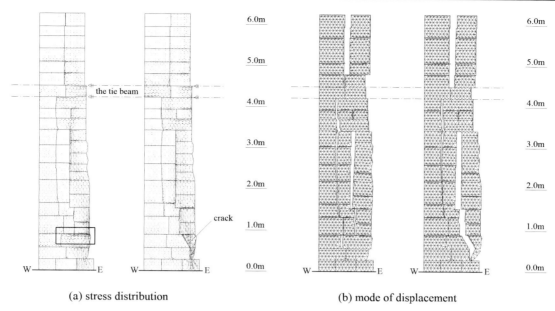

Fig. 6.2.8 Stress distribution (black: tensile stress, gray: compression stress) & mode of displacement

て分析を行い，次に，実際に生じている亀裂を模擬し，亀裂に沿って不連続面を作成したモデルにて検討を行った。加えて，繋ぎ梁の有無での性能の違いを比較するために，繋ぎ梁の位置に水平拘束が有る場合と無い場合の比較を行った。荷重条件として，自重に加えて，水平荷重として分布荷重を設定した。

まず，亀裂が存在していない状態を仮定した水平荷重作用時の応力図を示す（Fig. 6.2.8 (a)）。応力の発生モードが観察される亀裂発生箇所に一致し，亀裂発生箇所近傍で，亀裂の原因となりうる引張り力が発生していることがわかる。次に，実際に生じている亀裂を模擬し，亀裂にそって不連続面を作成した解析結果からは，亀裂があることで顕著に変位が増大し耐力が低下する結果であった。変位モードを比較すれば，亀裂があることにより，底面が回転中心となり転倒による崩壊モードが現れていることが窺える（Fig. 6.2.8 (b)）。

次に，繋ぎ梁の有無での性能の違いを検証した。繋ぎ梁が無い場合は，繋ぎ梁が有る場合に比べて大きく崩壊荷重が低減される結果であった。繋ぎ梁の有無でこうした性能の違いがあることからも，繋ぎ梁の修復も実施される必要があると考えられる。

6. まとめ

前述した内容を総括すると，バイヨン中央塔の上部構造においては，次のような具体的な対策が求められる。頂部においては，目地モルタル充填および鎹工の修繕，部分的な崩落防止工の設置，内壁の構造補強部材の修繕，

cause of crack initiation were analyzed. Then, a model with discontinuities along the cracks was used to simulate the actual cracks. In addition, a comparison was made between the performance with and without horizontal restraints on the location of the connecting beams in order to compare the difference in performance with and without the connecting beams. In addition to the self-weight, a distributed horizontal load was used as the loading condition.

First, assuming the absence of cracks, the stress diagram under horizontal loading is shown (Fig. 6.2.8(a)). It can be seen that the mode of stress generation coincides with the observed crack initiation point, and that a tensile force, which could be the cause of the crack, is generated near the crack initiation point. Next, a model with a discontinuity along the crack was used to simulate an actual crack. The model shows the mode of collapse as the displacement of the cracked stone at the bottom increases. A comparison of the effect of the presence of cracks on the displacement and the bearing capacity of the cracked stone shows a significant increase in displacement and a decrease in bearing capacity. Comparing the displacement modes, it can be seen that the presence of cracks causes the bottom surface to become the center of rotation, resulting in a collapse mode due to collapse by toppling (Fig. 6.2.8(b)).

Next, we examined the difference in performance with and without connecting beams. The collapse load without the connecting beams was significantly lower than that with the connecting beams. It is considered that the difference in performance with and without the connecting beams indicates the necessity to repair the connecting beams as a future restoration.

頂部の防水対策。中段ギャラリーにおいては，繋ぎ梁の修復，亀裂を有する角部の補強・補修，部分的な崩落防止工の設置。副塔においては，部分的な崩落防止工，頂部の防水対策。以上のような具体的な対策を今後行うこととなる。

これらの対策は，これまでJASAが遺跡修復で実践・蓄積してきた保存修復手法の範疇にある。しかしながら，バイヨン中央塔は高い塔状の遺跡であることから，その修復工事の難易度は高く，多様な分野が連携して取り組む必要がある。

6. Summary

The following specific measures are required for the superstructure of the Bayon Central Tower. At the top, maintenance of the joint mortar filling and reinforcement, installation of partial collapse prevention work, maintenance of the structural reinforcement members of the inner walls, and waterproofing measures at the top. In the Middle Gallery, repair of connecting beams, reinforcement and repair of cracked corners, and installation of partial collapse prevention work. In the sub-tower, partial collapse prevention work and waterproofing measures at the top. The above specific measures will be implemented in the future.

These measures are within the scope of conservation and restoration methods that JASA has practiced and developed in the restoration of Bayon. However, the Bayon Central Tower is a tall tower-shaped ruin, and its restoration work requires a high degree of technical difficulty. This project will be undertaken under the collaboration of various fields.

References

1) JICA Report. Nippon Koei Co., Ltd. and Nihon Suido Consultants Co., Ltd., "The Study on Water Supply System for Siem Reap Region in Cambodia," JICA Report to Min. of Industry, Mines, and Energy, The Royal Government of Cambodia, June 2000

2) JICA Report. 国際建設技術協会，国際航業㈱, "The Topographic Mapping of the Angkor, Archaeological Area in the Siem Reap Region of the Kingdom of Cambodia", May 1998, 社調 1 JR 98-087

3) JSA Report, アンコール遺跡調査報告書 (1995-2001)

4) 岩崎好規，「カンボディア王国アンコールにおける地下水揚水問題」，サイバー大学紀要第 1 号，サイバー大学，(2009), pp. 129-148

5) 岩崎好規，アンコール地域の地下水問題，サイバー大学紀要第 2 号，サイバー大学，(2010), pp. 63-81

6) JICA Report カンボジア国シェムリアップ上水道拡張整備事業準備調査最終報告書2 2011, JR11-139

7) S.Yamada, M..Araya, A.Yoshida, T.Oishi, "Structural stability evaluation study applying a wind tunnel test and monitoring of Bayon main tower, Angkor Thom, Cambodia", WIT Transactions on the Built Environment , vol.171, pp.287-296, 2017

8) Y.Honda, S.Yamada, A.Yoshida, T.Oishi, M.Araya, Y.Tamura, "New Manufacturing Method of Wind Pressure Model for Complicated-Shape Architectural Heritage Applying 3D Scanning Data and 3D Printer", Journal of Wind Engineering, 2016, Volume 41, Issue 1, pp.24-27, 2016

9) M.Hayashi, S.Yamada, M.Araya, T.Koyama, M.Fukuda, Y.Iwasaki, "Study for reinforcement planning of masonry structure with cracks at Bayon main tower, Angkor", Advances in Discontinuous Numerical Methods and Applications in Geomechanics and Geoengineering, pp.247-252, 2012

10) Y.Iwasaki, M.Fukuda, T.Fujiwara, "Geotechnical Study during Dismantling of Southern Library, Bayon Temple and Structural Monitoring", Annual Technical Report on the Survey of Angkor Monument 2007, JASA, Tokyo pp.101-116, 2007

11) Y.Iwasaki, I.Yamamoto, M.Araya, "Stabilization of the Central Tower and Countermeasures for Long Term", The Bayon Master Plan, JASA, Tokyo pp.206-222, 2005

6.3 バイヨン浅浮彫の保存修復計画
Restoration and Conservation Project of the Bas-reliefs of the Inner Gallery, Bayon

松井 敏也　　河﨑 衣美
MATSUI Toshiya　　KAWASAKI Emi

1. 遺跡の保存と整備の基本方針と志向

　文化遺産や遺跡は，保存し活用するために保存整備が行われる。地域の住民に遺跡の内容を正しく認識してもらうために建物を復元し，遺構を露出したままで公開展示するなどの工夫が行われる。また，遺跡の寿命をより長らえるために遺構面を土やシートで被覆し，保護するなどの保存整備が行われる事例も多い。保存整備に伴って，遺跡の近くに案内所や簡単な展示施設などの機能を併設した管理事務所が設置されることも多く，より安心安全な遺跡の保存が進められることが多い。これらの保存と整備の結果によって，遺跡の劣化を未然に防ぎ，たとえ劣化が起きたとしても早期に発見することで，遺跡の価値への影響をできるだけ最小限に抑えることが可能となる。すなわち，遺跡を継続的に保存管理することによって，遺跡そのものが恒久的に保存されることにつながる。また，継続的な管理は補修を必要とし，結果として修理技術を向上させる。その過程で，遺跡の当時の築造技術や土木技術，遺跡をとりまく社会構造にふれる機会も生じるであろう。こうした古代技法を正しく理解することによって，修理技術がさらに向上するという好結果を招くことも期待できる。

　遺跡には現代の科学技術では解明しきれない情報が包摂されており，それらの情報を極力破壊しないように遺跡を恒久的に保護することも保存整備の目的のひとつとなる。また現代の遺跡の価値を定めているのは今確立されている学術分野からのものに過ぎず，いままだ未成熟もしくは未確立な学問が将来に確立されるかもしれない。そういった時代になった時にも，十分に応えられるような保護の方針が必要である。

　文化遺産はこれまで保存を第一義としてきたが，現代社会における遺産のあり方が変わり，いまは公開活用を

1. Basic Policies and Direction for the Preservation and Maintenance of Sites

　Cultural heritage and cultural sites are conserved and maintained so they can be used and preserved. In order to provide local residents and foreign tourists with a proper understanding of what these sites consist of, they are restored and publicly displayed, oftentimes exposing the remains to an open environment. To extend their lifespan, there are many cases where conservation efforts are carried out, for example, by covering the remains with protective soil or sheets. Along with conservation and maintenance, there are many cases where a management office runs information centers and places simple signage close to the site, which promotes a safer preservation. The results of these preservation and maintenance efforts allow us to prevent damage to the sites, or to detect it early, which helps minimize the impact on its value. In other words, the continuous preservation and maintenance of a site will lead to its own permanent conservation. Continuous maintenance requires repairing while improving previously used repair techniques. In the process, there are opportunities to experience what the construction and civil engineering techniques of the site were at the time, as well as the social structures that surrounded it. A proper understanding of these ancient techniques can be expected to lead to even better repair techniques.

　A site contains information that cannot be explained using modern science and technology, and one of the purposes of conservation is to permanently protect the ruins so that this information is, to the extent possible, not destroyed. The value of a modern site is determined only by the currently established academic fields, and there may be new, immature or unestablished academic fields rising in the future. We need conservation policies that can adequately respond to such a potential future.

　Previously, the primary purpose of preservation of cultural heritage has been strict conservation, but the way heritage

前提とした保存の方法を考えなくてはならない。公開活用とは，単に訪問者に見せる利用を考えていればいいのではなく，地域との連携をはかる文化遺産の保存と活用，地域の活性化や経済振興のための観光資源として活用，さらには教育，歴史，文化の拠点として情報を発信する役割をも期待されている。特に地域での役割は今後ますます重要度を増し，地域の力を援用しながらの保存と活用が望まれている。そのためには地域の拠点となるような役割を遺跡が担うことになるかもしれない。

2. バイヨン浅浮彫の保存の基本方針

遺跡の保存整備に際しては，遺跡の歴史的，芸術的意義や現代社会の中における本質的な遺跡の価値を明確にしなければならない。保存整備の基本的な理念として，まず遺跡の調査研究方法の充実と精度の向上をめざす必要がある。次に整備技術の向上が挙げられ，特に重要なことは現地の伝統的な技術を尊重し，これを保存し，後世に継承していくことも重要である。同時に，大規模に進む地球温暖化などの地球規模での環境変動に対応しなければならず，伝統的な技術だけでは近い将来劣化のスピードに追いつけなくなることも予想できよう。保存整備のために応用される現代科学材料や技術の開発と，伝統的技術の融合の中から生み出す独自の技術開発もまた重要と考える。

他方，遺跡の整備にあたっては遺跡周辺の景観の管理計画は重要性を増す。遺跡と現代の都市とはその距離が急速に縮まっており，都市の影響が遺跡に及んできている。たとえば観光客の増加に対応してホテルが増えると，シャワーやプール，食事などに用いる水量が増える。また従事する人も増えることからますます生活水を使うことになる。過剰な水の汲み上げは地下水位の低下を引き起こしかねず，それが遺跡の不同沈下を起こしかねない。遺跡と都市との共栄をバランスよく図るためには，最小限の植生の再生もありうるという考え方も据えておく必要がある。また，保存整備にあたっては，保存と活用に関する理念も明確にしておく必要がある。文化遺産としての学術的評価やその位置づけを明確にしておかなければならない。

こうした保存整備事業の後には，これを維持する体制が不可欠であるが，これからの遺跡の社会における役割を考えた場合，地域の住民や技能集団（石材や土木など），NGO，NPOなどの参画も欠かせない。特殊な専門家しかできない保存はもちろん存在するが，日常管理や劣化の早期発見，簡単なメンテナンス技術は地域である程度

is treated in modern society has changed, and now we must consider conservation methods that assume the sites will be used by the public. Public utilization does not simply mean using a site by showing it to visitors; it also means preserving and utilizing cultural heritage in collaboration with the local community, using it as a tourism resource for regional revitalization and economic development, and more. Sites are also expected to play a role in disseminating information as a base for education, history, and culture. In particular, its role in the local community will become increasingly important in the future, and conservation and utilization should be carried out while leveraging the power of the local community. To this end, sites may play a role as regional hubs for education and tourism.

2. Basic Policies for the Preservation of the Bayon Bas-reliefs

When preserving and developing a site, we need to understand its historic and artistic significance as well as its essential value in modern society. As a basic philosophy for preservation and maintenance, we first need to aim at enriching and improving the accuracy of current site research methods. Following this, we need to improve maintenance techniques, respecting the local traditional techniques in particular, their preservation, and their passing on to future generations. At the same time, we must respond to global environmental changes such as global warming, which is progressing at a large scale, considering that traditional technologies alone are not expected to keep up with the speed of deterioration in the near future. We believe that it is also important to develop unique technologies that are created by combining modern scientific materials and techniques for conservation and maintenance with traditional techniques and materials.

Regarding site maintenance, management plans for the landscape that surrounds a site have become increasingly important. The distance between sites and modern cities is rapidly shrinking, and the influence of the cities is extending to the sites. For example, if the number of hotels increases in response to an increase in the number of tourists, the amount of water used for showers, swimming pools, meals, etc. will increase. Additionally, the number of people engaged would increase, leading to a multiplied demand for domestic water. Excessive water pumping can cause the groundwater level to drop, which can lead to the uneven settlement of archaeological sites. In order to achieve a well-balanced co-prosperity between sites and cities, it is necessary to keep in mind that minimal vegetation regeneration is possible. In addition, when carrying out conservation and maintenance, the preservation and utilization philosophy need to be clear. The site needs to be academically evaluated and its position as

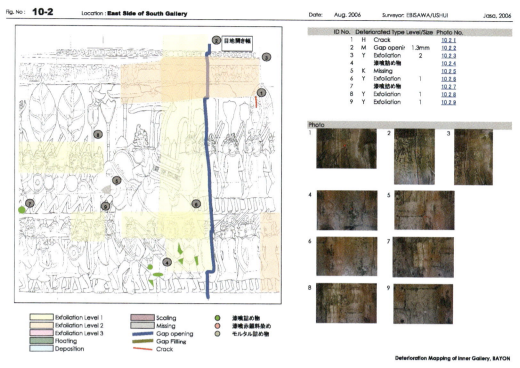

Fig. 6.3.1 Damage diagnosis of a Bas-relief (created by Takao Ebisawa in 2006)

はカバーできることを念頭に置かなければならないであろう。そのためには遺跡を研究する学術研究の拠点と地域との交流活動ができる場所の構築が展開できければ理想的である。

以上のような検討を経て，実際の施工に至ることができる。

3．浅浮彫の保存修復計画

(1) 状態の観察

基本的には上にあげた保存整備方針に沿った保存修復計画を立てるのが順当である。浅浮彫の損傷状況の確認と把握（カルテの作成）は当然のことである。Fig. 6.3.1は損傷状況をいくつかのパターンに分けた観測の結果である。このような記録は保存状態を把握するためには非常にわかりやすく，有効である。これを定期的に行うことは，バイヨンの浅浮彫の中でどの場所にどのような劣化が進行しているのかを知ることができる。

浅浮彫の表面が綺麗な状態（汚れていない）の場合は比較的劣化の識別はしやすいが，汚れや着生物などが繁茂していると劣化の正確な進行の把握は難しくなる。レーザー光を用いた計測を定期的に行うことで汚れの下で進む劣化の把握が可能になっている。

こうした損傷状況を明確にし，修復事項をパターン化し，修復対策を技術的見地から個別に検討することが求

a cultural heritage site must be understood.

After carrying out such conservation and maintenance projects, a system to preserve this structure is essential, and when considering the future role of a site in society, it is important to have the participation of local residents, skill groups (e.g. stone and civil engineers), NGOs, NPOs, etc. Of course, there are aspects that can only be conserved by specialized experts, but we must keep in mind that daily management, early detection of deterioration, and simple maintenance techniques can be covered locally to some extent. To this end, it would be ideal if we could develop a base for academic research to study the sites and a provide a place for dialogue with the local community.

Following the considerations explained above, the actual conservation and restoration can begin.

3. Bas-relief Conservation and Restoration Plan

(1) Condition Assessment

Fundamentally, a conservation and restoration plan should be established in line with the conservation policies listed above.

Naturally, the damage to the Bas-reliefs must be revised and understood (through a record of conditions) first. Fig. 6.3.1 shows the results of an assessment that divides the damage conditions into several patterns. Such records are very easy to understand and effective in grasping overall conditions. By regularly updating them, we can know where and what kind

められる。それぞれに見合った修復のための材料実験を行い，さらにこれを実証するための技術的課題もある。もちろん保存修復は長期に渡ることから，自然環境，微気象のモニタリングを行い，変動の先を読んでいかなければならない。様々なシミュレーションの活用も視野に入れる。

浅浮彫の回廊全域について水分の漏れの痕跡や被覆したモルタルに生じた亀裂等の有無，水漏れの有無を調査する必要がある。回廊内部への水分の浸入や，被覆モルタルの亀裂等の発生にともなう水漏れがみられる場合には，早急に保全の対策を講じなければならない。しかし，その保護対策は大規模なものになり，遠大な計画のもとに遂行することになる。

状態観察後に劣化や立地環境，機能用途ごとに修復方法を練る。次にその一例を示す。

・剝離膜（表面の堅い板状のもの）を，崩落しないように固定する処置，あるいは，すでに剝離している部分の補修。

・剝離面が崩落してしまい，あとの状態が粉状化を呈している部分の強化。

・浅浮彫が部分的に欠損，あるいはブロック自体にひび割れがある部分の処置。

・ブロックが部分的に欠損，欠落しているために周囲のブロックまでが不安定になっている箇所の補強措置。適切な材料による一時的な補強・強化策，さらには擬岩等の応用もありうる。

・風化し，粉状化した部分の崩落防止策を講じる。

⑵クリーニング方法

ほとんどの浅浮彫は汚れており，これをそのまま強化処置などを行うと，汚れたまま保存されることになり強化の効果が十分に得られない。汚れは主に微生物によるもので，菌や藻類，地衣類などがほとんどである。また表面が綺麗な浅浮彫でも何かしらの微生物が存在する可能性がある。保存修復にはこれらの汚れを取り除き，浅浮彫を表現する砂岩のみを出すことが必要である。たいていのクリーニングでは水を用いるが，水とブラシだけのクリーニングではブラシで汚れを取っているようでも，そこにあった汚れを水で薄めて広げているだけで，しばらくするとより広範囲に汚れが広がることになる。

方法1　陽イオン界面活性剤

水に陽イオン界面活性剤を少量まぜ，殺菌をしながら水とブラシで洗うものである。これによりクリーニングされた部位から広がる汚れは殺菌されており，広範囲に広がっていくことを抑制できる。ただしブラッシングを伴うことから，汚れの下の浅浮彫が脆弱である場合，力

of deterioration is progressing in the Bayon Bas-reliefs.

If the surface of the Bas-relief is clean (not dirty), it is relatively easy to identify deterioration, but dirty or overgrown surfaces hinder the accurate determination of the deterioration progress. By regularly conducting measurements using a laser light, it is possible to understand the deterioration that develops under the dirt.

From a technical standpoint, we need to clarify the damage conditions, identifying repair patterns and considering repair measures on an individual basis. There are also technical challenges when carrying out material experiments to identify the restoration that is appropriate for each piece in a demonstrable manner. Of course, conservation and restoration work take a long time, so it is necessary to monitor the natural environment and the local microclimate in order to anticipate future changes. Using a variety of various simulations can also be considered.

The entire area of the engraved gallery needs to be investigated to find any traces or indications of water leaks or cracks in the covered mortar. If the water enters or leaks into the gallery interior through, for example, such cracks, immediate conservation measures must be taken. However, such protective measures may widen and be carried out within a far-reaching plan.

After the conditions assessment, restoration methods are determined based on deterioration, local environment, and functional use. An example is shown below.

· Fix the peeling film (hard plate-like surface) to prevent it from collapsing, or repairing the part that has already peeled off.

· Reinforce the brittle areas where the peeled surface collapsed.

· Treat the areas where the Bas-relief block is partially missing or where the block itself has cracks

· Reinforce the areas where the surrounding blocks are unstable due to partially missing or completely missing blocks. Temporary reinforcement and consolidation using appropriate materials, measures may include using artificial stone.

· Take measures to prevent weathering and brittle parts from collapsing.

⑵ Cleaning Methods

Most of the Bas-reliefs are dirty, and if consolidation is applied as they are, they will remain dirty, missing the full strengthening effect. Dirt is mainly caused by microorganisms, such as bacteria, algae, and lichens. Even if a surface looks clean, there is a possibility that some kind of microorganism is present. For conservation and restoration, we need to remove these contaminants and expose only the sandstone that makes up the Bas-relief. Most cleaning methods involve water, but when a surface is only cleaned with water and a brush, even if the brush seems to be removing dirt, it is diluting the dirt that

Fig. 6.3.2 Left: before treatment, right: two and a half years after treatment (the left side remained untreated)

加減によっては浅浮彫にダメージを与える危険性がある。屋根や床などのクリーニングには効果的であろう。陽イオン界面活性剤には，例えば塩化ベンザルコニウム溶液などがある。これは人の手指の殺菌や家財道具の消毒にも使われるもので安全に使用できる。

方法2　光合成阻害剤

ブラッシングにより汚れの下の浅浮彫を損傷する恐れがある場合や石に強く固着する一部の地衣類などは光合成阻害剤が効果的である。これは藻類の光合成を阻害する物質を塗布することで，その生育を抑制し，枯死させる。地衣類は藻類と菌類の共生体であり，藻類が枯死すると共生体である菌類が生育できず，石の表面から剥がれ落ちる。この方法は1㎡あたり200gの塗布が必要で方法1と比較して経済的な負担がかかる。またその効果は長い時間がかかり，バイヨンの環境では1年半から2年かかるが，この方法はスプレーやハケで表面に塗るだけであり，ブラッシングを用いないとてもマイルドな処置になる。微生物が枯死しているだけであり，その表面を綺麗なまま維持する効果はなく，放っておくと新しい微生物が着生する。そのため，効果が十分に現れた時点で次の強化処置などをする必要がある。

Fig. 6.3.2に石に固着した地衣類を本法で処理した例を示す。

方法3　WASh法（Water Apply Solar-heat cleaning method）

これは水と太陽熱を利用したクリーニングである。微生物に水分を与えた状態（生物的に活動している状態）で熱をかけることで微生物にダメージを与える処置である。この熱は太陽光が利用でき，石に着生した微生物にまず水を与え，蒸発しないようにラッピングし，そのまま太陽下で2〜4日間放置し，その後ラップを取り除き，放置する。これも方法2と同様，数年かけて枯死する。太陽光による熱と与えられた水でサウナ状態になった石の表面の微生物が壊死する。方法1と2と大きく異なることは薬剤を使わず，環境に優しくコストもかからない。

was there with water and spreading it, so after a while, the dirt actually spreads over a wider area.

Method 1: Cationic Surfactant

This is a method where a small amount of cationic surfactant is mixed with water, so that water-and-brush cleaning is carried out while sterilizing. As a result, dirt that spreads from the cleaned area is sterilized and can be prevented from spreading over a wider area. However, since brushing is involved, if the Bas-relief under the dirt is fragile, the Bas-relief might be damaged, depending on the amount of force applied. This cleaning method is effective for roofs, floors, etc.

Cationic surfactants include, for example, benzalkonium chloride solution. It is also used to sterilize people's hands and household goods, and is safe to use.

Method 2: Photosynthesis Inhibitor

Photosynthesis inhibitors are effective in cases where brushing may damage the Bas-relief beneath the dirt, and in cases where lichens strongly adhere to the stone. This method involves applying a substance that inhibits the photosynthesis of algae, suppressing their growth and causing them to die. Lichens are symbionts of algae and fungi, and when the algae die, the symbiotic fungi cannot grow and fall off from the stone surface.

This method requires 200g of coating per square meter, which is more expensive than Method 1, also takes a long time to take effect. In the environment of the Bayon it may take one and a half to two years. This method is a very mild treatment that only requires spraying or brushing the surface lightly, and does not require abrasive mechanical cleaning. The microorganisms simply die, and there is no cleaning effect, so if the surface is left alone, new microorganisms will reappear. Therefore, it is necessary to take a subsequent consolidation treatment once the effect is fully achieved.

Fig. 6.3.2 shows an example of this method on a stone surface with lichens.

Method 3: WASh Method (Water Apply Solar-heat cleaning method)

This is a cleaning method that uses water and solar heat. This treatment damages microorganisms by applying heat

Fig. 6.3.3 Left: before treatment, Right: 2 years after treatment

ただ太陽光の強さが処理の効果を左右する。

Fig. 6.3.3に石に固着した地衣類を本法で処理した例を示す。

方法4　一時的覆屋の設置

微生物は当然のことながら，水と光（日光）が生育には欠かせない。回廊の上に覆屋を架けると数年で微生物層が衰退することを確認した。この方法は上記の3つの方法と比べて石に非接触で行える利点がある。ただ覆屋の敷設には足場の確保が伴うほか，景観に配慮が必要であろう。

3.　強化と透湿調整

(1) 強化について

強化とは経年劣化で強さが失われた石を強くすることである。強くするとは石の性質を持ったまま強くすることであり，石の吸放湿特性であったり，質感，色なども考慮して選ぶ必要がある。バイヨンにおける15年間の暴露試験により，石の劣化の傾向を把握し，強化剤にテトラエトキシシランモノマーおよびオリゴマーの混合物を用いることにした。混合割合はモノマー：オリゴマーが6：4を基準とし，石の劣化状態に合わせて割合を変化させる。この強化剤は空気中や石材中の水分と反応し，ガラス（SiO_2）とエチルアルコールとなる。ガラス内部にはエチルアルコールの蒸発に伴う空隙がつくられ，石の吸放湿特性を損なわずに強化ができる。ただ，ガラスが硬すぎると強化後の石に何かしらのストレスがかかった場合にガラスよりも石が割れるため，石よりも若干弱く設定し，ストレスを強化剤のガラスが受け止め逃すことで石を守る。またこの強化剤は石の空隙を充填するため，強度が向上するのだが，あまり劣化進行が進んでいない石には内部へ浸透せず，弱い部分に多く含浸することができる。

while they are moist (biologically active). The heat can be generated by sunlight, and the microorganisms on the stones are first moistened, wrapped to prevent evaporation, and left in the sun for 2 to 4 days. After this, the wrap is removed and the stone is left as it is. As with Method 2, this method also takes several years to cause the organisms to wither and die. Microorganisms on the surface of the stone are in a sauna-like environment due to the heat from sunlight and the water that is applied to it, causing necrosis. The major difference from methods 1 and 2 is that no chemicals are used, which makes it more environmentally friendly and less costly. However, the sunlight strength may cause variations in the effectiveness of the treatment.

Fig. 6.3.3 shows an example of this treatment on lichens on a stone using this method.

Method 4: Installing a Temporary Roof

Microorganisms naturally require water and light (sunlight) to grow. We confirmed that, if a roof was built over the gallery, the microbial layer on the Bas-reliefs would decline in a few years. This method has the advantage that it can be used without directly interacting with the stone, unlike the three methods described above. However, installing a temporary roof requires securing scaffolding, and the effect on the landscape must also be considered.

3. Consolidation and Moisture Permeability Regulation

(1) On Consolidants

Consolidation means reinforcing the stones that have lost their strength due to aging. To consolidate a stone, it needs to be strengthened while its properties are retained, so when selecting a stone to treat, its moisture absorption and release characteristics, texture, color, etc. must be considered. After 15 years of exposure tests at the Bayon, we followed the tendencies in stone deterioration and decided to use a mixture of tetraethoxysilane monomer and oligomer as a consolidant. The mixing ratio is based on a monomer: oligomer ratio of 6:4, and the ratio was changed according to the deterioration state of the stone. This consolidant reacts with moisture in the air and the stone material, forming glass (SiO_2) and ethyl alcohol. Voids are created inside the glass as the ethyl alcohol evaporates, making it possible to strengthen the stone without impairing its moisture absorption and release properties.

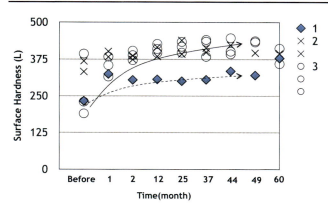

Fig. 6.3.4 An example of the consolidation treatment

バイヨン回廊で試験処理した事例の一つを Fig. 6.3.4 に示す。処理前は強度値（L）が200から400の値で分布していたことに対し，処理後は360から400程度となり石の硬さが一様になっていることがわかる。この場所での塗布量は1㎡あたり450gである。様々な環境下にある6ヶ所での試験を行い，強度は平均で1.6倍に，1つの石あたりの硬さのばらつきはおよそ1/3にまで強化することができた。当然ながら強化による石の吸水率などは変わらない。

⑵ 透湿調整の役割

透湿調整剤は石の呼吸のことであり，水の染みやすさとも言える。従来撥水剤が石の処理には使われることが多かったが，撥水作用により石の呼吸が止まり，水分の蒸散や浸透ができずにさらに劣化を深刻な状況にすることが多かった。排水施設や回廊の屋根部分に関しては，本来，雨水が抜け落ちるようなものではなかったはずであり，不透水性の機能を回復させることが必要である。屋根の石材は暑い時には表面温度が60℃近くにもなることがわかっている。バイヨンを構成する砂岩は60℃まで加温すると，自然冷却時になんらかの音が発生していることがアコースティックエミッション調査からわかっている。これは石の鉱物同士が擦れ合うことで発生していると推測され，強化処理剤後の透湿調整剤の塗布により軽減することがわかった。

回廊の浅浮彫ではこのような高温になることは考えられにくい一方で，強化処置だけでは処置をした石の周りと水分吸放湿性が大きく異なったままであることが考えられる。できれば回廊に発生する水のストレスを分散させて軽減することが理想である。そのため，周囲の石や，地形なども考慮し，透湿調整剤による処置が必要となる。

我々の試験ではシランモノマーオリゴマー系を採用した。以下にその一例を示す。Fig. 6.3.5の中央の石は当初全面に着生物に覆われていたが，右半分を塩化ベンザ

However, if the glass is too hard and certain stress is applied to the consolidated stone, it will break before the glass does. Thus, the agent needs to be set so it is slightly weaker than the stone, so that the strengthened glass absorbs and reacts under stress, protecting the stone material. Additionally, since this reinforcing agent fills the voids in the stone, while it improves its strength, it does not penetrate into the interior of the stones that have not undergone significant deterioration. Thus, the consolidant tends to be absorbed in the weak areas.

Fig. 6.3.4 shows the results of one test in the Bayon gallery. Before treatment, the strength values (L) were distributed between 200 and 400, but after treatment they ranged from 360 to 400, indicating that the hardness of the stones become more uniform. The application amount at this location is 450g per square meter. Tests were conducted at six locations under various environments, and the strength increased by an average of 1.6 times, while the variation in hardness per stone was reduced to approximately 1/3. Naturally, the water absorption rate of the stone does not change with consolidation.

⑵ **Role of the Moisture Permeability Regulator**

Moisture permeability regulators allow the stone to breathe, and reportedly also control the ease with which water stains the surface. Water repellents were traditionally used to treat stones, but they often stop the stones from breathing, making it impossible for water to evaporate or penetrate, leading to even more serious deterioration. Regarding the drainage and the roofs of the galleries, they were originally not supposed to allow rainwater to permeate through, so they need to be restored to serve their original functions. It is known that the surface temperature of the roof stones can reach nearly 60 degrees Celsius in hot weather. Acoustic emission studies have shown that when the sandstone that makes up Bayon is heated to 60 degrees Celsius, it makes a noise as it cools down naturally. This is possibly caused by the stone minerals rubbing against each other, and it was found that it could be alleviated by applying a moisture permeability regulator after the consolidant is applied.

While it is unlikely that the Gallery Bas-reliefs would experience such high temperatures, it is possible that the moisture absorption and desorption properties of a stone that underwent consolidation treatment alone differs from those that undergo the full treatment. Ideally, the water stress that occurs in the Gallery should be dispersed and alleviated. Therefore, it is necessary to consider the surrounding stones and topography and use a moisture permeability regulator.

In our tests, we used a silane monomer-oligomer system. An example is shown below. Initially, the entire surface of the stone in the center of Fig. 6.3.5 was covered with epiphytic organisms, but the right half was cleaned using a benzalkonium chloride solution. Afterwards, the lower half of the cleaned area (lower right part of the stone) was treated

Fig. 6.3.5 Test area using cleaning, consolidation, and a moisture permeability regulator

with a consolidant and a moisture permeability regulator. The numbers indicate the moisture content measured from the surface, and it can be seen that the moisture content is comparable to that of the surrounding stones that are untreated.

4. Landscape and Repairs

Fig. 6.3.6 shows an example of a damaged Bas-relief, for which there are two main possible treatments: one is to approach the flaked area that shows the internal new surface, and the other is to approach the original surface that has not peeled off yet. If we apply conservation-restoration alone, for example, by cleaning and consolidating the embossed parts, the parts that have fallen off will remain as they are. This would allow deterioration factors (such as rainwater) to enter from around the edges of the peeled parts. This condition would also draw attention and become a hindrance when viewing the Bas-reliefs. Therefore, we repair the peeled off parts of the Bas-relief after applying treatment. They also need to be filled with a material that resembles the original stone to ensure structural stability and conformity.

A material that resembles stone, called pseudo-rock, is created by stirring epoxy resin and water until it forms a foam, and then mixing it with sandstone powder. This material needs to match the color and tone of the variously deteriorated Bas-reliefs, to have filling and shaping properties, and also to follow the physical properties of the stone at the construction site, all while remaining attached. As a result of testing dozens of different blending ratios for 5 years, we decided to add 2

ルコニウム溶液を用いクリーニングした。その後，クリーニング部分の下半分（石の右下部分）を強化および透湿調整剤で処置を行った。数字は表面から計測した水分率を示し，周囲の処置をしなかった石と同程度の値を示していることがわかる。

4．修景，補修

Fig. 6.3.6に損傷した浅浮彫の一例を示す。大きく2つの処置が考えられよう。一つは剥落が生じ，内部の新たな部分が現れている箇所へのアプローチであり，もう一つはまだ剥離が起こらず，当初の表面が残存している箇所へのアプローチである。浅浮彫のクリーニング，強化等の保存修復だけでは剥落した箇所はそのままであるため，剥落箇所の周縁から劣化原因（雨水など）が入る危険性がある。また浅浮彫の鑑賞時にも目が留まってしまい，妨げになる。そこで，処置後の浅浮彫に対し剥落箇所の補修を行う。また，構造上の安定を確保するために石に似せた素材で充填する必要もある。

石に似せた素材は擬岩と呼ばれ，エポキシ樹脂と水をフォーム状になるまで撹拌し，それに砂岩の粉末などを混和することで製作する。様々に劣化した浅浮彫の色調に合わせながら，充填性，整形性はもとより，施工箇所の石の物性に追随し剥離しないことが求められる。数十種類の配合比を5年間曝露し検討した結果，エポキシ樹脂1に対し水を2加え，それに篩で粒度を調合した砂岩粉末を重量比で3.45添加したものを基本とした。Fig. 6.3.7に剥離箇所の亀裂に充填した擬岩（白線内）を示す。

Fig. 6.3.6 Flaking Bas-relief surface

Fig. 6.3.7 Repair with artificial-rock (marked by the white line)

Fig. 6.3.8 Filled roof gaps (white area)

Table 6.3.1 Roof Filler Formulation Proportions

Type of sand	Sand			Lime	Clay	Water
	< 0.85 mm	0.85 ≪ 2 mm	2 mm以上			
Crushed stone	164	36	0	70	80	70

擬岩は施工後，上記の強化剤，透湿調整剤で処理することも可能である。

5. 屋根の処置

回廊浅浮彫の保存にとって，回廊屋根，塔の隙間処置は重要である。浅浮彫を構成する砂岩の劣化のほとんどに水が関係しており，この水をどのように処置するかは保存修復の要である。回廊と塔は構造的にも不安定であり，理想的には解体し当初に近い形で屋根の機能を復元することが良いが，大規模遺跡では時間的，経済的な事由により現実的ではない。そこで，現状の屋根にできた隙間を埋める材料が必要になった。範囲が広大であるためできるだけ現地で取得でき，安定的な供給が望める材料を用いた。

5年の経過観察から，Table 6.3.1に示す配合とした。色が合わない場合はMnO₂を数g添加する。施工後の写真をFig. 6.3.8に示す。まだ充填材料の色調が明るいが，経年により周辺の石と馴染む。本来，バイヨンにはこのような目地材は使われていないため，将来の大規模整備や必要な時にはいつでも除去できるような施工処理が求められる。

6. 日常管理

このような保存処理はメンテナンスフリーではない。

parts of water to 1 part of epoxy resin, and then added 3.45 parts by weight of sandstone powder, which had been sieved to match the stone particle size. Fig. 6.3.7 shows the artificial-rock (marked by the white line) that filled the crack where peeling occurred. After making the artificial rock, it can be treated with the above-mentioned consolidants and moisture permeability regulators.

5. Roof Treatment

For the conservation of the gallery Bas-reliefs, the gaps in the gallery roof and tower need to be considered. Water is involved in most of the deterioration of the sandstone that makes up the Bas-reliefs, and how to deal with this water is the key to conservation and restoration. The galleries and towers are structurally unstable. Ideally, they would be dismantled and restored to return the roof's original function to the extent possible. However, this is not practical for large-scale ruins due to time and budgetary constraints. Thus, we needed a material to fill in the gaps in the current roof. Because the scope is vast, we used materials that could be obtained locally and that could be consistently supplied.

Based on observations that spanned 5 years, the formulation shown in Table 6.3.1 was adopted. When colors do not match, several grams of MnO_2 are added. Fig. 6.3.8 shows the conditions after application. The color of the filling material is still bright, but over time it has blended in with that of the surrounding stones. Originally, this type of joint material was not used in the Bayon, so an application process needs to be developed that allows for future large-scale maintenance or removal whenever necessary.

適切なメンテナンスにより保存処理の効果が長続きする。表面に堆積した汚れは劣化の要因となるため定期的なクリーニングは必要である。特別な技術は必要ではなく，屋根や床の清掃と柔らかいブラシやブロワーなどによる浅浮彫表面の優しい清掃である。活用や観光のあり方，環境の変動などにより今後どこにどのような劣化が生じるかは不明であり，早期の発見のために絶えず清掃することは重要である。もし劣化などの変化に気付いた際はその場の状況を記録するシートも必要であろう。これを蓄積することで劣化のポテンシャルが高い箇所を把握でき，予防的保存のアプローチが可能になる。

また，含水率や表面硬度など計測機器による定期的な診断や，ハリケーンや長期的な長雨，地震などの大規模な自然災害に対して，たとえば事前にシートをかける補強をするなどの対応ができる体制の構築が必要である。

7. さいごに

15年におよぶ保存処理剤の曝露試験，さまざまな劣化への試験施工とその評価を経て，保存修復計画の立案となった。浅浮彫の保存に必要と思われる課題を全てクリアできたとは言えないが，保存材料の経年変化も把握でき，またそれらの技術的改良への指針も得ることができた。砂岩浅浮彫は芸術的，歴史的にも非常に価値が高く，それを損なわずに劣化や損傷を修理するにはこれからの活用計画，管理計画，観光計画，都市計画などさまざまな計画との調整が必須である。浅浮彫は非常に脆弱化しており，これまでは大丈夫であった使い方であってもすこしのインパクトで壊れる恐れが十分にある。それを関係機関に周知し，理解してもらいながら進めることが，浅浮彫に負担をかけずに保存することへの一歩となる。

遺跡は過去のものではあるが，現在まで残ってきた遺跡をどのように今の社会全体で共有することができるのか，浅浮彫の保存を通して考えていかなければならない。

6. Daily management

This kind of conservation process is not maintenance-free. Proper maintenance will ensure the long-lasting effects of the conservation treatments. Dirt that accumulates on the surface causes deterioration, so periodic cleaning is necessary. No special skills are required, as it only involves cleaning the roof and floors and gently brushing the raised surfaces with a soft brush or blower. It is unclear where and what kind of deterioration will occur in the future due to factors such as use, tourism, and environmental changes, so consistent cleaning is important for early detection. Additionally, record sheets are necessary for when changes such as deterioration are noticed. By accumulating this information, we can identify areas with high deterioration potential, facilitating a preventive conservation approach.

In addition, we need to establish a system to regularly diagnose moisture content and surface hardness using measuring equipment, and to respond to large-scale natural disasters such as hurricanes, long-term rains, and earthquakes by applying reinforcement sheets in advance.

7. Conclusion

Building on 15 years conducting exposure tests with conservation treatments while creating and evaluating tests for various types of deterioration, we drew up a conservation and restoration plan. Although we cannot say that we were able to overcome all the issues that affect the preservation of the Bas-reliefs, we were able to understand changes over time in conservation materials, and we were also able to obtain guidelines to make technological improvements. Sandstone Bas-reliefs have great artistic and historical value, and in order to repair them without causing additional damage, we need to coordinate various plans such as future use plans, management plans, tourism plans, and urban plans. The Bas-reliefs have become extremely fragile, and even though they have been used successfully until now, they might break even upon a slight impact. Sharing this information with the relevant organizations and gaining their understanding will be the first step toward preserving the Bas-reliefs without burdening them.

Sites may be a thing of the past, but we must consider how they have remained until today, and how we can share them with today's society through the preservation of these Bas-reliefs.

6.4 バイヨンの景観保存について
Conservation of Landscape of Bayon

中川　武　　石塚　充雅
NAKAGAWA Takeshi　　ISHIZUKA Mitsumasa

1. はじめに

　JSA/JASAはバイヨンの存在が永続することを望んでいる。そのための重要な課題の一つが景観整備の長期計画の成就である。

　バイヨンにおいては20世紀前半にEFEO（フランス極東学院）によって基礎的な記録作業，崩落石材の除去及び整理作業，そして各種整備修復作業が進められた。これらの作業の過程はEFEOが作成した各種活動・研究記録資料の他，現地においても倒壊の危険性のある壁体を支えるコンクリート柱，危険箇所を接合する鎹，基壇や壁体へのセメント充填等，当時の整備・修復の痕跡を今でも多く確認することができる。現状バイヨンがある程度の状態を保持できているのはこれらの処置によるところが大きいが，それから100年近く立ち，現在新たに危

1. Introduction

JSA/JASA hope that the presence of Bayon will be permanent. One of the important issues for this purpose is the achievement of long-term plans for landscape maintenance.

In the first half of the 20th century, École Française d'Extrême-Orient (EFEO) carried out fundamental recording work, removal and arrangement work of fallen stones, and various maintenance and restoration work at Bayon. The process of this work can be verified in the various activity and research records compiled by EFEO and also there are many traces of restoration that can still be seen at the site, such as concrete pillars that support walls that are at risk of collapsing, clumps that connect structural dangerous parts, and cement fillings into parts of foundations and walls. The fact that Bayon is able to maintain its current state to a certain level is largely due to the measures at the time. However, we can see many places in dangerous states after around 100 years.

JSA/JASA has been carrying out restoration and maintenance work mainly at Bayon since the beginning of the project. After we implemented restoration work of Northern and Southern libraries of Bayon, we are currently working on landscape improvement work on the East façade of Bayon, mainly focusing on the improvement of East Outer Gallery.

Along with these conservation and improvement works, various studies for the permanent stabilization of the Central Tower of Bayon and conservation of the Bas-relief of the Inner Gallery of Bayon have been implemented, and these are at the stage where actual measures will be taken

Fig. 6.4.1 Present situation of Bayon

253

険な状態となっている箇所も少なくない。

　その中で，JSA/JASAはプロジェクト当初からバイヨンを中心に修復・整備作業を行っており，これまでにバイヨン南北経蔵の修復の他，現在バイヨン外回廊の整備を中心としたバイヨン東面の景観整備作業を進めている。またこれらの作業と並行して，バイヨン中央塔の恒久的安定化および内回廊浅浮彫の修復に関する検討がこれまで進められており，今後具体的に対策を実施する段階となってきている。また最近ではアプサラ機構による独自のバイヨン危険箇所に対する各種調査・修復・整備作業が進められている。

　上記の中で，改めてバイヨン全域の整備に関して長期的なスパンで計画を検討・整理する必要がある段階となっていることから，本項にて必要な点を改めて整理したい。

2. 長期計画において必要となる検討事項

　以下長期計画を検討する上で必要となる検討事項を整理する。

①リスクマップの作成・更新

　これまでにJSA/JASAによってバイヨンの危険箇所に関するリスクマップの作成を行い，近年ではアプサラ機構によってバイヨンのみならず，アンコール遺跡全域の各遺構に関するリスクマップの作成が進められている。

　今後に関してもこのリスクマップを定期的に更新し，寺院内の危険箇所を随時把握しておく必要がある。

②基礎記録資料の統合・更新

　これまでにバイヨンにおいてはEFEOによる各種図面および写真記録データ，1990年代以降においてはJSA/JASAによる修復・調査に伴う図面や写真等の各種記録データ，東京大学と連携したバイヨン全域の3Dデータ，そして近年ではアプサラ機構による修復・調査に伴う各種記録データが存在している。またバイヨン周辺においてはJSA/JASAも参加したシドニー大学を中心としたKhmer Archaeology Lidar Consortiumによるライダーデータも存在している。

　それらのデータの存在はいずれも重要なものである。しかし今後さらに長期計画を詳細に検討していく上で，バイヨンの建造過程における度重なる増改築とそれに伴う複雑な形状，その修復過程，そしてその中で生じている多様な課題を把握するため，3Dデータをベースとしたバイヨン各所の詳細図面および記録，周辺の詳細地形

based on the results of studies. In addition, APSARA National Authority has recently been carrying out their own various surveys, restoration work, and maintenance work at the identified dangerous areas in Bayon.

Given the current situation, we are facing the situation the necessarily to reconsider and organize the long-term plan for the arrangement regarding the entire Bayon. Therefore, we would like to reorganize the necessary points in this section.

2. Necessary considerations for long term plan

The following is a summary of necessary considerations for long term plan.

1, Preparation and updating of risk maps

In the past, JSA/JASA has prepared risk maps for Bayon, and recently, APSARA has been preparing risk maps not only for Bayon but also for the entire Angkor site.

In the future, it will be necessary to update this risk map periodically and to keep track of dangerous parts in the temples.

2, Integration and updating of basic recording materials

Until now regarding Bayon, there are various drawings and photographic record data by EFEO. And since the 1990s, there are also various recorded data such as drawings and photographs accompanying restoration and investigation by JSA/JASA and 3D data of the entire Bayon area in collaboration with JSA/JASA and the University of Tokyo. In recent years, there is various recorded data from restoration and investigation works by APSARA. In addition, there is also lidar data around Bayon by the Khmer Archeology Lidar Consortium centered by the University of Sydney, in which JSA/JASA also participated.

This data is important. However, as we consider long-term plans in more detail, updated versions of various basic materials will be additionally required such as detailed drawings and records of various parts of Bayon based on 3D data, and detailed topographical data of the surrounding area of Bayon in order to grasp the repeated expansions and renovations during the construction process of Bayon and the resulting complex shape, restoration process and various issues generated from these factors.

In the future, it is necessary as a long-term plan to integrate this data through software such as 3D data or GIS, and to create a platform that can share the updated status with related organizations whenever the current status will be updated.

3, Short-term and temporary reinforcement measures for highly urgent dangerous areas

After determining dangerous parts and organizing their

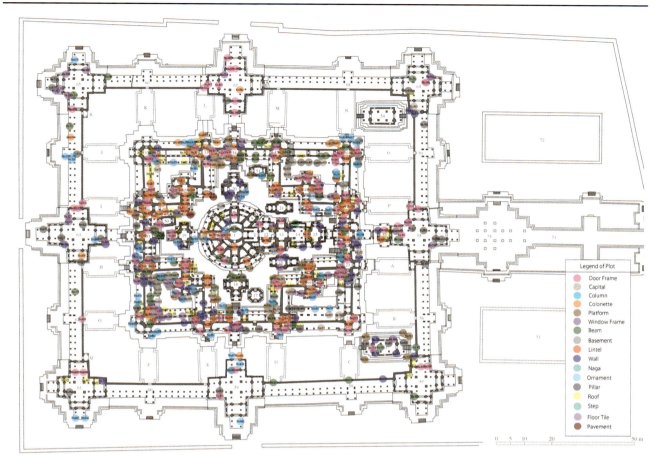

Fig. 6.4.2 Risk Map of Bayon (JSA/JASA)

データ等，これまでの資料をさらに更新した各種基礎資料が必要となってくる。

そして将来的には3DデータもしくはGIS等のソフトを通じて，これらのデータを統合し，現状が更新された際には，随時更新状況が関係機関で共有できるプラットフォームの作成も長期的な計画としては必要となってくるであろう。

③緊急性の高い危険箇所への短期的・暫定的な補強対策

危険箇所の整理を行い，それらのデータを整理した上で，緊急性の高い危険箇所に関しては状況に応じて短期的・暫定的な補強対策が必要となってくる。その場合には建築構造・地盤構造の専門家と共に，複合的に補強方針を判断し，対応する必要がある。ただし，補強方針によっては新たに崩壊のリスクを助長する可能性もあるため，慎重に検討する必要がある。またこの補強は全体の長期的修復との調整で，あくまでも短期的・暫定的な補強に留めなければならない場合があることに留意する必要がある。

④各種モニタリング

危険箇所および整備・修復箇所を中心として定期的，

Fig. 6.4.3 3D data of Bayon (The University of Tokyo)

data, short-term and temporary reinforcement measures will be required depending on the situation for highly urgent dangerous parts. In such cases, it is necessary to determine reinforcement policies and take appropriate measures with structural and geotechnical experts. However, depending on the reinforcement policy, there is a possibility that it may increase the risk of collapse, so careful consideration is required. Furthermore, it should also be noted that these reinforcements may have to be limited to short-term and temporary reinforcements in coordination with the overall long-term restoration.

4, Various monitoring

It is necessary to establish monitoring systems that can

かつ長期的に運用可能なモニタリング体制を構築する必要がある。これらのモニタリング結果に応じて，適宜整備計画を更新していく必要がある。

⑤散乱石材の長期的かつ段階的な整理・記録・原位置同定作業

バイヨンの景観整備における大きな課題の一つがバイヨン内外に存在する6万個近くの散乱石材である。これまで各個別の修復時に，周辺散乱石材の整理・記録・原位置復帰作業が試みられてきたが，依然として難題であることに変わりはない。将来的には出来る限りこれらの散乱石材の原位置を特定し，再設置作業ができることが望ましいであろう。これまでは技術的な限界もあり，散乱石材の原位置が十分に同定できていないものが多くあった。しかし近年は3Dおよび写真測量の技術が発展している状況があるため，今後はこれらの技術を活用し，散乱石材を段階的・組織的に記録し，その上でそれらの散乱石材の3Dデータおよびバイヨンの現状の3Dデータを活用して現位置を特定できるようなプログラムを関係機関と連携して開発すると散乱石材の大規模原位置同定作業に活路が開けてくる可能性がある。

⑥バイヨン内外の水利施設の整備作業の検討

バイヨンはその複雑な建造過程に伴い，内外に数多くの水利施設の痕跡を有している。アンコール遺跡の保存における大きな課題の一つとしていかに基壇基礎構造内部の版築盛土への水の影響を軽減できるかがある。それに加え，地球規模の温暖化に伴う気候変動による降雨状況の変化はカンボジアにも影響を及ぼしており，今後長期的な降雨を想定したリスク軽減のための対策が必要とされる。そのためバイヨン内外の水利施設の現状を今一度整理し，その上で現状バイヨンでどのように水利計画を行うのが一番有用であるかをシュミレーション等を通じて改めて整理し，その成果を踏まえて長期的な整備方針を検討していく必要がある。他方これらの水利施設の整備・修復が有用となる可能性があるが，同時に構造的支持力が減少し，長期的にはリスクとなる可能性もある。そのため，整備・修復前の慎重な各種シュミレーションおよび検討が非常に重要となってくる。

⑦段階的な各区域毎の整備作業

上記の検討を踏まえた上で，段階的な各区域毎の整備作業を行う必要がある。その際には建物の連続性を鑑みて，基本的には局所的にではなく，危険度の高い箇所から各区域毎に整備していくことが効果的であると考えられる。

be operated periodically and over a long period of time, mainly focusing on the hazardous areas and the areas to be maintained or restored. The maintenance plan should be updated according to the results of this monitoring.

5, Long-term and gradual arrangement, recording and identification of scattered stones

One of the major issues in the landscape development of Bayon is the nearly 60,000 scattered stones that exist inside and outside Bayon. Until now, in each individual restoration work in Bayon, attempts have been made to arrange, record, and return the stones scattered around each restoration site to their original locations, but dealing with scattered stones has remained as difficult task in Bayon. It would be desirable to be able to identify the original locations of these scattered stones and re-install them in the future as much as possible. Until now, many of the scattered stones have not been sufficiently identified as to their original location due to technical limitations. However, as 3D and photogrammetry technologies have developed in recent years, if we will record the scattered stones step by step and methodically by using these technologies and we can develop programs in collaboration with related organizations to identify the original locations of the scattered stones automatically by utilizing the 3D data of those scattered stones and the current 3D data of Bayon, we are possible to a new path for large-scale in-situ identification of the scattered stones of Bayon.

6, Consideration of maintenance work for water management facilities inside and outside Bayon

Due to its complex construction process, Bayon has numerous traces of water management facilities both inside and outside. One of the main important tasks in preservation of Angkor is how to reduce the impact of water on the compaction soil structure inside the foundation structure of the platform. In addition, changes in rainfall conditions due to climate change associated with global warming are also having an impact on Cambodia, so future measures are needed to reduce the risk of long-term rainfall impacts. We need to confirm the current status of water management facilities in and around Bayon once again, and reconsider the best water management plan for Bayon at the present state through the simulations. Then long-term maintenance policies based on the results can be considered. On the other hand, while this maintenance and repair work of these water management facilities are possible to be useful, these are possible to be the risks in the long term by reducing structural support capacity up to the situation. Therefore, it is extremely important to carry out various careful simulations and studies before maintenance and restoration.

7, Gradual maintenance work for each area

Based on the above considerations, it is necessary to carry

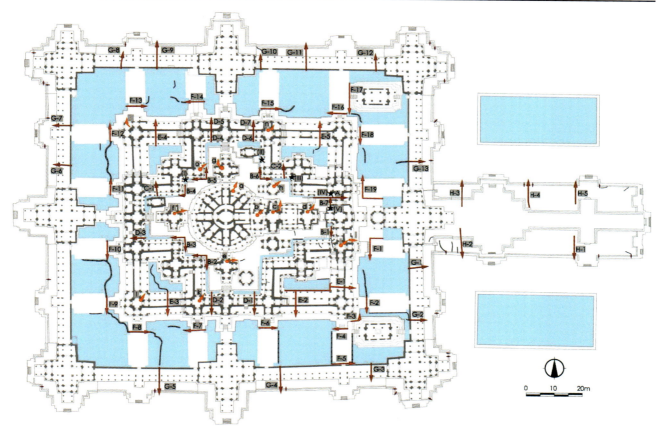

Fig. 6.4.5 Drainage system of Bayon (SO Sokuntheary 2007)

整備に際しては基壇および上部構造の変形が少ない区域においては基本的には上部構造および基壇外装砂岩材の部分解体・再構築，そして目地詰め整備に留める最小限の整備方針が基本的には好ましいと考えられる。他方で危険度が高く，変形が大きい区域に関しては建築構造，地盤構造調査を慎重に行い，その成果を踏まえ，場合によっては，整備の域を超え，本格的に修復方針を確定して作業を進めていく必要があるだろう。

また周囲を含めた植栽は寺院全体の景観の永続性にとって重要な意義があり，遺跡保存に弊害を及ぼしそうな巨樹の伐採についても各区域毎の整備作業との調和が図られる必要があると考えられる。

⑧観光との調和

これらの整備作業を進めていく上で，観光との調和をいかに行うかも非常に重要である。バイヨンの崩壊要因を軽減すること，そしてカンボジアにおける宗教施設としての機能・重要性を尊重することは非常に重要であるが，その一方アンコール遺跡，特に他に類を見ないバイヨンは体感することにより，その魅力，そしてカンボジアを越えた世界的な重要性を理解できる寺院である要素が強いことから，本寺院の価値およびその修復の普遍的意義をカンボジア内外に周知するためにも，長期的なス

out gradual maintenance work in each area. For this work, by considering the continuity of each building, it is effective to carry out the maintenance work in each area within a certain range rather than just parts limited to the high-risk areas.

In the areas that there are low deformations of the platform and superstructure, minimum maintenance policies, which is basically limited to partial dismantling and reconstruction of the superstructure and foundation exterior sandstone materials and joint filling treatment, is basically preferable. On the other hand, for areas with high risk and large deformation, it is necessary to implement a careful survey regarding the building structure and ground structure, and based on the results, in some cases it may be necessary to go beyond maintenance and decide on a full-fledged restoration policy and proceed with the work.

Furthermore, since the vegetation around Bayon has an important significance for the permanence of the temple's overall landscape, it is better to consider to harmonize with the maintenance policy of each area when considering cutting down large trees that are likely to harm the preservation of the monument.

8, Harmony with tourism

In proceeding with these maintenance works, it is also extremely important how to harmonize with tourism. It is extremely important to reduce the factors contributing to the

パンでいかにカンボジア内外からの観光と整備作業を調和していけるか検討することが重要である。

⑨カンボジア人による自立した調査・研究・保存修復体制の確立とそのための人材育成

1992年よりアンコール遺跡での修復・調査研究が活発化してから，当初は日本を含む海外のチームが主導して修復・調査研究が進められてきたが，現在は多くのカンボジア人専門家および現場スタッフが主体的に活動するプロジェクトも増加しており，その中核をなしているのがアプサラ機構である。その中で，将来的にはアンコールにおいてはアプサラ機構のカンボジア人スタッフが主体となり，バイヨンを含むアンコール全域での整備・修復作業が進められることが望ましい。そのためにはアンコール遺跡の活動に資するカンボジア人専門家および現場スタッフが育成される長期的な体制が構築できるよう，1990年初頭から継続して活動している外国チームの一つとしてカンボジアおよびアプサラ機構に引き続き協力していく必要があると考えている。

その上でこれまでにカンボジアおよび海外チームの尽力の結果，現在アンコールに関わる多くの建築および考古のカンボジア人専門家が育成されているが，今後カンボジア人によって各種調査・研究および修復活動を自立して実施・運用できるためにはさらなる分野の専門家の育成が急務であると考えている。特にアンコール遺跡においては建築構造及び地質・地盤基礎構造の専門家の育成が必要であると考えている。この分野は従来体験的技術としてカバーされてきたが，自立した形で問題点の発見からその解決のための工夫のプロセスを世界的に評価されるレベルで進めるためには，理論的研究に裏付けられることが必要である。その上で十分な技術を獲得するにはある程度継続的な訓練が必要となり，時間がかかるが重要なプロセスであると考えている。またこれらの専門家が自立して実験を行える体制が構築できることも必要である。そのためには専門家の育成と共に，カンボジアの現状および未来に即した設備および試験体制の構築を検討していく必要がある。

加えて，最終的な施工のクオリティは専門家と共に，現場作業スタッフの技量に左右される部分も大きい。1990年代以降のアンコールにおける活発な修復活動の結果，多くの現場作業スタッフが育成されているが，他方で高齢化が進んでいる状況もある。また多くの現場作業スタッフは近隣の村出身であることが多く，今後もアンコールのリビングヘリテージとしての価値を継続していくためには近隣の村の方々の遺跡に対する自発的な意欲と連携した長期的な修復体制の構築は重要であると

Bayon collapse and to respect its function and importance as a religious facility in Cambodia. On the other hand, by strong experiencing the Angkor, especially the Bayon, which is like no other, visitors can understand its charm and its global importance beyond Cambodia deeply. Therefore, in order to spread awareness both inside and outside Cambodia of the value of Bayon and the universal significance of its restoration, it is extremely important to consider how to harmonize maintenance work with tourism from inside and outside of Cambodia over a long-term span.

9, Establishment of an independent system for investigation, research, preservation and restoration system by Cambodians and human resource development for this purpose

After restoration and research at Angkor became active in 1992, international teams including Japan initially had led the restoration and research activities. But currently, the number of projects in which many Cambodian experts and field staff are actively working is increasing, and APSARA is at the core of these projects. In the future, it is desirable that the Cambodian staff of APSARA take the lead in carrying out maintenance and restoration work of Angkor, including Bayon. In order to build a long-term system for training Cambodian experts and field staff who will contribute to the activities of the Angkor, we believe it is necessary to continue to cooperate with Cambodia and APSARA As one of the international teams that has been operating continuously since the early 1990s.

As a result of the efforts of Cambodia and international teams, many Cambodian experts in architecture and archeology related to Angkor have now been trained. However, in order for Cambodians to be able to carry out and operate various surveys, research, and restoration activities independently in the future, we believe that there is an urgent need to develop more experts in various fields. Especially we believe that it is necessary for the Angkor to train more experts in architectural structures, geology, and geotechnical engineering. These fields have traditionally been covered as experiential techniques. Therefore, in order to be able to independently proceed with the process of discovering problems and devising solutions at a level that is recognized worldwide, it is necessary to be supported by theoretical research. Moreover, acquiring sufficient skills requires a certain amount of continuous training, so it takes time, but we believe it is an important process. It is also necessary to build a system in which these experts can conduct tests independently. Therefore, in addition to training experts, it is necessary to consider building equipment facilities and testing systems that are adaptable to Cambodia's current situation and future.

The quality of restoration finally depends on the skills of the on-site staff as well as the experts. As a result of continuous

考えられる。我々のプロジェクトにおいてはこれまでノコール・クラウ村を中心としてアンコール遺跡近隣の住民の方々と長年連携してきたが，今後も長期的，かつ継続的な連携のもとで各年代の現場スタッフの人材育成に寄与していく必要があると考えている。

3. まとめ

バイヨンはその建造過程および構造の複雑さから，アンコール遺跡の保存において検討しなければならない課題の多くを有している。そのためバイヨンの長期的な整備計画を考えることは，すなわちアンコール遺跡全体の長期的な整備計画を検討することにも繋がると考えている。その意義を十分に理解した上で，今後もアプサラ機構およびカンボジアの方々とアンコール，そしてバイヨンの現在および未来にとって何が重要なのか共に考え，そして活動を行っていく必要があると考えている。

active restorations at Angkor since the 1990s, many field workers have been trained, but at the same time they are becoming old. In addition, as many of the field workers are from nearby villages, in order to continue to keep the value of Angkor as a living heritage, it is also important to establish a long-term restoration system that works with the voluntary desire of people in nearby villages to preserve Angkor. In our project, we have been collaborating with residents near the Angkor for many years, centering on the Nokor Krau village. We hope to continue to support to develop human resources of field staff of all ages through long-term and continuous collaborat5ion.

3. Conclusion

Due to the complexity of its construction process and structure, Bayon has many issues that must be considered in the preservation of the Angkor. Therefore, we believe that considering a long-term maintenance plan for Bayon will also lead to considering a long-term maintenance plan for the entire Angkor area. Based on fully understanding its significance, we hope to continue to work together with APSARA and the people of Cambodia to think about what is important for the present and future of Angkor and Bayon, and to carry out activities together in harmony.

References
1) SO Sokuntheary, "Study on the Drainage System of the Bayon in the Angkor Thom, Cambodia", PhD thesis, 2007

第 7 章　バイヨンは希望となりえるか，結語に変えて

Chapter 7　Could Bayon Become Hope or not, Instead of Conclusion

中川　武
NAKAGAWA Takeshi

1. アンコール・ワットとバイヨンの保存が意味するもの

　バイヨンのみならず，およそ世界の文化遺産の保存修復の課題は，アテネ憲章（1933年）やベネチア憲章（1964年）などの世界的な枠組みで協議されてきた。私たちJSAのアンコール遺跡救済活動の参画は，ベネチア憲章を部分修正した1994年のオーセンティシティに関する奈良ドキュメントの考え方をバックボーンとしてきた。アンコールでの体験により，バイヨン憲章（2003年）や，アンコール憲章（2012年）の取組にも参加してきた。特に1993年以来のアンコール国際調整会議（ICC-Angkor）の積み重ね，そして何よりも，カンボジア人スタッフを含めた各国チームとカンボジア政府機構アプサラの探求と今現在アンコール遺跡がカンボジア人と世界の人々からどのように考えられているかに関わるであろう。その意味で私達のバイヨンの問題も，私達JSA/JASAがバイヨンとは何か，その謎の意味は何か，遺跡の劣化の状態と原因は何か，それに対して，これまでどう行動し，そしてこれからどのように対処しようとしているのか，その具体的な方法と保存の思想のようなものを，各々の個別分野の，30年のまとめとして報告したのが以上の文章である。したがって，アンコール・ワットとバイヨンの保存が意味するものは，私達にとっては以上の報告が全てというほかない。しかしそれではあまりに，「木で鼻を括る」ようなものなので，現時点で，改めてバイヨンに対する総合的な想いをまとめておきたい。

　アンコール・ワットはクメール建築の歴史的集大成と呼ぶにふさわしく，高さや広さの建築規模の面だけでなく，建築形式や浅浮彫装飾の技術的完成度の高さ等々においても歴史を包括する一定の到達点に達していると言えるだろう。

　では，アンコール・ワットが達成した建築の美と力はどのように考え，評価することができるだろうか。高塔のシルエットは，源流であるインド建築にもない，柔らかな優雅さがある。回廊の浅浮彫は，ただ長大であるだけでなく，高密度でダイナミックな動きにより，魅力的なストーリーを展開する。そして，何よりも重厚で集中的な石造建築の重力感が広い境内と周囲の森の空間に解き放たれていく融合感に絶大な魅力があるし，美しいと感じられる。しかし，ここで注意しておきたいのは，このようなアンコール・ワット，即ちクメール建築の正統の美と力は決して，形の大きさやものの重力を巨大化し，強めることによって発揮されているのではないこと

1. What Restoration of Angkor Wat and Bayon Means

　The issues of conservation and restoration of not only the Bayon but also the world's tangible cultural heritage have been discussed in global frameworks such as the Athens Charter (1933) and the Venice Charter (1964). JSA's participation in the Angkor Archaeological Park restoration and conservation has been the backbone of the idea of authenticity promulgated in the Nara Document of 1994, which partially amended the Venice Charter. We have also participated in the Bayon Charter (2003) and the efforts for the establishment of the Angkor Charter (2012) based on our experience. In particular, the accumulation of knowledge from the International Coordinating Committee for the Safeguarding and Development of the Historic Site of Angkor (ICC-Angkor) since 1993 and, above all, the quest of the international teams, Cambodian staff, and the Cambodian government organization APSARA National Authority, as well as the Ministry of Culture and Fine Arts will be linked as to how the Angkor Monuments is now considered by Cambodians and people around the world. In this sense, this book summarizes our concreted methods and ideas of conservation that what Bayon is, what is the meaning of the mystery, what is the state and cause of the deterioration of the site, how we have been acting and how we are going to act on it, as the achievement of 30 years activities. The above text is a summary of 30 years of research in each related field of conservation and restoration. Therefore, this report highlights and summarizes what we have to said and done about the conservation of Angkor Wat and Bayon, and what the sites means to us.

　Angkor Wat is worthy of being called the historical culmination of Khmer architecture, and it can be said to have reached a certain point of historical comprehensiveness, not only in terms of its height and size, but also in terms of its architectural form, the technical perfection of its bas-relief decoration to mention only a few of the many unique attributes.

　Then, how can we view and evaluate the achievements of Angkor Wat in terms of the architectural beauty and power? The silhouette of the high tower has a soft elegance that is not found in Indian architecture, which is also the origin of Angkor. The bas-reliefs in the gallery are not only long but also dense and dynamic, telling fascinating stories. Above all, the sense of gravity of the massive and intensive stone architecture spreads to the monuments site and surrounding beautiful forest. It is a sence of fusion attractive and beautiful. However, it is important to note that the legitimate beauty and power of Khmer architecture, is not derived from the enormity

である。クメール建築はアーチ構造を採用しない組石建築故に，版築土層による基壇を重ねながら，大きく，高く，そして広くしてきたことに起因している。アンコール・ワットは壮大な建築であり，そこに魅力がある。しかし，決して強大ではない。クメールも王権であるが故に強大さを欲した。だが，弱く，たゆたうような版築構造を選び続けた。これだけ広大な版図を築いたクメール帝国であれば，これほどまでに石造建築を造り続けたアンコール建築技術であれば，頑丈かつ，安定的で強大な記念碑の建造も可能だったのではないだろうか，しかしそうはせず，もう一つの未知を選んできたように思われる。ここにクメールの基本的な秘密があるように思う。

3.3「クメール建築設計方法研究とバイヨン（溝口）」にて概要が報告されているが，私達JSAがクメール建築史調査で最も力を入れてきたのが，建物の実測とその建築設計方法の分析である。そこから得られた重要な結論の一つが，左右対称形に配置されるクメール建築群の中心軸線と伽藍敷地の中心線を尺度と各部の寸法決定方法（つまり設計方法）に準拠しながら，巧妙にズラしていることの発見であった。たとえばアンコール・ワットの場合，外回廊伽藍敷地の大きさを，他の累計から考えて，当初は120 vyama（vm）×120 vm（1 vmは4 hasta（造営尺実長≒412㎜，肘尺））である正方形を念頭において計画を出発した。しかし，西側正面外回廊南北長さ110 vmとし，東西長さを130 vmと南北で残した10 vm分を足して，東西に長い伽藍としている。当然，伽藍中心線と建物中心軸は一致していた。そこからまず，正面向かって右側の回廊長さを2 vm分削る。中心軸はそのままだから，実際の回廊中の目に視えない中心線と中心軸との間に，2 vm/2（≒1648㎜）分のズレが発生し，左右の回廊長さに2 vm分の差が生まれる。視た目で左右対称とするために向かって左側の回廊柱間は，柱間寸法を少し狭くしたうえで，柱間数を右側より2つ増している。アンコール・ワットの楼門（ゴープラ）の幅寸法は約1.6m×2＝3.2mなので，目に視えない敷地中心線は，ほぼこの楼門の壁芯を通ることになり，敷地中心線が来拝者に踏まれる恐れはない。アンコール・ワットはこれを意識した上でのズレの創出か否かは分からないが，寺院によってずれの寸法値は異なる。しかし，ズレ創出の方法は，数値は異なっても，ほぼ同様の手筈である。

世界の中心を占めるべき聖なるものは，祠堂や伽藍敷地や都市の中心を避けなければならないという禁止の意識は，仏教以外のインドの伝統的宗教観に共通している。ヒンドゥー教寺院で注目されるのは，インドからの影響を強く受けたインドネシア・プランバナンの寺院群の配置である。中央祠堂（本尊）の位置が敷地の中心からはっ

and strength of the massive form but the serenity of massive feeling it radiates. Khmer architecture consists of a stone structures that has been made larger, higher, and wider by building on top of each other with a platform made of layers of sandy soil without arches. Angkor Wat is a magnificent structure, and that is its charm. But it is by no means mighty. The Khmer architects also wanted a powerful structure for their kingship. However, they continued to choose a weak and faltering imperfect structural design. The Khmer Empire, which had built such a vast territory, could have possibility built more sturdy, stable, and powerful monuments with the Angkorian architectural technology but it seems that they did not do so and chose another unknown technique. Here, I think, lies the basic secret of Khmer.

As outlined in 3.3, we at JSA have focused on the actual measurement of buildings and analysis of their architectural design methods in most of our research. One of the most important conclusions that we have reached, is the discovery that the central axes of Khmer monuments, which are arranged symmetrically, and the center line of the temple are cleverly displaced while conforming to the scale and the method of determining the dimensions of each part (i.e., the design method). For example, in the case of Angkor Wat, considering the size of the Outer Gallery in terms of the cumulative total of other buildings, the plan was initially started with a square of 120 vyama (vm) x 120 vm (1 vm = 4 hasta (actual length of building scale ≒ 412 mm, cubit)) in mind. However, the west front Outer Gallery is 110 vm from north to south, and the east-west length is 130 vm, plus 10 vm left over from the north-south side, resulting in a long east-west temple compared with the initial plan. Naturally, the center line of the temple and the central axis of the building were coincident. From the initial plan, the length of the gallery on the right side facing the front was shortened by 2 vm at first. Since the central axis remains the same, a gap of 2 vm/2 (≒ 1648 mm) is generated between the invisible central line and the central axis in the actual gallery, resulting in a difference of 2 vm in the length of the left and right corridors. In order to make the building symmetrical, the column spacings on the left side of the Gallery are slightly narrower than those on the right side, and the number of columns is two more than on the right side. Since the width of the gopura of Angkor Wat is approximately 1.6 m x 2 = 3.2 m, the center line of the site, which is not visible to the eye, runs almost through the center of the wall of the gopura, thus preventing visitors from stepping on the center line of the site. It is not known whether Angkor Wat created the displacement with this in mind or not, but the size of the displacement differs depending on the temple. However, the method of creating the displacement is almost the same, even if the dimensional values are different.

The awareness of the prohibition that a sacred object that should occupy the center of the world must avoid the center of the shrine, temple site, or city is common to traditional Indian

きりとズレていることが視認できるように小塔で示されているのである。それに対して同様の影響を受けたと考えられるアンコールでは，私たちが実測した全ての寺院群の中心軸線と敷地の中心線が，はっきりと設計方法として算出され，裏付けられてズレているのである。アンコール・ワットは規模が大きく，見た目ではそれとは気付かないが，おそらく知る人ぞ知るというふうなものであろう。しかし，そこにどのような意味があるだろうか。

　例えば1999年頃までは遺跡入場の規制などはまだ無くて，満月の夜のアンコール・ワット中央塔群のテラス上に腰かけて，西側参道の方を眺めていた。夜の帳が降りると同時に，思わぬほど近くのジャングルの中から，鳥や昆虫の鳴き声が一斉にやってきた。青い月光が西方だけは遠くの山際まで目が届き，かすかに残る赤い残照の中にまどろむように溶け合っている。当時まだ，周囲にほとんど人がいなかったせいか，アンコール・ワットと私と原始の森，世界に囲まれている私，という気分になってくる。そういえば，中央段台テラスの上から参道を振り返るように眼をやると，内回廊と中回廊の間の境内の広さが，中回廊と外回廊の間では少し広がり，周壁，環濠，そして周囲の森と，かつては多分一面の水田であったに違いない外の世界へと広がっていくようだ。要するに三重の回廊や境内の広がりが，リズムを刻むように，あるいは池に投じた小石が水紋を広げていくように，中心から周辺へと何かがヒタヒタと広がり満ちていく感覚がある。かつて東南アジアの国の村々では，祖先が北方の山々から降りてきて村を開拓した，あるいはヒマラヤから聖なる力が高山に降臨し，村々に祀られるようになったと信じられてきた。だから祖霊神を象徴する寺院群の中心軸と祖先が切り拓いた場所を象徴する寺院境内の中心線という2つのカミの併存に，後からやってきた新しい神々や文明の力がそこに乗っかってきたのではないか。クメールの寺院や聖地に，祠堂群の中心軸と敷地の中心線を目立たぬように，しかし2つの価値軸によって立つことを表明するために確実に確保した。このようにして，新しい神や文明や権力と元からある歴史や自然環境との調和が大切であることをクメールの人々が受け継いできたことの証左とその中味を，寺院配置や佇まいの，インドやインドネシアとクメールの違いの中に見出し，想像せざるをえなかった。アンコール・ワットの中心部の段台テラスから外を視た時，気持ちが広がっていくように感じたり，周囲の森と溶け合っているように感じるのは偶然ではなく，動かし難い共有感覚の表現によるものだと思う。自然やそこに流れる脈々とした伝統的共通感覚の力が，アンコールの聖なる空間を創造してきたに違いない。私達JSA/JASAの科学的総合研究は，回

religious views without Buddhism. Notable among Hindu temples is the layout of the Prambanan Temple Complex, Indonesia, which was strongly influenced by India. The location of the central shrine (the principal image) is indicated by a small tower so that it can be seen as being clearly displaced from the center of the site. In contrast, at Angkor, which is thought to have been similarly influenced, the center axis of all the temples we have measured and the center line of the site are clearly calculated and supported by the design method. Angkor Wat has a large scale and is probably well-known to those who know it, although it is not noticeable to the naked eye. But what does this mean?

Until around 1999, for example, there were still no entry pass to the Angkor Monuments, and I was sitting on the terrace of Angkor Wat's central tower complex on a full-moon night, looking toward the western approach. As soon as the night curtain fell, the chirping of birds and insects came in unison from unexpectedly close by in the jungle. It could be seen only the westward illuminated by blue moonlight, and the sight was mixed with red afterglow. Perhaps it was because there were few people around at the time, but I began to feel like I was surrounded by Angkor Wat, myself, the pristine forest, and the world. When I look back at the causeway from the top of the central terrace, it seems that the space between the Inner and Middle Galleries widens a little between the middle and Outer Galleries, and then spreads out to the perimeter wall, the moat, the surrounding forest, and the outside world, which must have once been covered with rice paddies. In short, there is a sense that something is spreading and filling the area from the center to the surrounding area, as if the three-layered galleries and the expanse of the temple grounds were marking a rhythm, or as if pebbles thrown into a pond were spreading a pattern of water. In the past, villages in Southeast Asian countries believed that ancestors came down from the northern mountains to settle their villages, or that a sacred power descended from the Himalayas to the high mountains and came to be worshipped in their villages. Therefore, the coexistence of two gods, the central axis of the temple complex symbolizing the ancestral gods and the central line of the temple precincts symbolizing the place carved out by the ancestors, must have been carried there by the new gods and forces of civilization that came later. They designed the central axis of the temple and the central line of the site were discreetly but surely secured in Khmer temples and sacred sites to express that they stood by two axes of value. In this way, I cannot help imaging the intension to harmonize the new gods, civilization, and power, with initial history, and natural environment, in the differences of layout plan and appearance of the temples between India, Indonesia, and Khmer. When I looked out from the terrace in the center of Angkor Wat, I felt as if my feelings were expanding and blending with the surrounding forest, which was not an accident but an expression of an unmovable common sense, I

りまわっていえば，そのことを明らかにしてきたことに他ならない。

2. アンコールの森と水と村

アンコール・ワットはクメール建築の総合的な意味での歴史的な到達点であったと既に述べた。正統とはそのことである。では，以上のようなクメールの伝統的空間感覚からいえばバイヨンはどうなのだろうか。

先の3.3「クメール建築設計方法とバイヨン」では，バイヨン創建時は，ヒンドゥー寺院として，伽藍は確かに左右非対称に計画されたが，後の仏教化時にそれは解消された，その名残が南側外回廊の屈曲として痕跡が残っている，そしてバイヨンの本格的仏教化を基点としてクメール帝国の歴史は変容した，と興味深い指摘を残している。

バイヨンの現状は，当然直線であるべきところが湾曲していたり，驚くべき細部の納まりがあったり，寸法のバラツキが大き過ぎたりと，設計方法の分析には極めてやっかいな難題である。バイヨンについてもEFEO（フランス極東学院）による膨大な実測図の労作があるが，何しろ詳細な寸法値が記載されているものが少ない。JSAでも以前に全体測量を試行したが，納まりがつかないままに中断していたが，近年3D測量と写真測量と手計りを駆使して，細部から全体までバイヨン実測図決定版の作製に取りかかったところである。

バイヨンは高密度な建築の集積であって，しかもメタモルフォースのように変容を重ねてきた。しかも彫刻だけでなく，組石方法も，熟練工人による，アドホックな，ある意味ではその場しのぎではあるが，極めて巧妙に，素早く建造された建築である。結果的にバラついた寸法や驚くべき納まりが残されているのは当然だったかもしれない。しかし計画は必ず存在したハズである。私たちはこれからもトライを重ねるが，アンコール遺跡の建築設計方法に興味を持った人は是非その研究に参加していただきたいと思う。これも以前からトライしてきたが，少しずつ進展しているところである。現状バイヨンの近辺には環濠が確定されていないこともあって，アンコール・トムのおよそ3km×3km城壁の外のお堀がバイヨンの環濠を兼ねているのでは，という前提のもとに，GPSを使った広域測量を行った。その時の暫定的な結論では，バイヨンはアンコール・トムの中心点からははっきりとズレて立地していたのである。もしそうであれば，後に仏教寺院に改宗したからといってどうすることもできない。私たちは今はまだ信頼できる数値は出せないが，ア

believe. I am sure that the power of nature and the traditional common sense that flows through it has created the sacred space of Angkor. Our comprehensive scientific research at JSA has revealed this indirectly.

2. Forest, Water, and Village in Angkor

We have already mentioned that Angkor Wat was a historical achievement in the overall sense of Khmer architecture, and in its orthodoxy. Then, how is Bayon in terms of the traditional Khmer sense of space as described above?

In the previous section 3.3, "Dimension planning method in Khmer architecture and the Bayon", the section described that when the Bayon was built, it was planned as a Hindu temple with asymmetrical architecture. However, when the temple was converted to Buddhism, the traces of change were left as the bend in the southern Outer Gallery. The history of Khmer Kingdom was transformed based on the full-scale conversion by Jayavarman VII to Buddhism and is manifested in the Bayon.

The current state of the Bayon is an extremely difficult to analyze in terms of the design method, as there are curves in what should naturally be straight lines, surprising details, and too many variations in dimensions. There are a large number of drawings of the Bayon by EFEO, however the drawings with detailed dimension values are very few. JSA also tried to measure the entire Bayon in the past, but it was suspended temporally without being able to settle on the exact dimensions. In recent years, we began to produce the drawing of Bayon with detailed dimensional values based on 3D scanning and photogrammetry.

Bayon is an accumulation of high-density architectural elements that has been transformed through some sort of metamorphosis into one unique homogeneous structure. Moreover, not only the sculptures but also the stonework was, in a sense, ad hoc. All phases of construction and decoration executed by craftsmen with great skill while at the same time quickly erecting the temple component. In the end, it may have been natural that the resultant disparate dimensions and surprising fittings would have remained unaltered. However, a plan must have existed. We will continue to try elucidate the Bayon, and we hope that those who are interested in the architectural design methods of the Angkor Monuments will participate in our research. We have been encouraging participation for some time, and we are gradually making progress.

Since the moat encircling Bayon has not yet been determined, we conducted a wide-area survey using GPS based on the assumption that the moat outside the 3 x 3 km walls of Angkor Thom may also serve as the moat encircling Bayon. The conclusion was that the Bayon was located at

ンコール・トム敷地の中心点を外してバイヨンが設定されている、と少なくとも私は考えている。

それは何を意味するのか。アンコール・ワットの時代では、伽藍敷地は祖先が切り拓いた聖なる土地、即ち自然に依拠した生活と伝統的価値観の象徴であった。それと新しい神、文明、国家を象徴する新しい建築群とその中心軸が調和して共存することが空間に表象されたクメール民族の哲学であり、価値観であり、共同的な空間感覚であったと言えよう。この時、伽藍敷地は自然の表象であり、世界を象徴するものであった。しかしバイヨンにおいて、伽藍が都市に拡大した時、アンコール・トムという首都を越えて、クメール帝国の隅々までも含めた世界との調和という意識を強めることにもなったと言えそうだ。このことは単なる妄想の飛躍ではない。

バイヨン外観の一番の特徴は、いくつもの沈潜した表情の尊顔に見つめられている、という感覚によって視るものの内面が泡立てられることである。これはかつてあった中央塔の四面仏が落下喪失していることもあろう。中心性がやや希薄になっていることである。奈良の大仏はその絶対性が外観建物にも顕在しているため、明快な秩序を強制してくる。もし残存していたとしても中央塔の尊顔と他の、数多くの尊顔の大きさは、どれも高さが2m内外であること、四面仏の多くが後の時代に半眼や瞑想形に掘り直されて、群をなして迫ってくるため、より悲しげな、反省を強いてくるような気持ちになるのである。それに対して、バイヨンの内観といえば、一つ一つの塔は彫刻のようなものだから、内部空間は、中央塔群回りとして考えると、特に太陽が真上から照りつけてくる日中、ここを巡っていると、あらゆる方向から、あらゆる神々によって射すくめられ、もう降参するしかない白昼夢の世界に彷徨うことになる。これは実は興味深い感受の世界であって、建物の外観によって内向的な意識を、そして内観によって自己意識が世界の隅々にまで飛ばされるという体験だと言えそうである。ヒンドゥー教も仏教もアジアの古代社会の共同意識が生み出した自己意識の絶対化であると言えよう。自分が自分に支配されるという構造である。アンコールの伝統社会では共同性がなじみ深い自然や身近な習俗とその延長であるため、無意識に支配されてきたと考えられる。しかしバイヨンの時代は、版図の拡大による未知の世界の新たな発見があり、そして仏教思想による個人の意識が庶民層にも登場してきたように、バイヨン外回廊の浅浮彫を見ると思われる。

西洋諸国がアジア、特に前アジア的古代に興味を持ち始めたのは18世紀からで、これは西洋・近代合理主義のもとに世界を制覇したことと対になっていた。19世

a distinctly off-geometric center point from the center of Angkor Thom for a reason. If so, there is nothing to prohibit the temple from later converted to a Buddhist temple.

What does it mean? In the era of Angkor Wat, the site of the temple complex was a symbol of the sacred land carved out by their ancestors, i.e., a life relying on nature and traditional values. The harmonious coexistence of the central axis of the new architectural complex, which symbolized a new god, civilization, and nation, was the philosophy, values, and communal sense of space of the Khmer people. At this time, the site of the temple complex was a representation of nature and a symbol of the world of the gods. However, when the complex of Bayon expanded into a city, it also strengthened the sense of harmony with the world, including all corners of the Angkor Empire, beyond Angkor Thom, the capital city of Angkor. This is not a mere leap of imagination, but a statement of protection, and harmony within all parts of the kingdom.

The most distinctive feature of the façade of the Bayon is that the viewer's inner self is awakened by the sensation of being gazed upon by a number of transcendent, spiritual faces. This may be due in part to the loss of the face of the Central Tower. The centrality has become slightly diluted. The absolute nature of the Great Buddha of Nara is evident in the exterior architecture, which enforces a clear sense of order. Even if the faces had survived, the Central Tower and many of the other faces would have been 2 m or less in height, and many of the faced would have been re-engineered in later periods into half-eyes or meditative forms and would have loomed in groups, making us feel as if we were forced to reflect on them in a sadder way. The exact configuration is unknown. In contrast, considering the spatiality of the Bayon, when I walk around the Central Tower, during the day time, all of gods face to me from all directions and I fall into a trance that I had no choice but to surrender to the spirits. This is actually an interesting world of perception It is an experience in which the façade of a building transports one's introverted consciousness and one's introspection to all corners of the world. It could be said that both Hinduism and Buddhism are a release of the sense of self created by the communal consciousness of ancient Asian societies. It is a structure in which the self is governed by the self. In the traditional society of Angkor, the community was governed unconsciously because it was an extension of nature and familiar customs and practices. However, in the Bayon period, the new discovery of a expanded mysterious world by enlargement of territory and the appearance of individual consciousness through Buddhist philosophy in the general population seems to be seen in the bas-relief in the Outer Gallery of Bayon.

Western countries began to take interest in Asia, especially in pre-Asian antiquity, since 18th century, which was paired with the conquest of the world under Western modern

紀末からの，EFEOのアンコール研究はフランスのインドシナ植民地支配の一環だけだったとは言わないが，ポルポト内戦以降の1980年代末にカンボジア・アンコールを視る眼は変わったように思う。18世紀以後世界の普遍性であった西洋近代合理主義では，世界はもう立ちいかないのでは，という思考である。近代文明の再考は1960年代に始まるが，アンコール研究では80年代末だった。それまではアンコールの美の解明が研究の目的であったが，なぜその美が生み出されたのか，という問題に関心がシフトしたように思われる。それはEFEOだけでなく，日本も含めたアンコール研究全体の傾向であったと思う。では近代の反省がアンコールの何に向ったのだろうか。

　大まかにみて，四大古代文明が人類史を原始から離脱させたと言われる。各古代文明は周辺から多くのものを集めて形成され，様々な道筋があっただろうが，古代文明が形成された後，周辺はどうなるのか，という問題をここでは考えてみたい。文明の中心と周縁の関係を，かつては構造主義歴史観による考察が多く見られた。近年柄谷行人が，中心―周辺―亜周辺の関係を『世界史の構造』の中で論じられている。私は建築様式の伝播を中国―朝鮮半島―日本，および中国―北ベトナム―中部ベトナムの関係の中で考察してきた。ここでは先に述べたインド―インドネシア―クメールの関係として述べると，分かりやすいと思う。聖なるものを空間の中心から避けるという方法について，とにかく避ける（インド），はっきり分かりやすいように避ける（インドネシア），何となく以心伝心で避ける（クメール）という違いがあるように思う。高度な中心から押し寄せる波は避けようがないので，過剰に受けてしまう（周辺）のに対し，適当な距離を隔てているが故に，良いものは自分の環境や事情に応じて，選択的に受容する（亜周辺）という方法である。古代―古典古代―中世―近代の歴史的展開は巨視的には自然史的な必然である。古代を全面的に受け入れた周辺は中心と運命を共にするしかないだろう。しかし，中心のいいものを自分勝手に受け入れて，そこにだけある自然環境と自分達だけの伝統と，まず調和させることを第一義に考えてきたクメールのやり方は，世界古代文明の古層にありながら最先端でもありうるような環境調和思想である。また，外からのヒンドゥー，仏教の視線（バイヨン外観）と個人の中の土地霊，祖霊との交換（バイヨンの白日夢）を通して，今，ここから脱出する夢を無意識のうちに視ることができるアンコールの歴史とバイヨンの新しい地平が注目される。

　アンコール遺跡に入っていくと，すぐ近くに深い森がある。その森は一年中，カサコソと枯葉が鳴り，木漏れ

rationalism. From my point of view, EFEO's interpretation of Angkor, seems to have changed at the end of the 1980s, after the Pol Pot regime. I think, They had doubt the world could no longer stand on the basis of Western modern rationalism, which had been a universal principle since the 18th century. The rethinking of modern civilization began in the 1960s, but it was not until the end of the 1980s that I began to study Angkor. Until then, the goal of research had been to elucidate the beauty of Angkor, but interest seems to have shifted to the question of why that beauty was created. I think this was the trend not only in EFEO but also in Angkor studies as a whole, including Japan. Then, what did the reflection of modernity turn to in Angkor?

Roughly speaking, four major ancient civilizations are said to have taken human history out of its primitive state. Each ancient civilization was formed by gathering many things from the periphery and had many different paths, but here we would like to consider the question of what happens to the periphery after an ancient civilization is formed. The relationship between the center and the periphery of civilization was once often considered from a structuralist historical perspective. Recently, Karatani Kōjin has discussed the center - periphery - sub-periphery relationship in his "The Structure of World History". I have examined the spread of architectural styles in the context of China - the Korean Peninsula - Japan and China - North Vietnam - Central Vietnam relationships. I think it is easier to understand the relationship here as the India - Indonesia - Khmer one I mentioned earlier. There seems to be a difference in the way of avoiding sacred objects from the center: avoiding them anyway (India), avoiding them in a clear and obvious way (Indonesia), and avoiding them slightly (Khmer). The waves coming from the center cannot be avoided, so peripheral area is received excessively, while those sub peripheral area is accepted selectively according to one's environment and circumstances, as they are separated by an appropriate distance. The historical development of ancient - classical antiquity - medieval - modernity is macroscopically inevitable on the view from natural history. The periphery that fully accepts antiquity will have no choice but to share its fate with the center. However, the Khmer make a choice to accept the tradition that is harmonized with nature and their traditions from the center. This is an environmental harmonization philosophy that could be the most advanced in the ancient civilization of the world, even though it is in the ancient layer of the world. Also, through the exchange between the Hindu and Buddhist gaze from outside and the land spirits and ancestral spirits within the individual, it is confirmed the history of Angkor and Bayon's new horizon, where one can unconsciously see the dream of escaping from here and now.

As you enter the ruins of Angkor, you can see a deep forest nearby. The forest is hot all year round with the rustling of dead leaves and the sun shining through the trees. Although it is the dry season and the earth is cracking, you can hear the

日が暑い。乾期で大地がひび割れているのにどこからか、ヒタヒタと水が押し寄せてくる音がする。街は喧噪であふれていることと対になっているようだ。近代に疲れた人々は何を夢見たのだろうか。

　アンコール遺跡の敷地の中心線と聖なる建物の中心軸がそれとなく維持され，バイヨンの基壇版築土層がオリジナルな方法で修復されなければならない。なぜそれらが保存されなければならないか。その謎が解けたら，アンコール遺跡もバイヨンも甦るだろう。アンコールの森と水と村は再生するだろう。それができたら近代以降の新しい歴史が始まるだろう。それが希望である。

sound of water rushing in from somewhere. It seems to be paired with the fact that the city is full of hustle and bustle. What did tired people for modernity dream ?

The central line of the Angkor site and the central axis of the sacred temples must be maintained, and the foundation of the Bayon must be restored in the original way it was built. Why must they be preserved? When the mystery is solved, both the Angkor Monuments and the Bayon will be restored. The forests, waters, and villages of Angkor will be restored. Once that is done, a new history after the modern era will begin. That is a hope.

Biography of Authors｜執筆者略歴

Chapter 1｜第 1 章

NAKAGAWA Takeshi
中川　武

JSA Director General / JASA Co-Director / Professor Emeritus, Faculty of Science and Engineering, Waseda University
JSA 団長／ JASA 共同代表／早稲田大学 理工学術院 名誉教授
Dr.Eng.
工学博士

1. T. Nakagawa, Y. Iwasaki: The significant meaning of the conservation of authenticity about block planning and foundation structure at Bayon temple and other Angkor's ruins, The 12th International Symposium on Architectural Interchanges in Asia, Pyeongchang, Korea, 2018.
2. T. Nakagawa: Research on the Ancient Architectural and City Ruins of Phnom Kulen and Quarries in the Surrounding Area, The 17th Science Council of Asia Board Meeting and International Symposium, Manila, Philippine, 2017.
3. T. Nakagawa: Bayon Great Buddha Restoration, Reconstruction and Reinstallation Project, The 15th Science Council of Asia Board Meeting and International Symposium, Siem Reap, Cambodia, pp.55-58, 2015.

Chapter 3｜第 3 章

IWASAKI Yoshinori
岩崎 好規

Adviser, Geo-Research Institute / Honorary Doctor from St. Petersburg State University of Architecture and Civil Engineering, Russia/ Ph.D. from Karaganda State Technical University, Kazakhstan/ Dr.Eng. from Kyoto University/ M.S. in Geotechnical Engineering, UC, Berkeley / P.E.
一般財団法人 GRI 財団（地域地盤環境研究所）顧問／サンクトペテルブルク州立建築・土木工学大学（ロシア）名誉博士／カラガンダ州立工科大学 Ph.D.（カザフスタン）／京都大学 博士（工学）／米国加州立大（バークレー校）M.S. ／技術士
M.S. in Geotechnical Engineering / Ph.D. / Dr.Eng. / P.E.
博士（工学），技術士

1. Y.Iwasaki, M.Fukuda: Preservation of the main tower of Bayon temple, Angkor, Cambodia, Geotechnics and Heritage -Historic Towers, Taylor & Francis Group, London, pp.191-227, 2018.
2. Y.Iwasaki, Y.Akazawa, M.Fukuda, J.Nakazawa, K.Nakagawa, I.Shimoda, T.Nakagawa: Dismantling for reconstitution of N1 Tower of Prasat Sour Prat, Angkor Thom, Cambodia, Geotechnical Engineering for the Preservation of Monuments and Historic Sites, CRC Press, A Balkema Book, pp.455-463, 2013.
3. Y.Iwasaki: Geotechnical Overview of Sustainable Conservation and Development for the World Heritage Area of Angkor, Cambodia, Chapter 6, World heritage in Asia, Geotechnics and Earthquake Geotechnics towards Global Sustainability, Geotechnical Geological, and Earthquake Engineering, Vol.15, Springer, pp.89-113, 2011.

FUKUDA Mitsuharu
福田 光治

Geotechnical Engineering Advisor, Taisei Geotec. Co., Ltd.
大成ジオテック株式会社 技術顧問
Dr.Eng., P.E.
博士（工学），技術士

1. M. Fukuda, Y. Iwasaki: Interpretation on Unsaturated Character of Foundation Fills of Angkor Complexes, Geotechnical engineering magazine, Vol.67(9), pp.8-11, 2019.
   福田光治，岩崎好規，本郷隆夫，下田一太：カンボジアアンコール遺跡基壇盛土材料締固め曲線の不飽和土特性としての解釈（特集 不飽和土の地盤特性），地盤工学会誌，Vol.67(9)，pp.8-11，2019.
2. M. Fukuda, Y. Iwasaki, T. Hongo, T. Koyama, R. Kuwajima, T. Nakagawa, M. Ishizuka: Strength Level of Sand Stone and Laterite Brock piled up at Bayon temple, Angkor by Equotip Rebound Hardness, Proceeding of the 51st Annual Convention of Japanese Geotechnical Society, pp.133-134, 2016.
   福田光治，岩崎好規，本郷隆夫，小山倫史，桑島流音，中川武，石塚充雅：アンコール遺跡砂岩とラテライトの風化レベルと強度，第 51 回地盤工学研究発表会講演概要集，pp.133-134，2016.
3. M. Fukuda, Y. Iwasaki, T. Nakagawa, M. Araya, S. Yamada, I. Shimoda: Bearing Capacity of Foundation of Angkor Ruin and Reconstitution, 58th Geotechnical Symposium, Japanese Geotechnical Society, pp.241-248, 2013.

福田光治，岩崎好規，中川武，新谷眞人，山田俊亮，下田一太：アンコール遺跡基壇の支持力と再構築，第 58 回地盤工学シンポジウム発表論文集，地盤工学会，pp.241-248，2013.

OKOCHI Hiroshi
大河内 博

Professor, Faculty of Science and Engineering, Waseda University
早稲田大学 理工学術院 教授
Dr.Eng.
博士（工学）

1. .Uchiyama, H.Okochi, N.Katsumi, H.Ogata: The impact of air pollutants on rainwater chemistry during "Urban-induced heavy rainfall" in downtown Tokyo, Japan, Journal of Geophysical Research: Atmospheres, 2017.
2. N. Katsumi, S. Miyake, H. Okochi, Y. Minami, H. Kobayashi, S. Kato, R. Wada, M. Takeuchi, K. Toda, K. Miura: Humiclike substances global levels and extraction methods in aerosols, Environmental Chemistry Letters, 1-7, 2019.
3. Y. Wang, H. Okochi, M. Igawa: Characteristics of Fog and Fog Collection with Passive Collector at Mt. Oyama in Japan, Water Air Soil Pollut, 232, Article number: 260, 2021.

MIZOGUCHI Akinori
溝口 明則

Former professor, Faculty of Science and Engineering, Meijo University
元 名城大学 理工学部 教授
Dr.Eng
工学博士

1. T. Nakagawa, A. Mizoguchi eds: PREAH VIHEAR ARCHITECTURAL STUDY ON THE PROVINCIAL SITES OF THE KHMER EMPIRE No.2, Chuo Koron Bijutsu Shuppan, 2018.
   中川武 , 溝口明則監修：プレア・ヴィヘア　アンコール広域拠点遺跡群の建築学的研究　2，中央公論美術出版，2018.
2. T.Nakagawa, A.Mizoguchi eds: KOH KER AND BENG MEALEA ARCHITECTURAL STUDY ON THE PROVINCIAL SITES OF THE KHMER EMPIRE, Chuo Koron Bijutsu Shuppan, 2014.
   中川武 , 溝口明則監修：コー・ケーとベン・メアレア　アンコール広域拠点遺跡群の建築学的研究，中央公論美術出版，2014.
3. A.Mizoguchi, T.Nakagawa, K.Sato, I.Shimoda: THE ANCIENT KHMER'S DIMENSIONAL PLANNING AT THE PRASAT THOM IN KOH KER: Study on the dimensional plan and the planning method of Khmer architecture No.5, J. Archit. Plann., AIJ, 75(653), pp.1751-1759, 2010.
   溝口明則，中川武，佐藤桂，下田一太：プラサート・トムの伽藍寸法計画：クメール建築の造営尺度と設計技術に関する研究 (5)，日本建築学会計画系論文集，第 75 巻，第 653 号，pp. 1751-1759，2010.

NARUI Itaru
成井 至

JASA Technical Assistant / Researcher, Faculty of Science and Engineering, Waseda University
JASA 技術補佐／早稲田大学 理工学術院 研究員
M.Arch.
修士（建築学）

1. I. Narui, T. Nakagawa, A. Mizoguchi, M. Koiwa, M. Ishizuka, C. Kuroiwa: Consideration on the Initial Plan about the Corridor with Pillar in Angkor Site -Study on Preah Khan de Kompong Svay, Cambodia part 3, Summ. Tech. Paper of Annual Meeting, AIJ, pp.839-840, 2017.
   成井至，中川武，溝口明則，小岩正樹，石塚充雅，黒岩千尋：アンコール期大型寺院における列柱回廊の計画方法の分析　カンボジア　コンポン・スヴァイのプレア・カーン寺院に関する研究（3），日本建築学会大会学術講演梗概集，日本建築学会，pp.839-840，2017.
2. I. Narui, T. Nakagawa, M. Koiwa: On the Dimensional Plan in Prasat Sambor Monuments in Sambor Prei Kuk Monuments – Study on the technique of planning methods in times in Pre-Angkor period (1), J. Archit. Plann., AIJ. Vol.84 (760), pp.1463-1472, 2019.
   成井至，中川武，小岩正樹：サンボー・プレイ・クック遺跡群北寺院群における祠堂平面計画－プレ・アンコール期における造営技術の研究　その 1，日本建築学会計画系論文集，第 84 巻，第 760 号，pp.1463-1472，2019.
3. I. Narui: Architectural Study on Sambor Prei Kuk Monuments, Waseda University Master's Thesis, 2018.
   成井至：サンボー・プレイ・クック遺跡群の建築学研究」，早稲田大学修士論文，2018.

NISHIMOTO Shinichi
西本 真一

Professor, Department of Architecture, Nippon Institute of Technology
日本工業大学 建築学科 教授
Dr.Eng.
工学博士

1. S. Nishimoto: The Construction Process of Bayon Temple, Ars Buddhica, Vol. 274, pp.97-110, 2004.
   西本真一：バイヨン寺院の建造過程，佛教藝術 274，pp.97-110，2004.
2. S. Nishimoto, S. Yoshimura, J. Kondo: Hieratic Inscriptions from the Quarry at Qurna: An Interim Report, British Museum Studies in Ancient Egypt and Sudan, The British Museum, pp.20-31, 2002.
3. S. Nishimoto (assistant editor): Bayon I; The Faces of the Towers, Part 1, Plates (T.Nakagawa ed.), Japanese Government Team for Safeguarding Angkor and UNESCO, Tokyo and Paris, 1999.

MIZUNO Saya
水野 さや

Professor, School of Humanities, College of Human and Social Sciences, Kanazawa University
金沢大学 人間社会学域 人文学類 教授
Doctor of Arts
博士（文学）

1. S. Mizuno: The View about the Fēng-shén (the Deity of Wind) Who is a Relative of the Attendants of the Sahasrabhuja-Avalokiteśvara, Bulletin of Kanazawa College of Art, Vol.67, pp.86(21)- 73(34), 2023.
   水野さや：千手観音諸眷属像における風神に関する一試論，金沢美術工芸大学紀要，第 67 号，pp.86(21)-73(34)，2023.
2. S. Mizuno: Establishment and development of the Eight-Devas (八部衆) Statue, Chuo Koron Bijutsu Shuppan, 2017.
   水野さや：八部衆像の成立と展開，中央公論美術出版，2017.
3. S. Mizuno: History of Buddhist Statues in Korea: from the Three Kingdoms period to the Joseon dynasty, Nagoyadaigaku Shuppankai, 2016.
   水野さや：韓国仏像史：三国時代から朝鮮王朝まで，名古屋大学出版会 , 2016.

TABATA Yukitsugu
田畑 幸嗣

Professor, Faculty of Letters, Arts and Sciences, Waseda University
早稲田大学 文学学術院 教授
Ph.D. in Area Studies
博士（地域研究）

1. Y. Tabata: A RESOURCE MANAGEMENT STRATEGY IN THE ANGKORIAN STONEWARE INDUSTRY, Preah Nokor No.2, pp.69-80, 2021.
2. Y. Tabata: Chronological Framework of Ceramic Trading in Angkorian Cambodia, in Sumio Fukami (ed): Multidisciplinary research in the ancient history of Southeast Asia, pp.37-49, Osaka, Research Institute of St.Andrew's University, 2016.
3. Y. Tabata: Recent Developments in Southeast Asian Archaeology, Asian Research Trends New Series, No.10, pp.59-75, 2015.

UCHIDA Etsuo
内田 悦生

Professor, Faculty of Science and Engineering, Waseda University
早稲田大学 理工学術院 教授
D.Sc.
理学博士

1. E. Uchida, Y. Kobayashi: Siliceous sandstones used in local Khmer temples in Battambang, Ta Keo, and Kampong Cham Provinces, Cambodia. Heritage, vol.7, pp.608–620. 2024.
2. E. Uchida, Y. Lu, L. Du: Non-destructive investigation of sandstone blocks used in the Wat Phu temple in Laos and the Banteay Chhmar temple in Cambodia. Heliyon, vol.9, e16357, 2023.
3. E. Uchida, R. Watanabe, R. Cheng, Y. Nakamura, T. Takeyama: Non-destructive in-situ classification of sandstones used in the Angkor monuments of Cambodia using a portable X-ray fluorescence analyzer and magnetic susceptibility meter. Journal of Archaeological Science: Reports, vol.39 ,103137, 2021.

MATSUI Toshiya
松井 敏也

Professor, Faculty of Art and Design, University of Tsukuba
筑波大学 芸術系 教授
Ph.D.
博士（学術）

1. T. Matsui, E. Kawasaki, M. Sawada: New Results of Conservation Science Reseach at the Bayon temple in Cambodia, 2017 International Symposium of Stone Conservation, pp.157-167, 2017.
   松井敏也，河﨑衣美，澤田正昭：カンボジアバイヨン寺院における保存科学の新展開，2017 International Symposium of Stone Conservation, pp.157-167，2017.

2. T. Matsui, E. Kawasaki, Y. Atomi: Studies on the vibration by tourists and epiphytes on stone at the Borobudur, 100 TAHUN PAS-CAPEMUGARAN CANDI BOROBUDUR, Balai Konservasi Borobudur, pp.77-91, 2012.

   松井敏也, 河﨑衣美, 跡見洋祐：ボロブドゥール寺院における観光客による振動と石材着生生物の調査, 100 TAHUN PASCAPEMUGARAN CANDI BOROBUDUR, Balai Konservasi Borobudur, pp.77-91, 2012.

3. T. Matsui, M. Sawada, S. Inoue, T. Ebisawa, E. Kawasaki, Y. Atomi, T. Nakagawa: A Study on Conservative Material for the Bas-Reliefs of the Bayon Temple in Angkor Monuments, Proceedings of the International Conference on Conservation of Stone and Earthen Architectural Heritage, 2014 ICOMOS-ISCS International Conference Organizing Committee, pp.138-144, 2014.

   松井敏也, 澤田正昭, 井上才八, 海老沢孝雄, 河﨑衣美, 跡見洋祐, 中川武：アンコール遺跡バイヨン寺院浮き彫りの保存のための保存修復材料, 2014 ICOMOS-ISCS International Conference Organizing Committee, pp.138-144, 2014.

KAWASAKI Emi
河﨑　衣美

Researcher, Archaeological Institute of Kashihara, Nara pref.
奈良県立橿原考古学研究所企画部資料課主任研究員
Ph.D.
博士（学術）

1. E. Kawasaki, T. Matsui, Y. Atomi, Y. Aikawa, M. Okano, M. Yuki: Investigation for Conservation and Utilization of Buildings Made with Bricks: A Case of Tomioka Silk Mill, 2019 Daejeon International Symposium on Conservation of Cultural Heritage in East Asia, pp.71-77, 2019.

   河﨑衣美, 松井敏也, 跡見洋祐, 相川悠, 岡野雅枝, 結城雅則：煉瓦造建造物の保存活用のための調査－富岡製糸場の試み, 2019 大田 東アジア文化遺産保存シンポジウムⅠ, pp.71-77, 2019.

2. E. Kawasaki: Inorganic analysis of lichens for stone heritage conservation, Lichenology, Vol. 12, no. 2, pp.79-80, 2014.

   河﨑衣美：石造文化遺産の保護と地衣類の無機分析, Lichenology, Vol. 12, no. 2, pp.79-80, 2014.

3. E. Kawasaki, T. Matsui, Y. Yamamoto, K. Hara: The documentation method using lichens growing on stoneworks in order to protect cultural heritage stone monuments : the case of Angkor monuments of Cambodia, Lichenology, Vol. 11, no. 2, pp.39-52, 2013.

   河﨑衣美, 松井敏也, 山本好和, 原光二郎：石造文化遺産保存を目的とする地衣類の記録方法の確立に関する研究：カンボジア, アンコール遺跡の事例, Lichenology, Vol. 11, no. 2, pp.39-52, 2013.

KATAYAMA Yoko
片山　葉子

Guest Researcher, Center for Conservation Science, Independent Administrative Institution, Tokyo National Research Institute for Cultural Properties / Emeritus Professor, Tokyo University of Agriculture and Technology
独立行政法人国立文化財機構 東京文化財研究所 保存科学研究センター 客員研究員／東京農工大学 名誉教授
Ph.D.
農学博士

1. R. Iizuka, S. Hattori, Y. Kosaka, Y. Masaki, Y. Kawano, I. Ohtsu, D. Hibbett, Y. Katayama, M. Yoshida: Sulfur assimilation using gaseous carbonyl sulfide by the soil fungus Trichoderma harzianum. Applied and Environmental Microbiology, Vol. 90, e02015-23, 2024.

2. X. Ding, W. Lan, J. Li, M. Deng, Y. Li, Y. Katayama, J-D. Gu. Metagenomic insight into the pathogenic-related characteristics and resistome profiles within microbiome residing on the Angkor sandstone monuments in Cambodia. Science of The Total Environment, Vol. 918,170402, 2024.

3. T. Inaba, T. Hori, M. Tsuchiya, H. Ihara, E. Uchida, J-D. Gu, Y. Katayama. Microscopic evidence of sandstone deterioration and damage by fungi isolated from the Angkor monuments in simulation experiments. Science of The Total Environment, Vol. 896, 165265, 2023.

GU Ji-Dong
顧　繼東

Professor, Environmental Science and Engineering Research Group, Guangdong Technion-Israel Institute of Technology / Israel Institute of Technology
広東イスラエル工科学院 環境工学学科／イスラエル工科学院 教授
Ph.D.
学術博士

1. X. Liu, R. J. Koestler, T. Warscheid, Y. Katayama, J-D.Gu: Microbial deterioration and sustainable conservation of stone monuments and buildings, Nature Sustainability, Vol.3, pp.991-1004, 2020.

2. X. Ding, W. Lan, J. Li, M. Deng, Y. Li, Y. Katayama, J-D. Gu. Metagenomic insight into the pathogenic-related characteristics and resistome profiles within microbiome residing on the Angkor sandstone monuments in Cambodia. Science of The Total Environment, Vol. 918,170402, 2024.

3. T. Inaba, T. Hori, M. Tsuchiya, H. Ihara, E. Uchida, J-D. Gu, Y. Katayama. Microscopic evidence of sandstone deterioration and damage by fungi isolated from the Angkor monuments in simulation experiments. Science of The Total Environment, Vol. 896, 165265, 2023.

OISHI Takeshi

大石 岳史

Associate Professor, Institute of Industrial Science, The University of Tokyo
東京大学 生産技術研究所 准教授
Ph.D. in Interdisciplinary Information Studies
博士（学際情報学）

1. T. Nemoto, T. Kobayashi, M. Kagesawa, T. Oishi, H. Kurokochi, S. Yoshimura, E. Ziddan, M. Taha, "Virtual Restoration of Ancient Wooden Ships Through Non-rigid 3D Shape Assembly with Ruled-Surface FFD," International Journal of Computer Vision, 131, 1269–1283, 2023.
2. K. Ikeuchi, T. Oishi eds.: 3D Digital Archive, University of Tokyo Press, 2010.
   池内克史，大石岳史（編著）：3次元デジタルアーカイブ，東京大学出版会，2010.
3. T. Oishi, A. Nakazawa, R. Kurazume, K. Ikeuchi: Fast Simultaneous Alignment of Multiple Range Images using Index Images, Proc. The 5th Int'l Conf. 3-D Digital Imaging and Modeling, pp.476-483, 2005.

IKEUCHI Katsushi

池内 克史

Emeritus Professor, The University of Tokyo
東京大学 名誉教授
Ph.D. in Engineering
工学博士

1. K. Ikeuchi, D. Miyazaki: Digitally Archiving Cultural Objects, Springer, 2008.
2. A. Banno, T. Masuda, T. Oishi, K. Ikeuchi: Flying Laser Range Sensor for Large-Scale Site-Modeling and Its Applications in Bayon Digital Archival Project, International Journal of Computer Vision, Vol.78, No.2-3, pp.207-222, 2008.
3. K. Ikeuchi, T. Oishi, J. Takamatsu, R. Sagawa, A. Nakazawa, R. Kurazume, K. Nishino, M. Kamakura, Y. Okamoto: The Great Buddha Project -Digitally Archiving, Restoring, and Analyzing Cultural Heritage Objects, International Journal of Computer Vision, Vol.75, No.1, pp.189-208, 2007.

YAMADA Shunsuke

山田 俊亮

Assistant Professor, Faculty of Human Ecology, Yasuda Women's University
安田女子大学 家政学部 助教
M.Eng.
修士（工学）

1. S. Yamada, R. Hashimoto, T. Koyama, M. Fukuda, Y. Iwasaki: Study on evaluation method of reinforcement effect of dry masonry in historical monuments applying DDA, Structural Analysis of Historical Constructions, SAHC 2023, Volume 2, RILEM Bookseries vol.46, Springer, pp.41-50, 2023.
2. S. Yamada, M. Araya, A. Yoshida, T. Oishi: Structural stability evaluation study applying wind tunnel test and monitoring of Bayon main tower, Angkor Thom in Cambodia, Structural Studies, Repairs and Maintenance of Heritage Architecture XV, WIT Transactions on The Built Environment, Vol.171, pp.287-296, 2017.
3. S. Yamada, M. Araya, K. Fukushima: Seismic safety evaluation and reinforcement design of Honjo Brick Warehouse, Structural Analysis of Historical Constructions – Anamnesis, diagnosis, therapy, controls, pp.1650-1655, 2016.

HASHIMOTO Ryota

橋本 涼太

Associate Professor, Graduate School of Engineering, Kyoto University
京都大学大学院 工学研究科 准教授 Dr.Eng.
博士（工学）

1. R. Hashimoto, M. Kikumoto, T. Koyama, M. Mimura: Method of deformation analysis for composite structures of soils and masonry stones, Computers and Geotechnics, Vol.82, pp.67-84, 2017.
2. R. Hashimoto, T. Koyama, M. Kikumoto, M. Mimura: A study on the bearing capacity characteristics of masonry structure foundation in Angkor, Cambodia, Journal of Japanese Geotechnical Society Chugoku Branch, Vol.35(1), pp.137-144, 2017.
   橋本涼太，小山倫史，菊本統，三村衛：カンボジア・アンコール遺跡の石積構造物基礎の支持力特性に関する一考察，地盤と建設，Vol.35(1)，pp.137–144，2017.
3. R. Hashimoto, T. Sueoka, T. Koyama, M. Kikumoto: Improvement of discontinuous deformation analysis incorporating implicit updating scheme of friction and joint strength degradation, Rock Mechanics and Rock Engineering, Vol.54, pp.4239-4263, 2021.

KOYAMA Tomofumi

小山 倫史

Professor, Faculty of Social Safety Sciences, Kansai University
関西大学 社会安全学部 教授
Ph.D (Land and water resources sciences)
博士（資源・水資源工学）

1. T. Koyama: Geotechnical engineering issues for stabilization and restoration/preservation of Bayon temple, Angkor ruins, JSCE Magazine, Civil Engineering, Vol.105, No.8, pp.38-39, 2020.
   小山倫史：アンコール遺跡バイヨン寺院の安定化と修復・保存のための地盤工学，土木学会誌，Vol.105，No.8，pp.38-39，2020.

2. R. Kuwajima, T.Koyama, R.Hashimoto, Y.Iwasaki, M.Ishizuka: Geotechnical investigation and deformation analysis by 3-D laser scanning at Gopura 3rd, Preah Vihear Temple, Cambodia, Proc. of the 35th of JSSSCP congress, pp.20-21, 2018.
   桑島流音，小山倫史，橋本涼太，岩崎好規，福田光治，石塚光雅：プレア・ヴィヘア寺院第三ゴープラにおける地盤調査と3次元計測による変状分析，日本文化財科学会第35回大会研究発表要旨集，pp. 20-21，2018.

3. R. Hashimoto, M. Kikumoto, T.Koyama, M.Mimura: Method of deformation analysis for composite structures of soils and masonry stones, Computers and Geotechnics, Vol.82, No.2, pp.67-84, 2016.

Robert McCarthy

ロバート・マッカーシー

JASA Volunteer Staff
JASA ボランティアスタッフ

1. R. McCarthy: Study on Unearthed Stone and Sandy Soil Elements, Annual Technical Report on the Survey of Angkor Monument 2014 - 2015, JAPAN-APSARA Safeguarding Angkor, pp.99-108, 2015.

2. N. Yamamoto, Kou Vet, Lun Votey, R. McCarthy, Chhum Menghong: Excavation Survey, Annual Technical Report on the Survey of Angkor Monument 2012 - 2013, pp.81-88, 2014.

3. R. McCarthy: Hazardous Element Survey Report of the Bayon, Report on the Conservation and Restoration Work of the Southern Library of Bayon, Angkor Thom, Kingdom of Cambodia, BOOK II, JAPAN-APSARA Safeguarding Angkor, pp.330-360, 2011.

Chapter 4 ｜ 第 4 章

AKAZAWA Yasushi

赤澤　泰

Guest Junior Researcher, [Guest Assistant Professor], Waseda Research Institute for Science and Engineering
早稲田大学理工学術院総合研究所 客員次席研究員（研究院客員講師）
Dr.Engineering
工学博士

1. Y. Akazawa, T. Nakagawa, A. Mizoguchi: ON THE BASEMENT AND PLATFORM OF PRASAT SUOR PRAT TOWER Study of architectural techniques of Prasat Suor Prat tower in Angkor (Part 1) Japanese Architecture Planning, AIJ, 72 (613), pp.189-196,2007.
   赤澤泰，中川武，溝口明則：プラサート・スープラ塔の 基礎・基壇の構成と技法アンコ ール遺跡 ” プラサート・スープラ塔 ” の建築技法に関する研究（1），日本建築学会計画系論文集，第 72 巻，第 613 号，pp.189-196，2007.

2. Y. Akazawa, T. Nakagawa, A. Mizoguchi, J. Nakazawa, Y.Iwasaki, M. Fukuda: DEVELOPMENT AND RESEARCH OF THE RESTORATION METHODS FOR BASEMENT AND PLATFORM OF PRASAT SUOR PRAT TOWER N1, AIJ J. Technol. Des. Vol. 15, No.30, 567-572, Jun., 2009.
   赤澤泰，中川武，溝口明則，中澤重一，岩崎好規，福田光治：プラサート・スープラN１塔基礎基壇修復方法の研究開発，日本建築学会技術報告集，第 15 巻，3 号，567-572，2009.

3. Y. Akazawa, T. Nakagawa, A. Mizoguchi: ARCHITECTURAL MASONRY FEATURES FOR PRASAT SUOR PRAT Study of architectural techniques of Prasat Suor Prat tower in Angkor (Part 3), Japanese Architecture Planning, AIJ, 717, pp.2653-2659, 2015.
   赤澤泰，中川武，溝口明則：プラサート・スープラの組積技術的特徴 - アンコール遺跡 “ プラサート・スープラ塔 ” の建築技法に関する研究（3），日本建築学会計画系論文集，第 717 号，pp.2653-2659，2015.

TOMODA Masahiko

友田 正彦

Deputy Director General, Tokyo National Research Institute for Cultural Properties
独立行政法人国立文化財機構東京文化財研究所 副所長／文化遺産国際協力センター長
Master of Engineering / Senior Architect / Professional Engineer (Civil Eng.)
工学修士／一級建築士／技術士（建設工学）

1. M. Tomoda, K. Sothin (ed.): Report on the Restoration of the East Gate, Ta Nei Temple, Angkor, Cambodia, APSARA/TOBUNKEN, 2024.03.

2. M. Tomoda, N. Dorji, et al.(ed.): Vernacular Houses in Bhutan, Western Central Area, Thimphu, Punakha, Paro, Haa, Department of Culture, Ministry of Home and Cultural Affairs, Royal Government of Bhutan/Tokyo National Research Institute for Cultural Properties, 2021.03.

3. M. Tomoda, S. Russo, M. Landoni, C.Rellensmann: Guidelines for In-depth Condition Assessment of Monument at Bagan Archaeological Area, UNESCO Myanmar, 2016.01.

TSUCHIYA Takeshi
土屋　武

Former JSA Resident Expert, Restoration Planning
元JSA修復設計班 長期派遣団員
M.Engineering
修士（工学）

1. T. Tsuchiya: 1.4.1 Traditional Construction and Structural Method of the Bayon Period and the Techniques of Conservation and Restoraation, Master Plan for Conservation and Preservation of Bayon, The UNESCO/Japanese Funds-in-Trust for the Preservation of the World Cultural Heritage, pp.155-192, 2005.06.
   土屋武：1.4.1　バイヨン期の伝統構法と保存修復技術，バイヨン寺院全域の保存修復のためのマスタープラン，（財）日本国際協力センター，pp.155-192，2005.06.
2. T. Tsuchiya, T. Nakagawa, I. Shimoda, S. So, Y.Matsumoto: Maintenance Work and Suggestion for the Preservation and Development of the Sambor Prei Kuk Monument : Study on the Khmer Architecture in the Pre-Angkor Period (VI), Summ. Tech. Paper of Annual Meeting, F-2, AIJ, pp.639-640, 2002.06.
   土屋武，中川武，下田一太，ソ・ソクンテリー，松元佑介：緊急メンテナンスと保存開発への提案：プレ・アンコール期クメール建築の研究（VI），日本建築学会大会学術講演梗概集，F-2，日本建築学会，pp.639-640，2002.06.
3. T. Tsuchiya, T. Nakagawa, I. Shimoda, S. So: Damage conditions of the Sambor Prei Kuk Monuments : Study on the Khmer Architecture in the Pre-Angkor Period (IV), Summ. Tech. Paper of Annual Meeting, F-2, AIJ, pp.133-134. 2001.07.
   土屋武，中川武，下田一太，ソ・ソクンテリー：遺構の破損状況について：プレ・アンコール期クメール建築の研究（IV），日本建築学会大会学術講演梗概集，F-2，日本建築学会，pp.133-134，2001.07.

SHIMODA Ichita
下田　一太

Associate Professor, Faculty of Art and Design, University of Tsukuba
筑波大学 芸術系 准教授
Dr.Arch.
博士（建築学）

1. I. Shimoda, T. Haraguchi, T. Chiba, M. Shimoda: The Advanced Hydraulic City Structure of the Royal City of Angkor Thom and Vicinity Revealed through a High-resolution Red Relief Image Map, Archaeological Discovery, Vol.4(1), pp.22-36, 2016.
   下田一太，原口強，千葉達朗，下田麻里子：高解像能赤色立体図によって解明された王都アンコールトムとその近傍における高度な水利都市構造，Archaeological Discovery, Vol.4(1), pp.22-36, 2016.
2. I. Shimoda: Quarrying Technique of Khmer Monuments Sandstone Blocks, Japanese Architecture Planning, AIJ, Vol.79 (705), pp.2543-2551, 2014.
   下田一太：クメール建築の砂岩採石技法に関する考察，日本建築学会計画系論文集，第 79 巻，第 705 号，pp.2543-2551，2014.
3. I. Shimoda, S. Shimamoto: Spatial and Chronological Sketch of the Ancient City of Sambor Prei Kuk, Aseanie, Vol.29, pp.11-74, 2012.
   下田一太，嶋本紗枝：古代都市サンボー・プレイ・クックの空間と年代に関する素描，Aseanie, Vol.29, pp.11-74, 2012.

ISHIZUKA Mitsumasa
石塚　充雅

JASA Technical Assistant
JASA技術補佐
M.Arch.
修士（建築学）

1. M. Ishizuka, T. Nakagawa, A. Mizoguchi, I. Shimoda, K. Sato: Study on arrangement planning of Chau Sray Vibol, Summ. Tech. Paper of Annual Meeting, F-2, AIJ, pp.423-524, 2011.
   石塚充雅，中川武，溝口明則，下田一太，佐藤桂：チャウ・スレイ・ビボールにみる配置計画に関する一考察」，日本建築学会大会学術講演梗概集 F-2，日本建築学会，pp.423-524，2011.
2. M. Ishizuka: Principle of the placement plan in the Khmer district large size temple, Master's Thesis, Laboratory of Architectural History, Waseda Univ., 2012.
   石塚充雅：クメール地方大型寺院にみる配置計画の原理，早稲田大学建築史研究室修士論文，2012.
3. M. Ishizuka, T. Nakagawa, A. Mizoguchi, I. Shimoda, K. Sato: Annexes so Called 'palace' at Beng Mealea (1-1) -Studies on Beng Mealea Monuments, Cambodia (1), Summ. Tech. Paper of Annual Meeting, F-2, AIJ, pp.591-592, 2010.
   石塚充雅，中川武，溝口明則，下田一太，佐藤桂：ベン・メアレア寺院の〈宮殿〉と呼ばれる付属建物に関する考察（1-1）－カンボジア ベン・メアレア遺跡群に関する研究（1），日本建築学会大会学術講演梗概集 F-2，日本建築学会，pp.591-592，2010.

Chapter 5 | 第 5 章

So Sokuntheary
ソ・ソクンテリー

Deputy Director of Department of Land Management, Housing and Demography, National Authority for Sambor Prei Kuk /
Honor Head, Architecture and Urbanism Department, Norton University
サンボー・プレイ・クック機構 土地管理・住宅・人口統計部副部長／ノートン大学 建築都市学科 名誉長
Dr.Architecture
博士（建築学）

1. S. Sokuntheary, I. Shimoda, T. Nakagawa: Central Tower N1 of Sambor, Sambor Prei Kuk Monuments, The 15th Science Council of Asia Board Meeting and International Symposium Proceeding, pp.112-117, 2015.05.
2. S. Sokuntheary: Study on the drainage system of the Bayon temple in the Angkor Thom, Cambodia, Doctoral Dissertation submitted to the Graduate School of Science and Engineering, Waseda University, 2007.10.
   ソ・ソクンテリー：カンボジア，アンコール・トム内バイヨン寺院の排水システムに関する研究，早稲田大学大学院理工学研究科学位請求論文，2007.
3. S. Sokuntheary, T.Nakagawa, S.Nishimoto: DRAINAGE LAYOUT OF KHMER TEMPLES IN THE ANGKOR COMPLEX : Orientation of the drains and the methodology of the drainage system arrangement, J. Archit. Plann., 71 (605), 2006.
   ソ・ソクンテリー，中川武，西本真一：クメール建築，アンコール遺跡における排水システム設計に関する研究：排水路における方位とそのシステム設定方法，日本建築学会計画系論文集，71（605），pp.207-213，2006.

Chhum Menghong
チュン・メンホン

Acting Secretary General of Cambodia National Commission for UNESCO
カンボジアユネスコ国際委員会事務局長代理
Dr.Arch.
博士（建築学）

1. C. Menghong, I. Shimoda, T. Nakagawa: CONSTRUCTION AND UTILIZATION DATING OF TEMPLES BASED ON EXISTING REMAINS INSIDE THE CITY COMPOUND - Structure of the ancient Khmer city of Isanapura(Part 1), J. Archit. Plann., AIJ. Vol.78 (690), pp.1865-1874, 2013.
   チュン・メンホン，下田一太，中川武：都城の基本構造と関連する寺院遺構の建立と利用年代—クメール古代イーシャナプラの都市構造に関する研究（その1），日本建築学会計画系論文集，第 78 巻，第 690 号，pp.1865-1874，2013.
2. C. Menghong: Surface Collection at Surrounding Area of Beng Mealea Site, KOH KER AND BENG MEALEA - ARCHITECTURAL STUDY ON THE PROVINCIAL SITES OF THE KHMER EMPIRE", pp. 188-197, Chuo Koron Bijutsu Shuppan, 2014.
   チュン・メンホン：ベン・メアレア周辺の採集調査，ベン・メアレア遺跡群の建築的特徴，コー・ケーとベン・メアレア　アンコール広域拠点遺跡群の建築学研究，pp.188-197, 中央公論美術出版, 2014.

YANO Kenichiro
矢野 健一郎

Representative Director, Yano Art Institute, Part-time lecturer at Hiroshima City University
㈲矢野造形技法研究所 代表取締役／広島市立大学芸術学部非常勤講師
Master of Fine Arts
芸術学修士

1. K.Nishimura, A.Maeno, K.Yano et al.: A study of the structure and visual environment of the Jodoji Amida Sanson statue, Bulletin of Faculty of Fine Arts, Tokyo University of the Arts, No.17, pp.15-45, 1982.
   西村公朝，前野曉，矢野健一郎，他 7 名：浄土寺阿弥陀三尊像の構造及び視覚環境の研究，東京藝術大学美術学部紀要，第 17 号，pp.15-45，1982.
2. T.Yamazaki, K.Yano: Study of medieval plastic technique, Bulletin of Faculty of Fine Arts, Tokyo University of the Arts, No.19, pp.1-19, 1984.
   山崎隆之，矢野健一郎：中世塑像技法の研究，東京藝術大学美術学部紀要，第 19 号，pp.1-19，1984.

SHIGEMATU Yushi
重松 優志

Sculptor / Buddhist statue sculptor / Restorers of Sculptures and Cultural Properties
彫刻家／仏師／彫刻文化財の修復家
Ph.D in Cultural Property Protection
博士（文化財）

1. Y. Shigematsu: Study of structure and technique of statue in Nara period by reproduction of Shukongoujin standing statue of Todaiji Hokkedo,

Ph.D. dissertation of Tokyo University of the Arts, 2020.

重松優志：東大寺法華堂執金剛神立像の模刻制作を通した奈良時代塑像の構造・技法研究，東京藝術大学博士論文，2020.

2. Y. Shigematsu: Study on the modification of wooden core and its meaning by reproduction of Shukongoujin standing statue of Todaiji Hokke-do, The Japan Art History Society Eastern Division Meeting (Oral Presentation), 2020.

重松優志：東大寺法華堂執金剛立像の模刻制作を通した心木構造改変の検証とその意味，美術史学会東支部例会（口頭発表），2020.

SHIMODA Mariko
下田 麻里子

Doctoral Candidate, Graduate School of Letters, Arts and Sciences, Waseda University
早稲田大学大学院 文学研究科 博士後期課程
M.Architecture
修士（建築学）

1. M. Shimoda: "A consideration of the utilization of Bayon after 13th century and its conversion to Theravada Buddhism", Southeast Asian Archaeology, No.43, pp.23-40, 2024.

下田麻里子：バイヨン寺院の 13 世紀末以降の活用と上座部仏教化に関する検討，東南アジア考古学，第 43 号，pp.23-40，2024.

2. M. SHIMODA: "A Typological Study of Theravada Buddhist Monasteries in Angkor Thom, Cambodia, Journal of Architecture and Planning, The Architectural Institute of Japan, Vol.87, No.797, 1347-1358, 2022.

下田麻里子：カンボジア，アンコール・トム内の上座部仏教遺構の類型学的研究，日本建築学会計画系論文集，第 87 巻，第 797 号：1347-1358，2022.

3. M. SHIMODA: "Study on the Construction Period of Theravada Buddhist Monasteries at Angkor Thom in the Late 13th - 16th Centuries", Southeast Asian Archaeology, No.41.pp.5-23, 2022.

謝　辞

　JSA/JASAのプロジェクトは一貫して，ユネスコ文化遺産保存日本信託基金によって遂行されました。プロジェクトの進展と拡がりによって，その都度重機購入のための日本政府の文化に関する無償資金協力，日本政府見返り資金，専門家派遣のための独立行政法人国際交流基金によってカバーされてきました。バイヨン内回廊浅浮彫の描き起こし，尊顔写真集の撮影については，財団法人文化財保護振興財団，フランス極東学院などの支援を得ました。また，プロジェクトの当初より下記の企業，機関，個人の皆様より御支援を受けました（順不同，企業名や団体名は当時のものを記載する）。

　株式会社大林組，株式会社クボタ建設，株式会社鴻池組，佐藤工業株式会社，株式会社間組，前田建設工業株式会社，アップルコンピュータ株式会社，伊藤忠商事株式会社，株式会社トーメン，丸紅ケミカル株式会社，Broncolor，富士写真フィルム株式会社，株式会社ニコン，ニコンカメラ販売株式会社，コメット株式会社，大日本印刷株式会社，株式会社西東京商事，ソニー株式会社，株式会社スタジオBAKU，CULTURE MOTION "Appassionato"，日本化成株式会社，コニシ株式会社，ショーボンド化学株式会社，三共株式会社，アサヒボンド工業株式会社，アサヒボンド工業会，株式会社アジケン，株式会社INAX，宇部興産株式会社，恒和化学工業株式会社，全国ビルリフォーム協同組合連合会，大日本インキ化学工業株式会社，株式会社東邦アースティック，日本建築仕上材工業会，日本樹脂施工協同組合，日本接着剤工業会，太平洋セメント株式会社，株式会社文化財保存計画協会，株式会社MUSA研究所，レオン工業株式会社，日東電工株式会社，ライオン株式会社，信越化学工業株式会社，三菱マテリアル株式会社

　以上の皆様からの長期に亘る絶大な御支援に対して，簡略ですがここに記載して御礼申し上げます。

　第三フェーズからは現地活動名をJSAからJASAへと変更し，カンボジア人エキスパートならびに現場スタッフの基本給，カンボジアで調達可能な資機材費，そして現地オフィスの電気・水道代をカンボジア政府アプサラ機構の支出によりました。

　以上はプロジェクト運営のための直接経費ですが，第三フェーズからは修復計画のための基礎調査，実験等の研究費と日本人専門家の派遣費などは，主に日本政府文部科学省の科学研究費助成事業によっています。

　本プロジェクトに関連した技術指導協力のプロジェクトとして，日本ユネスコ協会連盟，公益財団法人ユニオン造形文化財団，高口洋人を代表とする早稲田仏教会，清水寺，三和澱粉工業株式会社，佐野勝司氏等の支援をいただいています。

　さらに，本プロジェクトの裾野を広げるための間接的な活動として，アンコール・トム周辺の村の子供たちへの教育支援としてアンコールやまなみファンド（AYF），株式会社三田商会，NPO法人GREEN WIND ASIAなどの支援を得ました。また，バイヨン本尊仏のレプリカ作製と修復や子供たちのバイヨンにおける写生大会について，カンボジア人旅行者からこれらの活動への支援金をいただいています。これらを含めて，以上の物心両面にわたる御支援に対して衷心より御礼申し上げます。

Acknowledgements

JSA/JASA projects have been consistently funded by the UNESCO/Japanese Funds-in-Trust for the Preservation of the World Cultural Heritage. As the projects have developed and expanded, the projects have been supported by the Japanese Government's Cultural Grant Assistance, and Counterpart Fund, Government of Japan, for the purchase of heavy equipment, and by the Japan Foundation for the dispatch of experts. The drawing of the bas-reliefs of the Inner Gallery, Bayon and the photography of the portraits of Face Towers in Bayon were supported by FOUNDATION FOR CULTURAL HERITAGE AND ART RESEARCH and École française d'Extrême-Orient. We have also received support from the following companies, institutions, and individuals since the beginning of the project. (Names of companies and organizations are listed in no particular order and as they were at the time of support)

OBAYASHI CORPORATION, Kubota Construction Co., Ltd., KONOIKE CONSTRUCTION CO.,LTD., Hazama Corporation, MAEDA CORPORATION, Apple Computer, Inc., ITOCHU Corporation, TOMEN Corporation, Marubeni Chemicals Limited, Broncolor, Fuji Photo Film Co., Ltd., Nikon Corporation, COMET Corporation, Dai Nippon Printing Co., Ltd., Nishi-Tokyo Corporation, Sony Corporation, Studio-BAKU Co. Ltd., Culture Motion "APPASSIONATO", Nihon Kasei CO.,LTD., Konishi Co., Ltd., SHO-BOND Chemical Co., Ltd., Sankyo Co., Ltd., AsahiBond Kogyo CO., LTD., Asahibond Association., AJIKEN Co., Ltd., INAX Corporation, Ube Industries Ltd., Kowa Chemical Industries Co., Ltd., Japan Building Repair Federation, Dainippon Ink and Chemicals, Inc., TOHO EARTHTECH,INC., Japan Building Coating Materials Association., japan resin execution contractor's co-cop, Japan Adhesive Industry Association., Taiheiyo Cement Corporation, Japan Cultural Heritage Consultancy, MUSA Laboratory Co., Ltd., LEON KOGYO Co., Ltd., NITTO DENKO CORPORATION, Lion Corporation, Shin-Etsu Chemical Co., Ltd., Mitsubishi Materials Corporation

We would like to express our gratitude for long-term and tremendous support from all.

From the beginning of third phase, the name of the activity in Cambodia was changed from JSA to JASA, and basic salaries for Cambodian expert and site staff and the cost materials and equipment that were available to be procured in Cambodia, and the electricity and water bills for the Siem Reap office were covered by the APSARA National Authority.

The above are the direct expenses for the project management, and the cost of the basic research for the restoration plan, the cost of experiments, and the dispatch of Japanese experts were mainly covered by Grants-in-Aid program for Scientific Research of Ministry of Education, Culture, Sports, Science and Technology (MEXT).

The following organizations have provided support for collaborative project in relation to the restoration and conservation project in Bayon: National Federation of UNESCO Associations in Japan, UNION Foundation For Ergodesign Culture, supporting by Voluntary Group of Waseda Buddhism Society represented by Prof. TAKAGUCHI Hiroto, Kiyomizu-dera, Sanwa Starch Co., Ltd., Mr. SANO Katsuji and the others.

In addition, as indirect activities to expand the scope of this project, we have been cooperating with Angkor Yamanami Fund (AYF), MITA & CO., LTD., and NPO GREEN WIND ASIA to support the education of children in the villages around Angkor Thom. In addition, we have received support from Cambodian tourists for making replica, restoration, reconstitution and reinstallation of the original Bayon Buddha image and for sketching competition with children in Bayon. We would like to express our sincere gratitude for the above material and moral support.

追　悼

　JSAプロジェクトが1994年11月に正式に開始されて以降，本年で30周年を迎えました。この間，シェムレアップで常駐された方々，短期専門家として現地で働いていただいた方々の内，以下の合計11人の方々がご逝去されました。

　　　平岩　義男
　　　小稗　哲夫
　　　桜田　滋
　　　山本　勇
　　　成田　剛
　　　新谷　眞人
　　　サオ・サム
　　　澤田　正昭
　　　朴　亨國
　　　新井　英夫
　　　中澤　重一

　皆さまの在りし日の姿を偲びつつ，現在までのプロジェクトの進展を，本書をもって皆様にご報告申し上げたいと思います。この中には，駐在中のシェムレアップで交通事故のため亡くなられた小稗哲夫氏がいます。またカンボジア人スタッフについては，棟梁のサオ・サム氏以外にも亡くなられた方々がいらっしゃいますが，プロジェクトの発足以来，カンボジア人スタッフの結束のために献身していただいたサオ・サム氏に，特に名を挙げて感謝申し上げます。

　現在プロジェクトに携わっている私たち全員が，皆さまがプロジェクトに注いでくださった想いを忘れず，プロジェクトの成功に力を注ぐことをお亡くなりになった皆さまの前にお誓いして，ご冥福をお祈り申し上げたいと思います。ありがとうございました。

Memorial Writing

This year marks the 30th anniversary of the JSA project since its official launch in November 1994. During this period, 11 people who have worked in Siem Reap as permanent residents or short-term experts passed away, as follows.

HIRAIWA Yoshio
KOGURE Tetsuo
SAKURADA Shigeru
YAMAMOTO Isamu
NARITA Tsuyoshi
ARAYA Masato
SAO Sum
ARAYA Masaaki
PARK Hyounggook
ARAI Hideo
NAKAZAWA Juichi

In remembrance of their past, we would like to report to all of you in this publication on the progress of the project up to the present time. Among those who have passed away are Mr. KOGURE Tetsuo, who get involved in a traffic accident in Siem Reap while residing in Siem Reap. In addition, other Cambodian staff members besides Mr. SAO Sum, who was the site leader also passed away, but in particular by name, I would like to thank Mr. SAO Sum who had been dedicated for the unity of Cambodian staffs from the beginning of project.

All of us who are currently involved in the project will never forget the feelings that they have put into the project, and we would like to express our deepest condolences to those who have passed away and pledge our commitment to the success of the project. I would like to express my gratitude.

カンボジア アンコール遺跡救済 日本政府チーム協力 30 周年記念誌

バイヨン
謎と希望への JSA/JASA30 年の挑戦
ⓒ

発 行
2024年11月30日

監 修
中川　武

編 集
日本国政府アンコール遺跡救済チーム

発行者
松室　徹

装幀
岡本洋平
(岡本デザイン室)

印刷
半七写真印刷工業株式会社

製本
松岳社

中央公論美術出版
東京都千代田区神田神保町1-10-1 IVYビル6階
TEL. 03-5577-4797

ISBN978-4-8055-0991-3